Cities of Commerce

THE PRINCETON ECONOMIC HISTORY OF THE WESTERN WORLD

Joel Mokyr, Series Editor

A list of titles in this series appears at the back of the book

Cities of Commerce

THE INSTITUTIONAL FOUNDATIONS OF INTERNATIONAL TRADE IN THE LOW COUNTRIES, 1250–1650

Oscar Gelderblom

PRINCETON UNIVERSITY PRESS

Princeton & Oxford

Published by Princeton University Press, 41 William Street, Princeton, New Jersey 08540
In the United Kingdom: Princeton University Press, 6 Oxford Street, Woodstock, Oxfordshire OX20 1TW

press.princeton.edu

Jacket Art: Map of Amsterdam, from *Civitates Orbis Terrarum* (c.1572), by Georg Braun (1541–1622) and Frans Hogenburg (1535–90); colored engraving by Joris Hofnagel (1542–1600). Private Collection/The Stapleton Collection. Photo courtesy of The Bridgeman Art Library.

Library of Congress Cataloging-in-Publication Data

Gelderblom, Oscar.
Cities of commerce : the institutional foundations of international trade in the Low Countries, 1250-1650 / Oscar Gelderblom.
   pages cm.— (The Princeton economic history of the Western world)
Includes bibliographical references and index.
ISBN 978-0-691-14288-3 (hardcover : alk. paper)   1. Benelux countries—Commerce—History—To 1500.   2. Benelux countries—Commerce—History—16th century.   3. Benelux countries—Commerce—History—17th century.   I. Title.
   HF3595.G45 2013
   382.09492—dc23
     2013004034

British Library Cataloging-in-Publication Data is available

This book has been composed in Sabon

Printed on acid-free paper. ∞

Printed in the United States of America

10 9 8 7 6 5 4 3 2 1

Voor mijn ouders

Contents

Illustrations

Tables

Acknowledgments

MANY PEOPLE AND INSTITUTIONS ASSISTED ME IN THE WRITING OF THIS book. I am grateful to the Netherlands Organisation for Scientific Research (NWO), the Research Institute for History and Culture of Utrecht University, the Department of Economics of the University of California, Los Angeles, the International Institute of Social History in Amsterdam, the Centre for Urban History at the University of Antwerp, the Paris School of Economics, and the Netherlands Institute for Advanced Study in Wassenaar. Debbie Tegarden, Joseph Dahm, Tom Broughton-Willett, Seth Ditchik, and other staff members at Princeton University Press have been a tremendous help in the preparation of this book.

I thank several publishers for permission to reproduce (parts of) articles that appeared in their journals: "The Decline of Fairs and Merchant Guilds in the Low Countries, 1250–1650," *Jaarboek voor Middeleeuwse Geschiedenis* 7 (2004): 199–238; "The Governance of Early Modern Trade: The Case of Hans Thijs, 1556–1611," *Enterprise & Society* 4, no. 4 (2003): 606–39; and "The Resolution of Commercial Conflicts in Bruges, Antwerp, and Amsterdam (1250–1650)," in *Law and Long-Term Economic Change: A Eurasian Perspective*, edited by Debin Ma and Jan Luiten van Zanden (Stanford, Calif.: Stanford University Press 2011), 244–76.

Many students and colleagues have offered stimulating comments on research papers and draft chapters, among them Dan Bogart, Lars Börner, Giuseppe Dari-Mattiacci, Mauricio Drelichman, the late Larry Epstein, Benjamin Guilbert, Don Harreld, Marjolein 't Hart, Danielle van den Heuvel, Naomi Lamoreaux, Bas van Leeuwen, Clé Lesger, Jan Lucassen, Ghislaine Lydon, Debin Ma, John Munro, Larry Neal, Sheilagh Ogilvie, Lodewijk Petram, Gilles Postel-Vinay, Dave de Ruysscher, Liesbeth Sparks, Oliver Volckart, Jan de Vries, Herman van der Wee, and Marietje van Winter. Special thanks go to Jessica Dijkman, Laura Guerra, Heleen Kole, and Jeroen Puttevils for excellent research assistance. I was also fortunate to present my work, in various stages of development, to audiences at the Centre for Urban History of the University of Antwerp, the Free University of Berlin, the Early Modern History Workshop of the California Institute of Technology, the University of British Columbia,

Cambridge University, Lund University, the Paris School of Economics, Stanford University, and our very own Economic and Social History Seminar at Utrecht University.

I owe a great debt of gratitude to colleagues who read the entire manuscript, sometimes more than once: Bas van Bavel, Tracy Dennison, Avner Greif, Stuart Jenks, Abe de Jong, Wijnand Mijnhardt, Roger de Peuter, Jeroen Puttevils, Francesca Trivellato, Jan Luiten van Zanden, the readers of Princeton University Press, and last but not least Maarten Prak. I especially thank Regina Grafe, Bruno Blondé, and Peter Stabel for what they taught me in our joint work on the organization of international trade in premodern Europe. From beginning to end I have enjoyed the friendship of Joost Jonker and Jean-Laurent Rosenthal, whose comments and encouragement have made this a much better book. By the same token, Joel Mokyr, the editor of this series, deserves my deep gratitude. He made me contemplate the lessons we can learn from history, and he patiently guided my efforts to expound my views. Needless to say, I alone am responsible for any errors that remain.

My family has always been there for me. When our son was born in November 2004, I assured Nathalie this book was almost done. As it turned out, she and Guus had to wait slightly longer to see it in print, but sharing this moment with them is a great gift. It is with equal gratitude that I dedicate this book to my parents, for their unconditional love and support.

Cities of Commerce

CHAPTER 1

Introduction

WHEN SPANISH TROOPS CAPTURED ANTWERP IN AUGUST 1585 THE CITY'S merchants faced a difficult choice. They could stay, if they accepted the sovereignty of Philip II, but commercial prospects were bleak since large groups of Flemish textile workers had already left for France, England, and Holland and Dutch rebels blocked the river Scheldt and the Flemish coast. An alternative was to move to Protestant London, but here the local business elite actively tried to exclude newcomers. The Atlantic ports of Rouen and Nantes offered good connections to many countries in Western Europe, but France was embroiled in civil war, just like the Northern Netherlands where Zeeland and Holland remained fully exposed to military action. Hamburg and Emden in northern Germany were safer havens, but their Baltic affairs languished. Eventually Amsterdam attracted most traders from Antwerp. The immigration there started with merchants who specialized in the exchange of grain and textiles with the Baltic region, but soon enough the Dutch port became the preferred destination of merchants with a much broader commercial outlook, including a considerable number of German, Portuguese, English, and Italian merchants.

Amsterdam's rise to commercial primacy was a remarkable achievement. Within fifteen years the city managed to create well-functioning markets for the widest possible variety of goods, financial services, and commercial information. This, in turn, enabled local and foreign merchants to build up large, diversified businesses with Amsterdam as the central node in their international network of trading agents. In the meantime, however, the Dutch Republic continued to fight Spain, exposing merchants on virtually every land and sea route to violence. In addition to this violence, newcomers in Amsterdam were confronted with agency problems that issued from the differences between their own contracting practices and those of other foreigners and local merchants. Amsterdam's response to these challenges differed markedly from the responses of many of its urban competitors. Instead of granting safe-conducts, consular jurisdictions, or other special rights to separate groups, the city created inclusive institutional arrangements to protect all merchants, regardless of their origin, wealth, religion, or economic specialization against violence and opportunism.

The creation of *open access* or *generalized* institutions made it easier for merchants to deal with the conflicts that issued from Europe's political and legal fragmentation, but the origins of these more inclusive commercial regimes are subject to debate.[1] Douglass North, John Wallis, and Barry Weingast, Daron Acemoglu and James Robinson, and others emphasize the formation of stronger states with the military means to protect trade and the legal powers to adjudicate conflicts between traders. In their view, a state like the Dutch Republic could credibly commit to the safety of merchants because effective constraints on its executive power legitimized both their military and legal interventions and the fiscal efforts to provide this protection.[2] One problem with this explanation is that the strongest states in late medieval and early modern Europe were also the most belligerent, witness the military operations of Genoa and Venice in the eastern Mediterranean or the Atlantic power struggle among the Dutch Republic, England, and France.[3] Moreover, the importance of strong states is difficult to square with the early expansion of European trade. When European merchants first started trading across longer distances in the eleventh and twelfth centuries, sovereign rulers wielded very little if any power because their territories were small and their fiscal and military resources limited.[4]

To explain the growth of trade in the absence of strong states, Avner Greif has pointed to the development of private order solutions for the problems of violence and opportunism. Peer pressure and the prospect of repeat transactions helped merchants to keep distant agents honest, while the formation of guilds allowed them to organize boycotts and keep rulers from preying on their property.[5] Private order solutions thus contributed to the growth of trade in two distinct ways: they reduced or even preempted the merchants' reliance on the government to enforce contracts, and they could stimulate local or central authorities to protect merchants and provide impartial justice.[6] But there also are problems with this explanation. Notably Sheilagh Ogilvie has argued that group formation could lead to regulatory capture and rent seeking. When local merchant guilds and chartered companies used their social capital and corporate power to exclude competitors, they could strangle economic

[1] Gelderblom and Grafe 2010: 485; Ogilvie 2011: 248, 313–14, 340–41, 387–90, 432.

[2] North and Thomas 1973: 6–8, 120–58; North 1981: 143–57, esp. 154; North, Wallis, and Weingast 2009: 22; Acemoglu, Johnson, and Robinson 2005: 562–63; Acemoglu and Robinson 2012: 428–62; Jones 2003: 85–90, 232–36.

[3] Findlay and O'Rourke 2007: 127–33, 238–62; Rosenthal and Bin Wong 2011: 92–93.

[4] Tilly 1990: 38–42; Blockmans 1994: 223–24.

[5] Greif 1989: 867–68; Greif, Milgrom, and Weingast 1994: 748–49; Greif 2006b: 58–90, 318–49.

[6] Curtin 1984: 13; Greif 2006b: 121–23, 318–38; Selzer and Ewert 2001: 150–54.

growth.[7] On the other hand, the historical record shows that local and foreign merchants were willing to forego a corporate status when local rulers stepped in to provide the necessary legal and commercial support for their private business operations.[8]

The aim of this book is to develop an alternative explanation for institutional change in European commerce that is not predicated upon the existence of strong territorial states or the ability of merchants to create private order solutions. Instead, I argue that the very problem of Europe's political and legal fragmentation also produced its solution, in the form of competition between urban governments that tried to attract trade through the continuous adaptation of their legal, commercial, and financial institutions. Cities may seem a most unlikely candidate because their political power was limited and their jurisdiction did not reach far beyond the city walls, but even though the law was local and international trade—by definition—was not, the cities' legal autonomy actually made it easier for municipal governments to adapt institutional arrangements to the needs of international traders.[9] At the same time, the financial resources of commercial cities, both taxes and loans, were so important for most sovereigns that they seldom clamped down on major entrepôts.[10] But even then, why did the magistrates of commercial cities act in the interest of the merchant community at large instead of favoring specific groups of traders or excluding others—rent seeking behavior that can be observed in many industrial towns?[11] One might argue that international traders formed the government of commercial cities.[12] But this was not always the case, witness Venice or Antwerp, and even when active traders did dominate the municipal government, like in Amsterdam or London, they typically belonged to a very small political elite that excluded not just foreign merchants but also many local traders from power.[13]

[7] Ogilvie 2011: 94–159, 414–26. See also Lindberg 2007: 59–61; Lindberg 2009: 611–23; and Gelderblom 2009: 226–32; for a theoretical exposition: Dessí and Ogilvie 2003.

[8] Gelderblom and Grafe 2010: 485–86. Compare Greif's discussion of the role of late medieval rulers in the decline of merchants' collective liability for debts (Greif 2006b: 309–49).

[9] On urban support for trade: Pirenne (1927) 1970: 92–92; Hohenberg and Lees 1995; on the ability of organizations to adapt as a key factor in institutional change: North 1990: 80–82; North 2005: 77–78, 108–12; on the legal autonomy of local governments: Bairoch 1988: 170; English 1988: 56–112; Epstein 2000: 151–55; Kadens 2004: 50–56.

[10] Tilly and Blockmans 1994: 22–27; see also Tilly 1990; Stasavage 2011: 132–55.

[11] Braudel 1977: 57–58; Ogilvie 2011: 41–93.

[12] On the alleged political power of commercial interest groups: Acemoglu, Johnson, and Robinson 2005: 550; North and Thomas 1973; North 1981: 154; Stasavage 2011: 14–16, 111–32.

[13] On the participation of merchants in the local government of Amsterdam: Lesger 2006: 144; for London: Brenner 1993: 79–91; on the exclusion of local and foreign merchants from political power: Gelderblom 1999: 240–44; Lindberg 2009: 615–16, 621; van Gelder 2009.

The motivation of commercial cities to create inclusive institutional arrangements, I argue in this book, issued not from the political franchise of their merchants but from the economic rivalry between these cities. Competition has long been recognized as a key feature of European history with a deep impact on the formation of states, technological change, and economic growth.[14] Yet the effect of urban competition on the organization of international trade has remained largely unexplored.[15] Premodern Europe was characterized by the existence of a large number of cities with the potential to become a major international market.[16] Commercial leadership periodically shifted from one center to another. Achieving a leading position required strong commercial ties with other cities, which in turn stimulated a welcoming attitude toward foreign traders and targeted efforts to adapt local institutions to their business needs. Urban competition thus created a constant impetus to adapt institutions to the needs of the merchant community at large, with the arrival of new merchants further adding to the menu of institutional choices.

To demonstrate how urban competition affected the organization of international trade at its cutting edge, this book analyzes the consecutive rise of Bruges, Antwerp, and Amsterdam to commercial primacy between 1250 and 1650. In doing so, we will be able to answer several outstanding questions regarding the organization of international trade before 1800. Why did institutional change continue in Europe for many centuries while it stagnated in other commercialized areas like the Middle East or China? Why was the adaptation of contracting institutions in Europe not confined to areas with strong cities and weak sovereigns, but instead affected every town with commercial aspirations even in absolutist states like France or Spain? On the other hand, competition between cities, or rather changes in their competitive strength, can also explain why in some of them, after long periods of openness toward foreign traders, the dynamic process of institutional change ended in regulatory capture by local elites. And finally, urban competition helps to explain why even ports at the very top of Europe's urban hierarchy, in spite of their very sophisticated commercial and financial institutions, eventually lost their competitive advantage, producing Fernand Braudel's now classic sequence of commercial capitals from Venice to Antwerp, Genoa, Am-

[14] See, e.g., Wallerstein 1976; Mokyr 1994: 562–63; Pomeranz 2000: 194–206; Jones 2003: 104–5, 123–24, 245–46; North 2005: 60, 137–38, 141–42; North, Wallis, and Weingast 2009: 133–34, 136; Rosenthal and Wong 2011: 119–26.

[15] Hohenberg and Lees 1995: 374; but compare Volckart (2002: 81–82), who describes how in late medieval Germany cities competed with local lords to provide security to merchants.

[16] De Vries 1984: 158–67, 263; Bairoch 1988: 178–81; Hohenberg and Lees 1995: 47–55, 106–13.

sterdam, and then London. But before we can answer these questions, we should consider in greater detail the dynamics of institutional change.

STATE FORMATION AND THE GROWTH OF TRADE

Modern theories of institutional change take the strength of sovereign rulers as a crucial variable to explain institutional continuity or change. The basic assumption is that sovereign rulers who are strong enough to protect the property of their subjects may also abuse these powers and harm the interests of their subjects.[17] England is a principal reference point in all of these theories that derive from the work of English political philosophers like Hobbes, Steuart, and Smith, who were among the first to identify the crucial role of sovereigns in the protection of private property. In particular, England's history before and after the Glorious Revolution (1688–89) has led political scientists and economic historians to argue that the establishment of constitutional government in 1688 was a prerequisite for the creation of more secure property rights, the improvement of contracting institutions, and the subsequent growth of British trade and industry in the eighteenth and nineteenth centuries.[18]

From an English point of view these causal inferences seem reasonable enough because royal interventions in England's economy had a long pedigree. In the thirteenth century kings already regulated payments and credit operations, opened their courts to local and foreign merchants, and chartered trading companies for the export of wool and cloth. In the early modern period the crown organized and reorganized London's chartered companies, introduced radical protectionist policies, and created a standing navy with the explicit goal of furthering England's commercial interests.[19] For many economic historians the Glorious Revolution was a fundamental breakthrough, not just in politics and public finance but also in foreign trade, because it ended the privileged position of a limited number of London merchants who until then controlled virtually every sector of international commerce.[20] According to Acemoglu, Johnson, and Robinson (2005) the political revolution was indeed caused by the emergence of a new group of merchants in England's rapidly expanding Atlantic trade.

[17] See, e.g., North 1981: 20–24; Olson 2000: 6–11; Greif 2006b: 91.
[18] North and Weingast 1989; Acemoglu, Johnson, and Robinson. 2005: 562–69. For the distinction between contracting and property rights institutions: Acemoglu and Johnson 2005.
[19] Harris 2000; O'Brien 2000; Ormrod 2003.
[20] On the organization of England's foreign trade, see Gelderblom 2009: 226–32, with references to the older literature. Dincecco 2011: 5–9 summarizes the debate on the political and economic effects of the Glorious Revolution.

Their growing political power would have forced the English crown to support institutional arrangements that benefited the merchant community at large.[21]

The English case is nevertheless a poor foundation for empirical generalizations about the role of central governments in the organization of trade because the political situation was very different from that in the rest of Europe. London was the main gateway for domestic producers and foreign traders, but it was also the country's political and administrative center, as a result of which the crown had very close ties to the local business elite. On the European Continent, whether in Spain, France, Germany, or the Dutch Republic, the major commercial cities were always at a distance from the seat of government. As a result, there was no Continental equivalent of the chartered companies that controlled England's exports to Europe, and even though several princes opened up their central courts to commercial litigation, they could not fulfill their promise to adjudicate conflicts between merchants from different legal backgrounds because proceedings were too slow and the professional lawyers too ignorant about mercantile usage.[22] Consequently, merchants on the Continent had to rely on the market facilities and legal services provided by individual cities to support their trade.

A further drawback of the model proposed by Acemoglu, Johnson, and Robinson is its exclusive focus on Atlantic trade. The political and economic demands of London's colonial merchants did not necessarily reflect the concerns of English traders who operated within Europe. Whereas the latter wanted the government only to facilitate private trading, the organization of trade in the Atlantic and particularly in Asia required a very specific combination of diplomacy, military effort, and foreign trading posts to control distant markets and withstand European rivals. Thus, the active involvement of the English crown in colonial trade was a sheer necessity, and altogether very similar to that of Venice and Genoa when they first ventured into the Islamic world in the eleventh century or, for that matter, any other colonial power in Europe in the sixteenth and seventeenth centuries.[23] As trade within Europe did not require this kind of intervention, and Continental princes in any case lacked the power to do so, England's particular institutional trajectory of the seventeenth century with the crown as the protagonist of institutional

[21] Acemoglu, Johnson, and Robinson 2005: 564–66; see also Acemoglu and Robinson 2012: 209–11, 362. Note, however, that according to Brenner (1993: 517) a new group of independent merchants, i.e., with no ties either to the crown or to the chartered companies, had gained political influence already in the 1640s.

[22] See chapter 5.

[23] Greif 1998: 26–27; Dursteler 2006; Findlay and O'Rourke 2007: 92–96, 143–87; Gelderblom, de Jong, and Jonker 2011.

change remains a poor guide to the institutional arrangements that supported the growth of trade within Europe before 1800.

Private Order Solutions

Now how could merchants prevent violent assaults or the opportunistic behavior of their agents without the support of sovereign rulers? The most extreme answer to this question is that foreign traders did not need the government because they relied on private order solutions instead. The history of European trade provides many examples of merchants organizing transactions privately. Whether in the Mediterranean, the Baltic Sea, or the Atlantic world, the commercial operations that emerge from account books and business letters invariably point to the crucial importance of personal relations in the organization of cross-border trade.[24] In the case of the Sephardic Jews or the Christians from Armenia it is very clear that merchants could build large commercial networks without any support of a home government.[25] The international diamond trade of the eighteenth century also suggests that informal agreements sufficed to close big deals, and in the first early modern stock markets of Amsterdam and London traders explicitly renounced government intervention.[26] It is not difficult to add more examples to show how friendship and kinship, shared cultural beliefs, and the prospect of repeat transactions helped merchants to keep agents honest. But would that prove that private order solutions can sustain international trade in a legally and politically fragmented world?

Yes, says Avner Greif, that is exactly what happened in Europe during the Commercial Revolution of the eleventh and twelfth centuries, when merchants developed several institutional arrangements to trade at arm's length without recourse to a third party. Jewish merchants trading between North Africa and Italy in the eleventh century, for instance, formed coalitions within which they shared information about agents in other locations. Their surviving correspondence suggests that regular interaction allowed the Maghribi traders to detect defaulters and to exclude them from future transactions, thus creating a strong incentive for individual members to honor their obligations.[27] Many more merchants in medieval Europe traded in guilds, *consulados*, and *hanses*—mercantile associations

---

[24] See, for instance, Häberlein 1998; Selzer and Ewert 2001; Mathias 2000; Gelderblom 2003c; Dursteler 2006.

[25] Yogev 1978: passim; Curtin 1984: 179–206; Israel 2002: passim; Trivellato 2009: 102–31.

[26] On stock markets: Stringham 2003: 15–17; Petram 2011: 107–14; Petram 2012: 151–68; Carlos and Neal 2011: 25–26; Murphy 2010: 83–87. On the diamond trade: Trivellato 2009: 238–50; Vanneste 2011.

[27] Greif 1989: 867–68; Greif 2006b: 85–89.

that paired a strong sense of community to collective liability for the debts of individual members and punishment through exclusion.[28] Some of these associations, the German Hanse in particular, were so well organized that they could credibly threaten foreign rulers to leave collectively in case they preyed on any one of their members.[29] Finally, quite a few legal and economic historians have argued for the existence of a medieval *lex mercatoria*, or law merchant—a uniform legal code distinct from existing Roman law, canon law, and common law, which would have emerged spontaneously from regular exchange between merchants from different local backgrounds.[30]

But were these collective arrangements truly self-enforcing? Did they allow merchants to govern long-distance transactions without any support from either central or local governments, or was there a constant interaction between public and private institutions? With regard to the coalition of Maghribi traders, Goldberg, Edwards, and Ogilvie and others have pointed out not only that they shared social norms and cultural beliefs, but also that their commercial transactions were subject to more formal rules enforceable by religious or lay judges.[31] The sole survival of business letters makes it difficult to determine conclusively whether the Maghribi traders operated in the shadow of the law or not, but for merchant guilds and other communal institutions such formal embeddedness is beyond doubt.[32] For instance, the law merchant referred to in several medieval texts actually comprised a narrow set of procedural rules instituted by local rulers to secure a speedy resolution of conflicts between visiting merchants.[33] Avner Greif has shown that the collective liability for debts that made it easier for merchants from different communities to trade with each other was anchored in customary laws allowing merchants whose property had been seized abroad to go to their local court to obtain compensation from the actual perpetrator.[34]

[28] On the history of merchant guilds: Gelderblom and Grafe 2010 and Ogilvie 2011, both with references to the older literature. See also Blockmans 2010a. On the collective liability for debts: Greif 2002: 182–90, 195–200.
[29] Greif, Milgrom, and Weingast 1994: 759–62; Greif 2006b: 105–8; see also Volckart and Mangels: 437. According to Ogilvie (2011: 206–16) there is very little historical evidence for the positive effects of boycotts on the security of merchants.
[30] Berman 1983: 333–56; Benson 2002: 128–30; Milgrom, North, and Weingast 1990: 5–6; Munro 2003: 550–51.
[31] Goldberg 2011: 9–13; Goldberg 2012: 150–64, 178; Edwards and Ogilvie 2012: passim. See also Trivellato 2009: 13–14, 157–58. For Avner Greif's refutation of the claims of Edwards and Ogilvie, see Greif 2012: passim.
[32] On the government support for the German Hanse, see Greif 2006b: 100–110, 318–20.
[33] Baker 1986: 347; Baker 2000: 88; Basile et al. 1998: 179–88; see also, on the nonexistence of the law merchant, Donahue 2004; Kadens 2004, 2012; Cordes 2005.
[34] Greif 2006b: 318–38; Börner and Ritschl 2002: 207; Börner and Ritschl 2009: 101–3.

The embeddedness of private solutions in a wider framework of public institutions is most apparent from the organization of medieval merchant guilds. Everywhere in Europe merchants trading in foreign countries delegated control to corporate groups to negotiate privileges with foreign hosts, to resolve conflicts between them, or to monopolize a certain branch of trade.[35] Since many guilds performed a wide range of social and religious functions as well, they are sometimes considered paragons of collective action, but as far as the historical record goes, the merchant guilds were always and everywhere instituted with the explicit license of both their home government and their foreign host. This should not come as a surprise given that the guilds were indeed created to bargain with foreign rulers, to establish jurisdictions abroad, or to shield markets from competitors. Obviously, well-organized groups could apply more pressure than individual merchants could to obtain additional privileges or get compensation for damages from their host, but as the membership of most merchant guilds was large and in constant flux, the ability to act collectively typically hinged on the formal control delegated to the guild leaders.[36]

Even if the history of Europe's merchant guilds confirms the importance of formal support for mercantile associations, this does not imply that merchants were unable to organize transactions privately. Surely there were many places where foreign merchants continued to organize in guilds until the eighteenth century, but in the commercial heartland of Europe merchants turned away from these formal bodies much earlier. In the Italian city-states, the Low Countries, and England merchants stopped delegating control to corporate groups and instead started building multilateral networks of relatives and friends who settled abroad with little or no formal support from their home governments. How could this be? Did commercial connections eventually become so dense that the prospect of repeat transactions sufficed to enforce contracts? Did the growing interaction between foreigners create a cosmopolitan culture that bridged the social distance between merchants with very different religious and cultural backgrounds? And should we then conclude that the self-enforcing institutions first observed during the Commercial Revolution of the eleventh and twelfth centuries reached their full potential only in the early modern period? Or did private order solutions even then depend on public support, albeit not from central governments but from the commercial cities that competed vigorously to attract international trade?

---

[35] Greif, Milgrom, and Weingast 1994: passim; Greif 2006b: 91–110; Gelderblom and Grafe 2010: 481–86; Ogilvie 2011: 91–159, and passim.

[36] Gelderblom and Grafe, 2010: 487–93.

Urban Competition

In the High Middle Ages rulers everywhere in Europe created markets and fairs for the sales of agricultural surpluses from the surrounding countryside.[37] In many towns this market infrastructure never went beyond the most basic facilities, but there were also regions where individual fairs coalesced into cycles of fairs attracting trade for months on end and cities with permanent markets and a large, international clientele.[38] Successful commercial cities, I demonstrate in this study, continuously adapted their commercial, legal, and financial infrastructure to secure the continued presence of these merchants. They replaced temporary stalls with permanent vending locations. They adjusted tariffs and taxes to changes in the scale and scope of trade. They firmly regulated the work of brokers, money changers, and hostellers, but resolutely changed the rules when economic conditions demanded it. More than once cities traded a policy of exclusive privileges to some for free competition between all merchants. This responsiveness to change raises two important questions. Why was it so much easier for cities than for sovereigns to develop institutions to support international trade? And what drove these commercial cities to constantly adapt institutional arrangements to the changing needs of the merchants?

The answer to the first question is rather straightforward: only cities commanded the financial and legal resources to provide the necessary public goods. In Europe before the Industrial Revolution most taxes were local taxes, and for cities it was relatively easy to fund port facilities, public vending locations, and the local court system from current revenue, notably because trade added considerably to their fiscal resources. Even the protection of merchants, whether through the city's own defenses or through armed escorts of trade caravans or merchant fleets, remained a local affair, at least until the later seventeenth century when England and France started to fund their royal navies from state revenues.[39] Cities were also the most likely providers of legal support because almost everywhere in Europe the law was local, and this gave urban magistrates considerable leeway in dealing with the Continent's legal fragmentation. They could accept the heterogeneity of contracting institutions and create consular jurisdictions to allow foreigners to settle commercial disputes according to their own rules, or they could incorporate foreign mercan-

[37]Pirenne (1927) 1970: 66, 135–38; Spufford 2002. For England: Britnell 2009. For Holland and Flanders: Dijkman 2011.

[38]Epstein 1994; Johanek and Stoob 1996; Cavaciocchi 2001; Munro 2001.

[39]Lane 1958; for the Netherlands, see Bruijn 1993; Sicking 2004.

tile usage into their local customs and open their local courts to adjudicate the maritime, commercial, and financial conflicts of all merchants.[40]

Now, what motivated cities to continuously adapt institutional arrangements? Late medieval and early modern cities did not develop theoretically founded economic policies to strengthen their competitive position, let alone what urban planners today would call city marketing to attract new entrepreneurs.[41] However, town magistrates did have an eye for new opportunities in manufacturing and trade, and they understood how specific rules or regulations could constrain or stimulate the urban economy.[42] Under these circumstances specific groups of entrepreneurs, whether artisans in manufacturing towns or merchants in trading centers, could have considerable influence on the institutions governing exchange. Still, even in cities run by merchants, the private interests of the political elite did not necessarily coincide with those of the larger business community. The real question therefore is under which circumstances local magistrates, whether traders, artisans, lawyers, or otherwise, were willing to put aside their private concerns and serve the merchant community at large.

This book argues that urban governments were motivated to adapt institutional arrangements because they expected to gain from the local concentration of regional and international flows of goods, money, and information. There were no predetermined winners of this competition because many cities in Europe had commercial potential. Local supply and demand for goods and services obviously differed between them, but the number of potential gateways within close proximity of each other was such that merchants always had a choice both for the location of their main seat and for the establishment of subsidiary branches.[43] Still, this urban geography would never have led a large number of cities to exert themselves if their competition had been a tournament with only one winner. Surely cities like Amsterdam and London stood at the very top of the urban hierarchy, and their gains from trade certainly were a prize worth fighting for, but the essence of international commerce was the interdependence of a large number of more or less central markets, who could still be very competitive despite a smaller range of goods and

[40]On contract enforcement by local governments, see Lane 1962: 24, 33, 36; Jados 1975: xii; Baker 1986: 349ff.; Nörr 1987: 196–98; Kowaleski 1995: 179–221; van Niekerk 1998: 1:198–200, 225–29, 245–46; Basile et al. 1998: 42, 69–70, 114; Volckart and Mangels 1999.

[41]Reinert 2009: 23–30.

[42]Duplessis and Howell 1982: 55–78; Davids 1996: 100–118.

[43]De Vries 1984: 161, 254–57; Lesger 2001; Lesger 2006: 17–99, 262–63.

services, and a more limited access to other markets.[44] Therefore the efforts of individual cities were directed most of all to maximizing their connectivity with other markets.

The potential benefits to individual cities were large. Not only did the growth of trade lead to the creation of a permanent commercial and legal infrastructure, but as foreigners immigrated and markets became thicker new forms of exchange emerged, for instance in debt finance, insurance, and stock trading. Increased imports and exports also induced the growth of local production and consumption, allowing cities to raise more taxes without damaging the economy. Consequently, commercial expansion strengthened the cities' bargaining position vis-à-vis that of the central government.[45] Sovereigns relied on commercial cities for taxes and loans, which not only increased their commitment to secure property rights and contracting institutions, but also induced their active support for trade, for instance through the issue of safe-conducts or legal privileges to foreign merchants. The growing strength of monarchs after 1500 was at least partially due to their symbiotic relationship with major trading centers, and thus, even in absolutist states where the domestic economy suffered from serious infringements on private property rights, the central government remained very forthcoming toward the commercial cities in their realm.

There were also systemic benefits that accrued to Europe as a whole. While medieval Europe had several commercial subsystems, each with its own institutional arrangements, the growing interaction between regions from the thirteenth century onward gave merchants and magistrates a wider menu of institutional choices on the local market, and it stimulated them to adopt contracting institutions that reduced the costs of trading with other cities. In the long run these institutional adaptations allowed Europe to catch up with the Middle East and China, where contracting institutions in long-distance trade were already highly developed and widely shared at the end of the first millennium. Indeed, after several centuries of urban competition Europe had developed a common set of contracting institutions—and these institutional arrangements were also more varied and sophisticated, a quality that would eventually make them the global standard in the nineteenth century.[46]

This obviously is a very optimistic appraisal, as if urban competition always and everywhere led to an optimization of institutional arrange-

[44] De Vries 1984: 122. Notably Braudel (1977: 88–89) and Wallerstein (1976) put much greater emphasis on the few winners that came to dominate world trade.

[45] Tilly 1990: 51–54, 58–61, 86–91; Tilly and Blockmans 1994; Stasavage 2011: 3–4, 132–55.

[46] Greif 2006b: 388–400; Kuran 2010: 3–11; Rosenthal and Bin Wong 2011: 70–72, 80–83.

ments. That was not the case. The impetus for change differed with the economic opportunities of individual cities. In highly urbanized industrial regions neighboring cities might compete fiercely to become the principal outlet for local manufactures, whereas a single town in an underdeveloped region might feel no competitive pressure at all. Cities that were centrally located were also more attractive for the more or less footloose merchants who plied their trade over long distances, than ex-centrically located towns—a geographical reality that explains why in the seventeenth century institutional adaptation was a much more pervasive force in the Atlantic ports than for instance in the landlocked market towns of Central Europe.

Perhaps the most serious constraint on institutional change was the actual deterioration of a city's economic outlook. When cities were pushed to the periphery of the international urban network they became more susceptible to rent seeking by local elites, who tried to shape local institutions to maintain their share of a shrinking pie. This is very clear in the case of Lübeck and Venice when their commercial primacy faded during the sixteenth century. But even though they took a more hostile attitude toward new entrants, their institutions nevertheless remained in sync with the international standard, simply because the remaining merchants continued to trade internationally. Indeed, the survival of institutional know-how was such that even after long periods of economic decline, cities could regain a prominent role in international trade, witness the reemergence of Antwerp as one of Europe's principal ports in the nineteenth century.

Why was the adaptation of commercial institutions such a pervasive force in Europe before the Industrial Revolution? Some historians have pointed to the rise of an international culture of commerce.[47] In their view the constant interaction between merchants from around Europe created common business norms and beliefs that helped to bridge the social distance between merchants from different religious and cultural backgrounds. But even if cultural beliefs, as a rule, have a deep impact on the nature of institutional change, in this case the timing is wrong because a cosmopolitan culture emerged only in markets where foreign groups had come to know each other really well.[48] Indeed, institutional change in European trade derived from the exact opposite of a common culture, that

[47]For Europe: Jacob 2006: 66–94. For Antwerp: Kint 1996b: 343–96; Van Damme 2010: 487–503. Compare Mokyr (2010: 188–94) for the rise of so-called gentlemanly capitalism in eighteenth-century England, and Trivellato (2009: 70–101, 248–49) on the cosmopolitan attitude of Portuguese merchants in Livorno.

[48]On the relationship between individualistic beliefs and the rise of institutions for impersonal exchange, see Greif 1994a: 941–42; Greif 2006b: 269–304; and North 2005: 78–80, 101.

is, the heterogeneity of the merchant community. In major commercial cities there always were many different groups of merchants, each with their own specific commercial, financial, and legal demands. Notably foreign merchants were easily tempted to move their business elsewhere, and to bind these footloose traders cities were forced to adapt institutional arrangements to their needs.[49] The pressure thus exerted resembles that of the boycotts Greif, Milgrom, and Weingast described for medieval merchant guilds, but it did not necessarily require collective action to get local governments to act because, by definition, any removal of a merchant strengthened a rival city.

So why would rulers compete through institutional arrangements rather than the use of force? Surely the leading cities were powerful enough to hurt commercial rivals through tariffs, embargoes, or outright warfare—and they probably did, considering the high incidence of violence in the history of European trade. However, there were so many competing states in Europe with one or more important markets in their territory that sovereigns were careful not to prey on merchants in these cities.[50] They not just feared the direct loss of fiscal revenue or a higher cost of capital, but also realized they would play into the hands of their political rivals, as foreign merchants in particular were footloose and would not hesitate to remove their business to ports outside their realm.[51] The value of having at least one major port in one's territory explains the close connections between the English crown and London's merchant elite—ever since the thirteenth century the city had been the principal gateway to the British Isles—and it also explains the sometimes very crude interventions of sovereigns on the Continent, such as the Habsburg clampdown on Bruges in the late fifteenth century and the reduction of La Rochelle and other Huguenot strongholds by the king of France in the seventeenth century. In both cases the crown confronted the cities head-on because their merchants could move to nearby ports with a similar commercial infrastructure that were firmly under the sovereign's control.[52]

[49] See Albert Hirschman's contention that exit can be a very effective incentive for firms to optimize their production process provided that only some of the customers are willing to do so. If no customer is willing to exit, there is no incentive for the firm managers to change the organization of their firm, but if all customers leave for the smallest inconvenience, a very unstable situation emerges (Hirschman 1970: 24).

[50] Tilly 1990.

[51] See Mokyr (2007: 24, 28–31), who has drawn attention to the existence in seventeenth- and eighteenth-century Europe of a very mobile international community of scholars whose development of new scientific ideas benefited from the attempts of competing princes to attract the most capable among them to their respective realms.

[52] For the siege of La Rochelle, see Robbins 1997: 355.

In brief, the political and legal fragmentation of premodern Europe that harmed trade on many occasions also created competitive pressure on cities to develop institutional arrangements to deal with these problems. Cities were the focal point of institutional change because their governments, regardless of the background of individual members, vied for a more central position in Europe's urban network. To a large extent this process was self-propelling because the growing connectivity between cities, and the related alignment of institutional arrangements, made it increasingly easy for merchants to relocate at low cost when economic or political circumstances changed adversely. And thus, in a world where merchants moved around easily and cities competed to increase their share in international trade, even in polities in which international traders were entirely without political voice, rulers had strong incentives to improve institutional arrangements.

THE CASE OF THE LOW COUNTRIES

To demonstrate how urban competition shaped the institutional foundations of international trade in premodern Europe, this book analyzes the business organization of local and foreign merchant communities in Bruges, Antwerp, and Amsterdam. Between 1250 and 1650 these ports succeeded each other as main hubs of long-distance trade in Europe. In 1300 Bruges was one of the first cities on the Continent to establish durable ties with the commercial worlds of the Baltic, the North Sea, and the Mediterranean. As more and more foreign merchants flocked to the Flemish port, it became the principal gateway of Northwestern Europe.[53] Antwerp took over Bruges's leading position in the late fifteenth century, and its appeal to international traders may have been bigger still as the city became the principal outlet for colonial wares imported through Spain and Portugal.[54] With the rise of the Amsterdam market after 1585 the commercial center of gravity in Europe definitely shifted to the North Sea area. Merchants in the Dutch Republic established direct trading connections with every known market inside and outside Europe, and by 1650 Amsterdam had become the undisputed center of world trade.[55]

The analysis begins in chapter 2 with a general discussion of the competition between neighboring ports that led Bruges, Antwerp, and Amsterdam to the adaptation of institutional arrangements to the needs of

[53] Murray 2005: 216–58; Blockmans 2010b: 249–63.
[54] Van Houtte 1953; Van der Wee 1963: 2:113–208.
[55] Barbour 1950; Israel 1989: 38–120; De Vries and Van der Woude 1997: 350–408; Jonker and Sluyterman 2000; Lesger 2006: 62–138.

international traders. For Bruges and Antwerp, where few local business-men traded abroad between 1300 and 1500, this competition revolved around the recruitment of foreign merchants. The special privileges they extended to merchants from Germany, England, France, Portugal, Spain, and several Italian cities, and their more general efforts to improve the cities' commercial and legal infrastructure, were designed to concentrate the sales of manufactures from the Low Countries in one location and to offer merchants from around Europe a platform to trade between each other. In the sixteenth century Amsterdam demonstrated a similar will-ingness to adapt institutional arrangements, first to increase its share in the Baltic grain trade, and then, after the fall of Antwerp in 1585, to become the principal gateway of Northwestern Europe. Contrary to the earlier efforts of Bruges and Antwerp to attract specific groups of mer-chants through extensive privileges, Amsterdam chose to treat all mer-chants, local and foreign, equally.

The remainder of the book explores the various combinations of private and public institutions that merchants in Bruges, Antwerp, and Amsterdam used to keep trading partners on their toes and to protect their trade against violence. Chapter 3 examines the cities' creation of spot markets as a means for foreign traders to find buyers or sellers and negotiate deals with them. On a practical level I will show how public vending locations were constantly adapted to the size and composition of the merchant community, and how the work of local hostellers and brokers was regulated to ensure the availability of current commercial information to all merchants at low cost. At a deeper level these adap-tations reveal exactly how far local governments were willing to go to attract trade. Initially hostellers in each of the three cities offered a wide range of services to foreign visitors. They provided accommodation and storage facilities, they acted as their brokers and commission agents, and they even acted as guarantors for debts outstanding. The crux of this ar-rangement was the merchants' obligation to use a broker for each and every transaction, albeit at very low cost. This division of labor served the foreigners well up until the moment they became permanent residents and started building their own information networks. Now they could find their own trading partners, and as they rented or bought their own houses and storerooms, they no longer needed the hostellers for accom-modation either. The urban magistrates drew the logical conclusion and reorganized the brokers' profession into a subservient group of informa-tion specialists—accepting the inevitable corollary of hostellers and bro-kers losing their leading position in the local market.

Still, these changes in the commercial infrastructure of Bruges, Ant-werp, and Amsterdam could not solve all information problems for mer-chants, notably because their permanent presence in the Low Countries forced them to trade at arm's length with merchants elsewhere in Europe. To organize these cross-border transactions, international traders relied on relatives and friends who either traded on a commission basis or became their formal partners. To instruct these foreign agents the merchants used extensive correspondence and kept private accounts to monitor their operations. Chapter 4 will show that these private arrangements were essential to the growth of the markets of Bruges, Antwerp, and Amsterdam, but it will also reveal the fundamental contribution local governments made to the governance of these cross-border transactions. At first the magistrates' support consisted mainly of the public registration of sales and overseas shipments, but in the course of time the local courts began to accept business correspondence and private accounts as legal proof in lawsuits. For merchants, even if they tried very hard to keep away from time-consuming and reputation-damaging legal proceedings, the creation of a general standard for the instruction of distant agents and the reporting of their results buttressed their private efforts to keep trading partners from cheating and shirking.

This complementary relation between private and public institutions is further explored in chapter 5 when we consider the various ways in which merchants dealt with actual disputes over business transactions. We review the available evidence on commercial litigation in Bruges, Antwerp, and Amsterdam to show that merchants used a combination of peer pressure, arbitration, local court proceedings, and, occasionally, appeals to central courts to end their disputes, albeit with an overwhelming preference for amicable settlement. The resolution of commercial conflicts not only reveals the willingness of urban magistrates to adapt local court proceedings to the merchants' private efforts to enforce contracts, but also reveals the deep impact the presence of a large and heterogeneous group of traders from different parts of Europe had on the process of institutional change. When foreign merchants started to settle in Bruges and Antwerp for longer periods they were granted consular jurisdictions that allowed the leaders of their *nations* to combine the formal representation of their home government with the registration of business transactions and the adjudication of commercial disputes according to the legal rules of their hometown. But as these merchants went beyond basic sales and purchases with merchants from different legal backgrounds they had to choose between the contractual prescripts of either one of the two parties. The magistrates of Bruges, Antwerp, and Amsterdam played a crucial role in facilitating this legal crossover because they allowed merchants to use arbiters to settle disputes amicably and according to their own chosen standard, and because they actively sought to append local customary law with foreign mercantile usage. And thus, just like the hostellers who lost their attraction as key intermediaries when merchants began to organize their own information networks, the consuls of the foreign nations in Bruges and Antwerp were superseded by the local judges of Bruges, Antwerp, and Amsterdam who adapted their court proceedings to serve the merchant community at large.

The final two chapters of the book turn away from agency problems that issued from Europe's legal fragmentation to focus instead on the violence issuing from the Continent's political fragmentation. The turbulent political history of the Low Countries in the late medieval and early modern period allows us to explore how political fragmentation influenced the organization of international trade. Initially, Bruges, Antwerp, and Amsterdam belonged to relatively small polities—the county of Flanders, the duchy of Brabant, and the county of Holland, respectively. In the first half of the fifteenth century the Dukes of Burgundy brought these areas under one rule, and their attempts at political, administrative, and legal centralization of the Netherlands were forcefully continued by Emperor Charles V and his son Philip II in the sixteenth century. As they built their states, the Dukes of Burgundy, the Habsburg kings, and the States General of the Dutch Republic also engaged in wars with other countries. Both these international conflicts and the constant struggle between local and central authorities caused serious damage to merchants, so much so that the Flemish Revolt (1483–92) and the Dutch Revolt (1568–88) ended the commercial hegemony of Bruges and Antwerp, respectively.

The Low Countries nevertheless remained at the heart of European commerce for two reasons. In chapter 6 I will demonstrate that it was not the political power of local or foreign traders that determined the protective efforts of local and central governments, but the merchants' ability to take their business to another city in case of conflicts. Europe's fragmentation implied that such a move would typically find them in another principality, and that created a powerful incentive for rulers to protect trade. But even if this reduced the incidence of violence against international traders, it was never enough to secure their complete safety. Chapter 7 therefore explores the various ways in which merchants dealt with losses. Urban competition mattered once again, not only for specific groups like the German Hanse, punctuating their demand for damages with removals to neighboring ports, but also for the merchant community at large that used the cities' increasingly sophisticated commodity and financial markets to share, spread, and transfer the commercial risks that issued from Europe's political and legal fragmentation.

CHAPTER 2

Commercial Cities

IN LATE MEDIEVAL AND EARLY MODERN EUROPE MANY TOWNS COMPETED to attract foreign merchants and join in the emerging market economy. It was a contradictory competition because rival cities had to collaborate to move up in the urban hierarchy. The most successful ports in the Mediterranean, the Baltic region, or the North Sea area invariably developed close connections to neighboring ports and to the cities in their hinterland that bought foreign products and supplied export commodities. Becoming a principal node in Europe's urban network also required commercial cities to recruit merchants from other places, to secure their safety while traveling abroad, and to facilitate their local sales and purchases. Urban competition thus offered powerful incentives for cities to adapt property rights institutions and contracting institutions to the needs of international traders.

Despite the obvious benefits of an open attitude toward foreign merchants, the historical record provides numerous examples of commercial cities that were much less forthcoming. In her recent work on merchant guilds, Sheilagh Ogilvie gives examples of urban elites using their political power to favor local traders and producers or, inversely, to grant excessive privileges to foreign merchants.[1] Larry Epstein showed that urban rivalry could lead to legal or fiscal obstructions of trade between cities, up to the point of armed conflict to thwart each other's commercial aspirations.[2] But even in a more optimistic scenario in which local governments make every effort to serve the merchant community at large, the institutional framework might remain deficient. On the one hand, urban competition could waste valuable resources as cities, in their effort to attract as many merchants as possible, built commercial facilities that were never used. The opposite could also happen. Cities might be unable to adapt to changing economic circumstances, not because the government was overly friendly with some merchants or hostile to others, but simply because merchants and magistrates had invested themselves in a particular way of doing business, making it too costly to change their ways.

Still the growth of European trade between 1000 and 1800 leaves no doubt that quite a few commercial cities were able to overcome the negative

---

[1] Ogilvie 2011: 44–75, 100–125.
[2] Epstein 2000: 147–55.

effects of urban competition and develop an institutional framework conducive to the growth of trade. Among them were Bruges, Antwerp, and Amsterdam, whose successive commercial leadership can help us understand under which circumstances urban competition led to an improvement of the organization of international trade rather than regulatory capture, institutional oversupply, or institutional sclerosis. What did the three cities do to obtain a central position in domestic and international trade? Did they offer strategic privileges to traders whose presence was deemed indispensable for the growth of trade, or rather develop a commercial and legal infrastructure that served the entire merchant community? And what happened when the commercial prospects of other ports improved: could well-designed institutional arrangements keep merchants from taking their business elsewhere?

THE GROWTH OF THE BRUGES MARKET

Bruges was the first city in the Low Countries to become a major international market. It was probably in 1134 that a flood created the Zwyn, an arm of the sea that secured Bruges's access to the North Sea, allowing its merchants to travel to England to buy wool and to Gascony to buy wine. Back in Flanders the wool and wine were sold at the fairs of Ypres, Messines, Lille, and Torhout—an annual cycle that Bruges itself was added to in 1200.[3] Meanwhile, merchants from Bruges, Ypres, Lille, and various other towns marketed Flemish cloth in England, Germany, and, from about 1180 onward, at the international fairs of Champagne, southeast of Paris, where woolens were exchanged for silk and spices carried by Italian and Catalan merchants.[4]

The close commercial connections between Flemish cities also led to collaboration abroad. The Flemish cloth traders in England and France were organized in *hanses*. This incorporation allowed the towns of Flanders to control the export of textiles. At the same time the delegation of magistrates of each of the towns to a judicial body called the Scabini Flandriae supported the adjudication of conflicts between merchants. The Flemish merchants also benefited from the bilateral agreements the Count of Flanders signed with neighboring rulers to secure the safety of their subjects in each other's territory. Yet despite these safe-conducts and the strict internal organization, the Flemish hanses abroad never obtained

---

[3]Van Houtte 1953: 180–83; Henn 1999b: 50–54; Blockmans 2010b: 107–17.
[4]Reincke 1942–43: passim; Ammann 1954: 17, 26–38; Van Werveke 1936: passim; Van Werveke 1953a: 7–35; Van Houtte 1966: 30.

a formal status similar, for example, to that of the Germans who occupied the London Steelyard.[5]

The Flemish presence in foreign markets did not last. In the course of the thirteenth century, political and economic changes in England, Germany, and France forced their almost complete retreat.[6] First, various German towns raised their tariffs to bar Flemish traders from their markets. By the end of the century, active trade with Germany was reduced to a fraction of what it had been.[7] In England, merchants from Flanders also met with increasing competition from local wool exporters, all too aware of their commercial opportunities in Flanders. In 1294 the English king even established a formal staple on the Continent, with the merchants of the staple as the sole providers of wool.[8] Meanwhile, in France, higher tariffs, political turmoil, and outright assaults on foreign merchants ended Flemish visits to the Champagne fairs around 1280.[9]

But even if foreign competition damaged Flemish traders, their retreat from markets in England and France did not end Bruges's participation in international exchange. On the contrary, once the city had been granted the right to organize an annual fair in 1200, merchants from Cologne started trading Rhine wine for woolens in Bruges.[10] About the same time, improvements in shipping stimulated merchants from Lübeck, Hamburg, and several Baltic ports to carry their grain, timber, fish, and ore to the Flemish port. Around the middle of the thirteenth century, English merchants began offering their wool for sale in Bruges, while merchants and shipmasters from Galicia, Castile, and Biscay imported wool, iron, and wine.[11] In the late thirteenth century, merchant houses from Venice and Genoa stopped traveling to the Champagne fairs. Instead they began sending galleys with silk, alum, dyes, fruit, and spices to Bruges, where they employed agents to supervise sales, organize exports, and remit funds to Italy.[12] At the turn of the fourteenth century Portuguese and Scottish merchants had also become regular visitors in Bruges.[13]

[5]Van Werveke 1953a, 1953b; Blockmans 2010b: 112–17. See also chapter 7, "Prize Cases."
[6]Häpke 1908: 58–64; Reincke 1942–43: passim; Ammann 1954: 38–49; Van Houtte 1966: 31–32.
[7]Postan 1987: 185; Paravicini 1992: 99–100.
[8]Carson 1992: 130–31; Nicholas 1979: 23.
[9]Van Werveke 1953a: 20–23; Munro 2001: 14–24; Bautier 1953: passim; Thomas 1977: passim.
[10]Rössner 2001: 49–50.
[11]Verlinden 1939: 56–58.
[12]Vandewalle 2002: 27–30; Henn 1999b: 53; Häpke 1908: 157. To be sure, Italian merchants also continued to carry goods overland, over the Alps, and through southern Germany: Van Houtte 1982: 173.
[13]Pohl 1977: 23; Rooseboom 1910: 5.

The city's commercial ascent ultimately depended on its central position in Flanders' urban network. The production and export of textiles was the linchpin of the Bruges market. In 1322 the Count of Flanders designated Bruges as the official staple for all cloth produced in his territories. The importance of textiles was threefold. First, it stimulated imports of wool from England and Spain. Second, it attracted merchants from Venice, Florence, Genoa, Rome, and Lucca who exchanged the local products for their own high-value commodities. Third, and perhaps most important, German traders sold Flemish cloth to the Baltic and Central Europe, while importing timber, iron, and hides from these markets to Bruges. A large part of the foreign imports was sold to local customers, but transit trade between alien merchants also did occur.[14] In addition to this textile economy, Bruges imported bulk commodities such as grain, wine, and salt, in large quantities from England, France, and other parts of the Low Countries.

In the fourteenth century the fairs were no longer the focal point of exchange, but trade nevertheless remained seasonal. Commercial transactions were concentrated in April, May, and June, when the annual fair was held and the galleys from Venice, Genoa, and Florence arrived in the outposts of Damme and Sluis.[15] Merchants from Flanders, Germany, and Italy used the fair to settle their accounts, and transfer funds abroad.[16] Not surprisingly, the number of foreign merchants soared in springtime. Payments of local excises on beer and wine by merchants from Lübeck, Cologne, and various other Hanseatic cities in the second half of the fourteenth century show that from April to June 100 to 150 German merchants were present in Bruges, while in the remainder of the year there were never more than 50.[17]

As Flemish textile merchants traded in hanses when they traveled abroad, most alien merchants in Bruges were allowed to form associations with fellow traders from their hometown or home country. The initial recognition of these foreign nations (*vreemde naties*), as they were commonly referred to, issued from bilateral agreements between the Count of Flanders and foreign authorities. In exchange for safe-conducts given to Flemish merchants in England, parts of France, and various towns in Germany in the twelfth and thirteenth centuries, visitors from these territories were promised similar protection of their person and goods in Bruges.[18] In 1252 merchants from the Holy Roman Empire were the first

[14]Stabel 1997: 138–45; Brulez 1973: 21–26.
[15]Blockmans 1992a: 42.
[16]Paravicini 1992: 118; Lesnikov 1973: passim.
[17]Paravicini 1992: 101.
[18]Murray 2005; Greve 2001: 272; Blockmans 1992b: 220; De Roover 1948: 14–15; Vandewalle 2002: 34; Nicholas 1979: 24; Rooseboom 1910: 10; Bartier and Nieuwenhuysen 1965: 47–48; Van Houtte 1982: 171; Maréchal 1951: 27, 40.

to receive more extensive privileges, including the reduction of toll tariffs, the preservation of the ownership of goods in sunken vessels, and protection against seizure of their goods by other merchants.[19] But the Countess of Flanders denied them permission to have their own trade settlement outside the city walls.

A more formal association of alien merchants in Bruges began to take shape once their numbers began to grow in the late thirteenth century. A first concession, made to German and Spanish traders in 1282, and later extended to other groups, was permission to trade with other foreigners every day of the year, provided local brokers mediated all sales.[20] In the first half of the fourteenth century earlier safe-conducts were confirmed and new ones granted.[21] To further accommodate foreign traders in the fourteenth century most nations also obtained consular jurisdictions that allowed them to adjudicate commercial conflicts among themselves.[22] It was a well-considered intervention. The legal privileges placed the foreigners outside the local law, at least in internal disputes, but the urban magistrate controlled by local traders and artisans did not object as the livelihood of the city's middling groups depended on their presence.[23] Still, no foreign compounds were established in the city. The foreign consuls simply occupied nation houses in the town center, while local mendicant orders accommodated the meetings and religious services. Accommodation remained a private affair dominated by the city's more than one hundred hostellers.[24]

Foreign merchants dominated the Bruges market throughout the fourteenth and fifteenth centuries, but it is not easy to determine exactly how many alien traders lived and worked in Bruges at any point in time. The more or less extensive privileges of the various nationalities do show that more than a dozen foreign nations were formally represented in Bruges. Among them were merchants from Venice, Genoa, Milan, Florence, Lucca, Piacenza, and the German Hanse and several firms from southern Germany, Scottish staplers, and traders from Portugal, Castile, Aragon, and Navarre.[25] The number of members of each foreign nation is

---

[19] Stein 1902; Vandewalle 2002: 28, 30.

[20] Henn 1999a: 216–17; Stützel 1998: 25–26; Beuken 1950: 41; Greve 2000: 38.

[21] See chapter 6.

[22] See chapter 5.

[23] Murray 2005: 113–17, 228–29.

[24] Rössner 2001: 226–39; Beuken 1950: 41; Van Houtte 1983; Murray 2000: 12–13; Murray 2005: 196–205; Greve 2000: passim; Greve 2001: passim.

[25] Van Houtte 1982: 171–89; Vandewalle 2002: 32–39; Maréchal 1951: 26, 30; Brulez 1973; Paviot 2002: 45–48; Rooseboom 1910: 3. Merchants from Ireland received the freedom to trade in Flanders in 1387, but there is no trace at all of any Irish community residing in Bruges: Bartier and Nieuwenhuysen 1965: 244–46.

far more difficult to determine, if only because it could vary enormously in the course of one year.

The account books of a local money changer, kept between April 1366 and April 1368, reveal the names of 220 merchants from Germany, the Iberian Peninsula, Italy, and the British Isles—but this may have been just a fraction of the total number of foreign visitors.[26] More precise indications on the size of the various merchant communities date from the mid-fifteenth century, when the foreign nations participated in processions to celebrate Bruges's reconciliation with Philip the Good in 1440, and the accession of Charles the Bold in 1468. Table 2.1 shows that by far the largest nation at the time was the German Hanse, with at least one hundred, and in the high season perhaps as many as two hundred merchants. Most other nations counted a few dozen members only. Thus, the Venetian, Genoese, Florentine, Lucchese, Milanese, and Portuguese consuls each represented between twenty and thirty merchants, while merchants from Castille, Aragon, Navarre, and Biscay may together have numbered up to fifty. Besides, there were small contingents of Scottish and southern German merchants, but their exact number is unknown.[27] Merchants from the Staple Company in Calais continued to travel to Bruges to sell wool until the late fifteenth century, but English broadcloth was marketed in Antwerp instead.[28]

During the high season the number of foreign merchants must have exceeded this more or less permanent community of four hundred men, but perhaps not by that much, given the changes that had occurred in the composition of Bruges's international trade since the late fourteenth century.[29] Cheaper broadcloth from Brabant, Holland, Italy, and especially England had slowly but surely put an end to the export of traditional Flemish woolens. Instead, lower quality *new draperies* produced around Flanders and very expensive dyed cloth manufactured in the cities found their way to Northern, Central, and Southern Europe.[30] This offered new opportunities for local entrepreneurs to become international traders, but their number remained limited. Meanwhile foreign traders bought an in-

[26] Murray 2000: 7; De Roover 1948: 20. There were also French (233), Flemish (413), and Brabantine (125) account holders, but there is little evidence for their active involvement in long-distance trade: Blockmans 1992a: 50–53.

[27] Bruges also hosted merchants from Piacenza, Siena, Pisa, and Bologna, but there is no trace of any formal organization of these merchants: Vandewalle 2002: 37.

[28] Munro 1966: passim; Nicholas 1979: passim; Murray 2005: 218, 221–22, 236–41, 264.

[29] Based on surviving inventories of some of Bruges's hostels Jim Murray estimates the number of beds available to foreign visitors in Bruges around 1370 at 700 to 900. These guests, however, would include apprentices, clerks, shipmasters, perhaps sailors, and maybe even the families of some merchants. Murray's own estimates for merchants in the fourteenth century are considerably lower as well: Murray 2005: 95–97, 193.

[30] Munro 1972: 1–3; Munro 2008; Stabel 1997: 144–50.

TABLE 2.1. Estimated composition of Bruges's merchant community (permanent residents) in the mid-fifteenth century

Origin	Number
Germany (Hanse)	100
Venice, Genoa, Florence, Lucca, Milan	150
Castile, Aragon	50
Portugal	25
Scotland	10?
Southern Germany	10?
Low Countries	50?
Total	ca. 400

Sources: De Roover 1948: 20–21; Despars 1840: 3:431–32; Gilliodts-Van Severen 1901–2: 65; Greve 1997: 159; Murray 2000: 7; de la Marche 1850: 524–25; Paravicini 1992: 101; Van Uytven, 1995: 261; Pohl 1977: 24; Van Houtte 1982: 126.

creasing number of luxury manufactures, including tapestries, jewelry, paternosters, and paintings.[31] These high-value commodities were available throughout the year in Bruges, but four times a year merchants could visit the fairs of Bergen-op-Zoom and Antwerp to find a ready supply of English and South German textiles, and a large variety of manufactures from other parts of the Low Countries.

THE FAIRS OF BRABANT

Bruges essentially owed its commercial success in the fourteenth and fifteenth centuries to Flanders' thriving textile industry and its central location between foreign markets. London, the city's principal foreign competitor, also had a thriving domestic textile industry, but the English port lacked Bruges's easy access to Continental trading routes. Bruges's rivals within the Low Countries suffered other shortcomings. In the Northern Netherlands there were few towns with extensive foreign connections. Amsterdam had been founded only in 1250, and it did not make its debut in international trade for another century, when Hamburg merchants started trading beer on a regular basis.[32] From the 1350s the fairs of Deventer attracted merchants from Holland who exchanged cloth and dairy products for wine, timber, and manufactures brought by Germans from Westphalia and the Rhineland.[33] The single most important port in the

[31]Van Houtte 1966: passim; Van Houtte 1982: 141–47; Blockmans 1992a: 43–44.
[32]Smit 1914: 34–54; Kaptein 2004: 117–24.
[33]Sneller 1936: 41–45, 94–114; Feenstra 1953: 222–27; Irsigler 1996: 31; Weststrate 2008: 156–76.

Northern Netherlands before 1400 was Dordrecht, situated at the mouth of the rivers Rhine and Meuse, which hosted German and English merchants trading wine and cloth from the late thirteenth century.[34] But even if the city was a convenient stopover for the English and the Germans—in 1358 and 1388 it even served as a temporary seat of the Bruges *Kontor*, that is, the German nation—it had little to offer to other foreigners.[35] Attempts of the Count of Holland and Zeeland to lure Italian, Spanish, and Portuguese merchants to his territories failed altogether.[36]

The only serious competition for Bruges as the major hub of international trade came from the fairs of Antwerp and Bergen-op-Zoom, established in the first half of the fourteenth century.[37] As early as 1296 the duke of Brabant had extended safe-conducts, toll exemptions, and the right to establish a separate jurisdiction to English merchants in his territories.[38] In 1315 a similar set of privileges was extended to all foreigners.[39] In the following decade the fairs of Brabant were established. These fairs were held four times a year, in Antwerp at Whitsun and St. Bavis (October 1) and in Bergen-op-Zoom at Easter and All Saints' Day.[40] The strength of the Brabant fairs, like that of the earlier fairs in Flanders, lay in the interaction between local manufacturing and foreign trade. Antwerp and Bergen-op-Zoom attracted a considerable number of merchants and artisans from the Low Countries, as well as English wool exporters and cloth dealers and even a few Italian merchants.[41]

Antwerp's promising start was compromised in 1356 when the Count of Flanders, Louis of Male (r. 1346–84), seized upon the problematic succession of Duke John III of Brabant to attack the city and submit it to Flemish rule.[42] In a very explicit attempt to strengthen Bruges's position as the leading international market, Louis de Male forbade the foreign nations in Bruges to travel to Brabant and granted English merchants access to Flanders. The fines paid by foreign merchants visiting Antwerp in 1389 and Bergen-op-Zoom in 1401 suggest trade in Brabant did not come to a complete halt, but in this period Bruges was the dominant

---

[34] Dijkman 2011: 124–41.

[35] Beuken 1950: 60–118; Seifert 1997: 82–89, 115–29.

[36] Van Houtte 1982: 189.

[37] The best overview of Antwerp's commercial history up to 1600 remains Van der Wee 1963: vol. 2. For Bergen-op-Zoom: Slootmans 1985.

[38] De Smedt 1951: 63, 77–78, 86.

[39] Gotzen 1951: 466; Rössner 2001: 50; Henn 1999b: 56. Nuremberg merchants had already received toll exemptions in 1311: Häpke 1908: 117–19.

[40] The Antwerp fairs were instituted between 1317 and 1324, the fairs of Bergen-op-Zoom between 1337 and 1359: Van Houtte 1953: 189; Slootmans 1985: 1:6–7; Kortlever 2001: 626–27.

[41] Van Uytven 2004; Slootmans 1985: 1:6–8; Van Houtte 1982: 188.

[42] Blockmans and Prevenier 1999: 54–56; Slootmans 1985: 1:8–10.

market by far.[43] Only after 1405, under the rule of John the Fearless, did Antwerp and Bergen-op-Zoom become international markets in their own right again.[44] The growth of English exports of broadcloth, and the refusal of Bruges to import them, brought English merchants back to Brabant. Endowed with ducal and urban privileges, they traded their cloth for wine, fustians, alum, spices, copper, iron, and metal wares brought by merchants from the Rhineland and southern Germany.[45] By 1480 up to 40 percent of the English cloth exports was destined for Antwerp, from where it was re-exported primarily to Germany.[46] In addition to this, the fairs in the fifteenth century attracted hundreds of artisans from various parts of Brabant and Flanders, including Bruges, who sold their local produce to foreign customers.[47]

The precocious growth of the Brabant fairs changed Bruges's commercial outlook. Its resident foreign merchants were attracted by the growing variety of manufactures available in Bergen-op-Zoom and Antwerp.[48] In the mid-fifteenth century Italian merchants wrote home that trade in the Flemish port stalled during the fairs. In 1430 Bruges's magistrate explicitly forbade merchants to visit Brabant's fairs, but to no avail. Hundreds of artisans and merchants, local and foreign, regularly traveled to Brabant and even bought houses there.[49] The German Hanse formally decided to remove its staple from Bruges to Antwerp for the duration of the latter's fairs.[50] Neither Bruges's donation of a square in 1457 nor the erection of a spectacular Hanse house at the square between 1478 and 1481 could prevent the German merchants from importing and exporting an increasing share of their merchandise via Antwerp.[51]

The growth of trade in Brabant notwithstanding, Bruges remained the leading foreign market in the fifteenth century. Italian, Castilian, and German merchants were still firmly based in the Flemish port and actually bought houses, including, most famously, the partners of the Medici house who in 1466 took up residence in the Hôtel Bladelin, a walled residence with a small courtyard and a large room on the ground floor, to carry out banking operations. The purchases of foreign merchants and local elites continued to provide many artisans in Bruges with a livelihood. Local

[43]Gilliodts-Van Severen 1871–85: 4:158, 201; Slootmans 1985: 1:121–23; Van der Wee 1963: 2:20–28, 37–41.
[44]Van der Wee 1963: 2:49–56, 73–80; Slootmans 1985: 1:17.
[45]Munro 1972; Jenks 1996a; De Smedt 1951: 43–108; Rössner 2001: 49–50, 82–84.
[46]Munro 1966: 1143. Van der Wee 1963: 2:80–83.
[47]Slootmans 1985: 1:286–97; Van Houtte 1953: 193.
[48]Munro 1966: 1139–40; Blockmans and Prevenier 1999: 215; Paravicini 1992: 107–8.
[49]Greve 1997: 157; Dumolyn 1997: 72; Van Houtte 1953: 193.
[50]Beuken 1950: 150–53; Maréchal 1951: 31, 35; Blockmans and Prevenier 1999: 165.
[51]Rössner 2001: 72–76; Paravicini 1992: 99–100, 105–6.

entrepreneurs even got involved in the finishing of English cloth—in direct competition with Antwerp.[52] The financial market, centered upon the Bourse square, proved a great asset. Italian merchant bankers provided credit to numerous private merchants through bills of exchange, arranged loans for the Dukes of Burgundy, and helped the Church to remit the revenues of papal tithes to Rome.[53]

Antwerp, at the same time, was not immune to the vicissitudes of international politics. Particularly disruptive were conflicts between the Dukes of Burgundy and the king of England. The latter's fiscal policies, and the obligation to buyers of English wool in Calais to pay in cash and bullion, led the Dukes of Burgundy—supported in at least one instance by Bruges—to impose three successive embargoes on English cloth imports to Brabant and Flanders (1434–39, 1447–52, and 1464–67).[54] It was only when the cities of Flanders revolted against Maximilian of Austria in the 1480s that Antwerp could aspire to succeed to Bruges. Maximilian, who upon the death of his wife Mary of Burgundy in 1482 was named regent on behalf of his son Philip the Fair, wanted to become Count of Flanders in his own right. To force Bruges to accept, he ordered all foreign nations to move to Antwerp in 1484, where they would receive the same privileges and compensation for possible damages. At first the aliens did not comply, but when Maximilian's troops appeared before the city in the spring of 1485, they used the Brabant fairs as an excuse to leave Bruges.[55] Their departure was only temporary because in June of the same year Maximilian captured Bruges and reestablished his authority. However, in June 1488 Maximilian instructed the foreigners to leave Bruges once again, this time to punish the town magistrate for his humiliating imprisonment in the preceding months.[56] The merchants complied and for several years had no opportunity to return because Bruges and Sluis continued to fight Maximilian.[57]

FROM BRUGES TO ANTWERP

When peace was finally restored in 1492 Bruges had lost its momentum. Antwerp's magistrate had confirmed earlier privileges of the Dukes of Burgundy safeguarding the property of foreign merchants, and in addition

[52] Brulez 1973: 8; Geirnaert 1992: 80; Blockmans 1992b: 215–19; Dumolyn 1997: 60–61.
[53] Van der Wee 1963: 2:109–11; Blockmans and Prevenier 1999: 166; Paravicini 1992: 114–15.
[54] Van Houtte 1953: 201, 203; Munro 1966: 1141; De Smedt 1951: 88–89.
[55] Maréchal 1951: 31.
[56] Goris 1925: 38.
[57] Munro 1966: 1150–51.

granted them tax privileges equal to those they had enjoyed in Bruges.[58] In 1491 Maximilian had also granted Antwerp the staple of Italian alum, indispensable for the finishing of textiles.[59] Meanwhile Bruges tried very hard to bring about the return of the foreign nations. Already in 1488 the city had forbidden foreigners from selling merchandise bought at the Brabant fairs.[60] The town magistrate also proposed additional privileges and exemption from excise duties for aliens. Even their long-time commercial rivals, the English exporters of broadcloth, were invited to transfer their trade to the Flemish port.[61] Indeed, in 1493 Bruges reached an agreement with representatives of almost all communities about their return.[62] However, even if the consuls were inclined to move back to the Flemish port, their fellow merchants were not.

One trump card held by Antwerp was its acceptance of the import of English cloth. In 1496 the city benefited from the Magnus Intercursus, a peace treaty signed between the dukes of Burgundy and the king of England. This event marked the beginning of a lasting peace and formalized the position of the Brabant fairs as the only outlet for English cloth on the Continent. The Company of Merchant Adventurers committed to offering all their cloth for sale in Antwerp and Bergen-op-Zoom.[63] A further stimulus to the growth of the Antwerp market was the Portuguese penetration of Asia. In order to obtain silver and copper from Central Europe for export to the new colonies, the Portuguese king chose to make Antwerp the pepper staple for Northern Europe in 1498.[64] Twelve years later twenty-odd Portuguese merchants were formally recognized as a nation with a distinct legal status. Between 1498 and 1548 the Portuguese king also appointed individual merchants in Antwerp as royal factors. The factor supervised the sale of spices, organized commercial and financial transactions for the king, and informed him about commercial and political matters. The factor did not head the Portuguese nation, however, nor did he function as their diplomatic representative.[65]

It was not long before other merchant communities formalized their presence in Antwerp. Genoa, Florence, and Lucca established a consulate around 1515.[66] Merchants from Aragon and Catalonia appointed

---

[58] On the internal organization of foreign nations in Antwerp: Van Houtte 1953: 205.
[59] Munro 1966: 1149.
[60] Van Houtte 1953: 193.
[61] Munro 1966: 1150–59.
[62] Maréchal 1951: 48–54.
[63] Van der Wee 1963: 2:123.
[64] Van Houtte 1961: 260; Van der Wee 1963: 2:124–30; Maréchal 1951: 42; Goris 1925: 230.
[65] Goris 1925: 38, 215–36, 371–72.
[66] Maréchal 1951: 42–44.

consuls in 1527.[67] Even merchant communities without a formal representation in Antwerp reoriented their trade. The German Hanse retained its Kontor in Bruges, but its members—especially those from the Rhineland—were focused entirely on the Brabant fairs.[68] Wool exporters from Burgos and Bilbao had formally established their wool staple in the Flemish port in 1493, but they fetched cheap textiles at the markets of Bergen-op-Zoom and Antwerp for export to the colonies.[69] Basque and Castilian merchants also apprenticed their sons with friends and relatives in Brabant.[70] The Scottish staple was removed to Zeeland.[71] Merchants from southern Germany and France did not acquire a formal status but nevertheless concentrated their trade in the Scheldt port.[72]

In the first decades of the sixteenth century trade in Antwerp was still seasonal. The high season fell between Easter and Whitsun, when new broadcloths from England arrived together with the first shipments of grain from the Baltic and the big wagon trains carrying silk, fustians, copper, silver, and other valuable commodities from southern Germany and Italy.[73] As time progressed, however, transactions spilled over to the time between fairs. To accommodate this growing commercial activity, Antwerp and Bergen-op-Zoom prolonged each of their fairs with two, three, or even more weeks.[74] Even Bruges tried to take advantage of the growing trade by organizing yet another fair in January, right between two of Brabant's fairs. This, however, did not lead to the return of the foreign nations, and the city could do little more than complain about how the fairs of Brabant together lasted for about two-thirds of the year.[75]

[67] Maréchal 1951: 46; According to Goris (1925: 59) merchants from Biscay also appointed consuls in Antwerp at the beginning of the sixteenth century. Merchants from Navarre and Andalucia remained in Bruges: Vandewalle 2002: 40–42.

[68] Rössner 2001: 92.

[69] Maréchal 1951: 47–48; Van Houtte 1961: 260–61; Munro 1966: 1149; Munro 1972: 183–84; Van Houtte 1953: 194.

[70] Goris 1925: 31.

[71] Maréchal 1951: 42. The removal of the Scottish merchants to Zeeland was the logical outcome of their regular trade with Middelburg and Veere since the middle of the fifteenth century. They left Bruges already in the 1490s, but the official settlement of the Scottish staple in Middelburg was realized only in 1522. In later years the staple was moved to nearby Veere. Meanwhile the Scottish merchants continued to buy and sell in Bruges in the sixteenth century: Rooseboom 1910: 19–21, 29–40, 56, 61.

[72] Harreld 2004: 69; Coornaert 1961: 2:23–28.

[73] Van Houtte 1953: 191; Doehaerd 1962–63: passim; Herborn 1984: passim. The number of ships arriving from England between 1537 and 1568 shows a strong seasonal pattern until the late 1540s: De Smedt 1954: 276. Sailings from Antwerp to Southern Europe in 1540 suggest a similar seasonality: Goris 1925: 162–67.

[74] The first extensions occurred in the fifteenth century; after 1500 it became standard procedure: Van Houtte 1953: 193; Kortlever 2001: 629.

[75] Van Houtte 1953: 185, 194.

Meanwhile the Antwerp market gradually eclipsed the fairs of Bergen-op-Zoom. The Scheldt port boasted a larger supply of local manufactures, including extensive facilities to finish English cloth, and probably had better access to the Brabantine and Flemish hinterland.[76] Even manufactures from Bruges were often sold in Antwerp.[77] By the 1530s the annual number of visitors of the Bergen-op-Zoom fairs had dropped by 25 percent. In 1534 the town magistrate complained that prolongation of trade in Antwerp prevented merchants from coming to their fairs.[78] The final blow was dealt in 1541, when Charles V shifted the dates for settlement of bills of exchange in such a way that all financial transactions had to be concentrated in the Scheldt port. A few years later merchants from within and outside the Low Countries had withdrawn from Bergen-op-Zoom altogether.[79]

The growth of trade in Antwerp effectively created a permanent market. Whereas in the late fifteenth century the Church of Our Lady still rented 92 percent of its stalls for the duration of the fairs only, by 1547 permanent leases of shops, stalls, and other commercial buildings accounted for 95 percent of the church's trade-related income.[80] The city council, largely made up of nobles, jurists, and patricians with no direct involvement in international trade, nevertheless recognized its importance and provided several nations with their own storage facilities.[81] Individual investors also built warehouses that were let to foreign merchants. The most notable improvement was undoubtedly the New Bourse, opened in 1532. Although textiles, leather and hides, jewelry, tapestries, and paintings were traded in separate facilities, other commodities were sold at the Bourse, which also was the focal point of payments, insurance, remittance of bills of exchange, and miscellaneous credit operations.[82]

By the mid-sixteenth century the composition of Antwerp's trade closely resembled that of Bruges a century earlier. As Wilfrid Brulez's reconstruction of commodity flows to and from Antwerp in the 1560s reveals, the city had become a major market for foreign imports and local exports, but it also functioned as a transit station for goods from one part of Europe to another. Imports from France, Italy, Spain, Portugal,

---

[76] Van Houtte 1953: 194; Van Houtte 1982: 190.
[77] Gelderblom 2008: 10–13.
[78] Van Houtte 1953: 195, 196.
[79] Slootmans 1935: 8–20; Rössner 2001: 94.
[80] Van der Wee 1963: 2:329.
[81] On the limited participation of merchants in 1490–99 and 1550–59: Kint 1996b: 303–13. Wouters (2004: 905, 915, 917, 929, 930, 933) has demonstrated that between 1520 and 1555 very few active merchants were elected in Antwerp's city council. On the absence of merchants in Antwerp's magistrate between 1550 and 1565: Marnef 1996: 40.
[82] De Roover 1953a: 1012–14; Ehrenberg 1896: 14–17, 21.

and the Baltic area all exceeded two million guilders, and although some silver may have flowed to these markets most imports were balanced by sales of local manufactures or re-export of foreign goods. From Antwerp merchants could consign goods to partners or commission agents in commercial cities across Europe, and to organize this multilateral trade, more and more foreigners stayed for long periods.[83] Alien traders still used local hostels, but a growing number of them rented or bought private houses.[84] Consequently, as Tables 2.1 and 2.2 show, by 1560 the number of resident merchants from Italy, Portugal, Spain, England, France, and Germany in Antwerp was more than three times the number in Bruges a century before.

One important difference between Bruges and Antwerp was that more and more merchants born and raised in the Low Countries began to participate in international exchange.[85] The competitive edge of the latter merchants lay in the marketing of local produce, including agricultural surpluses and a variety of (finished) textiles, tapestries, jewelry, paintings, furniture, and metal wares. They were not given preferential treatment by the local magistrate, but their detailed knowledge of these products, personal relations with producers, and easy access to foreign buyers in France, Germany, England, and the Baltic area allowed the indigenous merchants to compete with foreigners.[86]

And then in 1566 Iconoclasm struck the Low Countries. In the course of a few months dozens of churches were robbed of their statues and other religious artifacts. Aristocratic petitioners asked for toleration of the Protestant faith. Initially their demands were met, but the conflict escalated with the arrival of the Duke of Alba in 1567. His persecution of Protestants and dissident noblemen and his efforts to enforce royal authority met with strong disapproval. In 1572, after several years of growing resistance, civil war broke out in Holland. The political and military unrest did not fail to produce its effect on Antwerp's merchant community. Already when Alba arrived in 1567, a first wave of Protestant merchants fled to England and Germany. The next year the English Merchant Adventurers decided to move to Stade in northern Germany. In the early 1570s Catholic merchants from Brabant and Flanders started moving to the Iberian Peninsula.[87]

---

[83]To be sure, many merchants continued to come for short periods only. This was true for the Merchant Adventurers who focused on the fairs (De Smedt 1954: 124–25) and for Spanish and Portuguese *viaenezes* who visited the fairs (Goris 1925: 31). Italians merchants who came to check on their agents also stayed for short periods only (Goris 1925: 31).

[84]Beck 1982: 767–68; De Smedt 1954: 8–16.

[85]Gelderblom 2000: 40–48, with references to the relevant literature.

[86]Gelderblom 2003b: 250–54; Putterils 2012.

[87]Stols 1971: 1:49–95.

TABLE 2.2. Estimated composition of Antwerp's merchant community (permanent residents) around 1560

Origin	1560
Italy	100
Portugal	100
France	150
Spain	150
Germany	300
England	300
Low Countries	400
Total	**1,500**

Sources: Brulez 1975: 128–31; De Smedt 1954: 123–28; Goris 1925: 54; Pohl 1977: 29, 38, 63, 73; Gelderblom 2000: 43–45.

The largest drain on Antwerp's merchant community followed the Spanish Fury of 1576. Spanish soldiers who had not received their pay pillaged houses of rich merchants and killed hundreds of citizens. The outburst of violence spurred German, Spanish, and Italian merchants to move elsewhere or return home. Only small groups of foreigners remained, most notably a few dozen Portuguese merchants.[88] And yet Antwerp's trade did not come to a standstill. Many local merchants continued their trade with France, England, the Baltic area, the Iberian Peninsula, and Italy, and some even started to explore new markets in Russia, and on the west coast of Africa. As a result, in July 1584, when Spanish troops began their siege of Antwerp, the city may still have counted about a thousand international traders—the vast majority of whom were born and raised in the Southern Netherlands.[89] Fourteen months later the city fell to the Duke of Parma and hundreds of merchants moved to the Northern Netherlands.

AMSTERDAM BEFORE THE DUTCH REVOLT

The dominant role of Antwerp notwithstanding, other towns in the Low Countries did participate in foreign trade in the sixteenth century. Bruges held on to its Spanish wool staple, and continued to export

[88] Gelderblom 2000: 71. On the Portuguese community in Antwerp: Pohl 1977.

[89] Based on estimates by van Roey 1963: 84–118. I have previously argued that there were as many as 1,600 merchants in Antwerp in 1585 (Gelderblom 2003b). However, little is known about the scale and scope of their operations, so a lower estimate of 1,000 long-distance traders seems closer to the mark.

Flemish manufactures directly to the Iberian Peninsula.[90] Towns like Lille and Douai in the south of Flanders also exported textiles on their own account. In the Northern Netherlands, Middelburg gained a large share in the wine trade with France, while Dordrecht continued to dominate river traffic to Germany.[91] Seaports and industrial towns in the province of Holland specialized in the export of herring, butter, cheese, peat, beer, and textiles. Most important, Amsterdam emerged as the principal supplier of shipping services to merchants in Antwerp, and the leading port for trade in grain, timber, salt, herring, and perhaps even wine and textiles, with the Baltic area. Especially between 1540 and 1565 Amsterdam's commercial expansion became closely linked to the growth of the Antwerp market.[92]

Amsterdam's trade with the Baltic dated back to the late fourteenth century when Dutch shipmasters began to travel regularly through the Danish Sound to sell salt, herring, and cloth and fetch grain, timber, tar, and pitch.[93] In the first decades of the fifteenth century the growing Dutch presence in the Baltic triggered diplomatic missions and armed interventions from the German Hanse, but these proved to no avail.[94] The Truce of Copenhagen (1441) ended the privateering war between Lübeck and Holland that had started in 1438, and secured the continuation of Dutch trade with the Baltic.[95] While several Hanseatic ports continued to refuse access to shipmasters from Holland, various small, irregular ports (*Klipphäfen*) and the city of Danzig allowed the Dutch to expand their operations in the East.[96] Meanwhile, the Dukes of Burgundy made a serious effort to conclude treaties with Holland's principal trading partners in order to protect the property of all merchants involved in the Baltic trade—a strategy reminiscent of the bilateral agreements of the twelfth and thirteenth centuries:[97]

> In order for the alien merchant to choose to settle and establish his business in the cities of this land, various treaties and minutes were

[90]Van Houtte 1982: 430–33.
[91]On Middelburg: Enthoven 1996: 5–6. For a reconstruction of Middelburg's formal claims to the wine staple in the Low Countries, see Wijffels 2003: 289–93. On Dordrecht: Tracy 1990a: 53–60.
[92]Blockmans 1993: passim; van Zanden 1993b: 357–67; Lesger 2006: 17–61.
[93]Smit 1914: 88–161; Henn 1999c; Kaptein 2004: 121–23.
[94]Seifert (1997: 173–418) provides an exhaustive analysis of the growing tensions between Holland and the Hanseatic League in the first half of the fifteenth century but also points to the continued interdependence of their commercial activities.
[95]Blockmans and Prevenier 1999: 90–93; Tracy 1990a: 16–17; Seifert 1997: 275–320.
[96]Posthumus 1953: 177, 182. On the cooperation between merchants from Holland and the German Hanse: Seifert 1997: 89–91, 205, 212; Seifert 1995: 88–91.
[97]Blockmans and Prevenier 1999: 91, 95.

drawn up with the realms of Denmark, Norway, Sweden, the principalities of Schleswig, Holstein, Wenden, and other Hanseatic and Eastern cities, stipulating that merchants from both cities can freely and
with all kinds of merchandise frequent the lands of Holland and the
East, provided they pay the old toll.[98]

Northern German merchants were the first foreigners to trade in Amsterdam on a regular basis. In 1358 the Hamburg beer traders in the
city were referred to as a company (*gheselscap*) led by two aldermen
who were expected to follow the same rules as the Germans residing in
Dordrecht at the time.[99] Initially the merchants and shipmasters from
Hamburg may have enjoyed a separate jurisdiction in Amsterdam, but it
became quickly obsolete as the city adopted the maritime law of Visby—
which was also used by the Germans—to settle conflicts among merchants,
shipmasters, and their crew.[100] Besides, the magistrate created the opportunity for nonresident merchants to bring their disputes before the local
court twice a week (see also chapter 5).[101] What remained of the corporate organization of Hamburg merchants in Amsterdam in the fifteenth
century was a religious brotherhood that worshipped at St. Paul's altar
in the Old Church.[102]

German merchants became more important for Amsterdam in the first
decades of the sixteenth century when imports of Baltic grain rose from
less than twenty thousand tons in 1480 to more than fifty thousand tons
in 1540. In the same period growing quantities of beer, herring, timber,
salt, and textiles were traded. Amsterdam's protests against the levying
of a customs duty (*congégeld*) on the re-export of grains in the 1520s
and 1530s explicitly referred to the consequences this might have for
the presence of foreigners.[103] This would suggest that merchants from
Danzig and other Baltic ports had been able to step up their business in
the grain trade, even if few of them seem to have settled permanently in
Amsterdam during this period. The urban registration of new citizens
that survives from 1533 onward, reveals no German buying the city's
freedom before 1540.[104] The only well-documented example of a foreign
merchant living permanently in Amsterdam at the time is that of Pompejus Occo, born in East Friesland, who acted as the agent of the south
German merchants Jacob and Anton Fugger and for the Danish king

[98]Noordkerk 1748: 1:chap. 26 (translation by OG); see also chaps. 19 and 20.
[99]Smit 1914: 58–59; de Melker 2002: 38.
[100]Breen 1902: 11–12; Van den Auweele 1977: 220–26.
[101]Breen 1902: 10.
[102]Rössner 2001: 198–200; de Melker 2002: 38.
[103]Meilink 1923a; Van Tielhof 1995a: 132–38.
[104]Amsterdam City Archives, *Poorterboeken* (digital file).

Christian II.[105] Meanwhile, a wealth tax levied in 1545 suggests that by then Amsterdam's local merchant community counted some hundred individuals each owning property worth at least 1,000 guilders.[106]

The number of aliens in Amsterdam certainly rose during the 1540s when merchants in Antwerp accepted the city's role as the principal grain market of the Low Countries. Merchants from Antwerp—Germans and locals alike—began to travel to Amsterdam to fetch grain. Many of them stayed for only a few weeks with one of at least twenty different hostellers.[107] Others bought the local citizenship and moved to the Dutch port permanently. For example, Francois du Gardijn, born in Valenciennes, settled in Amsterdam as an agent of a grain trading firm with partners in Emden, Antwerp, and Lisbon.[108] Amsterdam also attracted immigrants from the Baltic area, like Danzig merchant Cornelis Loeffsz, who arrived around 1550 and for twenty-odd years imported wheat, rye, and timber from Poland.[109] For lack of sources we cannot calculate the exact share of German and Antwerp merchants in Amsterdam's grain trade, but rough estimates suggest they may have financed up to half of all grain shipments.[110]

THE AMSTERDAM MARKET AFTER 1578

With the outbreak of the Dutch Revolt in 1568 Amsterdam temporarily lost its attraction to merchants. Adherents of the Protestant faith, among them several local and foreign merchants, were threatened with persecution. In 1572, moreover, the city council chose to support the Spanish king in his military operations in Holland, which led to a naval blockade of the port by Watergeuzen, rebel troops loyal to William of Orange. Because of these events many merchants decided to leave the city and settle in other ports in Holland, Germany, and even Poland.[111] The crisis lasted until the spring of 1578 when the Catholic city council reached an agreement with William of Orange about their defection to the rebel cause. Shortly after the signing of this Satisfactie, the civic militia ousted the Catholic magistrates and replaced them with Protestant regents.

[105] Nübel 1972: passim.
[106] Meilink 1922: 272–74.
[107] Around 1520 between fifteen and twenty hostellers were located on the town's principal street: Leeuw-Kistemaker 1974: passim; Wijnman 1963: 61–62.
[108] Van Tielhof 1995a: 81; Gelderblom 2000: 86.
[109] Van Tielhof 1997: passim; van Tielhof 1995b: 101–5.
[110] Tracy 1983: 311; van Tielhof 1995a: 185–227.
[111] Van Tielhof 1997: passim; van Tielhof 2002: 16–18; Gelderblom 2000: 84–88.

The defection of Amsterdam to Orange's side and the simultaneous deepening of the crisis in the southern provinces allowed the city to re-conquer its leading role in the Baltic trade, but in addition to the merchants returning from their voluntary exile, dozens of merchants from the Southern Netherlands also decided to move to Amsterdam in the early 1580s, notably to continue their trade with northern Germany, Poland, and Russia. With the siege of Antwerp in 1584, and the subsequent fall of the city in August 1585, immigration in Amsterdam intensified. By 1590 more than two hundred merchants born and raised in Brabant and Flanders had settled in Amsterdam. The Spanish capture of Antwerp and the subsequent naval blockade of both the river Scheldt and the Flemish coast ended the mutually beneficial division of labor between Antwerp and Amsterdam, and replaced it with the concentration of all trade in foodstuffs, raw materials, textiles, and other manufactures in the latter city. This reorientation of trade, however, did not happen overnight as a considerable share of merchants from the Southern Netherlands chose to settle in rival ports, like Middelburg, Rouen, London, and Hamburg, instead. Middelburg in particular benefited from its favorable location at the mouth of the river Scheldt, and it was not until the early 1590s that merchants from the Northern and Southern Netherlands became convinced of Amsterdam's superior prospects.[112]

From then on the Amsterdam market expanded very rapidly.[113] Merchants added agents in central Germany, France, and England to their network, and they started shipping merchandise to Italy. Trade embargoes made direct trade between the Dutch Republic and the Iberian Peninsula difficult, but Spain and Portugal needed foreign trade as much as Holland, and quite a few traders in Amsterdam used agents in Hamburg and Antwerp to work their way around the boycott of these two markets. Independence from the Spanish crown also allowed merchants in the Dutch port to venture into new markets in Africa, America, and Asia, which added an indispensable and very profitable element to their trade: the large-scale import of spices, sugar, dyes, diamonds, and other colonial wares.

In the first half of the seventeenth century Amsterdam became the single most important market in Europe. Holland's merchant fleet comprised a staggering 1,750 vessels, allowing the city's merchants to take their goods everywhere in Europe at very competitive rates.[114] The traditional trade in grain, herring, salt, and timber between the Baltic area and Atlantic coasts of France and Iberia also expanded, and already in 1617

[112]Israel 1989: 28–29, 38–42; Lesger 2001: 88–102; Lesger 2006: 85–99.
[113]See, e.g., Israel 1989: 43–79.
[114]De Vries and Van der Woude 1997: 357–62.

a separate corn exchange opened its doors to allow dealings between several hundred grain traders. The immigration of Flemish craftsmen and the proximity of industrial towns like Haarlem and Leyden turned Amsterdam into a major exporter of textiles and other luxury manufactures. Colonial trade was the fourth pillar of the city's prosperity with imports of sugar, spices, silk, dyestuffs, and many other exotic products making up the widest range of goods available anywhere in Europe. The growth of commercial transactions in turn made the Dutch port an important clearing house for international payments, facilitated by the Exchange Bank (est. 1609) as well as a major market for gold and silver, short-term credit, and marine insurance.

Amsterdam boasted a very thick market for virtually every kind of product, financial or otherwise, but the number of permanently resident foreign merchants remained very small in comparison with Bruges or Antwerp. Considering the war between Spain and the Dutch Republic, it made good sense for Castilian merchants to continue trading in Bruges and use overland routes in France for their wool exports to Flanders. However, there were not many Italian merchants in Amsterdam either. After the fall of Antwerp only members of the Burlamachi, Calandrini, and Diodati families, which had moved from Lucca to Antwerp in the 1560s, relocated to Holland.[115] German, English, and Portuguese merchants did settle in the Dutch port, but in the first decades of Amsterdam's commercial expansion their total number probably did not exceed one hundred (Table 2.3). In fact most of the Portuguese settling in Amsterdam after 1595 did not even come from Antwerp. They were sent as agents by Lisbon merchants.[116] Thus, the bulk of Amsterdam's merchant community consisted of traders from the northern and southern parts of the Low Countries.

One might be tempted to explain the small numbers of foreigners in Amsterdam by the city's refusal to extend privileges to foreign nations. When merchants from the *Oostersche natie* (i.e., the Hanse) asked for special privileges in 1586, the city simply refused.[117] The States General issued safe-conducts to various groups of foreigners, but its appeal to local governments to do everything they could to accommodate the wishes of the English and Portuguese merchants failed.[118] Amsterdam turned down requests from the Company of Merchant Adventurers to establish their

[115] Bicci 1981, 1990; Gelderblom 2000: 75, 154–55. See also unpublished notes by Johannes van Dillen on Italian merchants in Amsterdam: Amsterdam City Archives, Manuscript Collection 5059: inv. no. 139.

[116] Israel 1983: 508; Israel 2002: 94–96.

[117] Häpke 1908: 366–67.

[118] Vlessing 1995: 223; Japikse and Rijperman 1915–70: 4: no. 276; 5: nos. 267, 420, 467–68, 591, 754; 6: no. 722.

TABLE 2.3. Estimated composition of Amsterdam's merchant community in 1585 and 1609

Origin	1585	1609
Amsterdam	350	500
Southern provinces	75	450
Northern provinces	50	250
Germany	25	75?
Portugal	0	25
England	0	20
Total	500	ca. 1,300

Source: Gelderblom 2003b: 262–64.

court in the city because they attached greater value to the presence of so-called *interlopers*—English merchants who did not submit themselves to the authority of the company (see also chapter 3). The Court of Merchant Adventurers therefore settled in Middelburg in 1582, and later moved on to Delft (1621), Rotterdam (1635), and Dordrecht (1655). Even the Portuguese merchants that formed a close-knit community in Amsterdam and continued to refer to themselves as the *Portugese natie*, enjoyed no formal jurisdiction.[119] The result was that the German, English, and Portuguese merchants who did settle in Amsterdam played by the same rules as merchants from the Low Countries.[120]

The refusal to grant economic or legal privileges to foreign merchants did not issue from a hostile attitude toward alien merchants. Surely the native families that controlled the town council managed to bar even the most prominent newcomers from political power, but they were nevertheless very hospitable toward foreigners.[121] Walloon merchants, for instance, were given permission to establish their own French-speaking congregation, and English merchants were given a former Catholic church to worship in. The city also allowed Portuguese Jews and Lutheran Germans their own places of worship. What the lack of privileges does reveal, however, is a deliberate policy to stimulate competition between merchants. Under pressure from the States General the city had to accept the Dutch East India Company's control of the Asian trade, but

[119] Ordinances about the *Joodsche* or *Portugeese Natie* from 1616, 1622, 1659, 1670, and 1698 exclusively referred to marriages, religious matters, and poor relief. They did not include legal or economic privileges: Noordkerk 1748: 2:470–75.

[120] Between 1630 and 1650 the kings of France, England, Prussia, Denmark, Sweden, and Poland occasionally appointed commercial agents in Amsterdam. These representatives, however, played no role in the business organization of merchants from these territories: Schutte 1982: 48, 137, 363–64, 473–74, 529–30, 546–47.

[121] Gelderblom 1999; Lesger 2001: 142–48; Lesger 2006: 141–50; see also Dudok van Heel 1984.

otherwise the urban government made every effort to secure the freedom of individual merchants to trade in the products and markets of their choice. A separate legal status clearly did not fit this policy. Instead, the city magistrate determined that the person and goods of all merchants should be treated equally in equal circumstances.[122] Foreign merchants could even obtain freedom in Amsterdam at low cost, but few of them did because there was little to gain. Equality before the law in all commercial and financial matters obviated the need for formal citizenship.[123]

CONCLUSION

From the thirteenth century onward the principal ports of the Low Countries competed with each other and with commercial cities in neighboring territories for a place in the international hierarchy of markets. Initially foreign traders whom Bruges and Antwerp believed were crucial to their commercial position obtained extensive economic and legal privileges, but this special treatment alone was insufficient because merchants could easily obtain privileges in other locations—even before they actually moved there. What mattered most to international traders was direct access to a wide variety of local and foreign products, which could be achieved without privileges. Indeed, as time went by foreign merchants were increasingly willing to settle in the Low Countries without any kind of special status. That is to say, the magistrates of the three ports remained very keen to accommodate international traders but moved from giving a separate status for the foreign nations to offering political, legal, and commercial support to the entire merchant community.

Bruges, Antwerp, and particularly Amsterdam developed more inclusive commercial regimes in which all merchants were treated equally and the commercial infrastructure served the merchant community at large. Admittedly, in the 1550s Antwerp still granted the German and English nations their own compounds (see chapter 5), but this was very much a defensive strategy aimed to retain merchants whose presence was deemed indispensable for the local economy. Competition among the three cities also explains why trade could thrive in a politically very unstable world. Because Bruges, Antwerp, and Amsterdam shared similar geographical

---

[122] Noordkerk 1748: 2:502 (Extract from Compostboeck, February 6, 1607); see also *Handt-vesten* 1613: 227–35; *Handtvesten* 1639: 102, 112.

[123] On the rights of Amsterdam citizens: Prak and Kuijpers 2002. A citizen's right to become a member of local guilds was irrelevant for merchants, with the possible exception of a few impoverished merchants wishing to enter the brokers' guild (Stuart 1879: 61). Actively participating in local politics was an almost impossible ambition given the concentration of power in the hands of a very small group of Amsterdammers (Gelderblom 1999).

advantages and did everything they could to attract international traders, it was relatively easy for merchants to move their business to a nearby location, as a result of which neither the Flemish Revolt nor the Dutch Revolt put an end to the central position of the Low Countries in the European economy.

The willingness of the magistrates of Bruges, Antwerp, and Amsterdam to adapt local institutions resulted from the footloose character of foreign merchants, which made local rulers very concerned about their possible departure to another location.[124] But how did this lead to actual changes in the institutions that governed trade? For even if there existed a strong coincidence of wants between foreign merchants and local magistrates, adapting institutions to the needs of merchants required fundamental legal reforms, whether through the creation of consular jurisdictions or the amendment of local customs with foreign mercantile usage. Such changes tested the limits of the legal and political power of individual cities. The three ports may have had considerable autonomy when it came to the organization of local exchange and the protection of merchants within their city walls, but their legal authority ended at the city gate, which may have left the organization of border-crossing transactions beyond their control. On top of that there was the constant threat of violence directed against trade, from the wars fought by the sovereign rulers of the Netherlands, from repeated fiscal and political conflicts between the cities and the central government, and from occasional attempts by the cities themselves to use violence to strengthen their competitive position. Under such adverse conditions, why did so many merchants for such a long period choose to conduct their business from any one of these three ports?

[124]For a clear exposition of these fears, see Kint 1996b: 64, 343–96.

CHAPTER 3

The Organization of Exchange

Well-functioning local markets were part and parcel of the growth of long-distance trade in late medieval Europe. In the eleventh and twelfth centuries the expansion of Mediterranean trade led to the concentration of hundreds, sometimes thousands of traders in Venice, Genoa, Constantinople, and Cairo. Here they either visited public vending locations or each other's designated quarters to inspect goods, negotiate prices, and close deals.[1] Local markets of this size did not exist in Northern Europe before 1300.[2] Instead, the periodic fairs of Champagne, and to a lesser extent those of Flanders, South-East England, and the Rhineland, allowed face-to-face meetings of foreign traders during a limited time. At the fairs, facilities for storage and measurement of merchandise, as well as set days for display, delivery, and payments, reduced information costs for visiting traders and curbed opportunistic behavior.[3] But as the Champagne fairs started to decline in the late thirteenth century, foreign merchants began to look for a permanent location in Northwestern Europe to trade with each other.

In the previous chapter we saw that Bruges responded very successfully to this new demand, transforming its annual fairs into a year-round exchange, with more extensive storage facilities and permanent vending locations to allow merchants to search trading partners and negotiate deals with them on a day-to-day basis. As a result Bruges remained the most important international market of the Low Countries until the late fifteenth century, and as Antwerp and Amsterdam in the sixteenth century also readily transformed their periodic market it would seem that institutional

---

[1] The classic account of the Commercial Revolution remains Lopez (1971). Constable (2003) describes in great detail the physical infrastructure that supported exchange in the Mediterranean. Peter Spufford (2002) very vividly renders the daily operations of merchants in this period.

[2] The biggest permanent market in Northern Europe before 1300 was Cologne. See Hirschfelder 1994: passim.

[3] For the history of the fairs of Champagne, see Bautier (1953). Several recent studies of the institutional foundations of the Champagne fairs, e.g., Milgrom, North, and Weingast (1990), Munro (2001), and Edwards and Ogilvie (2013), remain tributary to Bautier's empirical work. Wedemeyer Moore (1985) gives a very detailed description of the daily functioning of the English fairs.

adaptation was trivial, an inescapable consequence of urban competition. But the creation of a permanent market infrastructure actually required the dismantling of existing arrangements and the private interests associated with them. In this chapter we explore the willingness of urban magistrates to make such adjustments through an analysis of the changing role of hostellers and brokers.

Hostellers were key figures in the organization of trade in the late Middle Ages. Their premises served not only as accommodation for temporary visitors but also as storage facility and trading venue, while the hostellers themselves acted as brokers and commission agents for their guests.[4] Their intervention was very convenient as long as trade was seasonal, but once merchants began to settle permanently in Bruges, Antwerp, and Amsterdam and move into their own houses with their own storage facilities, their daily presence at the local market allowed them to develop their own information network. These changes greatly reduced their demand for the multiple services of the hostellers-cum-brokers, and the town magistrates, recognizing their loss of purpose, chose to terminate the dominant role of these local intermediaries.

To uncover the dynamics of this institutional change, this chapter builds on Frederic Lane's observation, now more than fifty years ago, that merchants always used more than one institution to solve their problems, while at the same time the institutions they used had multiple purposes.[5] We explore the combination of services offered by the hostellers of Bruges, Antwerp, and Amsterdam, the benefits this created for temporary visitors, and the changes in the cost-benefit calculus of individual merchants when they became permanent residents. To illustrate the ability of resident traders to pass over local intermediaries and organize their own information supply, I reconstruct the business of one merchant, Hans Thijs, a jeweler from Antwerp who settled in Amsterdam in 1595. His surviving account books allow us to examine his operations in local markets for jewelry, leather, grain, spices, and even short-term loans, and the redundancy of brokers in most of these transactions. This analysis reveals to what extent the urban magistrates were willing, in the interest of the merchant community at large, to end the privileged position of the hostellers or, more accurately, to align the financial reward for their services with the value they added to the business of individual merchants.

---

[4]The role of hostellers is described by Van Houtte 1950–51; see also Murray 2005: 196–205 and Grafe 2005. For a general overview of the functions medieval brokers could perform: Börner 2006; Börner and Quint 2010.

[5]Lane 1958: 409–10. See also Ogilvie 2007: 667–71, 674–75; and Gelderblom and Grafe 2010: 478.

THE MARKET OF BRUGES

In the Middle Ages cities around the Mediterranean set up separate residences for visiting merchants.[6] The typical *fondaco*—or *funduq*, as it was
called in the Islamic world—was a gated building with an interior courtyard and one or two floors with bedrooms, stables, and storage space.
The premises were secured by local guards and provided visitors with a
safe place to spend the night, storerooms for their goods, and food and
shelter for their animals. The traders could also leave merchandise in the
custody of the fondaco's caretakers while traveling to other places. During the daytime the courtyard functioned as a marketplace for exchang-
ing goods with local buyers and sellers. At night the gates were locked
(not seldom from the outside) while the resident merchants socialized
or tended to their business. This creation of special quarters with multiple functions was attractive to strangers who often sojourned for only
brief periods abroad. At the same time it allowed host towns to supervise
transactions, tax trade, and (especially in the case of Christian traders in
Muslim markets) segregate local and foreign communities.

In Northern Europe German merchants appreciated the advantages
of such compounds, and in London, Bergen, and Novgorod, where they
were regular visitors, they were indeed granted such premises. The German merchants in Flanders initially did not need their own premises
because they merely visited for the duration of the fairs, but in 1252
merchants from Lübeck did ask permission from the Countess of Flanders to establish a trading post with separate jurisdiction near Damme,
just outside Bruges.[7] The countess refused, however, and the Germans
continued to lodge with hostellers while they congregated in the church
of one of the city's mendicant orders. This refusal, perhaps instigated by
the consideration that the Germans would come to Bruges anyway, set a
precedent for all other foreigners in Flanders. In the fourteenth century
most foreign communities did obtain nation houses in Bruges, but these
merely served as offices for the consuls and their aides, not as lodges,
warehouses, or marketplaces.[8]

---

[6]This paragraph is based on Constable 2003.

[7]Häpke 1908: 112; Rössner 2001: 44–46; Vandewalle 2002: 28, 30.

[8]Vandewalle 2002: 32–39; Gilliodts-Van Severen 1871–85: 5:326. In the fifteenth and
sixteenth century the nation houses of Florentine, Venetian, and Genoese merchants in
Bruges were sometimes referred to as *loges*: Gilliodts-Van Severen 1871–85: 5:357; 8:490,
491, 494, 516. Since in medieval Italy the term *loggia* was used for vending locations (Constable 2003: 186–89), the nation houses may have become marketplaces at some point. The
Genoese nation house was turned into a hall for cloth sales (*Saeyhalle*) after the Genoese
merchants moved to Antwerp in the early sixteenth century Gilliodts-Van Severen 1871–
85: 8:12.

The absence of separate quarters like the fondachi in Mediterranean ports did not harm merchants in Bruges because they had access to alternative facilities. As international shipping increased and more and more merchants frequented the city, the magistrate began to create public vending locations.[9] While in 1200 a foreign visitor would still have found the town center strewn with the temporary stalls of Flemish drapers, a century later the cloth trade was concentrated in a majestic cloth hall with bell tower. For money changers there was a designated area near the Belfort, known as the *Wissel*, or Exchange, where they offered their exchange and payment services.[10] In the fourteenth century the town magistrate turned the intersection of the streets where the nation houses of the Florentines, Venetians, and Genoese merchants were located into a daily exchange. This Bourse square, named after the hostel of the Van der Beurse family on the same intersection, was guarded by wardens, *Scaerwetters*, to make sure trade could go on undisturbed. In 1335 the town paid a gratuity to the bailiff "and his company" for supervising the fair day and night.[11] The supervision helped to prevent violence, but it also curbed more mundane nuisances. In 1466 Castilian merchants got permission from Bruges's magistrate to close off the street that they and other merchants and citizens used for the display and storage of merchandise. The measure should keep "indecent girls and other rabble from loitering about, as they have been doing for so long."[12]

It may be tempting to cite the Bourse square and other public vending locations as the principal reason for the absence of foreign compounds in Bruges, but there was an even more important private institution. Foreign merchants would have visited the Bourse square on a regular basis, but the bulk of their business was conducted in hostels, most of them located in the commercial quarter of the city. Around 1370 there were at least 120 hostels in the Flemish port, many of which lodged a specific group of merchants, for example, those from Germany, Castile, Portugal, France, Lucca, England, Scotland, or Hainaut.[13] The guests not only ate, drank, and slept in the hostel, but also met other merchants, stored merchandise, bought and sold goods, and changed money.[14] Hostels were the focal point of exchange in Bruges because many hostellers doubled as brokers,

[9]Murray 2005: 63–81.

[10]Murray 2005: 150–53.

[11]Gilliodts-Van Severen 1871–85: 7:562–63; 4:199. In 1411 Bruges paid guards who stayed overnight at the market to act immediately upon any disturbances that might arise: Gilliodts-Van Severen 1871–85: 4:178; 6:36.

[12]Gilliodts-Van Severen 1901–2: 88–89.

[13]Murray 2005: 181–85, 190–92, 226–27.

[14]Van Houtte 1983: passim; Rössner 2001: 226–39; Greve 2000: 37–44; Greve 2001: passim; Murray 2005: 181–210.

and from the late thirteenth century onward, all visiting merchants were required to hire a broker for every transaction that exceeded 5 pounds Flemish.[15] This obligation laid upon foreigners may seem unnecessarily costly,
but surely it was not a burden if brokerage fees were low and the information provided indispensable. In any case, many merchants stayed in Bruges
for periods too brief to acquire up-to-date knowledge of market conditions.

Their pivotal role in the organization of the market made the hundred-
or-more hostellers-cum-brokers into the leading local entrepreneurs in
Bruges. There were also many brokers without hostels, however. By the
mid-fourteenth century the membership of the brokers' guild probably
stood at more than four hundred.[16] The corporation had the right to
admit, discipline, and exclude members, and used this right to limit the
membership to local citizens.[17] Thus only once, in 1339, a small number of brokers from outside Flanders were admitted to the corporation.
Among them were two brokers from Lucca, Clais Barbezaen (Barbagialla)
and Gilles Visolle, who worked for merchants from the Lucchese nation
in the mid-fourteenth century.[18] The exclusion of newcomers never led
to a shortage of intermediaries because of another practice laid down in
the ordinance of 1303: hostellers were given the right to hire not just a
broker but also a clerk—not a member of the brokers' guild—to mediate
between merchants on the hosteller's behalf.[19] Presumably these hired

[15]Gilliodts-Van Severen 1883–85: 1:458; Greve 2000: 37–38. The privileges the Countess of Flanders granted to German merchants in 1253 explicitly referred to the intermediary
role of brokers: Greve 2000: 37–38; Höhlbaum et al. 1876–1939: 1:157–58; Van Houtte
1950–51: 3–4; Brokerage fees payable by the Germans were first specified in a charter in
1262: Gilliodts-Van Severen 1883–85: 1:458. For minor changes to these tariffs in the
fifteenth century, see Gilliodts-Van Severen 1871–85: 4:160; 6:199. In 1267 formal rules
for brokerage were set in all four Flemish fair towns: Van Houtte 1983: 186. According to
Van Houtte, Bruges's brokers guild was incorporated in 1293, with its monopoly formally
recognized by the city and Count in 1303: Van Houtte 1950–51: 3–5.

[16]In 1316 the names of 39 brokers and hostellers are mentioned as subscribers to a forced
loan issued by the town of Bruges for the funding of a fleet to protect ships sailing to and
from Flanders: Gilliodts-Van Severen 1883–85: 458. In 1340 Bruges mobilized 355 brokers
to serve in a militia of almost 5,500 Bruges citizens. Considering that some brokers must have
been too old to serve in the militia, and that some hostellers may have been counted among
the 579 poorters in the militia (Van Houtte 1950–51: 18), an estimate of 400 seems reasonable enough. On the admittance of foreigners as hostellers in 1339: Greve 1997: 153–63.

[17]As a result of the discretion of the guild leaders, entry fees were never used as an instrument to limit the membership. They were set at three pounds Flemish in 1303, and only in
1477 were they raised to six pounds Flemish: Van Houtte 1950–51: 8.

[18]Van Houtte 1950–51: 7–9; Lambert 2006: 24. But compare Murray 2005: 186.

[19]The only provision was that the town and the guild had registered the appointment.
Occasionally this clause even led the sons of foreign merchants to act as brokers: Van
Houtte 1950–51: 12–13.

brokers and clerks were paid a wage below the brokerage fees they generated, so as to make a profit for their principals.[20]

Forced mediation, entry barriers to the brokers' guild, and hired hands secured a regular income for the hostellers-cum-brokers, but was their strong position really in the interest of foreign merchants in Bruges? Would they not have preferred an open market for information? English wool traders bypassed local brokers several times and illicit brokerage occurred in the organization of overland transportation to Germany.[21] In 1307 German merchants even removed their business to nearby Aardenburg as a means to denounce, among other things, the high tariffs of Bruges's brokers.[22] The Count of Flanders supported their case, and in 1309 Bruges acquiesced, lowering some of the brokerage fees for the German traders.[23] In 1409 and 1419 foreign merchants complained about the payment of double brokerage on textiles purchased in other Flemish cities. Upon requests by Catalan traders the Four Members of Flanders tried to force the brokers of Bruges to give up their claim to brokerage fees, but they refused, and instead the Estates of Flanders decided to compensate the Catalans for their double fees.[24]

We should not read too much into these occasional protests and the intervention of the provincial and central authorities on behalf of foreign merchants, however, because the actual cost of brokerage was very, very low. We can use the brokerage tariffs negotiated between the local government and the German Hanse in 1360 (fees that remained unchanged thereafter) to estimate the actual cost of intermediation in Bruges.[25] Most tariffs are expressed in a sum of money per weight or measure for goods for which there is no price information but the few ad valorem tariffs listed, notably for silk, precious stones, and products not specified in the official list, reveal a charge of 0.8 percent—quite similar to incidental references found in the records of the Medici merchants.[26] Wheat prices from Saint Donatian's chapter in Bruges allow an annual calculation of

---

[20]This reading of the evidence may differ from that of Jim Murray, who argues that the guild ordinance of 1302 freed brokers from their dependence on hostellers (Murray 2005: 189). Note, however, that Murray also stresses the political dominance of the hostellers in the fourteenth century: Murray 2005: 113, 190.

[21]Van Houtte 1950–51: 25; Nicholas 1979: 28, 42, 44.

[22]Van Houtte 1982: 168.

[23]Beuken 1950: 64–66; Stützel 1998.

[24]Blockmans 1978: 479–80.

[25]Gilliodts-Van Severen 1871–85: 2:65–69.

[26]Two accounts that remain of the local branch of the Medici bank reveal that in 1441 the brokerage paid on the sales of 100 bales of almonds and 9 bales of cardamom was 0.5 percent and 0.7 percent, respectively: De Roover 1963: 146–47.

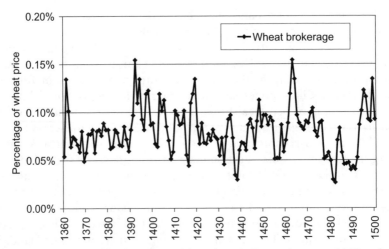

FIGURE 3.1. Estimated brokerage paid for wheat in Bruges between 1360 and 1500, expressed as a percentage of the price

the percentage share of the brokers' wage in the grain trade.[27] As Figure 3.1 shows, brokerage for grain—one of the principal German products— never exceeded 0.15 percent of the price of wheat between 1360 and 1500 (Figure 3.1)—a trifle compared to the physical costs of handling and transportation. In the early fifteenth century, German merchants estimated that brokerage, transportation, packaging, and tolls together added between 6 and 8 percent to the price of cloth purchased in Bruges.[28] Brokerage was only a very small part of these costs.

Commercial intermediation was so cheap because hostellers-cum-brokers earned a considerable part of their income providing additional services to their guests.[29] In the thirteenth century, when foreigners visited the fairs of Flanders, they closed all bargains on the spot. As soon as they moved beyond these spot transactions, however, they began to

[27]Prices from Verlinden and Craeybeckx 1959–73: 2:33–36. Not surprisingly, prices for wheat paid by several hospitals in Bruges between 1400 and 1500 yield a similar result. More importantly, a few prices for herring bought by Madeleine's hospital in Bruges in the second quarter of the sixteenth century (1535, 1536; and also 1573, 1583) suggest similarly low fees of 0.1 to 0.2 percent, when one applies the 1360 Hanseatic brokerage tariffs (Verlinden and Craeybeckx 1959–73: 2:76).

[28]Abraham-Thisse 2002: 68. James Murray arrives at the same conclusion but adds the detrimental effect of coin debasements on the brokers' wages: Murray 2005: 199–200.

[29]Note, however, that besides the hostellers-cum-brokers Bruges also had genuine brokers. Their income was secured because they were entitled to the full brokerage fees stipulated by the town magistrates: Van Houtte 1950–51: 12.

rely on hostellers as their local representatives. The larger hostels in particular became "one-stop shops" for storage, brokerage, eating, drinking, and sleeping, and although it was forbidden for brokers to associate with merchants, many hostellers developed exclusive agency relations with foreign merchants.[30] As factors they bought and sold goods, made payments, stood surety, organized shipments, or salvaged goods from shipwrecks, on behalf of their principal.[31] In the second half of the fourteenth century the city accepted that brokers signed contracts on behalf of foreign merchants.[32] This meant that temporary visitors, Germans in particular, could effectively extend their presence to the rest of the year, and thus lower their opportunity costs. Since brokers were required by law to keep accounts of their transactions, it was easy enough, at least after a deal was done, to find out whether they had acted in the best interest of their principals. Besides, both guild officials and the town magistrate saw to the proper application of guild regulations.[33]

The importance of hostellers-cum-brokers in Bruges was further enhanced by their representation of foreigners who traveled back home to attend their business. To prevent the breakdown of trade as a result of irrecoverable claims on absent traders, Bruges's hostellers were liable for their guests' debts.[34] The responsibility of hosts for wrongdoings of their guests was a general principle in medieval Europe, known as *gast-recht*.[35] In the case of merchants, this liability was limited to the goods and money they left with their host.[36] The *guest system* was certainly in place in Bruges in 1331 when the first instance of a hosteller standing surety for a guest is recorded.[37] In the privilege granted to merchants of the German Hanse in 1360, it was explicitly stated that hostellers and money changers in the city had to stand surety for them.[38] There are also various examples of visitors being identified by the name of their host, like "Jan Heldebolles gasten" in 1387.[39] In 1422 the liability of local

---

[30] Ehrenberg 1885; Van Houtte 1950–51: 22–24; Murray 2005: 196–210. A late but very well documented example of a hosteller who also acted as a broker, factor, and merchant in his own right is Wouter Ameide, who was active in Bruges from the late 1490s: Stabel 1996.

[31] Seifert 2000: 49. For a hosteller acting as guarantor: Lesnikov 1973: 241; Murray 2005: 190–215.

[32] Van Houtte 1950–51: 23–24.

[33] Van Houtte 1950–51: 21–22; Murray 2005: 196–205.

[34] Murray 2005: 194–96, 198–99.

[35] Peyer 1983: xii.

[36] For Florence: Szabó 1983: 87. For Bilbao: Grafe 2005: 20–25.

[37] Greve 2001: 281.

[38] Greve 2001: 273–80.

[39] Van Houtte 1983: 181.

hosts was written down in general terms: "a hosteller or broker vouches for sales by his guest in his house."[40]

This did not mean that the hostellers needed very deep pockets. Their liability for foreign guests was real, but it was limited to commodity transactions, most of which must have involved merchants they knew well. Jacob Scuetelare, for example, hosted the German merchant Hildebrand Veckinchusen for more than twenty years.[41] The few business ledgers that remain of hostellers show they mitigated risks by having a large number of guests with relatively small credit balances. Jacob Sconebergh, for instance, held accounts for several dozen guests besides a considerable number of local businessmen.[42] When hostellers deemed risks still too high, they could also shift it to guarantors, as in the case of two Bruges citizens who landed with a payment of 6,000 guilders to bail out "their" hosteller.[43]

The hostellers' key position in the local market suited foreign merchants very well as long as they did not settle permanently in Bruges. But as more and more merchants bought or rented their own houses in the late fourteenth and early fifteenth centuries they no longer needed an intermediary for every single deal negotiated in the local market. The growth of the Brabant fairs dealt a further blow to the brokers' profession as merchants increasingly carried out spot transactions on the Antwerp market. Once this erosion of the brokers' central position had begun, there was no stopping it. Declining demand for brokerage foreclosed any attempt to raise fees, and even if some of the leading hostellers' families retained their political influence, it was no use for the town magistrate to come to the rescue of the profession at large. On the contrary, growing worries about Antwerp's competition led the city to finally grant the German Hanse its own local compound in 1458. This slightly desperate effort to try to retain Bruges's leading role in the trade between the Low Countries and the Baltic area confirmed the demise of the hostellers as the cornerstone of the local market.

The permanent presence of merchants also overturned the guest system.[44] Merchants whose customers did not lodge with hostellers could also rely on the city's standard procedures for debt collection, that is,

---

[40] The liability of *brokers* for debts of their principals was first mentioned in writing in 1410: Greve 2001: 285, 289.

[41] Greve 2001: 285–88; Lesnikov 1973: 196.

[42] Murray 2005: 202–4.

[43] Greve 2001: 283; Gilliodts-Van Severen (1901–2: 57) reports the payment of almost 500 guilders to six Spanish merchants by three guarantors of the Bruges hosteller Josse de Bouchot in 1453. Bruges's money changers also used guarantors to back them: De Roover 1948: 333–34.

[44] Stabel 2002: 92–94; Gilliodts-Van Severen 1871–85: 2:48.

imprisonment or attachment of one's property, followed by summary proceedings before the local court to establish the validity of a claim.[45] These options had been available since the late thirteenth century, and in 1396 the town magistrate reconfirmed that this standard procedure for the collection of debts applied to all debtors and creditors, regardless of their origin.[46] Less than half a century later it had become the dominant enforcement practice in Bruges.[47] To prevent abuse, the local magistrates required merchants to always ask permission first, and they made provisions for release on bail and for the maximum number of days for a judgment to be passed.[48] Already in 1309 German merchants, clerks, and apprentices had been allowed to name a guarantor to prevent being arrested in commercial disputes with non-Germans.[49] In later years the same rule was laid down in the privileges of other foreign nations.[50] Conversely, the Bruges magistrate determined in 1396 that if a foreigner claimed debts from a local citizen, the latter should also give sufficient surety or render himself to the Steen, the local prison.[51] Just like the hosteller's liability for debts of his guests, these individual sureties were intended to prevent the breakdown of trade as a result of disputed claims. For instance, in 1448 two Florentine merchants stood surety for the patrons of the Florentine galleys in a conflict with Portuguese merchants about a sugar cargo. Their guarantees allowed the galleys to sail away from Sluis before the dispute was settled.[52]

In sum, the local authorities in Bruges worked hard to adapt the city's commercial infrastructure to the needs of foreign merchants. The fairs of the thirteenth century allowed visitors to engage in spot transactions in temporary but purpose-built vending locations, and when Bruges emerged as the most important market north of the Alps, the city supported brokers-hostellers in their role as providers of accommodation and storage facilities, and as middlemen in all sales and purchases involving alien traders. In the fifteenth century the intermediaries retained the right to mediate in all commercial transactions, but they lodged fewer

[45] Godding 1987: 69; Gilliodts-Van Severen 1901–2: 91.

[46] Gilliodts-Van Severen 1883–85: 441–49; Gilliodts-Van Severen 1901–2: 39.

[47] Surviving court records from the mid-fifteenth century do not reveal any hosteller being sued for debts of his foreign guests (personal communication, Bart Lambert and Peter Stabel).

[48] Gilliodts-Van Severen 1883–85: 286, 304–26; Gilliodts-Van Severen 1871–85: 2:31, 37, 39, 81.

[49] In 1309 the rule applied only to debts for which no written proof was available. In 1359 the rule applied to all debts: Gilliodts-Van Severen 1871–85: 2:49.

[50] Gilliodts-Van Severen 1871–85: 2:77–82, 136; Gilliodts-Van Severen 1883–85: 1:312–14; Gilissen 1958: 296.

[51] Gilliodts-Van Severen 1883–85: 1:445–47.

[52] Mallett 1967: 91.

foreigners, and the obsolescence of the guest system suggests they also lost their function as local agents for merchants abroad.

ANTWERP'S COMMERCIAL INFRASTRUCTURE

In Antwerp in the fourteenth and fifteenth centuries hostellers were also key figures in local exchange because most international traders stayed in town for short periods only. Until the first quarter of the sixteenth century the organization of the Antwerp market revolved around the two fairs, in the spring and in the autumn. This created a specific demand for accommodation, storage, and information that was readily met by the local hostellers. Many visitors rented rooms and storage space with them for the duration of their stay, and they mediated in the sales and purchases of goods.[53] A town ordinance from 1383 established that hostellers could represent foreign merchants while these were away.[54] Their right to broker deals was formally established in the rules laid down for the company (*geselscap*) of brokers in 1412.[55] The bylaws distinguished between *waarden* and *vremde makeleren*—hostellers and "alien" brokers—defining the latter group as those who did not own a hostel.[56] The "alien" brokers were allowed to mediate between buyers and sellers, but they had to hand over half of their fees to a hosteller, even if he had not been involved in the sale. The vremde makeleren also had to register their transactions with one and the same hosteller—an arrangement they could change once a year.[57] This service contract was very similar to that of the Bruges hostellers, as a later ordinance of 1437 determined that a waard could employ

[53] Some English merchants may have rented independent rooms and houses as in 1296 the city magistrate and the bailiff—the local representative of the duke of Brabant—promised reasonable rents that would not be raised during a visitor's stay. Slootmans 1985: 1:308–9, 317–18, 353–84; Prims 1927–49: 2:96.

[54] *Keurboek met den Doppen* (1419): 75–76; Nicholas 1979: 41–42.

[55] Ordinance, January 11, 1437, art. 9 (Dilis 1910: 419). To lure German, Spanish, and Italian merchants back to Bruges after 1492, the city magistrate relaxed the requirement to use brokers in Bruges: Munro 1966: 1149n6.

[56] Dilis 1910: 303, 416–17. The suggestion that the term *alien* in this particular ordinance has nothing to do with the citizenship of the brokers is based on the contents of two other specifications. One implied that if guests of two hostellers traded with one another, their hostellers would share the wage paid, whereas the involvement of an *alien broker* (*eenen vremden makelere*) would lead to a splitting in three of the wage. Another specification mentioned that if a merchant sold goods in another hostel without any mediation of the resident hosteller or an alien broker, he still had to pay half the brokerage to that hosteller. Neither rule would seem to require a distinction between local and foreign brokers, whereas being alien to the profession of the hostellers does make sense in this context.

[57] Dilis 1910: 419.

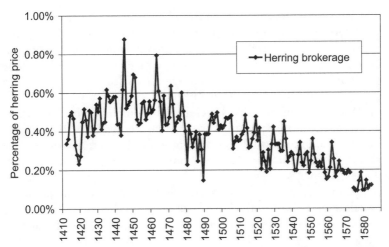

FIGURE 3.2. Estimated brokerage paid for herring in Antwerp between 1412 and 1584, expressed as a percentage of the price

Sources: The tariff for dry and wet herring was 8 groats Flemish per last (Dilis 1910). Van der Wee (1963: 1:Appendix 22, 277–86) gives prices for barrels of herring. To calculate the brokerage fee as a percentage of the price of herring, we estimated (courtesy Christiaan van Bochove) that a barrel contained 833 herrings, i.e., one last contained 10,000 herrings.

no more than two vremde makeleren.[58] Whether hostellers dominated the entire profession as they did in Bruges is doubtful, however, as separate rules existed for brokers of wine and grain from the late fourteenth century.[59]

Merchants in Antwerp accepted the forced mediation by hostellers because brokerage fees were kept very low. The tariffs set in 1412 for textiles, dyestuffs, metals, hides, and various foodstuffs and colonial wares suggest that brokerage did not weigh heavily on buyers and sellers. For example, the tariff for herring, 8 groats Flemish per *last*, translated into a brokerage fee of 0.4 percent to 0.7 percent until the 1480s, after which it steadily declined to about 0.1 percent in the second half of the sixteenth century (Figure 3.2). Brokerage for other bulky goods like grain, hides, wine, and metals—for which no tariffs were listed—could not have been much higher, as the 1412 ordinance determined that for such unlisted goods the tariffs current in Bruges would be applied. Meanwhile the few luxury products with an ad valorem tariff reveal a somewhat higher, but still modest brokerage fee for spices and dyestuffs at 0.4 percent of their value, and that of plate and mercer's wares at 0.83 percent.[60]

[58] Dilis 1910: 418.
[59] Dilis 1910: 413–17.
[60] Dilis 1910: 417.

The role of the hostellers changed when Antwerp took over Bruges's leading role in international trade during the last quarter of the fifteenth century. Initially the hostellers benefited greatly from the influx of traders who required accommodation and storage facilities. We catch a glimpse of these arrangements in June 1532, when Charles V ordered the arrest of the goods of merchants from Lübeck and other towns in the Wendische Viertel.[61] The emperor's secretary, accompanied by his sergeants and several town officials, visited six hostels known to be frequented by the Oisterlins. In the hostels' storerooms, and the warehouses and sheds attached to them, they confiscated numerous sacks of wool, as well as rawhides, copper, saltpeter, dyes, and various other commodities. Some hostellers may have made a separate business out of the supply of storage facilities. The host of the Engelburg declared that he had leased three warehouses to merchants from Lorraine, Westphalia, and England, respectively.

Foreign merchants who decided to stay longer in Antwerp, however, bypassed the hostellers and rented or bought their own houses instead. Almost two hundred merchants from France, Italy, Germany, England, Spain, and Portugal actually purchased the freedom of Antwerp between 1533 and 1567—a clear indication of their intention to settle. But even foreigners who continued traveling to the fairs increasingly passed over the hostellers. The city's customs of 1545 explicitly stated that tenants could not be evicted from houses and warehouses they rented during the fairs. Forty years later the local customs still contained a clause that determined that a house could not be repossessed while the fairs were in motion, in order to protect the merchants who used the premises for accommodation, storage, or sales.[62]

Instead of defending the central position of hostellers on the local market, Antwerp's magistrate invested in alternative vending locations and accommodation for foreign visitors. In 1476 English merchants were given a house with a relatively small courtyard that they used during the fairs to display and sell their cloth. This Engelse Pand had no storage facilities, but the nation had negotiated long-term leases of warehouses nearby. Since there was no sleeping accommodation either, the English merchants used hostels or rented their own rooms.[63] As tensions rose in Bruges in the 1480s, Antwerp opened a house with an interior courtyard in the Hofstraat for local and foreign merchants to exchange money and goods, and when this venue overflowed in the second quarter of the sixteenth

[61] Häpke 1913: 1:57–66.
[62] *Antwerpse Costumen* (1545), title 6, no. 48; *Antwerpse Costumen* (1582), title 34, no. 27.
[63] De Smedt 1954: 129–30.

century the city commissioned the building of a new exchange, which opened its doors in 1531.[64] The Nieuwe Beurs could accommodate hundreds of traders who traded not only merchandise but also bills of exchange, insurance policies, and short-term loans. In addition to this central marketplace, the city maintained several so-called *panden* for the sales of local manufactures such as tapestry, jewelry, and paintings.

The Company of Merchant Adventurers was the principal beneficiary of Antwerp's accommodation policy. In 1550 Antwerp's magistrate moved the Merchant Adventurers to the prominent Hof van Liere, a set of buildings in the northern part of town, with an orchard, garden, and four buildings, two stories high, set around three interior squares, with numerous bedrooms and store rooms.[65] The merchants could sojourn and trade here, and the Company of Merchant Adventurers could also perform its social and legal functions. Several members demurred, however, because they wanted a place closer to the Exchange or because they already had their own houses.[66] The nation leaders nevertheless accepted, presumably because a considerable number of merchants still commuted between London and Antwerp. They appointed one of the members as warden, responsible for the maintenance of the buildings and for the accommodation of English visitors. This merchant was also liable for goods the community members left in his custody.[67]

Antwerp's magistrate offered the Hof van Liere to the Merchant Adventurers because the English presence attracted other traders and boosted employment in the local finishing industry. Similar economic motives were behind the provision of warehouses to Holland's importers of leather and hides, and the construction of the Hessenhuis (1563) for the loading and unloading of horse-drawn carts traveling to and from Germany. The actual benefits to the foreigners were modest, however. When Philip II clashed with England over the capture of Spanish silver ships destined for Antwerp, the Merchant Adventurers moved to Hamburg where the town council provided premises as spacious as the Hof van Liere to accommodate their trade.[68] The financial support Antwerp offered in 1553 for the building of a new residence for the German Hanse could not retain the Germans either. The Oosterlingenhuis, completed in 1568, was at least as impressive as the English Hof van Liere or, for that matter, the Fondaco dei Tedeschi in Venice. The rectangular building measured 80 by 62 meters, and it had direct access to the river Scheldt. Its four wings were built around a large interior court, with cellars in

[64] De Groote 1976: 208, 215; van Niekerk 1998: 1:202–3.
[65] Soly 1977: 224; De Smedt 1954: 131–32, 144–46, 155–57; Schlugleit 1938–39.
[66] De Smedt 1954: 11–12.
[67] De Smedt 1954: 115–17.
[68] Lingelbach 1904: 274–75.

the basement, storerooms on the ground floor, and 130 bedrooms on the first and second floor. But the Germans did not really need such extensive premises—they had done without them for at least half a century—and the house never accommodated more than a handful of traders.[69]

The permanent residence of local and alien traders took away the Antwerp hostellers' competitive advantage as all-round agents for foreign visitors. As a result, the guest system that held hosts liable for their guests' debts also became obsolete. Antwerp's magistrate firmly established the individual legal responsibility of foreign and local traders, and it offered clear procedures for debt collection.[70] Portuguese merchants at issue with buyers or suppliers, for instance, started legal procedures seizing the merchandise of defendants.[71] Just like in Bruges the basic rule for such arrests was that Antwerp's aldermen had to give permission first.[72] When permission was granted, preference was to be given to the attachment of goods, rather than taking the owner of the goods into custody, and the value of goods attached was to correspond to the size of the claim.[73]

The permanent presence of local and foreign traders also ended the hosteller's control over Antwerp's brokers' guild. Resident merchants increasingly negotiated deals directly at the exchange, in one of the city's taverns, or at home, and the city therefore lifted the obligation to engage brokers in every single transaction.[74] This did not end the brokers' involvement in trade, however, because the Antwerp market expanded very rapidly. As the aggregate demand for commercial intermediation grew, the city allowed new entrants to the brokers' profession, and by the time

[69] Denucé 1938: xvii–xix.

[70] The oldest surviving bylaws of Antwerp, dating from the beginning of the fourteenth century, already recognized a creditor's right to arrest a debtor or his property for unpaid debts: FA, *Keurboek met de Doppen* (PK 94), art. 131; Gilissen 1958: 298–99; De Ruysscher 2009c: 308–69; De Smedt 1954: 591. Already in 1446 the privileges of the English merchants stipulated that whenever they were arrested for unpaid debts in Antwerp, they should be released immediately upon the provision of surety: De Smedt 1951: 92–93. The general application of individual legal responsibility in the sixteenth century is evident from the *Ordonnantie* (1532), articles 12, 13, 16, 22; *Antwerp Customs* (1545), title 1, arts. 20; title 4, arts. 19, 20, 24–26, 35, 36. For applications of the rule, Goris 1925: 355–59; De Smedt 1954: 592.

[71] See for instance the lawsuits in 1461, 1512, 1523, 1546, and 1567 recorded by van Answaarden 1991.

[72] *Antwerp Customs* (1545), title 4; *Antwerp Customs* (1582), title 27, art. 4.

[73] An important exception to the "permission first" rule was that creditors could always, without giving notice, attach the goods given to them as collateral—a crucial provision for the use of collateralized loans: *Antwerp Customs* (1582), title 28, art. 1.

[74] Among the loans contracted by Antwerp merchant Daniel de Bruyne between 1561 and 1566 there were several that were signed in a tavern. See, for example, his *Memoriael*, carta 33, 36: "Inde Swaen," a venue De Bruyne also used to play cards (carta 41). See also carta 33, for a loan contracted in the lender's house (FA, IB inv. no. 788).

the Nieuwe Beurs opened its doors in 1531, local *and* foreign brokers were allowed to mediate between buyers and sellers.[75] This transformation hurt the financial position of individual brokers. Without entry barriers to the profession competition between intermediaries increased, and most brokers saw their earnings decline to those of a skilled craftsman.[76] But even though they lost out individually, the brokers as a group still gathered and disseminated superior information about the supply and demand of goods, and increasingly also bills of exchange, short-term loans, and marine insurance. Because of this insiders' knowledge, the brokers were made responsible for the weekly publication of printed price currents from the 1540s onward.[77] These handwritten and later also printed overviews of the prices for goods traded on the Antwerp exchange were in great demand from merchants who used them to inform their agents and associates abroad about market conditions in the Scheldt port.[78]

Nonetheless the brokers found themselves in a subservient role. When in 1556 the Piedmontese merchant Jean-Baptiste Ferufini proposed the creation of a central insurance office run by four brokers, opinions were divided. Several dozen merchants in favor of a stricter regulation of the local insurance market supported the plan, but a much larger group of local and foreign traders thought nothing of the imposition of government control. They feared it would keep merchants from doing business in Antwerp, especially because the registration of insurance transactions would be in the hands of the brokers. This was the world upside down, they objected, and an outright denial of their freedom to organize trade according to their own preferences.[79] These protests convinced the town magistrate, who did enforce a common standard for the form and shape of insurance policies, but rejected a much stricter supervision of the market by brokers.

Hostellers and Brokers in Amsterdam

A close connection among the numbers of resident merchants, the duration of their stay, and the way commercial intermediation was organized also existed in Amsterdam. Since the late fifteenth century grain traders

[75] FA, Certificatieboek 1544, fol. 288 v, 290 (January 18 and 20, 1547), cited in Jansma 1943: 232. Dilis 1910: 319–33; Coornaert 1936: 134.

[76] Goris 1925: 180.

[77] Goris 1925: 99, 180–83, 188.

[78] Puttevils 2007: 46–48, 58–66, with references to the older literature.

[79] "[Q]ue les marchans estans libres et franches viendroient à estre esclaves et que la queue seroit plus que la teste, chose certainement monstrueuse et abominable." Génard 1882: 29.

from Hamburg, Danzig, and other Hanseatic towns sojourned in local hostels, where they stored their merchandise and transacted with other merchants.[80] They obtained up-to-date information about local customs and tariffs from their landlords. In 1474 Johannes Bethzoen declared that for eighteen years he had posted local tariffs in his hostel, De Witte Hond, on the Warmoesstraat, the city's principal street. Between 1450 and 1500 at least two other hostels frequented by Oosterlingen were located here.[81] The hostellers forged durable ties with their guests. In 1495, when Hamburg beer merchants obtained their own chapel in what is now known as the Old Church, the landlord of De Gulden Hand hosted their meetings and supported them financially.[82] Perhaps even the "guest system" embedded in the city's bylaws of 1413 still applied: "[N]o man shall host foreigners, rich or poor, unless he is willing to assume responsibility [for their behavior] on his own life and property."[83]

The hostellers were also among the principal intermediaries on Amsterdam's grain market.[84] In 1483 the town magistrate ruled that men who lacked the means to buy grain themselves were not allowed to buy it for others either, even if they did not make a profit from it.[85] Twelve years later, after complaints from alien merchants—Germans, presumably—that locals, pretending to be brokers, had cheated on them, all brokerage was forbidden. A self-declared broker caught red-handed would be banned for one year, and lose his right hand if he returned before the end of this term. It was also decided that disputes arising from such transactions would no longer be heard in the local court.[86] These rules did not apply to the expanding trade in oxen from Denmark and Northern Germany because it was administered by town officials. These *register-meesters* kept accounts of all transactions and settled claims between traders when the market closed—a clearing operation resembling that of periodic fairs.[87]

The general ban on brokerage became unsustainable once the number of resident grain traders began to grow. They could do without hostellers for accommodation or representation but they did need adequate infor-

[80] Breen 1902: 132.

[81] The De Gulden Hand house, also in the Warmoesstraat, was surely used as a hostel in 1502, but perhaps already in 1481 or even 1455. A hostel, In de Kauwe, probably also in the Warmoesstraat, is first mentioned in 1492. A fourth hostel in the same street was Het Poertgen, first mentioned in 1513. The evidence on hostels is summarized in Wijnman 1963: passim and Rössner 2001: 104–5.

[82] Wijnman 1963: 61; Bijtelaar 1957: 11–17.

[83] Breen 1902: 21.

[84] Van Tielhof 1995a: 191–94.

[85] Breen 1902: 186.

[86] Breen 1902: 304.

[87] Breen 1902: 395–99; cf. also Gijsbers 1999.

mation about potential buyers and sellers. In 1530 the city decided that brokers would be allowed to mediate, provided they had an official license. The next year a first group of eleven grain brokers was admitted.[88] In 1533 followed an ordinance that specified tariffs for various kinds of grains and seeds.[89] The brokers seized upon their official recognition to create a *bosse*, a communal purse, to support those of their colleagues who could not work due to illness.[90] To protect the brokers' livelihood the town magistrate began to clamp down on interloping brokers. For example, when in 1531 Jacob Jansen, also known as *de vliegende geest* (the flying ghost), was caught in the act of brokering, he was given the choice between four years exile or a fine of 6 guilders.[91] In 1544 *byloopers*, as the interlopers were called, were banished unless they paid a fine of 25 guilders.[92] These bans were repeated in the 1550s and 1560s, though, interestingly, the penalties were gradually reduced. In 1559 the fine was set at 12 guilders, or a banishment of one year, with two years banishment for a repeat offender.[93] In 1565 the fine was set at 12 guilders for the first and second offenses, with additional punishment for repeat offenders left at the discretion of the local court.[94]

From the 1530s onward both brokers and hostellers mediated for merchants in Amsterdam. Especially after the Peace of Speyer (1544) secured a free passage of Dutch ships through the Sound, dozens of German and Flemish merchants traveled from Antwerp to Amsterdam every year to trade grain, herring, hides, and textiles. By 1560 there were between fifteen and twenty hostels in the Warmoesstraat alone and quite a few landlords would have worked for guests visiting from Antwerp.[95] But there were also merchants—locals and some foreigners—who lived in their own houses, with their own store rooms, and they would have turned to the city's brokers. The growing demand for their services is evident from repeated admissions of new brokers during the Baltic trading boom, and in 1563 the brokers actually decided to split into two groups to hold their periodic meetings.[96]

After a deep slump in the early years of the Dutch Revolt the Baltic trade quickly recovered in the 1580s, and when Antwerp fell to the Duke of Parma in 1585 already some 150 alien merchants traded in Amsterdam.

[88] Van Dillen 1929: 85, 97–98.
[89] ACA inv. 366, no. 1043.
[90] Van Dillen 1929: 107–8.
[91] Van Dillen 1929: 99, 114.
[92] Van Dillen 1929: 169; Noordkerk 1748: 2:1062.
[93] Van Dillen 1929: 261–62.
[94] Van Dillen 1929: 308–9.
[95] Wijnman 1963: 61–62; Rössner 2001: 104–5; Leeuw-Kistemaker 1974: passim.
[96] Van Dillen 1929: 295–97.

TABLE 3.1. The regional origin of brokers, hostellers, and merchants in Amsterdam around 1600

Origin	Brokers, 1618 (%)	Hostellers, 1578–1606 (%)	Merchants, 1610 (%)
	(n = 439)	(n = 97)	(n = 1,000)
Amsterdam	17.1		40
Dutch Republic	23.0	36.1	20
Antwerp	16.2	17.5	23
Brabant[a] / Flanders	10.0	14.4	10
Wallony	5.0	6.2	2
Germany	10.0	11.3	<5
Portugal	2.3		<5
England	0.9	8.2	<1
France	0.7	3.1	<1
Other[b,c]	0.2	3.1	
Unknown	14.6	7.2	

[a] Includes Weert and Maastricht in Limburg.
[b] One broker from Italy.
[c] Two hostellers from Scandinavia, one from Switzerland.
Sources: On brokers: ACA 366, no. 1084. Portuguese brokers are not included in the 1618 membership list. Their number is based on the formal admission of 10 Portuguese brokers by the Amsterdam city council (Van Dillen 1929: no. 16). On hostellers: ACA Poorterboeken (digital file). The composition of the merchant community in 1610 is based on Gelderblom 2000, 2003b.

Hostellers were among the first to benefit from the city's change of fortune. Eventually the vast majority of newcomers would rent or buy their own house in Amsterdam, but as the extension of the city took time, and commercial prospects were very insecure at first, quite a few immigrants stayed with hostellers for some period. Between 1578 and 1606 almost one hundred hostellers, from elsewhere in the Dutch Republic (thirty-five), Flanders (thirty-seven), Germany (eleven), and England (eight), bought the freedom of Amsterdam (Table 3.1).[97]

Some hostellers may still have offered their guests a wide range of commercial services, but they no longer dominated the market as the majority of merchants took up a fixed residence in Amsterdam. The latter merely needed up-to-date information about supply and demand, and therefore the city emphatically chose to support brokers as the principal intermediaries on the local market.[98] As many goods were traded on a

[97] According to Visser (1997: 11) there were 518 hostels in Amsterdam in 1613, but his count probably includes drinking establishments.
[98] The following analysis builds on Gelderblom 2000: 102–4, 146–48. See also Go 2009: 70–118.

large scale for the first time, reliable information was at a premium, and the only way to meet the demand was to admit large numbers of foreign brokers. In 1618, when the city's brokers' guild decided to register its members' place of origin, the total membership stood at 430. As with the hostellers, the background of these intermediaries mirrored the rapidly changing composition of the city's merchant community. A third of the guild members came from the Southern Netherlands, a quarter from the Dutch Republic, a fifth from Amsterdam, and the remaining sixth from Germany and other European countries (Table 3.1). The membership even included a dozen Portuguese-Jewish brokers, although it was stipulated that they would contribute to, but not benefit from, the communal purse of the brokers.

The admission of brokers from abroad was a deliberate choice to improve the quality of information available to merchants. Many of the new brokers were specialized in products such as luxury textiles, dyestuffs, sugar, and spices, which had previously been traded in Antwerp. The city's regulation of brokerage fees mirrored this change. The tariffs set in 1579 comprised fifty mostly traditional products. Eight years later some thirty items were added, including various kinds of sugar and textiles, and the next tariff list drawn up in 1613 included no fewer than 173 commodities of all sorts.[99] To make their private knowledge available to the public the brokers were also charged with the publication of a weekly price current, which reported both exchange rates and commodity prices.[100] The regional origin of the men charged with the compilation of the price currents in 1585 speaks to the diverse composition of the commercial community: one was from Amsterdam, two from Antwerp, one from Bois-le-Duc, and one from Zwolle.[101] This is not to say that brokers exclusively worked for their fellow countrymen. On the contrary, they specialized in certain products and offered their services to the merchant community at large. The inventory of the estate of Jan Mathijsz Hendricx, a broker who died in 1594, listed the accounts of 163 customers from the Southern Netherlands, the Northern Netherlands, and Germany.[102]

Specialized brokers helped to clear the market for virtually every product in Amsterdam but called upon them only if they could not find a proper match themselves. The brokers' subservient position, apparent already in Antwerp in the mid-sixteenth century, can be demonstrated more pointedly in Amsterdam, through the analysis of the business dealings of the Antwerp merchant Hans Thijs who settled in the Dutch port

[99] ACA inv. 366, nos. 1043 and 1206; see also Stuart 1879, passim.
[100] McCusker and Gravesteijn 1991: 43–83; van Dillen 1929: 27.
[101] ACA inv. 366, no. 1071; McCusker and Gravesteijn 1991; Gelderblom 2000: 73, 150, 312.
[102] ACA NA 32–256/259v (15-11-1594)

in 1595. His account books reveal that brokers were involved in only a limited number of transactions in markets for leather, jewelry, shipping services, colonial trade, and credit.

An Antwerp Merchant in Amsterdam

In 1584 Hans Thijs, the eldest son of a jewelry merchant from Antwerp, traveled to Amsterdam to marry the only daughter of Augustijn Boel, a leather merchant also from Antwerp. Thijs and his father-in-law entered into a partnership to trade leather and hides, and for this business they moved to Poland in the spring of 1585. In Danzig they found a ready supply of rawhides, tanners who could prepare the hides, and shipmasters to deliver the leather to agents in Amsterdam and Hamburg. Hans Thijs also established himself as a jeweler, selling both his father's and his own jewelry to a wealthy clientele of noblemen and merchants in Poland and Lithuania. It was a profitable business but also a very demanding one because of time-consuming travels to regional fairs and noble residences. Being away from Danzig for weeks or months compromised other family and business obligations, and therefore Thijs repeatedly charged his servant Steffen Haller with the sales of jewelry in Königsberg, Torún, Reval, Cracow, Warsaw, and even Stockholm.[103] The jeweler also had to rely on relatives, his brother François in particular, to supply him with precious stones purchased in Frankfurt and Hamburg.

Upon his return from a short visit to Amsterdam in 1591, Augustijn Boel began to contemplate moving back to Holland. In the Dutch port, he had noticed, rawhides from Poland could be supplemented with imports from Russia, Sweden, Norway, and even North Africa and America (Terra Nova). The city also had experienced leather tanners, and the number of foreign outlets for leather was much larger. When two of Augustijn's younger brothers moved to La Rochelle in 1593, and wrote about the great opportunities to export leather from Holland to France, Augustijn Boel indeed decided to return to Amsterdam, and almost immediately after his arrival in 1594, he suggested to Hans Thijs that he should also move. The jeweler needed little prodding. He sent his wife and young children ahead to visit relatives in Germany, then made one last round of visits to several noble customers, and set sail to Amsterdam.

It took Augustijn Boel and Hans Thijs some time to sort out the organization of their leather business in Amsterdam. Before leaving Danzig in May 1595 Thijs had sent the remainder of their Polish leather

[103] BT 119, Letterbook Hans Thijs, 27-05-1591, 23-08-1591, 21-07-1592, 12-09-1592, 13-02-1593, 09-02-1594.

TABLE 3.2. The supply of leather, hides, and precious stones to Hans Thijs (and Augustijn Boel), 1589–1609

	Supply (guilders)	Suppliers	Gini index
Danzig			
Leather (1589–93)[a]	61,355	44	0.46
Precious stones (1589–94)	15,807	5	0.53
Amsterdam			
Hides (1595–1601)	78,157	46	0.51
Precious stones (1595–1609)	206,787	92	0.63

[a] Leather suppliers for 1594 not specified in the ledgers.
Source: BT 119, Ledger Hans Thijs (1589–1609).

to his father-in-law, but within a year these had sold out. To replenish their stock the two merchants placed orders with a leather merchant in Hamburg and with Thijs's former servant in Poland. From 1598 onward Thijs and Boel bought all their hides on the Amsterdam market, however. Their initial suppliers were the merchants who had acted as their sales agents before 1594. Several leather tanners also purchased hides on their account, and to further replenish the stock Hans Thijs participated in various lots bought by the Antwerp merchant Wilbert Simons van Os, and twice he bought hides from strangers through the intermediation of brokers. After 1598 Thijs and Boel no longer needed the help of others, however. They obtained two-thirds of their stock from twenty merchants with whom they had had no previous engagements (Table 3.2). Only three of these suppliers provided them with hides more than once.[104]

Hans Thijs followed his father-in-law back to Amsterdam because the city offered much better opportunities for the jewelry business as well. Leaving aside for now the direct access to markets around Europe—to which we will return in the next chapter—the Dutch port offered much better opportunities to buy precious stones, to commission the finishing of the gems and the production of jewelry to local artisans, and to sell this merchandise on the local market.[105] Once settled in Amsterdam, Hans Thijs purchased all his diamonds, pearls, rubies, and emeralds from Portuguese Jews and Antwerp immigrants in the city. Since there were only a dozen or so jewelers in the city, there was no need for brokers to

[104]BT 119, Ledger Hans Thijs 1599–1603, fol. 79. The involvement of brokers in the sales of hides and leather on the Amsterdam market is confirmed by tariffs for brokers drawn up by the city council in 1613. Tariffs were stipulated for eight different sorts of hides and Spanish leather (ACA inv. 366, nos. 1043, 1206). Earlier lists, from 1578, 1587, and 1596, did not specify fees for leather and hides.
[105]Gelderblom 2000: 135–38, 141–43; Gelderblom 2008: 24–30.

bring buyers and sellers together.[106] On the spot Hans Thijs measured the quality of gems and proposed a price for them. Exclusive relations with suppliers never developed. In fifteen years' time Thijs bought precious stones from no fewer than ninety-two different merchants. Even if five suppliers provided him with a third of his stock, transactions with them amounted to only 16 percent of all purchases. The transparency of the market for precious stones, at least for regular traders, is also apparent from the enforcement of the contracts of sale. Hans Thijs paid for gems received within twelve months.[107] With a relatively small group of buyers and sellers meeting regularly on the exchange, and no other place to find gems so easily, it would be foolish for the jeweler not to meet his obligations.

Along with the trade in precious stones came a finishing industry. "I have plenty of goldsmiths, cutters of diamonds and rubies here," Hans Thijs wrote in 1596.[108] However, the jeweler did not commission them right away. Rather, he bought finished stones from Simon van Middelgeest, who had worked as a diamond cutter for his father in Antwerp. Van Middelgeest now worked as a merchant, putting out the finishing of diamonds to local artisans.[109] In 1600 Hans Thijs took on the same responsibility. First, he asked several diamond cutters to provide samples of their work. Then he chose seven of them to work for him on a regular basis between 1600 and 1603. Demand for finished diamonds and pearls was such that, in March 1602, the jeweler promised two artisans in Antwerp that "he would keep them working" for the next twelve months, on the condition that they would not work for anybody else.[110] The immigration of dozens of goldsmiths from the southern provinces allowed Thijs to organize the production of rings, eardrops, bracelets, and neck-

---

[106] Only in 1607 and 1608 did Hans Thijs pay a brokerage fee to his brother's servant Hans Bodaen, for buying ten different lots of precious stones with an estimated value of 7,800 guilders (BT 119, Ledger Hans Thijs 1603–9, fol. 178). Three earlier mentions of brokerage in Thijs's ledgers relate to small sales of jewelry in Amsterdam: BT 119, Ledger Hans Thijs 1598–1603, fols. 84, 97, 124, 128; 1603–9, fol. 193). The first official quotation of brokerage fees for various sorts of gems by the city council in 1613 suggests that Amsterdam's market for precious stones was initially made by merchants rather than brokers in the 1590s: ACA 366/1043, 1206.

[107] Hans Thijs purchased 92 percent of his precious stones on credit. The maturity of the bills obligatory he wrote for this purpose ranged from six weeks to twenty-four months. The mean and median maturity of these IOUs was twelve months, however.

[108] BT 119, Letterbook Hans Thijs, 02-12-1596.

[109] In 1596 Hans Thijs wrote to his brother that Van Middelgeest was working with two "diamond mills" for him, and that he would be able to extend this number to four, if François was to commission the cutting of precious stones in Amsterdam (BT 119, Letterbook Hans Thijs, 02-07-1596). In 1598 Hans Thijs asked a correspondent in Antwerp whether he could recommend an apprentice diamond cutter who would be willing to work for Simon van Middelgeest for one year (BT 119, Letterbook Hans Thijs, 17-01-1598).

[110] BT 119, Goldsmithbook Hans Thijs, fol. 63.

laces along similar lines.[111] Already in 1596 he wrote to his brother that the work of these artisans would obviate the latter's carrying of "foreign" goods.[112] Between 1596 and 1603 three goldsmiths, all of Antwerp origin, received regular commissions. Though his goldsmith books for the following years have been lost, Thijs's ledgers suggest this putting-out system continued for many years.[113]

In Amsterdam Thijs also moved beyond the leather and jewelry business on a more regular basis. His miscellaneous sales rose to more than 4,500 guilders per year after 1595. Some of these transactions were return cargoes, shipped by foreign agents to channel revenues back to Hans Thijs. Thus, salt, wine, wool, dyestuffs, copper, hemp, and wax from both France and the Baltic were quickly disposed of—sold to cover the costs of purchasing and shipping—sometimes even with a small loss.[114] However, Hans Thijs also invested in wine, salt, grain, and spices in Amsterdam.[115] For this purpose he participated in incidental partnerships for the joint purchase of specific goods, and he bought shares in various merchantmen and their cargo. In Poland Thijs had already been a part owner of several ships, and he had been directly involved in the management of at least one of these ships. In Amsterdam, however, he left the monitoring of his investments to specialized *reders*. In return for a commission fee these fellow investors monitored the construction, maintenance, manning, freighting, and insuring of the ships, and after each voyage they rendered accounts to the shareholders.[116]

The most important agent for Thijs's investment in shipping in Amsterdam was the Antwerp merchant Berent Berwijns. After two participations in salt shipments organized by Berwijns, Thijs bought shares in seven

[111] Between 1578 and 1606, twenty-eight goldsmiths from the southern provinces bought the freedom of Amsterdam—a condition for guild membership. Until 1601 goldsmiths belonged to St. Eloi's guild. Hereafter they had their own guild (Briels 1971, 1972).

[112] BT 119, Letterbook V, Hans Thijs to François Thijs, 09-03-1596 and 02-07-1596.

[113] BT 119, Ledger Hans Thijs 1603–9, folio's 5, 49, 137, 168, 178, 189, 193.

[114] For example, in 1601, one of Thijs's agents in La Rochelle bought 79 barrels of Cognac for Thibaut de Pickere, an Antwerp merchant and business friend of François Thijs who resided in Amsterdam. Hans Thijs had agreed to pay for 29 barrels. When the wine was sold he received back his investment (BT 119, Ledger Hans Thijs 1598–1603, fols. 140–62). Also 10 parcels of "pastel de toulouse" a dyestuff, worth ƒ 300, were sold for ƒ 295, in September 1590 (BT 119, Ledger Hans Thijs 1598–1603, fol. 73). In much the same way Castilian wool, worth ƒ 639, was sold in 1600 ƒ 88 gulden below purchase prices (BT 119, Ledger Hans Thijs, 1598–1603, fols. 73, 147).

[115] In August 1600, Thijs wrote to his brother-in-law in Halberstadt, "I have divided my goods in three parts. [the first part] in elk skin, chamois leather and Spanish leather, the second [part] in jewelry, pearls, and their dependencies, [the third part] the shipping shares I now have to East, West India, Guinea, Saint Nicolas in Moscow [Archangel?] and other places. . . ." BT 133, Letter, Hans Thijs to Andries Bacher, August 20, 1600.

[116] Hart 1977: 111.

different ships that were also managed by him. Together with several ventures in ships managed by yet another Antwerp merchant Thijs was able to raise his investments in shipping from 1,600 guilders in 1589 to more than 18,000 guilders in 1603.[117] The participation in these shipping companies was also the basis for Hans Thijs's involvement in colonial trade. From 1595 onward dozens of joint-stock companies were established to explore the coasts of Africa, America, and Asia. In January and March 1598 Hans Thijs bought two shares of 750 guilders each in the *Oude Compagnie*, which outfitted ships for the second time after a successful first voyage to the East Indies in 1595. Thijs placed his investment with one of the directors of the company, the Antwerp merchant Dirck van Os. One year later, in the spring of 1599, Hans Thijs invested 1,200 guilders in a voyage of Amsterdam's united Africa company through his agent Berent Berwijns.[118] His main interest was in the Asian trade, however. Between 1598 and 1602 Hans Thijs and his father-in-law participated in eight different voyages to the East Indies, always placing their money with either Berwijns or Van Os.[119] These investments in the Asian trade proved extremely lucrative: in 1608 the average annual rate of return of the *voorcompagnieën* since 1598 stood at more than 25 percent.[120] No wonder Hans Thijs also invested in the Vereenigde Oost-Indische Compagnie (VOC; Dutch East India Company) in 1602. Initially he bought a share of 12,000 guilders in the Amsterdam chamber of that company, but by the time of his death the nominal value of Thijs's shares in the chambers of Amsterdam, Middelburg, and Enkhuizen had risen more than threefold to 42,000 guilders.[121] As it turned out, this share capital became a major factor in the financing of his trade.

Thijs seldom relied on Amsterdam's brokers to organize commodity transactions. Together with his father-in-law the jewelry merchant was able to build up his own local network of buyers and suppliers. Other merchants, immigrants from Antwerp in particular, helped him to organize investments in shipping and colonial trade. When Augustijn Boel retired from active trade in 1600, Hans Thijs suddenly faced a heavier workload, but he managed to replace his local leather sales with shipments to foreign agents in France and Italy. It was not until 1603 that he sold his remaining stock to two leather tanners in Amsterdam. Once freed from the leather sales Thijs was able to expand his jewelry trade,

[117] Gelderblom 2000: 281.
[118] In 1601 some of the revenue of this first shipment (f 228) was carried over in another shipment, but the ledgers of Hans Thijs do not show any continuation of investments in the Africa trade thereafter (BT 119, Ledger Hans Thijs 1598–1603, fol. 42).
[119] BT 119, Ledger Hans Thijs 1598–1603, fols. 28, 88, 108, 150, 200.
[120] Gelderblom 2003b.
[121] Gelderblom 2000: 144.

with average annual sales doubling from 13,500 guilders between 1598 and 1603 to 27,000 guilders between 1604 and 1609.[122]

The expansion of Thijs's trade between 1595 and 1609 was closely bound up with the growth of the Amsterdam money market. Credit was indispensable for merchants. The buying and selling of commodities required them to demand credit from suppliers and to extend credit to customers. Hans Thijs typically used bills of exchange to remit the revenues of foreign sales, and he wrote promissory notes—IOUs in modern parlance—to finance purchases of diamonds and other merchandise. These credit operations did not suffice to run his business, however. Longer term funding was needed to keep stocks of leather and jewelry, to invest in shipping shares and colonial trade, and to provide for delayed payments by debtors. Thijs partially met these requirements through the reinvestment of profits, but he needed more capital than that.[123] Another solution would have been to enter into partnership with his brother who moved to Amsterdam in 1599, but maybe because he deemed François's continuous travels too risky, Thijs never did. Instead he used loans to broaden the financial basis of his business.

Before 1598 Hans Thijs primarily borrowed from his brothers and sisters, notably the money they had inherited from their deceased father in 1592 (Figure 3.3). Thijs continued to use these family deposits after 1598, but he also entered Amsterdam's money market. Between 1598 and 1609 he borrowed from no fewer than 70 different merchants or their widows. In 1600 these loans already stood at 25,000 guilders, and in the following years Hans Thijs borrowed on average between 50,000 guilders and 70,000 guilders per annum. Thijs's credit operations benefited from the introduction of new loan collateral. From 1603 onward he borrowed on the security of his shares in the VOC. Regular transfers between shareholders turned these shares into a liquid asset that could be sold easily in case of a borrower's default.[124]

Brokers are conspicuously absent from the records Hans Thijs kept of his credit operations. The jeweler did rely on them for several purchases of VOC shares, but he negotiated loans directly with his creditors.[125] This was not because brokers were barred from the money market: the city set brokerage fees for financial transactions as early as the 1560s. Thijs

---

[122] Gelderblom 2000: 279.

[123] Reinvestment of profits certainly did not suffice to finance expansion. Whereas the returns on sales of rawhides seem to have been rather modest in the 1590s, tanned leather of different kinds generated gross profits between 5 percent and 12 percent. Such returns must have sufficed to cover the costs of trade and provide Thijs and Boel with an income to live off.

[124] Gelderblom and Jonker 2004: 659–65.

[125] BT Ledger Hans Thijs, 1598–1603, 1604–9, passim.

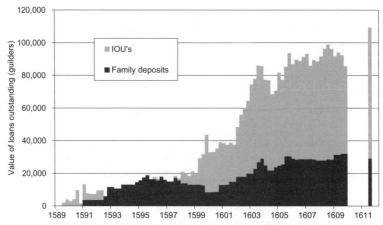

FIGURE 3.3. Funds borrowed by Hans Thijs from family members and funds raised with bills obligatory, 1589–1611 (quarterly totals)

Sources: 1589–1609: BT 119, Business Ledgers Hans Thijs, passim. September 1611: BT 113 (Journael E), fols. 3, 4.

simply managed to find his financiers without intermediation. Even kinship and common business interests seem to have been relatively unimportant to raise funds. Relatives signed less than 5 percent of his bills obligatory, and fellow jewelers provided only 15 percent of the funds. This is not to say that all lenders were passersby.[126] The seven biggest lenders provided almost 40 percent of total funds, while 60 percent of all lenders extended only 20 percent of the loans. By far the biggest lender (10 percent of all funds) was Simon van Middelgeest, the merchant and diamond cutter with whom Thijs had had many previous dealings.[127] Besides the prolongation of many loans, there certainly was an Antwerp connection, with between 55 percent and 60 percent of the credit extended to Thijs coming from immigrants from the southern provinces. The money market was not segmented, however, as local merchants consistently provided at least 25 percent of the sums borrowed.

The security offered by the use of shares as collateral is evident from a comparison of the interest rates paid by Hans Thijs to family members and other creditors (Figure 3.4). In Danzig the choice between the two groups of lenders was easily made. While interest rates on bills obligatory typically stood at 10 percent in Danzig in the early 1590s, family

[126]To measure the relative importance of all seventy lenders, we have calculated the total capital supplied by each of them (principal d maturity) as a share of total capital lent to Hans Thijs.

[127]BT 119, Ledger Hans Thijs 1595–98, fol. 21; Ledger Hans Thijs 1598–1603, fols. 5, 195; Ledger Hans Thijs 1603–9, fols. 42, 214; BT Journael E (Hans Thijs) fols. 3, 4.

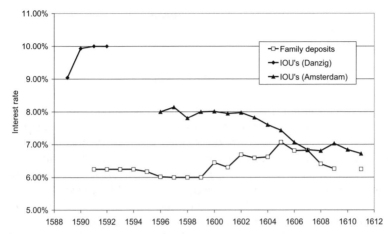

FIGURE 3.4. Average interest rate paid by Hans Thijs to family members and other creditors (1589–1611)

Sources: 1589–1609: BT 119, Business Ledgers Hans Thijs, passim. 1611: BT 113 (Journael E), fols. 3, 4.

deposits were provided to Hans Thijs for an average 6.25 percent. This interest gap was still considerable in Amsterdam in the late 1590s, but it narrowed markedly thereafter. While the average market rate dropped from 8 percent in 1598 to slightly below 7 percent in 1607, the average family rate rose to 6.75 percent and even 7 percent in the same period. In 1607 Hans Thijs paid as much interest (6.75 percent) to his relatives as to other lenders. Thereafter the family rate dropped again, to 6.25 percent, or half a point below the market rate.

The convergence of interest rates paid to relatives and other lenders reflects the rapid growth of Amsterdam's money market in the first decade of the seventeenth century. A growing demand for capital and the pledging of shares as collateral for loans made the purchase of IOUs attractive for wealth owners with surplus funds. In the case of Hans Thijs, he may have been obliged to raise the interest on loans from his relatives because they could credibly "threaten" him to deposit their money with other merchants in Amsterdam.[128] If a price differential remained after

[128]To be sure, some relatives of Hans Thijs found yet other outlets for their surplus funds. Between 1604 and 1616 Andries Bacher, the earlier mentioned husband of Magdalena Thijs, extended credit to more than 100 merchants and artisans in Hamburg, through the intermediation of a local merchant. The total value of the bills obligatory held by Bacher, amounted to ƒ 30,000 in 1614. Until 1610 the interest on these IOUs stood at 7 or 7.5 percent—thereafter rates of 6 percent and 6.5 percent also were negotiated (BT 143, cash register Andries de Bacher, 1604–16).

all, this probably was a reward for financial services he rendered to his brothers and sisters.

The Growth of the Amsterdam Market

The case of Hans Thijs shows that merchants who settled permanently in a foreign market did not need the combined services of a hosteller or the forced intermediation of a broker. They arranged for their own accommodation and storage facilities, and they gathered information through personal networks of suppliers, producers, and financiers. This private solution worked because commercial cities readily adapted rules and regulations to changes in the scale and scope of trade.[129] In their efforts to change the institutional framework of trade the rulers of Amsterdam carefully considered commercial and financial practices in Antwerp. The functioning of the local money market, for instance, went back to an ordinance of Charles V from the 1540s that had allowed merchants in the Scheldt port to use IOUs to borrow money for periods up to one year. The town magistrate also invited Flemish immigrants to testify to the rules followed in Antwerp, for instance in marine insurance and exchange operations, and the Antwerp customs of 1582 were reprinted several times in Amsterdam, either separately or in combination with other legal texts.[130] Notaries recorded private consultations of Antwerp merchants about business practices in the southern provinces.[131] The adoption of customs or mercantile usage from Antwerp did not imply any preferential treatment of merchants. In the fifteenth century Amsterdam's magistrate had decided to treat all merchants, regardless of their origin, as equal before the law, and this did not change.[132] In 1607, for instance, it was confirmed in a *turbe*—a formal declaration regarding business practices made by at least ten individuals—that Amsterdam's local laws and customs made no difference between citizens and strangers with regard to the attachment of goods for unpaid debts or insolvencies.[133]

Amsterdam, however, departed from Antwerp practice in one important respect, that is, the establishment of a Bank of Exchange in 1609.

---

[129] For a detailed reconstruction of information supply on the Amsterdam market: Lesger 2006: 214–57, which builds on Smith 1984: passim; see also van Tielhof 2002.

[130] *Rechten ende costumen van Antvverpen*, published in Amsterdam in 1613 by Hendrick Barentsz. Similar editions printed in Cologne and Hamburg may also have circulated in Amsterdam: Goris 1925: 34. On the consultations: Wachter 1639: 108; Oldewelt 1967: passim; Asser 1987: 105–6, with references to the older literature.

[131] See, for instance, ACA NA 1967/325 (August 14, 1609).

[132] Breen 1902: 159–61, 222; Noordkerk 1748: 1:33–46; 2:495–502, 577.

[133] Noordkerk 1748: 2:502; Wachter 1639: 102; *Consultatien* 1657–66: 1:302.

The Wisselbank was intended to strengthen Amsterdam's position as an international clearing house for bills of exchange through the mandatory settlement of bills worth 600 guilders or more. The bank allowed merchants to make payments through transfers between their respective accounts, and thus reduced their administrative burden, but its establishment nevertheless led to a storm of protest from cashiers who until 1609 had been the prime organizers of payments and discounting of bills both in Antwerp and Amsterdam. The city magistrate initially ignored the complaints but soon found out that the cashiers did provide a valuable service to the merchant community, so they had to climb down and readmit the cashiers in 1621, albeit without the right to settle bills in excess of 600 guilders.

The building of the Exchange, completed in 1611, was again grafted onto the Exchange of Antwerp. From now on merchants no longer needed to gather at the New Bridge or in one of the nearby churches, but in spite of this practical improvement, merchants and magistrates started bickering because the city seized upon the opening of the Exchange to reorganize the brokers' profession. To secure the concentration of trade at the exchange the city wanted a stricter regulation of the work of licensed brokers, and firmer measures against interlopers. For instance, nobody was to stay in the vicinity of the Bourse before or after trading hours.[134] The city also tried to turn brokers into pure information specialists: they were no longer allowed to act as agents for merchants not present at the exchange.[135] Hostellers also had to choose between brokering and the lodging of visiting merchants—doing both was no longer allowed.[136]

The city also considered lowering tariffs to bring more trade to the Beurs. It stated that lower brokerage was equitable since often large quantities of goods changed hand, which effectively limited the amount of work brokers had in mediating between traders. But the brokers, by now numbering 340, wanted higher, not lower wages. They argued that most of them dealt in small quantities only and needed the money to sustain their livelihood. They insisted that tariffs were higher in other towns, and that merchants were willing to pay higher tariffs to byloopers. The brokers rallied the support of almost four hundred merchants trading in a wide variety of goods. One of the formal requests signed by these merchants asserted that

> [interlopers] were ten, or more, to one, and they were virtually the only ones trading in silk, spices, and other merchandise, adapting to the time and taking what the merchants wanted and still want to pay,

[134]Van Dillen 1929: 61–62.
[135]Noordkerk 1748: 2:1060–74.
[136]Noordkerk 1748: 2:1060–62.

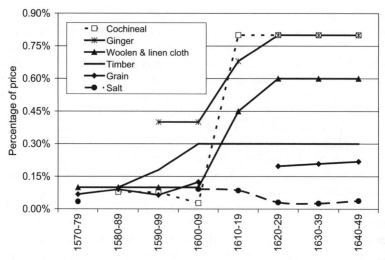

FIGURE 3.5. Brokerage paid on various products in Amsterdam between 1570 and 1650 expressed as a percentage of the price (decennial averages)
  Sources: ACA 366 inv. nos. 1043, 1206; Stuart 1879.

that is, as much as was given as brokerage for many years, and still today, in Antwerp.[137]

If this were true, higher tariffs could kill two birds with one stone: placate the brokers and quell illicit brokerage. And thus in 1613 the city council raised tariffs for many goods, some with more than 100 percent. Figure 3.5 shows that hereafter the average tariff for bulk goods like grain and timber amounted to between 0.15 percent and 0.30 percent of the wholesale price, while brokers in textiles and dyestuffs could charge between 0.2 percent and 0.8 percent.

At first sight the stricter regulation of commercial intermediation implemented after the opening of the Exchange was a sweeping victory for the officially registered brokers. Besides the higher tariffs, they also managed to convince the town magistrate that the number of formally admitted brokers should be reduced to three hundred, and that only citizens could be members of the brokers' guild.[138] Furthermore, higher fines were set for illicit mediation, and the brokers themselves were given the right to prosecute byloopers. From 1612 onward members had to report illegal brokers and the parties involved in their transactions, after which both merchants and intermediaries were fined.[139]

---

[137] ACA inv. 366, no. 1037 (translation by OG).
[138] Van Dillen 1933: 814.
[139] ACA inv. 366, no. 1287; van Dillen 1933: 813–16.

But things worked out differently for the brokers. For one thing, the cap on membership did not work. Several members decided to sell their right to mediate to outsiders at terms favorable to them but detrimental to the profession.[140] The expansion of the guild membership to 430 in 1618 shows the authorities quickly backed away from the set limits.[141] Most important, the byloopers simply continued their work outside the Bourse, on the quays, in taverns, or on their own premises.[142] The leaders of the brokers guild also complained that hostellers were reluctant to give up their brokerage.[143] Even if the number of illicit transactions prosecuted by the brokers guilds was small—between fifteen and twenty-five per year in the first five years—these records reveal that merchants from all backgrounds—Dutch, Flemish, German, English, French, and Portuguese—used byloopers, and not just for commodity trade (sugar, grain, diamonds) but also for insurance policies, freight contracts, and bills of exchange.[144] It was difficult to suppress illegal mediation because for merchants it did not really matter who put them in touch with potential buyers and sellers, as long as they made a profit.[145] Hostellers, warehouse keepers, and shipmasters could all deliver the goods. It was also difficult for the official brokers to catch a bylooper red-handed. Merchants had no incentive to tell on their intermediary—not even when they were cheated, for the local court refused to rule in disputes involving interlopers. After 1636, when every licensed broker was required to carry a staff, it became impossible to deny one's dealings with a bylooper, but this of course could not prevent the initial illicit transaction.[146]

Thus the position of brokers in Amsterdam was under pressure because many merchants were able to gather information by themselves, and in case they did need somebody else to find a buyer or supplier, they did not hesitate to use the services of an interloper. But brokers, even if they could not make the market, certainly helped clearing it, and therefore the city magistrate intervened and made for a new organizational model, in which commercial and financial intermediation was concentrated at the exchange, with official brokers who received slightly higher tariffs, and on top of that retained the right to publish Amsterdam's price

---

[140] Van Dillen 1933: 59–60, 342n1, 689–90, 814.

[141] Van Dillen 1933: 27.

[142] Van Dillen 1933: 341–42.

[143] ACA inv. 366, no. 1037, letter dated January 20, 1616.

[144] ACA inv. 366, no. 1287, fols. 1–25.

[145] Stuart 1879: 47, 67–69, 160.

[146] Van Dillen 1933: 474. The persistence of byloopers is all too clear from the description in *De Koophandel van Amsterdam*, published by Le Moine de l'Espine in 1694. This book mentioned 1,000 illicit brokers, next to 375 formally admitted brokers and 21 Jewish brokers (Jansen 1946: 38).

currents. The tariff structure and enforcement of the new rules was such, however, that merchants could minimize information costs, while brokers, just like in Antwerp, were reduced to a subservient position with a modest income.

Conclusion

The history of Bruges, Antwerp, and Amsterdam highlights the development of well-functioning local markets as one of the principal achievements of premodern Europe. What set successful commercial cities apart was not just the establishment of fair cycles, the creation of hostels and foreign compounds, or the building of exchanges. Their main achievement was the continuous adaptation of the commercial infrastructure to changes in international trade, even if this required the dismantlement of existing practices, or the relegation of intermediaries to a humbler position. This adaptation of institutional arrangements in Bruges, Antwerp, and Amsterdam helps to explain their central position in European trade, but it also exposes a more general dynamic of institutional development, where the growth of trade changes the costs and benefits of existing institutions, which in turn leads merchants and rulers to adopt new solutions.

The concentration of trade in local markets allowed merchants in premodern Europe to reduce transaction costs in several ways. For one, they could gather in a specific location to personally meet trading partners, negotiate deals, monitor transactions, and enforce contracts. The international fairs of Flanders and Brabant facilitated exactly this kind of simultaneous exchange. But as trade in Bruges and Antwerp began to spill over to the time in between fairs, foreign visitors could no longer keep up with their transactions. This created opportunities for local hostellers who could reduce merchants' transactions costs through the bundling of several functions, including the supply of commercial information, storage facilities, and accommodation. Many hostels in the ports of the Low Countries doubled as vending locations and as the hostellers formally represented their guests while they were abroad, their hostels became *one-stop shops* offering a combination of services at the lowest possible cost.

The hostellers lost this competitive advantage when foreign merchants settled permanently in the Low Countries. The foreign traders now had their own place to stay, and they could buy and sell goods throughout the year. The benefits of performing multiple functions that had once put hostellers in a superior position accrued to individual traders. Or at least part of the benefits did, because merchants still needed the host cities to provide public vending locations, while they also lacked the specialist knowledge to trade in each and every market segment. The response of Bruges, Antwerp, and Amsterdam was to reorganize their brokers' profession, to give merchants the choice to use them or not, and to increase competition between brokers to put pressure on the cost of their information services. These changes did not require extraordinary investments by town magistrates, but the reduction of hostellers and brokers was nevertheless remarkable. The prominent position of the medieval hostellers and the corporate status of the brokers could have made for sharp social conflicts. This never happened because the adaptation of commercial intermediation was a very gradual process that went hand in hand with a steady growth of trade, thus mitigating the impact of regulatory changes on the business of individual hostellers and brokers.

CHAPTER 4

Crossing Borders

SO FAR WE HAVE EMPHASIZED THE PIVOTAL ROLE OF URBAN GOVERN-
ments in the organization of European trade through the creation of well-
functioning markets frequented by local traders and visiting foreigners.
However, international trade by definition implied the transfer of money
and goods between markets, and this created an entirely different set of
delivery and payment problems.[1] In the Middle Ages the risks involved
in trade over long distances were so large that merchants traveled constantly abroad to exchange money and goods in person, thus leaving no
residual claims to be settled after they left. The costs of this itinerant
trade were high, however, not just in terms of travel expenses, but also
with regard to exposure to violent assaults and natural disaster and, perhaps most important, the investment opportunities foregone. To overcome these problems merchants increasingly worked with others who
either traveled with their money and goods or traded on their behalf
in foreign locations. This trade at arm's length was essential for the expansion of European trade between 1000 and 1800, but distant trading
partners might have been tempted to serve their own interests rather than
those of their principal.

An early solution for this problem was the writing of *commenda* contracts, which motivated agents to exert themselves because they cleared
a substantial part of the profits when transactions were successful. Such
contracts were already used by Islamic merchants between the eighth and
tenth centuries, and they were also an essential element of the transactions of merchants from Venice and Genoa in the eastern Mediterranean
from the eleventh century onward.[2] In the late medieval period, however,
the commenda was superseded by more durable partnerships between
relatives and friends, and by a much more loosely organized commission
trade within which money and goods were sent to foreign agents who
dealt with them in exchange for a small commission.[3] Notably the latter

---

[1] For a theoretical statement of the agency problems encountered by international traders, see Greif 2000: 253–56. See also Greif 1989: 857–59; Greif 2001: 5.

[2] On the origins of the commenda in the Islamic world: Udovitch 1970. For a summary
of the historical literature, see Harris 2008: 14–15. On the use of the commenda in medieval
Italy: Lopez 1971: 73–77; Lopez and Raymond 1955: 92–94, 174–76; Heers 1961: 160–61,
165; Hunt and Murray 1999: 61.

[3] On the widespread use of private limited liability companies in the nineteenth century:
Lamoreaux and Rosenthal 2005; Guinnane et al. 2007.

form required merchants to carefully monitor their agents because their fees bore no relation to the actual value of their transactions. So why did these agents not take the money and run?

The standard answer of trade historians is that commercial transactions were embedded in close-knit networks of relatives and friends where information about the past performance of prospective agents was readily available, agency relations were reciprocal, and shared social norms and cultural beliefs created strong incentives to honor obligations.[4] In many historical cases the combination of these elements has been shown to constitute a very stable private order solution of personal relations and reciprocity safeguarding the honest behavior of foreign agents.[5] Economic conditions did not always allow the careful breeding of confidence, however, as merchants sometimes needed to move quickly to capture a windfall or enter a new market. Even then they tried to recruit agents through recommendations of trusted partners and they tested them through trial consignments, but without personal ties, or the certainty that their services would be called upon again in the future, it must have been difficult to keep these distant agents from cheating.[6]

Several scholars have argued that public intervention was indispensable to sustain agency relations over long distances. Cities around Europe supported the creation of hanses, consulados, and guilds to stimulate the exchange of information between merchants traveling abroad; they also laid down standard formulas for equity and debt contracts in urban bylaws, and they set public standards for record keeping and correspondence between merchants, making it easier for merchants to enforce contracts with their agents.[7] The Venetian Republic went even further as local magistrates collected and distributed information about commercial operations in foreign markets to help resident traders seek out trustworthy agents abroad.[8] The obvious question to ask then is what the cities of Bruges, Antwerp, and Amsterdam did to help resident merchants build and maintain their international networks. As we will

[4]Curtin 1984; Mauro 1990; Mathias 2000; Selzer and Ewert 2001. But compare Trivellato (2009), who points to the benefits merchants drew from commercial ties with trading agents outside their network.

[5]See, for instance, for the Habsburg Netherlands: Brulez 1959, 1960; Baetens 1972. For the Dutch Republic: Lesger 1996; Veluwenkamp 1996; Kooijmans 1997; Gelderblom 2000; Wijnroks 2003; Antunes 2004. For England: Neal and Quinn: 2001; For Germany: Häberlein 1998. For the Mediterranean world: Dursteler 2006; Engels 1997; Van Gelder 2009; Fusaro 2012. For the Atlantic world: Bailyn 1955; Doerflinger 1986; Vanneste 2011.

[6]Greif 1989: 865; Gelderblom 2003c: 633.

[7]Gelderblom and Grafe 2010: 481–86, with an overview of the literature. See also Ogilvie 2011: 94–159.

[8]González de Lara 2008: 262–72. Milgrom, North, and Weingast (1990: 20) suggest that a similar function was performed by the judges presiding over the courts of the Champagne fairs.

see, self-organization was not sufficient for the proper functioning of international trade. Instead, urban magistrates were always present in the background to support the network-based trade of international merchants and promote the central position of their own city in the European economy.

COMMISSION TRADE

When Hans Thijs moved from Danzig to Amsterdam in the spring of 1595 he risked losing his carefully established clientele in Poland and Prussia. To prevent this from happening he left 3,250 guilders worth of jewelry with his long-time servant Steffen Haller, who was accustomed to traveling in the Baltic area to sell his master's merchandise. This time, however, he cashed his wage of 200 guilders without selling a single piece, returning the jewelry to Hans Thijs's brother François in March 1596. "He is a fantasist," Hans Thijs wrote to his brother, urging him not to rely on servants any longer.[9] François took over from Steffen Haller and in seven years' time he sold 43,000 guilders worth, or one-third of his brother's jewelry, in Frankfurt, Leipzig, Copenhagen, Danzig, Königsberg, Warsaw, Cracow, Constantinople, Avignon, Paris, Brussels, and Antwerp. The two brothers may not have been very close personally—in letters to relatives François's wife complained that Hans seldom visited them in Amsterdam when her husband was traveling—but they performed valuable services for each other. Hans kept his brother informed about political and economic developments, sold some of his merchandise, and made numerous payments on his behalf.

The situation of Hans Thijs in Eastern Europe resembled that of German and Italian merchants who began trading in Bruges in the thirteenth century. They expected to make a profit from sales and purchases in Flanders, but to achieve this they had to leave their money and goods in the hands of agents who might pursue their own advantage. An early solution for this problem used by merchants in Italy as well as northern Germany was the writing of commenda contracts. Between 1280 and 1320 Genoese traders recorded dozens of these contracts with notaries in Genoa to organize their trade in Flanders and England. The contracts united one active traveling partner who supplied his labor, and one or more passive partners who invested their money. Because the capitalists in Lübeck and Genoa could not directly observe their agents' performance, profits were divided according to a fixed formula, typically one-third for the active

---

[9] BT 119, Letterbook Hans Thijs, 24-04-1596, 25-06-1596; BT 119, Ledger Hans Thijs, 1595–98, fol. 25.

partner and two-thirds for the passive partners, which created incentives for the traveling merchant to exert himself. Rudimentary accounts rendered upon return sufficed to evaluate the agent's activity, especially since disclosure of poor results by the capitalists in Lübeck and Genoa would make it difficult for a merchant to find new financiers.[10]

In the fourteenth century foreign merchants in Bruges replaced the commenda contracts with commissions to fellow countrymen who settled in the city for a longer period. Notably Italian merchants with commission agents in cities around Europe were able to increase the scope of their international operations in this way, but Bruges's hostellers also contributed to the growth of such consignments. German, Italian, Spanish, Portuguese, and English merchants left their money or goods in the hands of local hostellers, who did not assume ownership but simply tried to buy or sell in exchange for a percentage fee.[11] In the fifteenth century this commission trade spread to Antwerp and Amsterdam.[12] A comment by one of the litigants in a commercial lawsuit regarding the seizure of property of a German merchant in Amsterdam in 1498 reveals just how solid the arrangement was:[13]

> It was the custom and usage among merchants in Amsterdam, trading with Eastern and Hanseatic towns, and elsewhere, that they sent their merchandise with their ships and servants to their factors and hostellers, who received and sold them, and returned the money or other goods, and all this in good faith and for their *pontgelt* [commission fee].

The private character of the commission trade is abundantly clear from this description, but that does not mean it was an informal solution, in the sense argued by Avner Greif for the coalition of Jewish traders from Northern Africa in the eleventh century.[14] Social sanctions must have played a major role in the commission trade of foreign merchants in the late medieval Low Countries, but their consignments implied formal agreements. Merchants wrote letters with detailed instructions, and hostellers, brokers, and money changers were required to keep written

[10]Cordes 1998: 308–14; Arlinghaus 2002: 249–53.

[11]Selzer and Ewert 2001: 140–42; Maréchal 1951: 27, 40; Murray 2005: 243; Lopez and Raymond 1955: 213; Cordes 1998: 222.

[12]Goris 1925: 215–16; Brulez 1959: 263–64, 374. The terms *consignment trade* and *commission trade* are both used in the literature to describe the sending of goods or money to agents abroad. In the seventeenth century consignments came to indicate shipments of goods to an agent who paid up (part of) the value of the goods beforehand: Jonker and Sluyterman 2000: 30.

[13]Poelman 1917: 2:1072.

[14]Greif 1989, 1993, 2006.

records of their dealings. In 1437, for instance, Antwerp's magistrate decided that the administration of hostellers was worth as much as two individual testimonies, provided the hosteller pledged an oath to the truthfulness of his books.[15] This was practical for the hosteller because it allowed the reviewing of earlier transactions and disclosure of relevant information to his customers, but the ex post verification of business deals on the basis of such records also allowed merchants to substantiate financial claims.[16] The convenience of this is clear from the insolvency of the widow of the Bruges money changer Diederic Urbaen in 1350. Forty-five creditors claimed money from the estate, but only twenty-seven of them could prove their transactions with entries in Urbaen's accounts. The guarantors of the money changer and his widow—liable for any losses incurred by them—saw their chance and disputed the other claims.[17]

The growing number of foreign residents in the ports of the Low Countries eroded the hostellers' role as commission agent because the merchants themselves started to operate in bilateral or multilateral networks of traders who bought and sold goods on each other's behalf. In the fourteenth century, for instance, German traders engaged in commission trade *auf Gegenseitigkeit* on the major commercial axis between Lübeck and Bruges.[18] Richard and George Cely, wool merchants from London, took commissions from both relatives and strangers when traveling to Bruges and Antwerp in the 1470s and 1480s.[19] In the mid-sixteenth century the Van der Molen family in Antwerp bought and sold merchandise for a broad group of Italian merchants, several of whom they had never met in person.[20]

Sustaining commission trade between relative strangers was possible because the size of individual sales and purchases was kept small and because merchants carefully picked their agents and closely monitored their performance.[21] In 1596, for instance, after his bad experiences with Steffen Haller, Hans Thijs wrote to another correspondent in Danzig, "I beg you, write me a little about the affairs of Abram Saem. How has he

[15] Ordinance, January 11, 1437, art. 6, cited in Dilis 1910: 418. See also Godding 1987: 439, 457–58; Greve 2000: 43.

[16] According to Godding (1987: 457–58) brokers were often asked to testify in commercial disputes, but he does not cite any evidence. According to Van Houtte (1950–51: 22) the testimonies of brokers who had witnessed sales were used in court as early as 1262.

[17] The ruling of Bruges's aldermen has not survived but clearly the lack of paper proof added to the creditors' difficulties in getting their money back. De Roover 1948: 265–67, 361–63.

[18] Cordes 1998: 249–50.

[19] Hanham 1985: 35–36, 39, 51, 52, 54, 215–16, 244.

[20] Brulez 1959: 488–90.

[21] See, for example, the business correspondence of Daniel van der Meulen: Jongbloet-Van Houtte 1986: 429, 456, 457.

done in the trade with Italy? And does he have good credit there?"[22] We do not know the correspondent's response, but Thijs never hired Saem. Shortly after this letter, Hans advised his brother François that leaving grain with their long-time Lübeck agent Andries Fagel might not be such a good idea: "[Y]ou should not trust Fagel too much, for he has had rye here and forgot to make a profit from it." Obviously this kind of information was passed on rather discretely: "This is secret, my dear brother, [but] one must keep an eye on things these days."

The foreign nations in Bruges and Antwerp may have offered a platform for the dissemination of information about merchants' reputation. For instance, the Lucchese nation in Bruges and the English nation in Antwerp regularly convened their members and organized the delivery of mail with their hometowns. These letters were the linchpin of the commission trade. They guided the international transactions of merchants in the Low Countries from the very first introduction of a potential agent to the final settlement of accounts.[23] In the fourteenth and fifteenth centuries the local directors of Italian firms in Bruges exchanged many hundreds of letters per year with the head of the company, the managers of other branches, and a host of clients and employees.[24] Hildebrand Veckinchusen received 546 letters in Bruges in the first two decades of the fifteenth century.[25] Between 1563 and 1606 Castilian merchants Simon and Cosimo Ruiz in Medina del Campo received almost 3,000 letters from agents in Antwerp; their principal correspondents wrote at least once every fortnight.[26] In the 1580s Flemish merchant Maarten Della Faille wrote between four and eight pages per week to his principal correspondents, while Dutch merchant Claes van Adrichem spent as much as 50 guilders per year (a quarter of the annual wage of an unskilled worker) on the correspondence with his agent in Poland alone.[27] The letters Hans Thijs wrote, first from Danzig and then from Amsterdam, increased from 33 in 1591 to 275 in 1598.[28]

In their letters, merchants asked agents to sell to the best of their abilities (*to synem besten to verkopen*) as if the merchandise was their own (*come de cossa proprio, al of 't mijn eigen ware*). To evaluate their agents'

[22]BT 119, Brievenboek V, Hans Thijs to Didrich Swarts, June 1596; see also BT 199, Brievenboek W, Hans Thijs to Didrich Swarts, December 4, 1596.
[23]For the role of business letters in the organization of early modern trade, see Trivellato 2009: 177–93. Monographs that use the business correspondence of merchants in Bruges, Antwerp, and Amsterdam include Vasquez de Prada 1960; Kooijmans 1997; Jonker and Sluyterman 2000; Gelderblom 2000.
[24]Grunzweig 1931, passim; De Roover 1963: 96–100.
[25]Stieda 1921, passim.
[26]Vasquez de Prada 1960, passim.
[27]Brulez 1959: 428–29; Jonker and Sluyterman 2000: 27.
[28]Gelderblom 2000: 284–86.

performance, merchants required correspondents to send copies of accounts.[29] When Hans Thijs checked the annual accounts sent by his agent Paulus Boel in Bordeaux in 1605, he noticed sales had been overestimated and immediately debited the commission wrongly charged on Boel's current account.[30] Merchants in major ports could also use public information generated by frequent arrival of merchants and shipmasters from other towns, and, from the sixteenth century onward, they increasingly relied on price currents to benchmark their agents' results.[31] Privately written reports on commodity prices may have circulated in Bruges already in the fifteenth century, but from the 1530s onward printed price lists in Antwerp gave foreign merchants an additional, independent yardstick to measure the performance of their agents. Following what might have been an earlier Venetian example, two currents were published, one for exchange rates, the other for commodity prices, based on information gathered by local brokers.[32] The surviving business letters of the Van der Molen merchants of Antwerp suggest that such price lists were habitually enclosed to share price information with traders abroad.[33]

The letters merchants sent to each other were couched in terms of friendship and courtesy, but the formal power of this correspondence should not be underestimated. As Francesca Trivellato has demonstrated for eighteenth-century Livorno, merchant letters also defined the formal relationship with correspondents.[34] In addition to detailed instructions to agents regarding the price, quality, and payment of goods, the letters sometimes contained verbatim transcriptions of powers of attorney passed before a local notary.[35] Marks written on bales, crates, and sacks were added to the letters to enable the correspondent to identify shipments, and they also served to allow retrieval in case of theft or privateering.[36] Samples of handwritings were enclosed to allow agents to recognize future bills of exchange, which had to be handwritten to get accepted.[37]

[29] Brulez 1959: 53–55, 373; Jongbloet-Van Houtte 1986: 146–47, 149, 193, 194, 198.

[30] BT 119, Ledger Hans Thijs, 1603–9, fol. 145.

[31] Compare the work of Dean Williamson, who has argued for late medieval Venice that information flows with other ports were so dense that principals could learn about the business environment their agents operate in, without asking them themselves: Williamson 2002.

[32] The earliest price currents (commodities and/or exchange) surviving in Italian towns are from Venice in 1585, Florence in 1598, and Genoa in 1619. In Germany, Hamburg (1592) and Augsburg (1592) had price currents before 1600. For an exhaustive overview of price currents in other parts of Europe in later years: McCusker and Gravesteijn 1991; see also McCusker 2005. McCusker has convincingly argued for the existence in Antwerp since the late 1530s of a price current for commodities, besides the printed listings of exchange rates: McCusker 1996.

[33] McCusker 1996: 313–21.

[34] Trivellato 2009: 177–93. For a Dutch example: Zijlstra 2012.

[35] Lopez and Raymond 1955: 379.

[36] Gilliodts-Van Severen 1871–85: 2:190.

[37] De Roover 1963: 127.

Courts recognized the legal value of these private writings, and already in the late fourteenth century the consuls of the Lucchese nation in Bruges accepted letters as proof in commercial disputes.[38] The aldermen of Bruges did the same from the fifteenth century onward, and in Amsterdam around sixteen hundred Portuguese merchants regularly used their business correspondence as proof in court proceedings.[39]

PARTNERSHIPS

Consignments were very convenient to organize simple sales and purchases in foreign markets, but merchants who wanted their agents abroad to make judgmental decisions about investments or buy and sell on credit needed more safeguards against opportunistic behavior. An early solution employed by Italian and German merchants in Bruges was the bilateral commenda—known as *colleganza* in Venice, *societas maris* in Genoa, and *Widerlegung* or *wederlegginge* in Lübeck—in which the active partner also contributed capital and thus shared in the costs and benefits of his own performance.[40] German traders pushed the boundaries of this contract even further as they signed wederlegginge for indefinite periods.[41] The *societas inter Flandriam et Lubeke*, for instance, was created by two merchants in 1316 for the joint investment of 1,000 marks of silver in shipments between Bruges and Lübeck.[42] The more common German strategy, however, was to write several commenda contracts simultaneously. This was the preferred mode of operation of Sivert and Hildebrand Veckinchusen,

[38]Lazzareschi 1947: 19–20, 23–27, 32–33, 66–68, 72–79, 86–95, 220–21. Merchants also turned to the consuls to formally register their letters to increase their legal value: Lazzareschi 1947: 228–29. In 1582 the publication of the verdicts of the *Rota* of Genua confirmed that an agency relation evidenced in business letters had legal force even toward third parties: Fortunati 1996: 84–85.

[39]SR nos. 114–15, 319, 359, 1478, 1731–732, 1738, 1786, 1799, 1803, 1808, 1813, 1842, 1853, 2318, 2327, 2369, 2650, 3059, 3204, 3355, 3356, 3399, 3429, 3472, 3556, 2764.

[40]Lopez 1971: 76–77; Lopez and Raymond 1955: 174–76; Cordes, Friedland, and Sprandel 2003: 22–24, 32–43; Edler de Roover 1941: 88, has argued that the bilateral commenda allowed a young merchant at the beginning of his career to accumulate wealth by reinvesting earnings from previous voyages. See also Udovitch 1970: 170–71.

[41]The *Widerlegung* was referred to as *societas, recta societas*, or *vera societas* in the publicly registered latin contracts in Lübeck in the fourteenth century: Cordes, Friedland, and Sprandel 2003: 3; Selzer and Ewert 2001: 140–41. A contractual agreement similar to an Italian unilateral commenda appeared only 17 times in Lübeck's register of *societates* between 1311 and 1360, versus 267 *Widerlegungen* (Cordes, Friedland, and Sprandel 2003: 14–17).

[42]Cordes, Friedland, and Sprandel 2003: 5, 6, 86, 87, 100. Regular *Widerlegungen* with several partners were not written, however, since this would have required additional arrangements for the liability of the passive partners toward each other. In Genoa, where merchants did participate in bilateral commendas with several passive partners, the contracts were always accompanied by a contract *in comuni ratione*, explicitly stating the joint and several liability of the passive partners: Doehaerd 1941: 1:120–26; Liagre-De Sturler 1969: lxvii.

two brothers from Lübeck who in the early fifteenth century wrote a string of *Widerlegungen* to organize their trade with Bruges.[43]

The bilateral commenda was well suited to raise more equity, but it did not allow partners to borrow money to expand their business, as the unfortunate history of the Venedischer Handelsgesellschaft, established in 1407, shows. This company united Hildebrand Veckinchusen and his brother Sivert with four other groups of two or three German merchants who each invested 1,000 Lübeck marks in what effectively was an extended Widerlegung. This combination of merchants located in Bruges, Lübeck, Cologne, and Venice set out to exchange silk from Italy for furs and amber from the Baltic area.[44] The partners could not closely monitor each other's behavior, but the profit-sharing rules created the proper incentives for each of them to put in their best effort. Initially business went rather well, and in 1409 the partners decided to reinvest profits, supply additional capital, and raise the total subscription to 20,000 marks.

The merchants went one step further, however, and allowed the agents in Venice to buy on credit. The Widerlegung did not allow credit operations, but the merchants now wrote separate powers of attorney to grant each other, and the partners in Venice in particular, permission to buy on credit. As soon as their play was established, things started going awry.[45] The large quantities of silk that were now being sent from Venice could not be sold in the north, and the merchants in Bruges and Cologne could not honor the bills of exchange drawn by their Venetian partners. The failure was in part the result of a political crisis in Lübeck that forced Sivert Veckinchusen to leave the town, and robbed the company of a major outlet. But nothing would have happened if the Venetian partners had not been allowed to buy on credit. If they had simply limited themselves to purchases to the amount of the company's capital, they would have incurred some costs for stocks unsold, but they would not have had to liquidate the company in 1414–15 with considerable losses (and anger) for those partners who had advanced their money to the Venetian associates.[46]

Italian merchants found a different solution to limit their liability with the creation of specific purpose partnerships.[47] Just like as with a general partnership, the partners in a *compagnia* were jointly and severally liable

[43]Irsigler 1985: 79; Lesnikov 1973: passim. On several occasions, the partnership of Hildebrandt and Sivert Veckinchusen acted as the passive investor in the *wederlegginge*: Cordes 1998: 309.

[44]Irsigler 1985: 85–86; Cordes 1998: 251–55.

[45]Cordes 1998: 255–60 and Seifert 2000: 49–50.

[46]Only one of the initial partners, Bode van Stocham, escaped the crisis because he had been bought out by the Veckinchusen brothers in 1411: Cordes 1998: 242–43.

[47]Lazzareschi 1947: 11–13; Lopez and Raymond 1955: 175, 291; De Roover 1963: 139–40, 260–61; Lopez 1971: 74.

for each other's actions, but only if these actions were in accordance with the purpose and duration of the company contract.[48] A specific purpose partnership could be established by private contract, for any kind of business ranging from a single voyage to a general trade for several years.[49] The earliest specific purpose partnerships for trade in the Low Countries were signed in the early fourteenth century by merchants from Genoa before notaries in their home.[50] Not much later the Bardi, Peruzzi, and several other Florentine merchants began to use similar company contracts to manage their branches in Bruges and London.[51] By 1377 specific purpose partnerships were common practice among the members of the Lucchese nation in Bruges, where the consuls registered the names of all their members, the partners they were associated with, and the employees in their service in Bruges, London, and Paris.[52] This recording practice mirrored that of the Corte dei Mercanti in Lucca, which required merchants to register, every year, the names of all employees and associates, in order to determine if merchants could be held liable for debts incurred by others.[53]

The proper functioning of specific purpose partnerships required a careful choice of associates and close monitoring of each other's activities—especially when partners worked in different locations.[54] In the fourteenth and fifteenth centuries the heads of Florentine houses visited their branches in Bruges or recalled their managers to report results. In the sixteenth century the Fuggers of Augsburg also hired inspectors to travel from branch to branch and check the books of the local managers.[55] This kind of hands-on monitoring was common enough among merchants in preindustrial Europe, but to some extent it defeated the purpose of a partnership because traveling was time-consuming and required merchants to have somebody else—a servant, wife, or associate—to look after their business while they were away.[56] Merchants who did decide to

[48]De Roover 1963: 142, 145.
[49]Gelderblom, de Jong, and Jonker 2011: 32–33.
[50]On Genoese notaries working in fourteenth-century Bruges: Murray 1983: 150–51; Murray, Prevenier, and Oosterbosch 1995: 92; Oosterbosch et al. 1998: 38.
[51]Hunt 1994; Padgett 2005: 2–3, 32, 37, 48, 54, 56, 58.
[52]Lazzareschi 1947: 11–13.
[53]Häpke 1908: 164; Lazzareschi 1947: passim; De Roover 1949: 61–62, 64–65.
[54]De Roover 1963: 85, 89; Grunzweig 1931: passim; Mus 1964: 44.
[55]Hunt 1994: 206–11.
[56]Spufford 2002: 25–29, 174–227. Around 1400 a voyage between Danzig and Bruges could take anywhere between ten and forty days: Stieda 1921: xviii. In the early sixteenth century a letter from Antwerp would reach Paris in less than two days, Rome in eleven days, Danzig in thirteen days, and Lisbon in thirty-eight days (Goris 1925: 136). As for the agency of merchants' spouses, the wives of German merchants can be shown to have worked alongside their men in the fourteenth century: Cordes 1998: 213–14. In 1517 a Spanish traveler noticed the aptitude of Dutch women in running a business and handling money: van Gelder 1917; In his *Descrittione di Tutti Paesi Bassi* (1567), the Florentine

travel often combined visits to several agents or took the opportunity to trade while traveling.[57]

A complementary solution was for all partners to keep detailed accounts of their own and the others' operations.[58] Periodic comparison of the accounts of both parties made it very difficult for agents to hide manipulations from their principals.[59] This was obviously true for accounts kept in the Italian style, that is, with double entries, but merchants from Augsburg and Nuremberg, who applied their own, slightly different rules, were also able to keep tabs on their partners and employees.[60] Before 1500 the accounts of merchants in northern Germany, France, England, and the Low Countries probably were too rudimentary to keep track of more complex credit transactions and substantiate financial claims in case of disputes.[61] They started collaborating in specific purpose partnerships only in the second quarter of the sixteenth century—about the same they adopted double-entry bookkeeping.[62] The Antwerp merchant Jan Della Faille, for instance, was taught the Italian style while he was apprenticed in Venice in the 1530s and 1540s, and then went on to use the new method in his own business with various partners.[63] The famous printer Christoffel Plantijn was introduced to double-entry bookkeeping during his association with one Venetian, and two Antwerp merchants between 1563 and 1567.[64]

Lodovico Guicciardini noted the active participation of women in trade and their abilities to keep accounts and speak several languages. French merchants in the sixteenth century gave powers of attorney to their wives: Coornaert 1961: 2:39, 68–69. See also for Antwerp van Aert (2005) and for Amsterdam van de Heuvel (2007).

[57] Doehaerd 1941: 115.

[58] Jongbloet-van Houtte 1986: 60–61, 71, 84, 88, 92, 94, 101–4, 179, 183–85, 192, 215, 219, 243, 281–83.

[59] Grunzweig 1931: 6, 21, 125; Brulez 1959: 19–20.

[60] Davids 2004: 236; Karpinski 1936; Cordes 1998: 205–60; Arlinghaus 2002: 240–48.

[61] Cordes 1998: 200–260; Arlinghaus 2002. No *compagnia* contracts are found among the few fifteenth-century Dutch, Flemish, and English merchants whose letters or accounts have survived: Posthumus 1953: 1, 10, 25–27; Stabel 1996; Hanham 1985; Denucé 1934: 198–215. Compare the more traditional accounts of the independent Flemish merchants of the Despars family in the 1470s and 1480s (Mus 1964: 55, 58–59) with the double-entry accounts of the Bruges broker and merchant Wouter Ameide, who worked as factor of several Florentine firms around 1500 (Stabel 1996: 79–83, 75–97). In the mid-sixteenth century merchants in Lübeck could still pledge an oath before the local court to repudiate liability for debts of partners in what was known as a *vulle mascopey* (a full company) in the Hanseatic world (Cordes 1998: 264–67, 269–71).

[62] Brulez 1959: 66, 557, 558; Pohl 1977: 217–18; Goris 1925: 212–15; Strieder 1962; Coornaert 1961: 2:44. On the formal training of double-entry bookkeeping to merchants in Antwerp and Amsterdam in the second half of the sixteenth century, see Davids 2004: 238–41, 245.

[63] De Waal 1934: 6.

[64] Edler 1937: passim; De Roover 1956: 109–11.

TABLE 4.1. Balance sheet of the Compangnye op Dansick in 1585

Assets		Liabilities	
General debts	81,454	Segher Boel	53,009
Miscellaneous goods	34,195	General debts	7,634
Cash with Guillam Boel	961	Capital	54,779
Total	**116,611**	**Total**	**116,611**

Source: BT Memoriaal AB, fols. 89v–90r.

The importance of double-entry bookkeeping for the management of partnerships is very clear from the Compangnye op Dansick, which Hans Thijs's father-in-law, Augustijn Boel, created with several relatives in 1581. His brother Guillam moved to Danzig in 1581 and Augustijn settled in Amsterdam in 1582. Another brother and a brother-in-law remained in Antwerp. The four men signed a partnership agreement with a total capital of 32,100 guilders, with Augustijn subscribing 5,000 guilders.[65] The main purpose of the company was to ship textiles and dye-stuffs from Antwerp, via Amsterdam and Hamburg, to the Baltic area. At the end of each trading season Guillam Boel took stock of the company's assets and liabilities and sent his brothers and brother-in-law a balance sheet, for inclusion in their private ledgers (Table 4.1).

When Augustijn Boel left the Compangnye op Dansick in 1585 to begin his partnership with Hans Thijs, the company was doing very well. In four years' time the capital stock had grown by 22,000 guilders—an average annual return on investment of 14.3 percent. This rapid growth was due to the partners' reliance on the credit of Seger Boel in Antwerp and Guillaum Boel in Danzig. Allowing the two brothers to buy and sell on credit greatly increased the company's turnover. At the same, however, it exposed the partners to considerable credit risks, and this in turn required close monitoring through regular correspondence, detailed recording of transactions, and the periodic rendering of accounts.[66]

PAPER PROOF

Merchants valued proof of business transactions on paper. Trading over long distances obviously required them to relay information through letters and excerpts from account books, but once established this paper economy also served other purposes, provided the government lent its

---

[65] BT 119, Memoriael Augustijn Boel, fol. 127v.
[66] Gelderblom 2000: 90–99; Jongbloet-Van Houtte 1986: 430; Wijnroks 2003: 86–87.

support. Written records made it easier to monitor agents, especially when they were involved in complex border-crossing ventures.[67] Moreover, letters, bonds, quittances, contracts, or account books could serve to substantiate claims if and when the arbiters, consuls, or local justices adjudicating conflicts accepted the documents as legal proof.[68] The magistrates of Italian cities would be the first to accept the entire range of account books, letters, and privately drafted contracts as legal proof in the fourteenth century, but earlier rulers already declared that merchants should not be burdened with complex requirements to proof commercial and financial transactions.[69] One early means to make it easier to prove debts outstanding was the tally—a wooden stick carved with transactions and then split in two for both parties to have one part.[70] Compared to the ordeals that still reigned in criminal cases, tallies and oral testimonies were a marked improvement, but they were not ideal. An anonymous late-thirteenth-century English writer on litigation practices between merchants described the production of both tallies and testimonies as "hard and very tedious and a kind of burden and continuous obstacle."[71] To relieve merchants from this burden, the fair courts of Champagne and the hosts of fairs in southeastern England allowed informal writings to be presented as proof of transactions.[72]

In Flanders, the first trade-related changes in requirements for proof date from the twelfth century. In 1127 merchants from St. Omer visiting the Flemish fairs were allowed to pledge an oath to prove their innocence, rather than reverting to older truth-finding devices, such as duels and ordeals. The same privilege was extended to merchants from Holland and Cologne in the second half of the twelfth century. Flemish merchants trading in the German empire received a similar right in 1173, and the concession was returned to *all* German merchants in Flanders in 1252.[73] The towns of Flanders also supported trade and finance through the public registration of private contracts.[74] In Ypres, one of the five hosts of the Flemish fairs, for instance, town magistrates wrote the *lettres de foires* that served foreign traders so well as a means of deferred payment from

[67]Cipolla 1993: 197–98.
[68]Baker 1986: 368; Cordes 2005: 57; Berman 2003: 348–56.
[69]Fortunati 1996: passim.
[70]Hunt and Murray 1999: 66–67. For the use of tallies by visitors of fairs in England (including Flemish merchants from Douai and Ypres), see Wedemeyer Moore 1985: 117, 296.
[71]Cited in Basile et al. 1998: 14.
[72]Benson 2002: 128–30.
[73]Planitz 1940: 112. On the legal status of sworn testimonies, see Oexle 1985.
[74]Van Caenegem 1965: 58–59; Murray 1983: 32, 34–36, 136–37. Godding (1987: 436–37, 453–55) argues convincingly that only commodity transactions that included real estate, or a departure from customary rules, required recording through gracious justice of the towns.

one fair to the next.[75] Similar procedures were followed in Bruges in the thirteenth century and later also in Antwerp and Amsterdam.[76] By the mid-fourteenth century Bruges employed no fewer than twelve clerks to produce written evidence for myriad transactions.[77]

Foreign merchants in Bruges, however, initially relied on public officials in their hometowns to record debt and equity contracts. The city of Lübeck, for instance, kept a *societates* register in the fourteenth century, which merchants used to document their temporary associations, *wederlegginge* mostly, for trade with the Netherlands.[78] In Italian city-states notaries pioneered the systematic production of written records for commercial purposes.[79] The first notaries were officials of the church and emperor, but by the twelfth century the bulk of them were appointed by local *comunes*. Their numbers were impressive: in 1288 Milan counted 1,500 notaries, Bologna had 2,000 in 1290, and Florence had 600 in 1338.[80] Merchants turned to notaries because their own accounts and letters still had limited legal value.[81] Real estate transactions, credit operations, partnerships, and other commercial contracts recorded by notaries, on the other hand, were put on the same footing as charters issued by clerical or imperial institutions.

The important role of notaries in the recording of business transactions and agency relations of Italian merchants who traded in the Low Countries can be gleaned from the protocols that survive in Genoa. As shown in Table 4.2, between 1280 and 1440 notaries wrote almost two thousand contracts for merchants who traded with Flanders, England, France, and Germany. Up until 1360 the bulk of their work consisted of recording simple sales and purchases, bills of exchange, and commenda contracts. Then, in the second half of the fourteenth century, a remarkable change occurred. Notaries virtually stopped the recording of bills of exchange, purchases and sales, and, albeit to a lesser extent, commenda contracts.[82] One might be tempted to argue that Italian notaries in Bruges

---

[75] Murray 1983: 35.

[76] The earliest evidence for Amsterdam dates from 1333: Verkerk 2004: 182, 193–94.

[77] Murray 1983: 136.

[78] Cordes, Friedland, and Sprandel 2003: passim.

[79] The following is based on Oosterbosch et al. 1998: 13–17.

[80] Van Caenegem 1965: 57; Lopez and Raymond 1955: 65, 71–74.

[81] Much of the evidence we have on commercial practices during the Commercial Revolution comes from notarial archives: Lopez and Raymond 1955: 229; see, e.g., the work of González de Lara (2002, 2008) on Venice and that of Van Doosselaere (2009) on Genoa.

[82] In Genoa in the fifteenth century the bill of exchange, previously written by notaries, turned into a document drawn up by merchants without any interference of notaries, that is, bills for important markets like Bruges, London, or Seville. Bills drawn on smaller cities and bills drawn by merchants unknown to the local merchant community were still passed before a notary: Lopez and Raymond 1955: 229–30; Heers 1961: 82–84.

TABLE 4.2. Notarial deeds signed in Genoa by merchants trading with the Low Countries and other parts of Northern Europe, 1280–1440

	1280–1319 (%)	1320–59 (%)	1360–99 (%)	1400–39 (%)
Purchases and sales	33	30	5	1
Transportation	7	7	53	70
(Insurance)	(0)	(2)	(47)	(68)
Debt / equity contracts	44	37	18	14
(Commenda)	(16)	(11)	(8)	(3)
(Bills of exchange)	(24)	(12)	(2)	(4)
Conflict resolution	3	8	13	9
Other agency relations	11	13	7	5
Nontrade	1	4	3	1
All deeds (n)	492	307	323	811

Sources: For 1280–1320: Doehaerd 1941: passim. For 1320–1400: Liagre-De Sturler 1969: passim. For 1400–1440: Doehaerd and Kerremans 1952: passim. Notarial deeds written between 1200 and 1280 are not included in the table because very few of them refer to direct trade between Genoa and Bruges.

took over from their Genoese counterparts, but there is little evidence to support this idea.[83] In fact, the number of notarial deeds signed in Genoa rose sharply after 1400. Much of this increase was the result of the introduction of a new kind of contract: the insurance policy. Between 1400 and 1440 two-thirds of the Genoese notarial deeds relating to trade with Northern Europe consisted of insurance policies. The likely explanation for this change in contracts written by notaries is the acceptance of privately recorded bills of exchange, deeds of sale, and commenda contracts as legal proof. This is also what happened to the public recording of wederlegginge in Lübeck in the fourteenth and fifteenth centuries: it simply stopped because merchants started writing private contracts instead.[84]

Unlike their counterparts in the Italian city-states, notaries in the Netherlands were rarely involved in the organization of long-distance

[83] Notably Tomaso de Stroppa from Genoa (1325–42): Guide de fu Maestro Medico (1345) and Bartholomeus de Arquato (1368–75). The few notarial deeds that survive from these men suggest they wrote debt contracts for trade with Italy, and they translated sundry documents: Murray 1983: 150–51; Murray, Prevenier, and Oosterbosch 1995: 92; Oosterbosch et al. 1998: 38.

[84] Cordes, Friedland, and Sprandel 2003: 19–21; In course of the fifteenth and sixteenth centuries the local court of Lübeck allowed merchants to submit their account books as proof provided they had been kept orderly and in their own handwriting: Cordes 1998: 203–4.

TABLE 4.3. Different kinds of certificates issued to local and foreign merchants in Antwerp (1488–1515)

Nature of certificate	Share (%)
Ownership of goods	56.0
Purchases and sales	12.6
Debt and equity contracts	6.5
Transportation	0.5
Conflict resolution	3.9
Agency relations	14.5
Other	5.9
Total	100.0

Source: Doehaerd 1962–63: passim.

trade before 1500.[85] In Bruges, for instance, foreign merchants turned to notaries mainly for wills and transfers of real estate. Only occasionally did the notaries authenticate private documents, write up oral testimonies, translate foreign letters, and draft texts to facilitate the pursuit of legal action.[86] Instead of notaries, merchants in Antwerp—and presumably also in Bruges and Amsterdam—relied on the noncontentious litigation by local courts.[87] Renée Doehaerd's edition of more than four thousand *certificaties* written by the Antwerp magistrat for local and foreign merchants between 1488 and 1514 suggests the aldermen and their clerks offered at least two valuable services (Table 4.3). First and foremost, the certificates provided formal proof of ownership of goods transported over land to Germany, France, and Italy (56 percent). This most likely was a precautionary measure that gave merchants a better chance to claim damages if anything went wrong on the way. It may have been for similar reasons that the town magistrates confirmed existing agency relations between merchants (15 percent) and registered incidental sales and purchases (13 percent). The number of certificates issued by Antwerp's aldermen—an average of 160 per year—was far too small to satisfy the merchants' need for paper evidence, however.

A more active involvement of notaries in the production of paper proof in the Netherlands dates from the regulation of their work by Charles V

[85]Notaries worked in the Low Countries since the late thirteenth century, but before 1500 their role was largely confined to administrative duties for town magistrates, central authorities, and the clergy: Oosterbosch et al. 1998: 44–65; Godding 1987: 437–38.

[86]Murray 1983: 152, 245–46. Gilliodts-Van Severen 1871–85: 8:144–47.

[87]Goris 1925: 87–90. On the limited use of notaries in Amsterdam before 1500: Van der Laan 1975: 183–85.

in 1525 and 1531, respectively.[88] In 1525 the Estates of Holland appointed four notaries in Amsterdam. Half a century later at least nine notaries worked in the Dutch port.[89] In Antwerp notaries started working for merchants from England, Germany, Portugal, Spain, and the Italian city-states on a regular basis in the 1530s. Several of them opened cabinets in the streets around the New Bourse, and some even specialized in dealings for merchants of a specific nation.[90] In the 1560s the demand for notarial services grew so fast that several unqualified men began offering their services. To prevent abuse the town magistrate moved to transfer a large part of the notaries' powers to its own secretaries. Foreign merchants protested, however, and the city settled for a more scrupulous admission of new notaries instead.[91] In Antwerp there were at least fifteen active notaries in 1585.[92]

The protocols that survive of notaries in Antwerp and Amsterdam allow an analysis similar to that of the notarial records of Genoese traders in the late medieval period. Table 4.4 compares the nature of deeds signed by German merchants in Antwerp in the mid-sixteenth century with those of Portuguese merchants in Amsterdam in the early seventeenth century. The more intensive use of notaries by the Portuguese in the Dutch port is glaring: they signed as many deeds as the Germans in Antwerp, but during a period that was three times shorter. Considering that the German traders in the Scheldt port were also more numerous in 1550 than the Portuguese Jews in Amsterdam in 1600, the notaries may have been more important for traders in the latter city—although confirmation of this assumption would require a simultaneous analysis of both groups in both towns.

Notaries in Antwerp and Amsterdam supported the trade of foreign merchants in at least three ways.[93] Besides the registration of simple sales and purchases, both German and Portuguese merchants turned to notaries for formalities related to problems with the enforcement of contracts.

---

[88] Nève 1975: 2:381–82. One indication for this change is the publication in Antwerp in 1496 of *Ars Notariatus*, a popular treatise compiled shortly after 1370 from various Italian texts on the work of notaries. In the second half of the sixteenth century Antwerp notaries produced Dutch editions of this work (Oosterbosch et al. 1998: 21–22).

[89] Van Dillen 1929: 311, 324.

[90] De Smedt 1954: 108–9.

[91] Goris 1925: 87–94.

[92] A minimum estimate of the number of active notaries in Antwerp can be derived from the surviving notarial protocols: for 1500 the protocols of one notary remain, for 1550 two, for 1565 five, and for 1585 sixteen: http://stadsarchief.antwerpen.be/Unrestricted/Folder.aspx?document_id=09041acf8000061a&format=pdf.

[93] For ease of exposition we disregard the obvious possibility that traveling merchants, like the Germans in Antwerp, had recourse to registration by notaries, or other officials, in their home ports.

TABLE 4.4. Different kinds of notarial deeds signed by German merchants in Antwerp (1525–69) and by Portuguese merchants in Amsterdam (1600–1614)

Nature of deed	Germans in Antwerp (%)	Portuguese in Amsterdam (%)
Purchases and sales	20	10
Debt and equity contracts	8	8
Transportation	4	19
Conflict resolution	38	41
Other agency relations	10	10
Miscellaneous	0	2
Nontrade	20	10
All deeds (n)	743	707

Sources: Strieder 1962: passim; Koen 1973–2001: passim.

They recorded the appointment of agents to collect debts, the naming of representatives in court, protests of bills of exchange, seizures of property, and the actual settlement of conflicts. In Amsterdam the Portuguese Jews also visited their notary to record disagreements about, and settlement of insurance policies.[94] Furthermore, merchants used notarial deeds to formalize the extension of agency relations beyond the closed networks of family and friends, especially through the signing of proxies, or the registration of debt and equity contracts.

There is one notable difference between the two samples: Antwerp notaries played no role in the maritime operations of the Germans, whereas Portuguese merchants regularly turned to a notary to write freight contracts. Merchants who had no ships at their disposal, or did not know which shipmaster to turn to, could call upon a local notary to search one for them. Notably Jan Franssen Bruyningh concluded more than six thousand freight contracts in Amsterdam between 1593 and 1624. Through his office, merchants from Holland, Flanders, Germany, Portugal, and England found shipmasters to move their goods around Europe.[95] To be sure, the intermediation of notaries helped to clear the market for transportation, but it did not make it: 90 percent of transportation services were allocated within firms, or provided through relational contracting.[96]

[94] In 1564 Amsterdam took the appointment of legal representatives in court proceedings out of the hands of notaries. From then on, these proxies had to be registered before the town secretary. A payment of no more than two stivers was required for registration and publication of the proxy: van Dillen 1929: 303.

[95] Winkelman 1971–83; IJzerman 1931; Hart 1978; van Royen 1990; Gelderblom 2000: 134, 151–55, 221–22.

[96] Christensen 1941: 260.

The number of notarial deeds that survive for German and Portuguese merchants in Antwerp and Amsterdam demonstrates that notaries registered only a fraction of the commercial and financial transactions in the ports of the Netherlands. The bulk of all transactions was registered in the private accounts of merchants. On average merchants visited their notary perhaps two or three times per year.[97] Shortly after 1600 a merchant from France denounced his government's imposition of the formal registration of partnerships by notaries. He had previously worked in Antwerp and declared that there it was common for merchants to write company contracts privately.[98] With the exception of freight contracts, the Portuguese Jews in Amsterdam used notaries only to write contracts with unusual specifications, to anticipate difficulties with trading partners, or to take action in case business deals had gone sour. These cases confirm our earlier impression from the official documents used by German and Italian merchants in Bruges before 1500: the public registration of private contracts, whether by town secretaries or notaries, covered only a small fraction of all commercial transactions. This does not imply that public registration was unimportant—it was often indispensable for merchants to start legal proceedings—but the bulk of the business of foreign merchants in the Netherlands was recorded privately, and this put a premium on the government's acceptance of private accounts, letters, and contracts as proof in court proceedings.

THE DOUBLE PURPOSE OF DOUBLE-ENTRY BOOKKEEPING

The acceptance of private documents as legal proof in the Low Countries may have originated in the shipping sector. In 1413 the Amsterdam *keurboek* stipulated the obligation of shipmasters to properly record transactions carried out on the joint account of the shipowners. If shipmasters did not hand over the accounts of their voyages to the associates (*veynoets*), they would have to deliver them before the local court (or anyone appointed by the court).[99] Given that the shipmaster's documents comprised expenses for a large number of items over a long period, and that revenues had to be divided between a large number of shareholders, with often different shares in the enterprise, it is not surprising that strict requirements for evidence were set at a very early date.

[97] Oosterbosch et al. 1998: 24; Nève 1975: 2:379–87. Between 1595 and 1625 the Portuguese Jews in Amsterdam signed a total of 3,200 notarial deeds. With an estimated average size of the Portuguese merchant community of 35 or fewer during this period (see Israel 1983), this comes down to three notarial deeds per person per year.
[98] Coornaert 1961: 2:43.
[99] Breen 1902: 28.

Foreign merchants in Bruges also relied on the accounts of individual shipmasters to prove their claims. This is apparent from a conflict between Spanish merchants who in August 1453 had loaded iron onto a ship in Spain to be sent to Flanders.[100] After part of the cargo had been jettisoned in a storm, the freighters tried to recuperate the remaining iron. However, those who had signed a charter party, presumably before a notary, challenged the claim of merchants who had only the shipmaster's daybook to prove their ownership of part of the iron. The case was brought before the Bruges aldermen's bench, which ruled that *arbitres, arbitrateurs et communs amis* should be named to settle the dispute. Although the very conflict suggests that ships' registers were still a controversial means to prove claims in Bruges, the arbiters' choice to reward all freighters part of the remaining cargo does suggest the merchant community was willing to recognize the evidential value of the shipmaster's accounts.

The next step, from ship's registers to account books as legal proof, originated in Italy, the cradle of double-entry bookkeeping.[101] First introduced in Genoa and Florence around 1300, double-entry bookkeeping was a powerful disciplinary instrument.[102] In the fourteenth century the courts of Venice, Genoa, and other Italian city-states increasingly allowed merchants to support claims with their own account books.[103] Benedetto Cotrugli, the earliest commentator on the system, wrote in 1458 that adequate records "not only preserve and keep in the memory [all] transactions, but they also are a means to avoid many litigations, quarrels, and scandals."[104] The very strict rules for recording revenues and expenses made tampering difficult.[105] These rules included the writing in one hand, the registration of transactions in a journal without blanks separating the entries, their transcription in a ledger with accounts for every agent, and cross-referencing between accounts of all entries debited and credited.

The benefits of double-entry bookkeeping were considerable. Early accounting historians emphasized the possibility of drawing up balances at the end of each year, which would have allowed merchants to regularly evaluate the profitability of their operations. Some merchants certainly did this, but surviving account books and instruction manuals suggest this

---

[100]The following is based on Gilliodts-Van Severen 1901–2: 58–60.

[101]In seventeenth-century Dutch tracts on the evidential value of merchant books, there are various references to Spanish and Italian legal treatises, as well as to the rulings of the *Rota Genuae*, the merchant court of Genoa established in 1528: Lichtenauer 1956: 16–17.

[102]Lopez and Raymond 1955: 359–60; Hunt and Murray 1999: 109–12, 154–58.

[103]Lopez and Raymond 1955: 212, 228–29; Doehaerd and Kerremans 1952: xi; Heers 1961: 372–73; Murray 1923. For developments after 1500, see Fortunati 1996.

[104]Benedetto Cotrugli, *Della mercatura et del mercante perfetto (il libro dell'arte di mercatura)*, cited in Lopez and Raymond 1955: 375–77, see also 409.

[105]Hunt and Murray 1999: 157–58.

practice spread only slowly.[106] Even without an annual balance merchants would have perused their ledgers to evaluate performance, however, and they also relied on them to liquidate estates in case of bankruptcy or the death of a merchant.[107] More important, however, merchants used their journals and ledgers to keep track of debts outstanding, payments due, stocks, and shipments to and from agents abroad. With the acceptance of private account books as legal proof, a merchant killed two birds with one stone, as his monitoring device now doubled as evidence in court.

Meanwhile the evidential value of private accounts was not limited to the registration of actual transactions. Partnership agreements, whether for one voyage or for a number of years, could also be recorded in one's own ledgers. First in Florence, but soon also in Genoa, Venice, and other ports, merchants could use such handwritten contracts as legal proof, although sometimes an oath was required to confirm their authenticity.[108] The English translation of Antwerp's first manual for double-entry bookkeeping, published by the heirs of the author, Jan Ympyn, in 1543 specified

> the whiche compaignie and parteners or felowship, ye shall first entre into your boke and declare their states, condicions and agrementes, and how thei did agree, and when to begin and how long to continu, referryng alwaies to the instrument of Endenture of couenauntes made betwene theim, where the couenantes and condicions more largely shall apere.[109]

In the Dutch Republic judges also inspected the account books of merchants to figure out the precise terms of agreements drawn up between them. One example is a legal advice given to the Court of Holland in 1617 regarding a dispute between two merchants and a dyer who together formed a partnership for the finishing of cloth. The lawyers who advised the court based their opinion on a thorough inspection of the accounts and daybooks of the company and one of their suppliers. Provided the supplier would declare under oath that his books revealed the truth, they argued, the contents should be considered as proof of the nature of the partnership.[110]

Italian merchants were among the first to insist on the use of business ledgers as legal proof in the Low Countries. In 1459 three Italian merchants found themselves in a conflict with a Spanish shipmaster about merchandise he had carried from Catalonia to Zeeland for them. The merchants discovered that the cargo, on arrival, was incomplete and dam-

[106] Yamey 1949; Arlinghaus 2002; Funnell and Robertson 2011.
[107] De Waal 1934: 10.
[108] Lopez and Raymond 1955: 229–30.
[109] *A notable and very excellente woorke* . . . , chap. 18, cited in de Waal 1934: 41.
[110] *Consultatien* 1657–66: 2:462.

aged. They held the shipmaster liable, but the latter refused to pay the surety he had pledged, for in his view it related only to the carriage. To prove his point he was willing to testify under oath, "like the laws and customs of Bruges require."[111] The Italians rebutted that according to these local customs, oral testimonies could only supplement other evidence. Besides, they had documents at their disposal to prove the shipmaster was wrong. The aldermen's bench followed the Italian interpretation and condemned the shipmaster to pay up his surety. While in this case it remains unclear what exactly constituted the documents, in 1466 the aldermen of Bruges used the "books and correspondence" of a company of two Spanish merchants to establish the liability of the associates before and after the dissolution of their partnership.[112]

The acceptance of private accounts as legal proof progressed slowly but steadily in the sixteenth century. In Antwerp, the members of the Portuguese nation still could not be forced to show their books or commercial secrets, unless their consuls suspected they did not pay enough contribution in relation to their turnover.[113] On the other hand, Antwerp's customs of 1545 already contained various articles that suggested the acceptance of merchants' accounts as proof. For instance, in case of bankruptcy, Antwerp merchants could escape imprisonment if they gave up their possessions, provided they had revealed all their goods, shares, and credits—a requirement that suggests business papers were commonly used in legal procedures.[114] In the 1560s a Flemish merchant went so far as to forge his books in order to substantiate his claims in court. He was found out, however, because the invented figures did not add up and did not match those in the books of his agents.[115] In 1567 several merchants explicitly declared before Antwerp's local court that "it was common legal practice that anyone who wanted to prove a debt, had to show his account books."[116]

In Amsterdam in the seventeenth century all documents related to a merchant's business, from receipts of local sales and handwritten debt recognizances to letters and account books, were accepted as proof.[117] Business associates were legally bound to keep records of their dealings for the company.[118] The books of the Dutch colonial companies were also

[111] Gilliodts-Van Severen 1901–2: 81–83.
[112] Gilliodts-Van Severen 1901–2: 90.
[113] Goris 1925: 51–52.
[114] *Antwerp Customs* (1545), title 15, art. 2; Van der Wee 1963: 2:347–48.
[115] Brulez 1959: 14, 22, 25.
[116] "Ende dattet nae recht notoir waere dat om probatien te doene eenyegelick schuldich ware te doene exhibitien van syne rekenboecken," cited in Van der Wee 1967: 1078n5.
[117] Lichtenauer 1956: 162–63.
[118] *Consultatien* 1657–66: 3:391–92.

accepted as legal proof.[119] Foreign agents had to keep a proper administration of the business conducted on behalf of their principal.[120] The evidential value of account books also applied to the accounts of deceased merchants, to the books kept by the merchants' wives, and to Christian and Jewish (i.e., Portuguese) merchants alike.[121] None of this made the records of public officials fully redundant. Besides the deeds drafted by the city's notaries, the administration of the brokers could also be used to prove outstanding claims, provided the entries matched those of the merchant who had asked for a broker's testimony.[122]

A crucial prerequisite for the acceptance of business papers, whether in Bruges, Antwerp, or Amsterdam, was that merchants followed standard procedures to record their transactions. A legal tract published in Antwerp in 1584 underlined that merchants had to use double-entry bookkeeping to preserve the evidential value of their ledgers.[123] Various Dutch jurists also stipulated the obligation of separate debit and credit entries, although they held different views on which part of books (waste books, journals, ledgers) were the most trustworthy evidence. Double entries considerably reduced the possibilities of fraudulent administration, especially if the accounts of all merchants involved in a dispute could be compared. Obviously, the thorough training of merchants in the *vasten stijl van boeckhouden* (fixed style of accounting), which expanded enormously in the sixteenth century, facilitated the acceptance of paper proof.

In Antwerp and Amsterdam various kinds of privately drafted contracts were also accepted as legally binding claims. In 1621 a turbe of Amsterdam merchants on bottomry loans put notarial and private contracts on equal footing.[124] Bills of exchange, IOUs, and bearer bonds sufficed to substantiate a claim.[125] Inventories of estates did not have to be drawn up by a notary, a rule that gave merchants considerable leeway in organizing the liquidation of a business in private.[126] A turbe of merchants gathered in 1596 to testify that a factor had the first claim to goods consigned to him, provided that he could prove this title "with his books or other reliable evidence."[127] To validate the documents submitted

[119] *Consultatien* 1657–66: 1:457, 475; Gelderblom and Jonker 2004: 653.

[120] *Consultatien* 1657–66: 3:81–83; Wachter 1639: 182.

[121] Lichtenauer 1956: 157, 162–63.

[122] Lichtenauer 1956: 159–60, 164.

[123] A legal treatise first published in Antwerp in 1584 stated that in the city it was well known that accounts not in accordance with the *stylus mercatorum* might not be accepted in a court of law: Lichtenauer 1956: 69. A similar rule applied in Holland in 1647 according to legal advice: *Consultatien* 1657–66: 4:522; Lichtenauer 1956: 163.

[124] Wachter 1639: 102.

[125] *Consultatien* 1657–66: 1:486–89; Lichtenauer 1956: 173.

[126] *Consultatien* 1657–66: 5:489.

[127] Wachter 1639: 100–101 (1596); Noordkerk 1748: 2:538–40. An early example of business ledgers used as legal proof in Amsterdam notarial records: ACA NA 32/74v (June 25, 1592).

as proof, merchants were often asked to confirm before a notary that the handwriting of the contracts, accounts, and paper claims was indeed that of the merchant involved.[128] Records well kept were also considered to be legal proof for an association between merchants. Thus, when the French government tried to impose the formal registration of partnerships by notaries shortly after 1600, a French merchant who had previously worked in Antwerp declared it had been common for merchants there to write company contracts privately.[129]

This legislation from below through *turben* reveals how sensitive urban magistrates, in this case from Antwerp and Amsterdam, were to demands from merchants. Equally important, however, was their choice not to substitute new rules for old ones but rather add mercantile usage to existing customs. This is not to say written documents were the only evidence accepted in commercial disputes. An ordinance of 1478 allowed shipmasters to declare under oath what cargo they had carried.[130] In sixteenth-century Antwerp oral testimonies were still highly valued. In fact, proceedings before the *extraordinarise rol*, designed especially for cases that involved foreigners, had to be based on testimonies.[131] The proxies Amsterdam merchants gave to their agents included the right to "sign, give, execute and draw up agreements, whether under his signature, in writing, legally or otherwise."[132] Merchants often used official declarations before a notary and witnesses to make disagreements known, but objections made in public and heard by several people also sufficed as legal proof.[133] A legal opinion concerning the nonpayment of sugar by a Portuguese merchant in 1641 details the different kinds of documents submitted to the jurists. They included translated excerpts from Simon Corea's journal and from his Portuguese broker's waste book, as well as three written declarations under oath by the same broker (before a notary, the town magistrate, and the jurists) and an excerpt from the administration of the Amsterdam weigh house.[134] Interestingly the jurists also specified that the ledgers of merchants and brokers were credited as legal proof only when accompanied by their oath—a specification that reminds us of the doubt several students of Roman law continued to have about this new practice.[135]

Finally, the gradual acceptance of merchants' account books as legal proof also sheds light on the puzzling fact that the first treatises on double-entry

[128]See, e.g., ACA NA 33 fols. 185–185v (July 31, 1598); ACA NA 62 fols. 143–44 (February 10, 1607).
[129]Coornaert 1961: 2:43.
[130]Breen 1902: 132.
[131]*Ordonnantie* (1532), title "Van den thoon," art. 6; De Ruysscher 2009c: 113–16.
[132]ACA NA 51/38 (March 27, 1597).
[133]*Consultatien* 1657–66: 5:757; 6:568.
[134]*Consultatien* 1657–66: 1:305, 461–63.
[135]*Consultatien* 1657–66: 1:340.

bookkeeping appeared very late, did not spread widely, and were very general in their description. The first full description of the method, in Luca Pacioli's *Summa de Arithmetica* (1494), was published almost two centuries after the first merchants began to use it.[136] Besides, this description and that of early followers like Ympyn were too general to have served as manuals to teach double-entry bookkeeping. Oral instruction by schoolmasters and on-the-job training by merchants were far more important for the diffusion of the new accounting skills—especially for merchants who wanted to rely on their books to support legal claims.[137] Yet the early texts on double-entry book-keeping were reprinted many times in the sixteenth century in Italy, and later also in local adaptations in the rest of Europe.[138] Why publish them? The logical answer would seem that the treatises on double-entry bookkeeping were a means to formalize the requirements for acceptance of books in courts of law. Pacioli explicitly referred to the evidential value of account books and commented on current practices in Italian cities to validate the ledgers of merchants. Instruction manuals published in various parts of Europe in the sixteenth century also insisted on the legal use of account books well kept.[139] Indeed, the first chapter of Ympyn's treatise in the 1540s explicitly stated that his work was "very commodious & profitable to all iusticiaries, because thei maie have knowledge to discerne al differences and alteracions that daily happeneth among Marchantes, as well by faute of evill kepyng of their bokes of accomptes as otherwise (as is used in Italy)."[140] Ympyn then copied Pacioli and explained how the consuls of mercantile courts in commercial cities in Italy allowed merchants to use their books to argue their case in conflicts with fellow traders.[141]

CONCLUSION

For local and foreign traders in Bruges, Antwerp, and Amsterdam personal relations with merchants in other ports were the basic means to secure smooth transactions. They developed long-standing agency relations, and besides the prospect of repeat transactions, family ties and friendship, shared social norms, and religious beliefs helped to secure their agents' compliance. These personal relations and the related incentives to cooperate gained in strength as networks became denser and the connectivity between merchants increased. And yet, the growth of these

[136] De Waal 1927: 54.
[137] Davids 2004: passim.
[138] Harreld 2006: 9, based on Hoock et al. 1991.
[139] De Waal 1927: 99, 123, 145, 227–28.
[140] De Waal 1934: 15.
[141] De Waal 1927: 54, 99–100; de Waal 1934: 22–23.

multilateral trading networks cannot be dissociated from the intervention of urban governments. For one thing, the efforts of Bruges, Antwerp, and Amsterdam to organize markets for money, merchandise, and shipping services, and the superior access to information this provided did not just facilitate local exchange, as we discussed in the previous chapter, but also stimulated merchants to choose these locations as the central nodes in their network of agency relations. Indeed, the local rulers deliberately positioned hostellers as information hubs, and in addition they allowed the foreign merchants to organize themselves and share information on foreign market conditions and trading partners.

The explicit aim of the local magistrates was to complement private order solutions. As soon as foreign merchants had developed their own local networks, hostels and nations lost their function as information hubs and the cities simply let it happen, concentrating instead on the supervision of local market exchange. A similar retreat can be observed in the organization of border-crossing transactions. At first public officials like notaries and town secretaries played an important role in the registration of contracts, testimonies, and legal proxies, but their involvement in the administration of trade rapidly decreased once merchants began to maintain regular correspondences and keep detailed accounts of sales and purchases, credit transactions, and even partnership agreements. The government's retreat from registration did not bother merchants because their own accounts were helpful for making proper business decisions, regular correspondence facilitated the instruction of trading partners, and the combination of both letters and ledgers made it easier to detect their agents' misinterpretation of agreements, mistakes, or outright fraudulent behavior.

Still, the merchants' private efforts to monitor distant agents paid off only because the government stood behind them. The local magistrates in Bruges, Antwerp, and Amsterdam determined the format business letters and ledgers should have and accepted these documents as evidence in court. An important tool was the turbe, a declaration of common usage, made by practitioners with the explicit purpose of adding current practices to the prevailing law. The time and effort merchants put into the proper recording of their business operations suggests that recourse to the law mattered a great deal to them—not because they wanted to take every single dispute to court but because a credible threat to do so raised the opportunity cost of agents who considered cheating them. This also implied, however, that merchants needed to have access to courts that could rule expeditiously and in accordance with their mercantile usages and customs. And this confronted both merchants and rulers with one of the most pervasive problems of the premodern economy: Europe's extreme legal fragmentation.

CHAPTER FIVE

Conflict Resolution

PREMODERN EUROPE WAS A PATCHWORK OF LOCAL AND REGIONAL JURIS-
dictions, each with its own legal traditions. Every commercial city had its
own local court applying local laws and customs to business disputes of
all kinds.[1] This legal fragmentation was never a problem for merchants
who traveled between fairs because their local hosts were both willing
and able to tailor court proceedings to the specific nature of their spot
transactions.[2] However, for merchants who settled abroad for longer
periods legal fragmentation was a serious concern. Their business was
the shipment of money and goods to agents in different places, and as
transactions extended beyond single jurisdictions, they had to reckon
with differences in contracting rules between localities. Yet these legal
complications did not prevent large numbers of merchants from different
parts of Europe from moving abroad and building extensive commercial
networks that sometimes spanned the entire Continent. How did they
enforce their border-crossing contracts if the law was local and the jurisdiction of the place they lived in ended at the city gate?

Douglass North has argued that, from the fifteenth century onward,
the creation of a central, state-sponsored court system mitigated the
problems of legal fragmentation.[3] The judges of central courts like the
Parlement in Paris, the Grand Conseil in the Burgundian Netherlands,
and the Reichskammergericht in the Holy Roman Empire would have
applied the same contracting rules to all merchants regardless of their
background.[4] In North's view, the state as legislator and independent
third-party enforcer made it easier for alien merchants to contract with
one another, and so contributed to the growth of trade.[5] This, however,
is a problematic proposition as the judges of the new central courts were
professional lawyers with a background in Roman law and very little or

---

[1]Volckart and Mangels 1999: 435–37; Epstein 2000: 7–8, 36, 159, 167; Kadens 2004:
46–47; Grafe 2012: 25–27.
[2]Thomas 1977: 451–52; Wedemeyer Moore 1985: 168–85; Irsigler 1996: passim; Epstein 2000: 77.
[3]North 1981: 24; see also Ogilvie 2011: 301–3.
[4]Coornaert 1961, 1:58; de Schepper and Cauchies 1993: 131–32.
[5]North 1981: 24; North 1991: 28–29. To be sure, North does acknowledge the efficiency enhancing effects of private enforcement mechanisms: North 1990: 108–9; Milgrom,
North, and Weingast 1990: passim.

no understanding of mercantile practice. Moreover, international traders had been able to sustain large, multilateral trading networks long before the creation of these central courts in early modern Europe, so there must have been other institutional arrangements to enforce commercial contracts.

The preferred explanation of most trade historians is that merchants carefully built networks of relatives and friends, and then used social sanctions or more or less implicit threats to withhold future business to discipline these agents.[6] This private order solution was certainly widespread in premodern Europe, but it presupposes the kind of routine trading that does not fit the many merchants that either allowed their trading partners full play or even dealt with strangers to explore new markets and products. Avner Greif and others have argued that these dealings at arm's length could still be governed without the support of rulers or relatives. Medieval merchants, for instance, created guilds whose leaders could be made responsible for the adjudication of commercial conflicts between members.[7] International traders may also have relied on a *community responsibility system* within which all members of a merchant community could be held liable for the default of any one group member.[8] Finally, some historians believe that the continuous interaction between traders from different parts of Europe created a lex mercatoria, or merchant law: a set of standard contracting rules which all international traders were to comply with.[9]

These institutional arrangements may have been widespread in medieval Europe, but it is doubtful whether they ever functioned without recourse to the law. In those instances where merchants invoked the existence of a lex mercatoria, they referred to procedural rules instated by local rulers to secure the speedy resolution of conflicts between foreign traders.[10] At the medieval fairs of England and Champagne, for instance, temporary courts were established to pass immediate judgment in conflicts between visiting merchants.[11] The functioning of the community responsibility system also hinged on government intervention as merchants whose money or goods were seized to compensate damages done by others, turned to their local courts for redress.[12] The same public embeddedness

---

[6] See, e.g., Lesger 1996: 72–73; Mathias 1995: 13–16; Selzer and Ewert 2001: passim; Ewert and Selzer 2010: 11–20.

[7] Gelderblom and Grafe 2010: 490–92; Ogilvie 2011: 251–68, with references to the older literature.

[8] Greif 2001; Greif 2006b: 318–38; Börner and Ritschl 2002, 2009.

[9] Berman 1983: 333–56; Benson 2002: 128–30; Milgrom, North, and Weingast 1990: 5–6; Munro 2003: 550–51.

[10] Baker 1986: 347; Basile et al. 1998: 179–88.

[11] Wedemeyer Moore 1985: 165–87.

[12] Greif 2006b: 328–36; Börner and Ritschl 2009: 102.

characterized the many hanses, consulados, and guilds of foreign merchants, whose ability to adjudicate conflicts issued from the explicit delegation of legal authority by their home government and the granting of consular jurisdictions by their hosts.[13]

But if all these so-called private, self-enforcing institutions functioned in the shadow of the law, one has to wonder to what extent the personal relations hailed by generations of trade historians as a sufficient safeguard against agency problems did not benefit from public support either. Admittedly, central governments may be unlikely candidates to have offered this kind of support, but that was not the case for urban governments whose legal autonomy did allow them to adapt court proceedings and local customs to the needs of merchants at issue with their trading partners.[14] The question then is how able urban magistrates were in designing formal procedures for the resolution of commercial conflicts that complemented the private practices of merchants, and to what extent they could adapt existing legal institutions when changes in the scale and scope of trade required as much.

AMICABLE SETTLEMENT

"Hildebrant, dear friend, do realize that I am surprised you did not give us our money, because we can make good use of it, and we need it. So we beg you that you do so, and send us the money." With these words Wilhelm Weits and Lamsin Kupere prodded Hildebrand Veckinchusen in August 1421 to pay his debts. Veckinchusen, a German trading in Bruges, had sustained large losses in the salt and textiles trade, and his financial difficulties had been exacerbated by his failure to retrieve a loan extended to German King Sigismund. At the time the letter was written, Veckinchusen was absent from Bruges as he attempted to obtain new lines of credit in Antwerp, Cologne, and Lübeck. He stayed for some time in Antwerp, where he met with friends and creditors in a local hostel to restructure part of his debts. In the meantime Veckinchusen's agent in Bruges, the hosteller Jakob Schotteler, was approached by other impatient creditors. Schotteler urged Veckinchusen to return to the city, which he eventually did. Together they managed to hold out for several months, until, in February 1422, the Genoese banker Joris Spinola lost patience and had Hildebrand Veckinchusen locked up in Bruges's debt prison.[15]

---

[13] Jados 1975, xii; Gelderblom and Grafe 2010: 485; Ogilvie 2011: 258–59.
[14] Lane 1962: 24, 33, 36; Baker 1986: 349–54; Nörr 1987: 196–98; Basile et al. 1998: 42, 69–70, 114; Volckart and Mangels 1999: 443; González de Lara 2008.
[15] Stieda 1921: letter no. 295; Irsigler 1985: 92–94; Rothmann 1998: 553.

Merchants recognized that their trading partners could face sudden cash shortages, and instead of jeopardizing their business relations with threats of litigation, they were often willing to stretch the terms of payment. The balances of current accounts were easily transferred to a following year, obligations were prolonged, or new bills of exchange were drawn to ease liquidity constraints. Creditors exercised restraint because any action that signaled a merchant's lack of creditworthiness could provoke a chain reaction of other creditors calling in debts, which could create difficulties for many more merchants. In general, delays of a few weeks or even months were accepted if the other party was believed to be honest.[16] But even if payment was not forthcoming, merchants did not immediately go to court. They would continue to pressure their debtors, and in the meantime consider the consequences of firmer action. Then, when debts issued from single transactions with traders outside the core of their business network, a merchant might simply write off irretrievable claims. For instance, in the mid-fifteenth century the Medici branches in Bruges and London reserved 10 percent of their profits to cover bad debts.[17]

Taking one's losses was not always possible, however. Too much money could be involved, the failed transaction might be part of a complex set of mutual obligations, or merchants expected too many future gains from the continuation of trade. Termination of such relationships was impossible without considerable losses, often to both parties.[18] But then a friendly solution might be impossible because of personal frictions, because of the social distance between trading partners, or simply because parties felt too strongly about their own rights.

To prevent the collapse of trade as a result of anonymity, animosity, or a lack of appropriate sanctions, foreign merchants in the Low Countries could turn to arbiters to complement their private efforts to enforce contracts. The mediation of two or more men, acceptable to both parties, with access to the necessary papers and testimonies, was impartial, expedient, and cheap. What is more, arbiters could deviate from legal prescriptions and propose equitable solutions to try to appease both parties.[19] For foreign merchants arbitration probably had the added advantage that arbiters could be asked to apply the rules of their own city or country. Evidence of arbitration between merchants can be found in

---

[16]Irsigler 1985: 77; De Smedt 1954: 587. Local customs in Antwerp and Amsterdam allowed merchants to charge interest for deferred payments: *Antwerpse Costumen* (1582), title 49, art. 17. For Amsterdam: Wachter 1639: 115–16. Compare the letter of the Amsterdam merchant Hans Thijs to his brother-in-law Andries Bacher, July 2, 1599: BT 133–B1.

[17]De Roover 1963: 323; Brulez 1959: 384.

[18]Lambert 2006: 105–8.

[19]Donahue 2005: 84; Kessler 2007: 65–105.

thirteenth-century England; by the sixteenth century it had become common practice throughout Europe.[20]

In Bruges arbiters may have mediated disagreements between foreign merchants as early as 1300.[21] The privileges of the English nation granted in 1359 specified that conflicts between members of this community and others should be resolved through arbitration by two Englishmen and two local citizens.[22] In the mid-fifteenth century no fewer than three-quarters of the disputes submitted to the local court by Spanish merchants were referred to arbiters.[23] For instance, a conflict between a Genoese merchant and two Spanish merchants was submitted to the maritime court of Damme in 1447, but it was resolved through arbitration by three men—a councilor of the Burgundian duke, a hosteller from Bruges, and a Portuguese merchant.[24] The procedure was straightforward. The parties each named one or two arbiters—mostly fellow merchants—while the local justices sometimes added other members to the committee. The arbiters began with the inspection of the evidence, heard the arguments of both parties, deliberated, and passed their judgment. Their ruling was confirmed by the local justices and sometimes registered with a notary.[25]

By the time Amsterdam emerged as Europe's leading commercial center, arbiters helped merchants to solve a variety of conflicts with business partners, buyers, sellers, shipmasters, or artisans.[26] The notarial deeds that survive of Portuguese merchants in Amsterdam show the involvement of arbiters in fifty-seven business conflicts between 1602 and 1627.[27] They ruled in simple cases about unpaid bills and the quality of merchandise, in more complex disputes about inheritances or the settle-

---

[20]Basile et al. 1998: 41; Godfrey 2002; Irsigler 1985: 86; Kowaleski 1995: 219.

[21]Des Marez 1901: 123, 149, 168, 173–74, 196, 199, 219. Greve 2000: 37–38.

[22]Nicholas 1979: 24.

[23]Gilliodts-Van Severen 1901–2: 35, 50–52.

[24]Gilliodts-Van Severen 1901–2: 29.

[25]Gilliodts-Van Severen 1901–2: 29–30; Goris 1925: 67–68. For similar procedures in Antwerp: Strieder 1962: 293, 294.

[26]For the role of arbiters in the resolution of commercial conflicts in Antwerp, see Puttevils 2012: 295–97. For individual cases: Goris 1925: 46; De Smedt 1951: 92; De Smedt 1954: 582; Coornaert 1961: 1:175–76. Mediation by arbiters in Amsterdam is first mentioned in 1489: Poelman 1917: 2:1024–25. See also Wijnroks 2003: 190, 227.

[27]SR 345 (344); SR 451; SR 458; SR 569; SR 601; SR 723–26, 728; SR 799; SR 1792; SR 1954; SR 2038; SR 3181; SR 3217; SR 3412, 3486; SR 3527; SR 876, 918; SR 1962; SR 2640; SR 2271; SR 3169; SR 2711; SR 91; SR 109; SR 178; SR 132, 133, 212, 341; SR 210, 217, 318; SR 556; SR 594; SR 792, 871, 892; SR 875, 877–79, 882, 889, 891, 897, 898, 901, 923, 924; SR 1093; SR 1367; SR 1416; SR 1441; SR 1511; SR 1524; SR 1704; SR 1811, 1812; SR 2031; SR 2078; SR 2092; SR 2234; SR 2323; SR 2406; SR 2485; SR 2701; SR 2842; SR 2828, 2910, 3145; SR 2988; SR 3065; SR 3100; SR 3137; SR 3154; SR 3296; SR 3318; SR 3401, 3453; SR 3513; SR 3550. Not included in this overview are disputes about marriage contracts, illegitimate children, and religious disputes.

ment of accounts between former partners, and also in maritime affairs such as damages from privateering and shipwrecks, insurance claims, and the enforcement of freight contracts. Arbitration was especially helpful when both parties believed they had legitimate claims, or the contract between them offered no clear-cut solution for a problem. The latter was the case in various conflicts between Portuguese merchants and shipmasters who had experienced delays, changed routes, used smaller ships, or sailed without taking in any cargo. Otherwise, arbiters were called in to escape court procedures and force a speedy resolution of conflicts.

Legal historians have shown that medieval law distinguished between two kinds of arbiters. On the one hand there were *goede mannen, amyable compositeurs*, or arbitrators, who were appointed by merchants, and whose judgment was based on equity. In this case parties typically chose one mediator each.[28] On the other hand there were arbiters appointed by local or central courts. They applied prevailing law, and as a result should be considered lay judges.[29] An attestation of a group of lawyers and solicitors in Amsterdam in 1615 bears out this distinction. The jurists declared before a notary that, if the local court had referred litigants to arbiters, they retained the right to appeal to their judgment. An arbitral decision was legally binding only if merchants had voluntarily submitted to arbitration.[30] The latter rule was confirmed by the Supreme Court, as evidenced by a company contract signed by two cloth traders in 1630. In the contract the partners determined that any future differences should be submitted to two or three goede mannen. "In conformity with a ruling of the Supreme Court," the contract stated, "the associates were bound by the decision of the arbiter, and had no right to appeal."[31]

Merchants who preferred the gentle hand of arbiters sometimes anticipated the mediation of goede mannen in company contracts, freight contracts, and insurance policies.[32] The broad acceptance of arbitration in Amsterdam is also demonstrated by the fifty different merchants from Holland, Flanders, and Portugal who acted as arbiters in the fifty-seven conflicts involving Portuguese merchants that were resolved in this way. In the second half of the seventeenth century Amsterdam's aldermen even kept registers with the names of men who in their profession were held to

[28] Godding 1987: 128; Le Bailly 2001: 181–82; Lichtenauer 1935: 354–56. For Antwerp: Goris 1925: 67.
[29] Le Bailly 2001: 181–82.
[30] Van Dillen 1929: 238.
[31] SR 1314.
[32] De Groote 1977: 207; van Niekerk 1998: 1:230–34. Between 1594 and 1600, 134 out of a total of 866 freight contracts specified the referral to arbiters in case conflicts would arise due to the route the ship had taken, delays, and freight costs: Winkelman 1971–83: 2:xlviii. For similar arrangements by Portuguese merchants, see SR 363, 2947, 3353.

be respectable and knowledgeable, and hence might be eligible to act as arbitrators should conflicts arise.[33] Only seldom did merchants refuse to submit to the mediation of arbiters. One such instance was the refusal of the English merchant Thomas Stafford to settle his affairs with Walloon merchant Pieter Denijs through arbitration, because "in the past Denijs (and his son) had slandered him, challenged him to fight, and even tried to stab and kill him at the Exchange." Stafford decided to bring the case to court.[34] But even in these circumstances it remained up to the court to decide whether or not a lawsuit was appropriate.[35] Thus, when in 1630 arbitration seemed impossible in a conflict about a merchant's sale of calfskins to a gold leather maker because the latter refused to cooperate, the merchant turned to the local court, which then forced the artisan to accept arbitration. Within a month after their intervention an amicable settlement was reached.[36]

Arbitration was an attractive solution for merchants because it was quick, because it allowed the application of a wider set of contracting rules, and because it provided the opportunity to decide matters in fairness rather than clinging to the letter of the law. Mediation was also attractive for the urban magistrate because it relieved the court system. Notarial deeds concerning Portuguese merchants in Amsterdam reveal that at least one-third of arbitral decisions in commercial disputes were referrals from local and occasionally also provincial courts.[37] The obvious aim was to speed up proceedings, as with a dispute that arose over the noncompliance with the terms of a freight contract signed in 1596 between a Dutch shipmaster and a Dutch merchant residing in Seville. Initially the case was brought before the local court of Amsterdam, which ruled in 1601. Both parties appealed to the Court of Holland, which suggested in July 1603 that the parties should try to reach an agreement with the help of arbiters. Each of the parties chose three arbiters, and these six men appointed a seventh to act as their chair. Within a month the arbiters had reached a legally binding verdict that included the payment of tolls, fines, and damages, the lifting of the seizure of goods and the freeing of a hostage in Seville, the return of business papers, and finally the pledging of sureties.[38]

[33] Gijsbers 1999: 244–45.
[34] ACA NA 729 B (April 8, 1636), NA 729B-174 (September 26, 1636).
[35] Noordkerk 1748: 2:577.
[36] Van Dillen 1929: 2:737.
[37] Out of 57 arbitral decisions, 19 were referrals from local or provincial courts: SR 345 (344); SR 451; SR 458; SR 569; SR 601; SR 723–26, 728; SR 1792; SR 1954; SR 2038; SR 3181; SR 3217; SR 3412, 3486; SR 3527; SR 876, 918; SR 1962; SR 2640; SR 2271; SR 3169; SR 2711; SR 2828, 2910, 3145.
[38] ACA NA 20 H, fols. 1–9 (August 17, 1603).

COMMERCIAL LITIGATION IN BRUGES

Amicable settlement, with or without the help of arbiters, was the preferred solution in business conflicts, but it was not always possible. Sometimes parties were irreconcilable or simply wanted to solve matters without delay. The latter constraint was felt in particular at the fairs of Flanders and Brabant, where traders met only at short intervals. The inclusion of Bruges in the cycle of Flemish fairs in 1200 required the city to offer visitors the possibility of resolving disputes on the spot. Unlike with the fairs in Champagne or South England, foreigners in Bruges were never referred to a temporary court. Rather, the local court, established around 1100, took on the responsibility to pass judgment in conflicts between visitors of the fairs. The oldest bylaws in Bruges, dating from 1190, 1281, and 1304, already stipulated that *schepenen* were expected to rule within three days (or eight, when the defendant was not present) in cases brought before them by foreign visitors.[39] In 1330 the Count of Flanders specified that during the fairs justice should be done at least twice a week, with the exception of the three days of display, and the three days before and after that, when traders should be left to themselves. In 1396 the city declared that procedures for local citizens and foreigners had always been equally expedient.[40]

The active role of Bruges's Schepenbank in the resolution of commercial conflicts can be gleaned from the twenty-one trade-related sessions it held between September 1333 and January 1334. Three years later this number had already risen to thirty-one.[41] It is difficult to establish what kind of disputes the aldermen's bench settled. A town ordinance of 1481 mentioned that conflicts between foreigners and between foreigners and locals had of old (*van ouden tyden*) been brought before the Schepenbank, but the substance of the proceedings is not mentioned.[42] The privileges given to the German merchants in 1360 are more precise, stipulating that the local court would deal with any conflict arising from the services provided by local weighers, brokers, shipmasters, workmen, and wagoners. In addition the authorities confirmed that within three days the court had to pronounce judgment in all disputed credit transactions involving German traders.[43]

The aldermen's bench played a very active role in the resolution of conflicts between foreigners, but nevertheless the city of Bruges, in conjunction with the Counts of Flanders, granted consular jurisdictions to

[39]Gilissen 1958: 293–94; Gilliodts-Van Severen 1883–85: 1:208, 249, 311; 2:266.
[40]Gilliodts-Van Severen 1883–85: 1:398, 447–48.
[41]Gilliodts-Van Severen 1883–85: 1:398.
[42]Gilliodts-Van Severen 1883–85: 1:114–16.
[43]Bartier and Nieuwenhuysen 1965: 493–94.

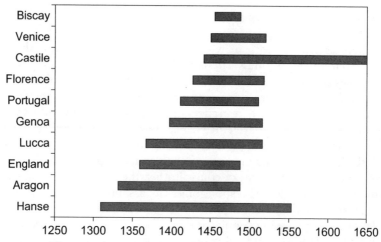

FIGURE 5.1. The consular jurisdictions of foreign merchant communities in Bruges, 1250–1650

Sources: Gilliodts-Van Severen 1883–85: 2:118; Gilliodts-Van Severen 1901–2: 44–45; De Roover 1948: 15; Van Houtte 1982: 175; Vandewalle 2002: 38–39.

foreign merchant communities. This legal privilege allowed consuls, appointed by the merchants or their home rulers, to adjudicate disputes according to the laws and customs of their own country. They ruled in maritime and commercial conflicts and in cases of insult and harassment, and they also administered noncontentious procedures, like the management of the estates of deceased merchants. Extant documents of the Spanish nation suggest that its consuls also resolved disputes through arbitration, thus providing a highly valued extension of private order solutions.[44]

The establishment of consular courts in Bruges is remarkable because of its timing. As Figure 5.1 shows, most foreign nations were given a consular jurisdiction a century or more after their initial arrival. German merchants had been regular visitors since 1200, if not much earlier, but they received their jurisdiction only in 1309. The merchants of Aragon obtained a similar privilege early on, in 1330, but there is no evidence that they appointed judges at this date. The great majority of aliens, including most of the merchants from the Italian city-states, received their separate jurisdiction in Bruges only in the fifteenth century. The number of consular courts peaked in 1450, when ten out of fourteen foreign nations had their own court. Only merchants from France, southern Germany, Scotland, and Milan remained without a consular jurisdiction.

Political considerations cannot explain the timing of the establishment of consular courts. Admittedly, in 1359 the English cloth traders—*not* the

---

[44] Gilliodts-Van Severen 1901–2: 28; Bartier and Nieuwenhuysen 1965: 493.

wool merchants—were granted a separate jurisdiction in Bruges because the city wanted to lure them away from Antwerp.[45] However, Italian and Iberian merchants had been present in Bruges for three-quarters of a century or more before they were given a consular court in the second half of the fourteenth century. The spate of consular jurisdictions created in this period was a direct consequence of the growing permanence of trade. In the late thirteenth century and much of the fourteenth century the majority of foreigners had stayed for brief periods only, which allowed them to turn to judges in their hometowns to resolve disputes. In this early period commercial conflicts involving foreign merchants in Bruges were adjudicated in the Corte dei Mercanti in Lucca, the Consulado del Mar in Barcelona, the Consulado of Burgos, the Uffici di mercanzia in Genoa, and the local court of Lübeck. As foreign merchants began to stay for longer periods in Bruges, the creation of consular courts was a very welcome innovation since it allowed them to settle disputes with business associates and trading partners while away but still on the basis of their own rules. The consuls were chosen from among their midst, which meant they had a keen eye for the commercial interests of the parties involved and that they valued reasonable, quick solutions.

The nature of the work of the consular courts can be gleaned from the *libro della comunità* of the Lucchese nation, a ledger with descriptions of disputes dealt with by the consuls between 1377 and 1404.[46] The first thing to notice is that the number of business conflicts described in the register is surprisingly small. In the quarter century covered by the libro, the consuls dealt with only thirty-four conflicts involving 50 out of a total of 235 merchants mentioned in the community's records in this period. The recorded lawsuits are very unevenly distributed over the quarter century covered by the Lucchese ledger. Two-thirds of the recorded proceedings date from the first five years in which the book was kept. Then followed a long period of great political unrest in Flanders (1383–89), during which only one verdict was recorded. The community lost at least half of its members in these years, and the remaining merchants complained that the community did not work properly.[47] The problems were exacerbated by a political regime change in Lucca that alienated a considerable part of the Lucchese community from their home

---

[45] Nicholas 1979: 24.

[46] De Roover 1948: 18–20; Lazzareschi 1947: passim. We cannot completely rule out the possibility that small and simple disputes between merchants were dealt with in oral proceedings, which have left no trace in the *libro della comunità*. However, the very detailed, sometimes day-to-day recording of proceedings makes this unlikely.

[47] In 1385 the consuls issued stricter rules for merchants who wanted to leave the community. Lazzareschi 1947: 120–21, 130. In two years (1383, 1385) no election of consuls was registered in the *libro della comunità*: Lazzareschi 1947: 116–17, 126, 152.

government.[48] The nation in Bruges was restored, however, in the early 1390s when a new house was purchased with the financial support of fourteen of its members. Until 1395 another ten lawsuits were recorded, but then the registration of verdicts stopped again (save one exception in 1402), perhaps because of renewed frictions within the community.[49]

The attempts to resurrect the consulate point to the continued desire of the Lucchese merchants to bring disputes before their own judges. The substance of the lawsuits recorded in the libro della comunità suggests that this court indeed served as a substitute for the Corte de Mercanti in Lucca. Of the recorded conflicts, twenty-five concerned financial claims that issued from all sorts of business dealings, including the delivery of goods, the dissolution of partnerships, and exchange operations. In several of these cases debts had not been paid because merchants had moved to London or Paris.[50] A further six verdicts concerned debts that remained after the decease of one of the nation's members.[51] That only three cases related to the transportation of goods was a direct result of the fact that the overland carriers, the conduttori di balle, fell under the jurisdiction of the local court in Lucca.[52] Besides substantial differences in the law applied, the Lucchese consuls also sought merchant-friendly solutions that did not strain business relations. They pronounced an actual verdict in fifteen of the recorded cases, but in another twelve conflicts they acted as arbiters. In two disputes an amicable settlement was reached even without the intervention of the consuls.

Obviously the creation of a consular court cost money, but these expenses did not weigh heavily on the nation because in exchange for modest membership fees it also performed other social and political functions. Moreover the consuls had more legal services to offer than just the settlement of commercial disputes. They could record private agreements between merchants, a service reminiscent of the noncontentious jurisdiction exercised by local courts, and they had the authority to discipline servants, apprentices, and sailors handling the merchants' money and merchandise. Indeed, in many of the grants of consular jurisdictions to foreign nations in Bruges these two groups—employees and sailors— were explicitly mentioned as submitted to the rulings of the consuls.[53]

[48] Lazzareschi 1947: ix, 146–48.

[49] Lazzareschi 1947: 256, 258.

[50] Lazzareschi 1947: 3–4, 14–17, 19–20, 29, 32–33, 43–47, 58–60, 70–72, 86–95, 101–10, 140–43, 162–65, 179–81, 186–87, 220–21; see also: De Roover 1949: 55.

[51] Lazzareschi 1947: 4–6, 23–27, 160–61, 187–88, 204–8, 242–43.

[52] Lazzareschi 1947: xxii. For the transportation cases dealt with by the Lucchese consuls in Bruges: Lazzareschi 1947: 21, 66–68, 260–62.

[53] Beuken 1950: 42; Gilliodts-Van Severen 1871–85: 2:130–39; Van Houtte 1982: 182; Bartier and Nieuwenhuysen 1965: 238–40, 469–79.

Thus emerged a multifunctional institution, attractive because, like the city's hostellers, it offered a multitude of services to merchants.

The exact combination of functions could differ between Bruges's foreign nations, however. German traders, for instance, were allowed to set up a consular court in Bruges as early as 1309, but at the time most of them were present in the port only during the trading season. Why would they want a consular jurisdiction if they returned home on a regular basis? One explanation lies in the staple rights granted to the German merchants in the early fourteenth century. To secure the compliance of all members, the aldermen of the German community had to be able to punish or possibly even exclude infringers. However, up until the formal recognition of the *Kontorordnung* of 1356 this was the responsibility of the Hanseatic diet led by Lübeck. A more urgent concern was the disciplining of the numerous German shipmasters and sailors frequenting Bruges since the thirteenth century. Damaged ships, lost cargoes, labor conflicts, and fighting sailors were real concerns for merchants and rulers and compelling reasons to ask for a consular jurisdiction in Bruges. This is also apparent from the first privileges granted to German merchants in Dordrecht by the Count of Holland in 1303, which included the right to try crewmembers who had fought aboard ships—provided there were no fatalities.[54]

And yet, not all seaborne traders obtained a consular jurisdiction. Shipmasters from Normandy and Brittany sailed regularly to Flanders in the fourteenth century and they must have faced problems similar to those of the Germans. In 1331 wine merchants from Saint-Jean-d'Angély and La Rochelle received privileges from the Count of Flanders, promising the protection of their person and goods from arbitrary confiscation, or any other damage. But they were not granted a separate jurisdiction. Instead, they were referred to the maritime court of Damme in case of disputes.[55] The judges in Damme ruled in conflicts between shipmasters, sailors, and merchants based on the articles of the French Rôles d'Oléron.[56] German merchants also used this maritime law, but they had their own adaptation of the original articles, known as the sea laws of Visby. The separate jurisdiction of the Germans allowed the application of these laws, whereas conflicts between French merchants and sailors could simply be adjudicated in Damme on the basis of the Rôles d'Oléron (see "Laws of Merchants" below).

German merchants valued the internal resolution of disputes, and they even threatened to exclude merchants who brought their cases before the

[54]Van Rijswijk 1900: 18.

[55]Bartier and Nieuwenhuysen 1965: 118–22.

[56]Gilliodts-Van Severen 1883–85: 1:285; 2:102, 395; Goudsmit 1882: 140–41; Nicholas 1979: 28.

local court instead. A similar prescription in the bylaws of the Venetian nation also suggests that the foreign nations preferred to stay away from the local legal system.[57] In reality, however, the consular courts and local courts functioned as complementary institutions. The Lucchese nation, for example, explicitly allowed its members to appear before the local court if this benefited a quick resolution of conflicts.[58] Thus merchants from Lucca appeared before the local court to deal with failed deliveries, arrests, and conflicts with employees and partners. A recent survey of cases brought before the aldermen's bench of Bruges reveals several hundred lawsuits in matters of insurance, payment and delivery, arrests, and myriad other cases involving members of virtually every nation.[59] The foreign consuls themselves appeared before the Schepenbank to support claims by their members, or they called upon local justices to settle an internal dispute. For instance, in 1458 Bruges's schepenen intervened to ensure that Catalan merchants paid the membership fee of their nation.[60] The aldermen of Bruges also heard appeals lodged by Lucchese, Castilian, and Portuguese merchants against the ruling of their own leaders, and they settled disputes between consuls from different nations.[61] Finally, the local court looked after the estates of deceased foreign merchants in case no relatives were present in Bruges, although conflicts regarding the division of estates were always referred back to the respective consuls.[62]

THE COURTS IN ANTWERP

In Bruges the legal differences between merchants from different parts of Europe set in motion two opposite developments. On the one hand, the city and the count discovered that granting consular jurisdictions was an attractive means to lure foreign traders. On the other, the regular interaction between merchants with different legal backgrounds stimulated the local magistrates to adapt their legal system to the needs of foreigners. Both developments surfaced in Antwerp as well, once foreign traders began frequenting the market. In 1296, thirteen years before the German merchants in Bruges obtained their consular jurisdiction from the Count of Flanders, the Duke of Brabant extended a similar privilege to mer-

[57] De Roover 1948: 18, 20.

[58] De Roover 1949: 55, 79; Lambert 2006: 157–62.

[59] Personal communication with Peter Stabel; see also van Niekerk 1998: 1:200–202; Nicholas 1979: 25; Gilliodts-Van Severen 1883–85: 2:106.

[60] Gilliodts-Van Severen 1901–2: 62–63, 79.

[61] De Roover 1948: 18; Lazzareschi 1947: 82–83, 87; Gilliodts-Van Severen: 1883–85: 2:117–18.

[62] Gilliodts-Van Severen 1883–85: 2:116.

chants from England. Whether the English immediately set up a consular court is doubtful, however. In the first half of the fourteenth century they traveled to Bergen-op-Zoom and Antwerp only for the duration of the fairs, where local justices habitually dealt with disputed payments and deliveries.[63] In 1308 Antwerp's magistrate had also granted the deans of the local cloth hall jurisdiction over all conflicts relating to the manufacturing and sales of cloth, the most important commodity traded by the English in Brabant—all of which suggests that the granting of a separate jurisdiction was a symbolic gesture from the Duke of Brabant, very much like the advances he made to Florentine and German traders in 1315.[64]

Probably only in the mid-fifteenth century did English merchants begin to rely on adjudication by the leaders of their own community.[65] In August 1446 Philip the Good confirmed the consular jurisdiction of the English merchants, and shortly afterward the city magistrate issued an ordinance to regulate its actual proceedings. This likely did not mean a comprehensive transfer of commercial litigation to the English consuls, however, as Antwerp also adjusted local court proceedings to the needs of the English cloth traders. For instance, in 1474 they were allowed to bring conflicts with local merchants and artisans before the Schepenbank rather than the cloth hall. Ten years later, when English merchants complained about the slow procedures before the aldermen, the town reviewed its appointment of local judges.[66] The privileges of the Company of Merchant Adventurers in 1496 confirmed the jurisdiction of the English Court but also promised the quick resolution of conflicts before the aldermen's bench.

As in Bruges, the adaptation of local court proceedings did not stop Antwerp from the creation of separate jurisdictions for other foreigners. On the contrary, it used these legal privileges to lure foreign merchants away from Bruges (Figure 5.2). In 1511 the city confirmed all earlier privileges of the Portuguese nation in Bruges, including the right to establish a consular court. The decline of Bruges also led to the transfer of the Genoese *massaria*, in 1522. In 1546 Charles V gave Florentine consuls the right to rule, in the first instance, in conflicts between members of their nation. In 1553, after lengthy negotiations with the town magistrate, the Kontor of the Hanseatic League was removed to Antwerp. Finally, around 1560, the merchants of Lucca were given the opportunity to name consuls to "resolve all conflicts between members."

---

[63] Slootmans 1985.
[64] Gotzen 1951; on the cloth hall: De Ruysscher 2009c: 57, 11, 129–31.
[65] Gotzen 1951:462–65; De Ruysscher 2009c: 117; De Smedt 1951: 111–12, 130–31.
[66] De Ruysscher 2009a: 106–12.

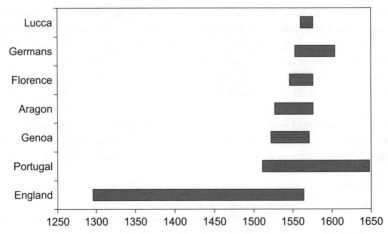

FIGURE 5.2. Consular jurisdictions of foreign merchant communities in Antwerp, 1250–1650

Sources: Antwerpse costumen 1570: 487; Antwerpse costumen 1582: 36; Liste Chronologique 1885: 295; Goris 1925: 58, 67, 71, 76, 79; Lazzareschi 1947: xxxiv–xxxv, 286–87; Harreld 2004: 66.

Like in Bruges, consular and local courts in Antwerp were complementary institutions. For instance, the Court of the Merchant Adventurers mainly dealt with three kinds of cases.[67] First, it punished public drinking, gambling, violence, and other objectionable behavior of its members. The disciplining of the community was specifically targeted at servants and apprentices, who were punished even more severely than the merchants of the company. Second, the court applied English law to contracting issues between members of the nation, and—if both parties agreed—between the company's freemen and other English traders. Finally, the consular jurisdiction helped the Merchant Adventurers to enforce their monopoly in the English cloth trade. The secretary of the court kept a register with the powers of attorney London merchants granted to freemen in Antwerp, and the transactions these agents carried out on behalf of their principals. This registration was a double-edged sword. It made the consignment trade more transparent as merchants, members or not, could inquire into existing agency relations. At the same time it made it easier to detect interlopers and punish their illicit trade with fines, confiscation of property, or even imprisonment pending their forced departure from Antwerp. As with the German merchants in Bruges, the consular jurisdiction served an additional purpose, that is, the protection of the members against competition from outsiders.

[67] De Smedt 1954: 32–36, 66–68, 98, 61–62, 66–69, 98, 106, 158–68, 183–91.

The Merchant Adventurers did not exclusively rely on Company officials in legal matters, however. They wrote many powers of attorney to solicitors to bring cases before the local judges. In 1537 the leaders of the English nation spurred the town magistrate to tighten the rules for the payment of bills of exchange, obligations, and insurance claims.[68] The Portuguese merchants in Antwerp also turned to their own leaders *and* local judges to solve problems. Every week two Portuguese consuls presided over a tribunal in which the members of the nation acted as a jury. Besides the correction of insults, scuffles, and other minor offenses, the consuls dealt with commercial and maritime conflicts, most notably the settlement of insurance cases. But merchants who disagreed with the consuls' rulings never hesitated to bring their case before the local court. This right to appeal was even written down in Antwerp's customs in 1582. The schepenen, in turn, always pointed to the consular court to resolve conflicts between shipmasters and sailors, which required the application of Portuguese maritime law.[69]

The exertions of the English and Portuguese community leaders notwithstanding, consular courts were less important in Antwerp than they had been in Bruges. Merchants from Florence, Germany, and Lucca had to wait several decades before they could appoint consuls, and merchants from Aragon, Castile, Venice, France, Holland, and southern Germany never obtained this privilege.[70] The German case suggests this did not harm trade in the least. The Germans moved to Antwerp in the late fifteenth century while their Kontor remained in Bruges. In Antwerp the merchants happily turned to the local court to settle disputes between them.[71] Conflicts between German merchants and sailors did not warrant a separate jurisdiction either because, when necessary, the local court applied the maritime laws of Visby. Hence Charles V's permission to remove the Kontor from Bruges in 1553—following an earlier agreement between Antwerp and the Hanse in 1546—was but a symbolic measure in addition to more substantial benefits (i.e., the building of the Oosterlingenhuis) to secure the prolonged presence of German traders in Antwerp.

The extent to which Antwerp's magistrates were willing to adapt legal procedures to the changing organization of trade is apparent from the change in their treatment of insolvencies. Before the sixteenth century the basic rule was that the first creditor to attach the property of a merchant was the first whose debts would be honored.[72] This "first come, first served" principle was applied in the Low Countries as well as in the German lands.

[68] De Smedt 1954: 1901, 576; De Smedt 1940–41: passim.
[69] Goris 1925: 40–41, 44–47.
[70] Goris 1925: 71, 80; Harreld 2004: 58–59; Coornaert 1961.
[71] Strieder 1962: 170, 178, 283–85.
[72] De Smedt 1954: 593.

It entailed considerable risks for merchants, however, because it created incentives for creditors to provoke bankruptcy, stand first in line, and snub other claimants. This not only was unfair but also harmed the merchant community at large as creditors further down the line could run into financial difficulties, which in turn might lead to further insolvencies. In France, Italy, and Spain, where all creditors were treated as equals, these problems were avoided.[73] Still, it was only in the sixteenth century that the magistrates of Bruges and Antwerp began to change insolvency proceedings. The most likely explanation is that before 1500, in case of insolvencies, most foreign merchants relied on their consular courts, which, even if the city supervised the arrest of goods, could settle debts according to their own rules. But from the moment they settled in Antwerp for a longer period and then started to develop credit relations with merchants from different legal background who could claim allegiance to different legal prescripts, reforms were required to secure an equal treatment of all creditors.

Town ordinances from 1516 and 1518 determined that in case of rogue insolvencies the order of attachment was of no consequence for the validity of the claims of creditors.[74] The only requirement for interested merchants was to report their debts outstanding.[75] Creditors from the Low Countries, Germany, and northern France had to come forward within forty days with their claims, and merchants in more distant markets were granted three months.[76] Officially these rules did not apply to bona fide insolvencies, but in practice merchants combined the new bankruptcy proceedings with older rulers regarding the cession of property to support amicable agreements between creditors and insolvent debtors. From the 1520s onward the typical procedure was for the legal authorities to draw up an inventory of the assets in the insolvent estate, after which the merchant or his heirs, in case the insolvency was discovered after his death, ceded the property to the collective creditors. The creditors then started to negotiate, and after they had reached an agreement followed the proportional distribution of the assets.[77] In 1556 merchants formally stated before Antwerp's town magistrate that the equality of all creditors applied to the insolvency of bona fide merchants as much as to bankruptcies.[78] The final consolidation of the procedure followed in the Customs of 1582 with the explicit stipulation that the rules applied to all merchants regardless of their origin.[79]

---

[73] De Ruysscher 2009c: 305–69, esp. 326–27. De Ruysscher 2009b.
[74] De Smedt 1954: 594; Goris 1925: 359. De Ruysscher 2009c: 320–23.
[75] *Antwerp Customs* (1582), title 67.
[76] De Ruysscher 2009c: 321.
[77] De Ruysscher 2009c: 320–59.
[78] De Ruysscher 2009c: 323; see also De Ruysscher 2008.
[79] *Antwerp Customs* (1582), title 65, art. 2.

To better serve the needs of merchants, other litigation procedures were adapted as well.[80] Following English complaints about the enforcement of debt contracts in 1537, for instance, Charles V insisted on a revision of the local court's terms to pass judgment. The city recognized the problem and from 1543 onward allowed merchants to bring simple contractual matters, most notably contested short-term debts, before the *extraordinaris rol*, a subcommittee of aldermen that met twice a week, and passed sentences within eight days. Matters that were less urgent but still required a speedy resolution could be brought before the *ordinarisse rol*, a similar subcommittee, also with two hearings per week, but sentencing was provided only within fourteen days. To be sure, the rollen were no courts of first instance like the Cloth Hall (1308) or the Orphan Chamber (1497); foreign merchants retained the right to submit their cases directly to the full Schepenbank.

Procedural problems nevertheless remained in one field, that of insurance conflicts. Already in 1459 Philip the Good had ruled that local courts should settle insurance disputes as quickly as possible. The aldermen of Bruges and Antwerp complied, but about eighty years later, in 1537, Antwerp's magistrate expressed the wish to hand over this particular function to the consular courts.[81] This desire was probably related to the different contracting rules applied by Portuguese, Castilian, Genoese, and Florentine merchants. Charles V, however, did not want referral to the consular courts and promulgated an ordinance that, among other things, instructed the local court to pass provisional judgments, in combination with a financial deposit made by the parties involved (*namptisatie*).[82] This was the first of a series of royal interventions to restructure legal proceedings, especially in matters of insurance. A second attempt dates from 1550, when counselors of Charles V, perhaps following the advice of Antwerp's magistrate, prepared an ordinance for the establishment of a mercantile court led by one of the schepenen and the consuls of four nations—the English, Portuguese, Genoese, and Florentine.[83] This court would have been authorized to deal with all conflicts arising between merchants trading at the Exchange. Thus, the plan would have created a mercantile court like the ones that existed in Italy and Spain, but perhaps anticipating protests from merchants and magistrates in Antwerp, the ordinance was never promulgated.

Instead, in 1551 the Castilian merchants in Antwerp asked for their own jurisdiction.[84] Just like the Germans, they were still officially submitted to

[80] Gotzen 1951: 305.
[81] Van Niekerk 1998: 2:201.
[82] Van Niekerk 1998: 2:201; De Smedt 1954: 576–78.
[83] De Ruysscher 2009c: 126–30.
[84] Goris 1925: 58–70.

the authority of the consuls of their nation in Bruges. In the 1520s and 1530s the consuls of Bruges actually came to Antwerp to adjudicate conflicts between merchants. However, according to the Antwerp members, their community leaders were incompetent in their dealings with conflicts in the Scheldt port. In particular, the Castilians wanted qualified judges to support the fulfillment of insurance policies, and hence asked for their own judges in 1551. In a petition to the Governess, the town magistrate of Antwerp endorsed the Castilian request and proposed the establishment of a consulate for all Spanish merchants, which would rule initially in commercial matters like the other nations in Antwerp. The magistrate of Bruges was furious and suggested the city might withhold its financial support of Charles V if the Spanish consulate—and the wool staple—would be removed to the Scheldt port. At this point the city of Antwerp decided to let the matter rest, and the Spanish merchants were left with their own arbiters, or *hombres buenos*, to settle insurance disputes.

In 1556 Jean-Baptiste Ferufini's plan to put brokers in charge of the registration of policies also met with fierce resistance. Ferufini was eventually appointed by the central government as superintendant in 1559, but his charge was limited to the visual inspection of policies and the registration of the names of ships insured. Merchants in Antwerp continued to write contracts privately and relied on either consuls or local judges to adjudicate conflicts.[85] In fact, in 1559 the Castilian merchants, in conjunction with the Antwerp magistrate, revived their attempts to create their own consular court in the Scheldt port. Bruges rallied the support of the Estates of Flanders, threatened to stop paying to the sovereign, and thus pushed the Governess to reject the plan in 1565. This time the Spanish nation in Bruges proved more forthcoming, however, as it laid down Castilian insurance customs in its Hordenanzas of 1569.[86]

This was not the end of the struggle among merchants, cities, and the central government over the boundaries of their jurisdiction in insurance matters. As political tensions grew during the 1560s, marine insurance became more important for merchants, but more cases of insurance fraud were also reported, which the central government used as a pretext to intervene again.[87] In 1569 the new governor, the Duke of Alba, actually forbade the writing of policies. This obviously was not a realistic proposal, but it created sufficient leverage for Alba to push through the appointment of a commissioner of the Registration Bureau in Antwerp, with deputies in Amsterdam and Middelburg. The new office was supposed to register all policies to the extent that entries could be used as legal proof

[85] Goris 1925: 189; de Groote 1976: 208.
[86] Goris 1925: 65–66; de Groote 1976: 207.
[87] Van Niekerk 1998: 1:203.

in case of disputed claims. Whether merchants complied with these rules is doubtful, however, for none of the remaining sources refers to such a substantial role for the bureau. There is some evidence that the new insurance officer and his clerks assisted in the calculation of averages in case of partial loss of cargo, but otherwise the city of Antwerp would seem to have retained its judicature in insurance matters.[88] When most foreign nations had left Antwerp in the late 1570s, the city's aldermen probably took on the majority of insurance disputes—for as long as it lasted, because in the 1590s the market for marine insurance moved to Amsterdam.

In sum, in the sixteenth century the city of Antwerp managed to develop a legal system capable of adjudicating the full range of commercial and financial conflicts because the town magistrate adopted foreign rules, because it reconsidered the duties of its various courts, and because it accepted arbitration to settle conflicts quickly and equitably. As a result of these attempts to accommodate its merchant community at large, the foreigners who traded in Antwerp needed their consuls ever less to resolve commercial disputes.

CONFLICT RESOLUTION IN AMSTERDAM

The shift of commercial primacy from Antwerp to Amsterdam set the magistrates of the Dutch port a similar legal challenge, but their response differed. Until 1578 Amsterdam's prime occupation had been the exchange of bulk goods with the Baltic area, but now it quickly became an all-round market with numerous Dutch, Flemish, and German merchants and traders from England, Portugal, and even Italy and France. The growing scale and scope of the market increased the variety and complexity of commercial and financial transactions between these merchants, and yet in spite of their different legal backgrounds, the city refused to create consular jurisdictions to support the enforcement of contracts between the foreigners. In the 1580s talks between Amsterdam's magistrate and representatives of the German and English nations of Antwerp about the removal of their formal seat to the Dutch port came to nothing. The Portuguese merchants did receive several safe-conducts from the States General but Amsterdam did not oblige with legal privileges.

The city did allow the establishment of separate churches, which created some opportunity for internal disciplining by religious leaders. The consistory of the English reformed church, for instance, corrected merchants whose behavior threatened a stable social order.[89] Especially in

[88] Van Niekerk 1998: 1:204–7.
[89] Carter 1964: 174–77.

the first years after the church's establishment in 1607 they dealt with failed payments and deliveries, conflicts between employers and employees, and bankruptcies. On rare occasions the elders even acted as arbiters in business disputes. The elders of the Dutch Reformed Church in Amsterdam—many of whom were Dutch and Flemish merchants—also played an active role in the resolution of commercial conflicts. Between 1578 and 1650 the elders of this church dealt with 247 insolvencies, many involving merchants.[90] The *imposta* board of the Portuguese community, established in 1622, had a slightly different function as it mainly prescribed behavior, warning against conflicts between brokers and *bylooper*, and issuing bans on gambling, trade in illegal coinage, and the carrying of arms near synagogues.[91]

But religious leaders never offered an alternative for formal litigation. Rather, they supplemented the private efforts of merchants to settle matters amicably. One obvious reason for their limited contribution was the sheer number of denominations in Amsterdam. By 1650 the city boasted about a dozen church communities, most of which counted merchants among their members.[92] This is why, for instance, the Portuguese imposta board, which was a collaboration between three Jewish congregations, could only issue warnings. Second, not all traders were active members of these churches. They may have been devout Christians but professed their faith in private. Among Flemish, German, English, and Portuguese Jews there remained many unaffiliated believers. Finally, the punishment of religious leaders was symbolic, and often temporary at that. When two Antwerp grocers had attempted to monopolize the supply of certain foodstuffs in 1590 they were merely reprimanded by their pastor and a churchwarden. The next year one of the merchants was already reelected deacon.[93] In the case of insolvency the English and Dutch Reformed Churches in Amsterdam followed an enactment of the reformed Synod of Dordrecht (1618), which excluded only fraudulent bankrupts from communion.[94] Involuntary bankrupts could continue to join the communion, provided they had reached an agreement with their creditors. The completion of the actual bankruptcy proceedings was always left to the creditors or the bench of aldermen.[95]

[90] Roodenburg 1990: 377–81; Gelderblom 2002: 29; Estié 1987: 64–65.
[91] Swetschinski 2000: 184, 218.
[92] Gelderblom 1999: 248–54; Carter 1964; Dijkman 2002; Swetschinski 2000: 175–76.
[93] ACA inv. 376 no. 1, fol. 315 (05-02-1587); ACA inv. 376 no. 2, fol. 26b (15-02-1590), fol. 55b (07-02-1591).
[94] Carter 1964: 170, 174–75.
[95] Roodenburg 1990: 377–81.

The dominant role of Amsterdam's magistrates in the resolution of commercial conflicts dated back to the fifteenth century. In 1413 the town magistrate ruled that conflicts between guests had to be resolved expeditiously by the Gerechte or aldermen's bench. In practice this meant that foreign merchants, when they sojourned in the city, could go to court twice a week.[96] Particularly important for the German merchants who frequented the city in the fifteenth century was Amsterdam's choice to apply the sea laws of Visby to maritime conflicts. This was the legal code used by the Hanseatic merchants themselves, and hence it obviated the need for a separate jurisdiction, or the referral of cases to the nation in Bruges under which the Germans in Amsterdam formally resorted (see the more detailed explanation of the Visby rules in the "Laws of Merchants" section below).[97]

Because the records of Amsterdam's local court are lost, it is impossible to determine exactly how intense the local judges' involvement with conflict resolution between foreign merchants was, but the few surviving prescriptive texts suggest that Amsterdam's Gerechte could adjudicate the full range of commercial and maritime conflicts between foreign merchants. If, for instance, a stranger's property was sequestered by a fellow town resident or countryman, the court would take on the issue, but if either of the two parties objected, the case was referred to their "daily judges."[98] Incidental references to actual disputes between local and foreign merchants in the second half of the fifteenth century confirm the court's adjudication of cases concerning payments, disputed arrests, freight charges, the ownership of merchandise, and the dissolution of partnerships.[99] Only in exceptional circumstances did the aldermen refuse to intervene in commercial matters. For instance, in April 1482, Amsterdam's aldermen's bench decided it would no longer rule in cases against Simon Modder, who on a daily basis threatened to hurt and actually did hurt creditors asking for payment. Modder himself would be fined or imprisoned if he misbehaved again.[100] In this case, however, withholding legal support confirms rather than denies the importance of the court's intervention in business disputes.

The immigration of large numbers of Flemish, Portuguese, English, and German merchants between 1580 and 1650 did not change the legal primacy of the local court. The local judges ruled in all conflicts, ranging from problems with shipmasters and employees to conflicts regarding the

[96] Breen 1902: 10; Wachter 1639: 116–18; Verkerk 2004: 182–92.
[97] Breen 1902: 11–12; Goudsmit 1882: 97–106; Van den Auweele 1977: 20.
[98] Wachter 1639: 90–92; Rooseboom 1656: 73–81.
[99] Poelman 1917: 2:683, 886–87, 889, 1000, 1024–25, 1048, 1061, 1064, 1072–73.
[100] Breen 1902: 178–79.

quality of goods delivered, and from unpaid debts to outright insolvencies.[101] All these proceedings were in Dutch, but foreigners could bring translators or rely on solicitors to defend their interests.[102] In conflicts with fellow countrymen, foreign merchants could ask Amsterdam's aldermen to apply the laws under which the disputed contracts were originally signed, and whenever the local judges felt merchants could settle conflicts between themselves they referred cases back to arbiters.[103]

A more serious problem was the local court outgrowing its strength. This was true not only in a practical sense for the very cramped premises of Amsterdam's city hall, but also with regard to the ever-increasing administrative burden created by the multiplication of lawsuits of all kinds. The city had no difficulty covering the legal costs with urban taxes and fees paid to those who appeared before the court, but the aldermen's bench threatened to become overburdened by the increased workload created by the immigration of more than one thousand merchants after 1585. The solution was found in the creation of subsidiary courts: the second institutional change, following the absence of consular courts, that set Amsterdam apart from Bruges and, to a lesser extent, Antwerp.[104] Between 1578 and 1650 Amsterdam set up a string of subsidiary courts led by commissioners with specialist knowledge. Directly or indirectly involved in the city's trade were the Orphan Chamber (1578) and the Insurance Chamber (1598), the commissioners of Minor Affairs (Kleine Zaken) (1611), the Chamber of Insolvent Estates (1627), and finally the commissioners of Maritime Affairs (1641).[105] Not all these subsidiary

---

[101]SR 19; 52; 83; 114; 115; 122; 183; 200; 221; 222; 223; 224; 226; 227; 231; 248; 251; 253; 344; 345; 451; 458; 459; 545; 548; 551; 569; 601; 643; 702; 717; 718; 720; 723; 724; 725; 726; 727; 728; 745; 752; 782; 793; 876; 923; 1031; 1032; 1038; 1041; 1042; 1042; 1045; 1049; 1067; 1068; 1071; 1072; 1081; 1088; 1115; 1196; 1216; 1244; 1250; 1255; 1365; 1366; 1368; 1382; 1395; 1517; 1562; 1592; 1600; 1611; 1613; 1620; 1674; 1688; 1771; 1792; 1834; 1850; 1894; 1954; 1957; 1962; 1971; 1997; 1999; 2016; 2023; 2038; 2089; 2126; 2141; 2145; 2210; 2252; 2273; 2281; 2313; 2319; 2428; 2467; 2474; 2512; 2518; 2539; 2560; 2582; 2608; 2609; 2614; 2625; 2640; 2654; 2711; 2734; 2747; 2754; 2967; 3009; 3028; 3028; 3122; 3122; 3148; 3149; 3181; 3209; 3210; 3217; 3234; 3248; 3273; 3378; 3379; 3380; 3386; 3412; 3417; 3436; 3486; 3527; 3538; 3551; 3552; 3605; 3633.

[102]Rooseboom 1656: 63–64.

[103]Consultatien 1657: 2:400. One exception was when foreign contracts implied actions to be taken in the United Provinces, in which case Dutch law was applied: van Niekerk 1998: 1:237.

[104]A Chamber of Insolvent Estates was created in Bruges in the 1520s. From 1477 the local court of Bruges occasionally ruled in shipping disputes. In 1500 the aldermen of Bruges began to serve as justices of the maritime court of Damme, and in 1566 its jurisdiction was transferred to the Bruges Schepenbank. Gilliodts-Van Severen 1883–85: 2:100–104, 315, 395.

[105]Rooseboom 1656: 18–22; Oldewelt 1962: passim.

courts were equally important. *Commissarissen van Kleine zaken* ruled only in minor commercial disputes, while merchants often excluded the involvement of the Orphan Chamber in their wills in order to protect their business interests.[106] The other courts did provide very valuable services, however.[107]

Amsterdam's capacity to adapt its legal institutions to the growth of international trade during its Golden Age can be demonstrated to good effect with its bankruptcy proceedings. Insolvencies in Amsterdam were dealt with according to the principles laid down in Antwerp's customs in 1582.[108] Notarial deeds from Portuguese merchants show insolvent merchants after 1600 handing over control over their assets to a collective of creditors.[109] The latter reviewed the estate's assets and liabilities and determined what percentage of debts outstanding could be restituted. It is difficult to judge the efficiency of this procedure. The surviving evidence on creditors' agreements typically relates to disputes that arose when some creditors claimed preference over others. In 1624, for example, the local court ruled in favor of Portuguese merchants who claimed 700 pounds from two merchants for a bill of exchange written only days before their insolvency became public knowledge. They claimed the merchants had known about their financial difficulties, which would give the Portuguese debt preference over all others.[110]

Determining the date of the insolvency was important to sort out claims of creditors. In principle, in both Antwerp and Amsterdam, a merchant was considered insolvent when he no longer appeared at the Exchange. The debtor himself, and sometimes even some of the creditors, would know about the financial difficulties before that, however. This could lead to disagreement about what to do with payments made or debts incurred after the insolvency had become apparent. The surviving Portuguese cases suggest the creditors, and sometimes the arbiters, judges, or even church officials, relied on the accounts of the insolvent merchants to determine the exact date of insolvency. It may have been the precision required for this inspection that led Amsterdam's magistrate to create the Chamber of Insolvent Estates in 1627. The town ordinance promulgated in 1643 to regulate its work determined that the commissioners of the chamber supervised the inspection of the debtor's accounts, formally declared insolvency, established which claims creditors

---

[106]Oudkerk 1938: 25, 28.

[107]Lichtenauer 1956: 141–43; Schreiner et al. 1991: 34; van Niekerk 1998: 1:208–14; Schöffer 1956: 76; Go 2009: 95–117.

[108]De Ruysscher 2008: 309–13; De Ruysscher 2009a: 473–74.

[109]SR 226, 227; 368, 369; 466; 715; 1133; 1365, 1368; 1592, 2141; 3148, 3149; 2539, 2608–9, 3028, 3122, 3378–80.

[110]SR 3148, 3149.

had, supervised the liquidation of the estate, and made the payments to creditors.[111]

The combination of a local court taking on general conflicts and a string of specialized courts for bankruptcies, insurances, exchange, and maritime law left very little for merchants to desire. Even so, in the second half of the seventeenth century, some merchants began to contemplate the creation of a separate court for all commercial conflicts, very much like the commercial tribunals in Spain, Italy, and France. A proposition to this end was made by former bookkeeper Johannes Phoonsen in his *Wissel-Styl tot Amsterdam*. Phoonsen proposed turning the local Exchange Bank into a *bank van judicature*. Conflicts between merchants that did not fall under the jurisdiction of the Chambers of Insurance and Maritime Affairs would initially be brought before the commissioners of the Wisselbank. Their jurisdiction would comprise "all differences concerning matters of exchange trade, sales or purchases, deliveries and payment; and contracts of trade, and their observance; liquidation and adjustments of accounts, as well as provisions, salaries, and pay of Commissioners, Factors, Bookkeepers and Servants &c. and generally all disputes and matters that arise in, or follow from trade."[112] Although a merchant tribunal was never created in Amsterdam, the very proposition shows the constant concern for the alignment of legal institutions with business practice.

THE CENTRAL COURTS

The legal autonomy of commercial cities allowed them to do what Douglass North and others generally attribute to the increasingly powerful central governments of early modern states: the adaptation of institutional arrangements to the needs of merchants. Bruges, Antwerp, and Amsterdam were so good at adapting their legal systems to the changing needs of foreign traders that the creation of central courts, first by the Burgundian and Habsburg rulers and then by the United Provinces, seems to have played no role whatsoever in the governance of international trade in these cities. The central government obviously had to approve the creation of foreign jurisdictions in Bruges and Antwerp, and sometimes it spurred the town magistrates to change specific procedures, but the local authorities generally needed little prodding, and merchants seemed satisfied with the legal options available to them locally. But was that really the case, or did foreign merchants value wider choices of legal options, and perhaps even the combined use of local and central institutions to discipline dishonest trading partners?

[111] De Ruysscher 2009a: 475.
[112] Phoonsen 1676.

From the fifteenth century onward the central government allowed foreign merchants to appear initially before the provincial and central courts and to appeal the verdicts of local judges there. The vast majority of cases brought before higher courts in Flanders, Brabant, and Holland consisted of disputes between ordinary citizens, public officials, villages, towns, and provincial authorities.[113] Nevertheless it was the privilege of a select group of people—nobles, ducal officials, widows, orphans, and foreign merchants—that their cases were heard initially by judges of the higher courts.[114] Thus in 1409 John the Fearless ruled that disputes between nonresident foreigners could be brought before the Council of Flanders in Ghent. In the mid-fifteenth century Philip the Good allowed foreigners to take their disputes to the Grand Conseil in Malines.[115] In the sixteenth century foreign traders in Antwerp could turn to the Grand Conseil initially, and after 1581 the Hoge Raad van Holland en Zeeland (Supreme Court) offered a similar privilege to merchants in Amsterdam.

Town magistrates may have balked at this infringement on their autonomy, but the impact on the resolution of commercial conflicts was in fact very limited. An exhaustive analysis of lawsuits before the Hof van Holland between 1457 and 1467 reveals only about ten trade-related cases per year, with an even smaller number of foreign traders among the litigants.[116] The same applied to litigation before the Grand Conseil in Malines. For the years between 1460 and 1580 Robert van Answaarden has documented sixty-one cases that involved Portuguese claimants, defendants, and occasionally also lawyers and witnesses—but only twenty-three of these were related to Portuguese long-distance trade.[117] It would seem that this kind of litigation simply cost too much time and money for merchants who wanted to settle disputes quickly.[118]

We can extend van Answaarden's analysis to the foreign merchant community at large using the published sentences of the Grand Conseil in

---

[113] Blockmans and Prevenier 1999: 47.

[114] The provincial and central courts heard cases in the first instance for a select group of people, including nobles, ducal officials, widows, orphans, and foreign merchants: de Schepper and Cauchies 1993: 162–64; Damen 2003: 6.

[115] Van Answaarden 1990: 11; van Answaarden 1991: 82.

[116] A total of 255 civil lawsuits made up only 22 percent of all cases brought before the court between 1457 and 1467. Fewer than half of these cases (122) concerned the law of contracts (either credit transactions or sales of goods), while another 30 cases were concerned with the transfer of real estate (Le Bailly 2001: 287–90). Among the 535 plaintiffs whose profession was recorded by the court, there were only 27 "traders, fishermen, and shipmasters," while among the 1,002 defendants, their number did not exceed 35. Foreigners numbered only 51 among the 3,057 persons who appeared before the court in this decade. Most foreigners who did appear before the court were pawnbrokers. Le Bailly 2001: 259–63, 266.

[117] Van Answaarden 1991: passim.

[118] Godding 1987: 125–26, 129; Le Bailly 2001: 182–89; Strieder 1962: 142, 153, 177, 184–85, 271, 281, 284, 295, 316, 324.

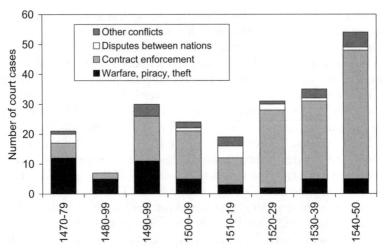

FIGURE 5.3. Sentences passed by the Grand Conseil of Malines in lawsuits involving foreign merchants, ordered by type of conflict (1470–1550)
Source: de Smidt 1966–79: passim.

the years between 1470 and 1550. This data set yields 221 trade-related lawsuits in which either claimants or defendants can be identified as foreign merchants.[119] The claimants and defendants whose origin was explicitly mentioned in the sentences (two-thirds of their total number) came from a variety of countries, including the Italian city-states (76), Castile and Biscay (49), the British Isles (47), and different parts of Germany (44), France (30), and Portugal (10). The sentences, summarized in Figure 5.3, reveal that merchants initially turned to the court only to settle prize cases—a subject to which we will return in the next chapter. After 1490 the majority of lawsuits concerned the enforcement of contracts, including failures to pay or deliver goods, the sales of collaterals on unpaid loans, and the imprisonment of debtors. A few cases involved matters of shipping and insurance. The Great Council also settled miscellaneous conflicts including disputes between foreign nations and failures to execute amicable settlements. Finally, it is important to note that not all 221 lawsuits implied great differences of opinion. In 38 cases the supreme judges merely formalized private agreements in noncontentious verdicts.

Measured by the number and nature of cases brought before the Grand Conseil, it is clear that the higher judges did not settle everyday disputes

[119]The number of "foreign" cases identified in the sentences published by De Smidt et al. (1966–79) probably underestimates the total number of cases involving foreign merchants, as it contains only ten of the fifteen commercial disputes involving Portuguese merchants that appear in van Answaarden's exhaustive survey in the same period (van Answaarden 1991).

between merchants. For merchants the principal function of the supreme court was to evaluate earlier verdicts by local or provincial courts. Already in the fourteenth century Louis de Male allowed his Flemish subjects to contest the judgment of local magistrates before the Council of Flanders. In the mid-fifteenth century Philip the Good gave all inhabitants of Flanders, Brabant, and Holland the right to lodge an appeal with their respective provincial courts against the verdict of local justices.[120] He also created the opportunity to appeal to the Grand Conseil de Malines against the verdicts of the provincial courts of Flanders and Holland.[121] To appreciate the importance of this measure, we can compare the total number of lawsuits before the Grand Conseil with the size of the resident foreign merchant community in the Low Countries and estimate the probability that a foreign merchant would appear before the Grand Conseil in any one year.[122] At 0.34 percent, these odds were very low, strongly suggesting that merchants settled the vast majority of their disputes elsewhere.

The limited involvement of the Great Council in the resolution of conflicts between merchants was a direct result of the amount of time it took the court to reach its decisions. When opportunities for appeal were first created in the mid-fifteenth century, merchants did not hesitate to use them to delay proceedings and postpone possible sanctions. To secure expeditious justice, the Burgundian dukes quickly decided to limit the possibilities for appeal to decisions of local courts.[123] In 1459 they stipulated that appeals would be allowed only in case of considerable damages. Besides, indemnities awarded in the first instance were to be paid awaiting final judgment. The beneficiaries could dispose of the money thus transferred, provided they gave sufficient surety. Also, surety was to be given for the expected costs of the appeal. Noncompliance with these rules resulted in a penalty of 30 guilders.[124] An explicit concern for a quick resolution of commercial conflicts is evident from Maximilian's decision in 1488 that no appeal to central courts would be possible on

[120]Le Bailly 2001: 10.

[121]Gilliodt van Severen 1883–85: 2:266; van Niekerk 1998: 197–98; Le Bailly 2001: 94, 203–8. Officially, the Parlement of Paris remained the supreme court in Flanders until 1521, but it never played a substantial role in commercial litigation in the fifteenth century: de Schepper and Cauchies 1993: 131–32; Gilliodts-Van Severen 1883–85: 2:340–41; Blockmans 1992b: 213–16. Verdicts of the Court of Brabant could not be appealed to the Grand Conseil: Puttevils 2012: 316–19.

[122]To calculate the probability we have assumed linear growth of the number of foreign merchants from 400 in Bruges in 1450 to 1,100 in Antwerp in 1550. Based on this interpolation, the average number of merchants present in any one year between 1470 and 1550 is 820.

[123]Gilliodts-Van Severen 1883–85: 2:35–39.

[124]Gilliodts-Van Severen 1883–85: 2:35–39, 55–58 (1464), 215–17 (1511).

judgments passed by the Antwerp court in conflicts arising from trade at Brabant fairs.[125]

The Grand Conseil may not be the best place to look for a direct involvement of the central authorities in the resolution of commercial conflicts, however. Provincial courts were first in line when merchants appealed to local verdicts. We can analyze the role of the Court of Holland in the settlement of commercial disputes through a representative sample of 212 Flemish traders working in Amsterdam between 1580 and 1630—one quarter of the total Flemish merchant community in this period.[126] Comparing this sample with the names mentioned in the extant sentences of the Court of Holland in the years between 1580 and 1632 shows 81 merchants from the southern provinces appearing as claimant and/or defendant before the court. Almost half of this group (36) was involved only in cases that were not directly related to long-distance trade, most notably contested wills, care for orphans, and the sale of real estate. As for commercial disputes, a total of 45 out of 212 Flemish merchants were involved in at least one case brought before the Court of Holland between 1580 and 1632. The total number of these commercial cases was twice as high (96) because several merchants appeared more than once.[127]

Two merchants from the sample were involved in a very high number of cases: Louis del Becque in thirteen cases and Isaac Lemaire in eighteen. The latter's appearance in ten cases involving the trade in VOC shares comes as no surprise, considering that Lemaire was the leader of the world's first and ultimately unsuccessful bear syndicate operating in Amsterdam in 1609 and 1610.[128] Indeed stock trading and conflicts regarding payment and delivery were the most common grounds for litigation, with seventeen cases for each category. Most of the other cases brought before the Court of Holland involved insurance policies (eight), freight contracts (six), insolvencies (six), and miscellaneous financial contracts (thirteen). Disagreements about company contracts (four) and labor conflicts (three) were very few and far between.

A simple measure to evaluate the involvement of the Court of Holland in the settlement of disputes is to translate the number of cases in the

[125] *Antwerp Customs* (1609), title 4.

[126] The sample was compiled by selecting all merchants whose surname ended with B, M, or P from the database "Merchants from the Southern Netherlands and the rise of the Amsterdam staple market (1578–1630)"; available on line: Persistent Identifier urn:nbn:nl:ui:13-p78-n3t.

[127] In 14 of these 96 cases the records do not indicate the actual issue at stake. However, given that both claimant and defendant in these cases were merchants, we have added them to the category commercial conflicts. If excluded, the number of cases would drop to 82, and the number of merchants to 36 (or 17 percent of the total).

[128] Petram 2011: 62–65, with references to the older literature.

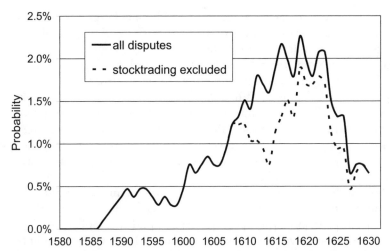

FIGURE 5.4. The probability that an individual Flemish merchant appeared before the Court of Holland to settle a commercial dispute in any year between 1580 and 1632 (five-year moving average)

sample to the entire Flemish merchant community. Doing this yields an estimated 385 cases brought before the court between 1580 and 1632— fewer than eight per year. A different and perhaps more accurate measure is the probability that an individual Flemish merchant appeared before the Court of Holland in any year between 1580 and 1632. This probability can be calculated by dividing the number of different merchants mentioned in cases starting in a particular year by the total size of the sample. The result, presented in Figure 5.4, reveals the odds of a Flemish merchant having a case adjudicated before the Court of Holland in a particular year were below 1 percent before 1607, rising to slightly over 2 percent around 1620, and then dropping again to less than 1 percent in 1627.[129] Compared to the Grand Conseil before 1550, merchants made more of the provincial court of Holland but still their court appearances were infrequent.[130]

[129] Even if the calculated probability does not distinguish between one or more appearances of a single merchant before the court in any one year, the underlying sample includes only *two* merchants (Lemaire and Del Becque) being engaged in *more than one* new case in one particular year.

[130] The odds for other merchants in Amsterdam were similar. A comparison of the names of all English merchants known to have worked in Amsterdam before 1630 (Dijkman 2002) with the extant sentences reveals only four cases before the Court of Holland. Assuming an average size of the English community of twenty merchants between 1600 and 1630, the probability of any one member appearing before the court in any one year was 0.67 percent.

The court cases demonstrate a twofold contribution of the Hof van Holland to the resolution of commercial conflicts. The spate of cases on VOC share transactions after 1607 suggests the court played an active role in determining the rules of the game of stock trading in the aftermath of Isaac Lemaire's speculation.[131] In addition to this, the court took on appeals on decisions of Admiralty courts, local courts, and their subsidiaries.[132] Merchants' appetite for going through an appeal procedure was limited, however, presumably because many years elapsed between an initial appeal and the final verdict. The fifty-odd cases for which we know the year of submission and the year of sentencing show an average duration of five and a half years.

Given the speed with which the Hof van Holland sentenced, it comes as no surprise that the number of commercial conflicts involving Amsterdam merchants brought before the Hoge Raad van Holland en Zeeland (Supreme Court) was smaller still. A survey of 1,094 cases brought before the Hoge Raad between 1582 and 1586 reveals only one nonresident merchant (an Antwerp citizen) bringing a case before the court initially—and this case was repealed before passing any verdict.[133] In later years the number of merchants appearing before the Supreme Court to settle a commercial dispute remained very small. This is apparent from the notarial deeds signed by Portuguese merchants in Amsterdam in the first decades of the seventeenth century. They reveal only five appeals of sentences from lower courts, one of which was actually repealed before a verdict was reached, in thirty years.[134] References to thirty-eight cases brought before the Court of Holland suggest this provincial court was slightly more important for the Portuguese merchants, but only in cases that divided parties to the extent that proceedings could last for years.[135]

[131] For a detailed analysis of the court cases dealing with the share in VOC trade, see Petram 2011: 21–22, 46–47, 72–73, 92–116.

[132] Out of 96 cases, 68 are explicitly referred to in the sentences as appeals to decisions by other courts. In 19 of these cases previous proceedings were referred: 13 times a local court, mostly that of Amsterdam, 3 times arbiters, once the Insurance Chamber, once the Court of Flushing, and once a referral back from the Supreme Court.

[133] Verhas 1997: case no. 509. Admittedly, most merchants moved from Antwerp to Amsterdam *after* 1585, but even at this early date the Flemish community counted already more than 120 traders: Gelderblom 2000: 189.

[134] SR 8, 14, 85, 184; SR 3551, 3552, 3605; SR 2539, 2608–9, 3028, 3122, 3378–80; SR 114, 115, 122. The case withdrawn: SR 3243, 3350.

[135] In addition to these thirty-eight, cases the notarial deeds contain nineteen powers of attorney to solicitors or attorneys "at the Court of Holland and the High Court of Holland." Other, more extensively documented legal proceedings suggest these powers of attorney were intended, first of all, to bring cases before the Court of Holland, not the Supreme Court. In addition to this, it must be stressed that these powers of attorney could have been precautionary measures that were not followed by actual proceedings. Furthermore, due to

Judged by the number of cases heard, the central courts' influence on everyday commercial dealings remained extremely limited. The provincial courts of Flanders, Brabant, and Holland and the Supreme Courts of Malines and The Hague could adjudicate cases between foreign merchants initially, but they were of little use for run-of-the-mill commercial disputes because their proceedings took far too long. The central courts' hearing of appeals against verdicts of local judges could have had a more profound influence on merchants' dealings, but only if they concerned new types of contracts, like Amsterdam's derivatives trade that emerged after the establishment of the VOC in 1602. In such cases the Hoge Raad may have played a role similar to that of supreme courts in common law countries today, but properly rating their contribution to the substance of commercial law requires a closer look at the way in which mercantile usage and local customs in general evolved between the thirteenth and seventeenth centuries.

The Laws of Merchants

Foreign merchants in Bruges and Antwerp valued their consular courts because of the speedy resolution of conflicts according to their own contracting rules. Their preference faded, however, as the town magistrates transformed their legal system, initially designed to support local market exchange, into a court system dealing with business conflicts of all kinds, irrespective of the litigants' legal origin. This was a major achievement, not because it was an expensive operation, but because it required substantial choices about the legal rules to apply to commercial disputes at hand. Every group of foreigners had its own contracting rules, and the same was obviously true for the local business community. How did they solve this legal divergence? Did the commercial legal system gradually converge toward an international standard? Did urban magistrates initiate the introduction of new rules? Or was this the one domain in which the central government played a key role?

Between 1475 and 1480 the leaders of the German Kontor in Bruges drafted a register with the rules and regulations that would apply to Hanseatic merchants and sailors in cases of business conflicts or damage to their property.[136] This Flandrischen Copiar included the fourteenth-century privileges of the Flemish counts, the maritime law of Damme (which was the Flemish edition of the Rôles d'Oléron), and a collection of

---

the general wording of the powers of attorney, it is possible that several of these powers of attorney relate to one and the same business conflict.

[136]The following is based on Jahnke and Graßmann 2003; see also Henn 2008.

rules and regulations regarding shipping matters, as promulgated by the Hanseatic League in the course of the fifteenth century. A first remarkable element is the strong emphasis on shipping issues. The Flandrischen Copiar specified, among other things, how to deal with such mishaps as lost cargo, undisciplined crew members, and piracy and privateering, and it spelled out the related liability issues with regard to bottomry loans, the joint ownership of vessels, and the liability of shipmasters, shipowners, and freighters toward each other. This emphasis on maritime issues in the Flandrischen Copiar confirms the earlier documented concern of the aldermen of the Kontor with issues of violence and opportunism in shipping operations between Flanders and Germany.[137]

For our present purpose it is the pragmatic mixture of shipping rules from different legal traditions that matters, however. The inclusion in the register of the maritime law of Damme is a clear indication of the German willingness to use the Flemish edition of the Rôles d'Oléron in case of disputes. At the same time, the fact that the Alterleute set additional rules, specific to the Kontor in Bruges, shows that this maritime law was no sacrosanct code but a legal tool that was adapted to local circumstances if necessary.[138] The way the Flandrischen Copiar was compiled— with disjoint bits and pieces of legislation—also shows that the German aldermen at the time had no intention of consolidating a finite set of contracting rules for financial and commercial transactions. Rather they made an effort to supplement whatever customary rules were regularly applied by German merchants with specific regulations of potentially contentious issues.

The obvious explanation for the lack of universal contracting rules in medieval and early modern Europe is the Continent's legal and political fragmentation. This certainly applied to Flanders, Brabant, and Holland, where towns could develop their own local customs independent of the central rulers.[139] For instance, Bruges retained its legal autonomy vis-à-vis the Count of Flanders until at least the fourteenth century: *stadsrecht* trumped *landrecht*.[140] In the fifteenth century the Burgundian dukes were able to set country-wide rules for the herring fisheries, linen production,

---

[137] See chapter 6.

[138] The bylaws of the German Hanse in London, Bergen, and Novgorod did not constitute a uniform legal code, either. Rather, they specified the proceedings to be followed by the merchant community and its leaders in case of disputes between members. Although this allowed for the resolution of conflicts between traders from different cities, the bylaws did not stipulate contracting rules. Besides, each of the four major branches of the Hanse had its own procedures. Dollinger 1964: 125–32, 489–90.

[139] See, for Amsterdam, Smit 1914: 22; Carasso-Kok and Verkerk 2004: 206.

[140] De Schepper and Cauchies 1993: 142; Godding and de Smidt 1980: 179; Gilliodts-Van Severen 1883–85: 251, 436.

and mint production, but these hardly amounted to an international commercial code, not even to a country-wide code.[141] More important— but of a much later date—was the supplementing of the maritime law of Visby with two placards issued by Charles V and Philip II, in 1551 and 1570, respectively. These new ordinances regulated marine insurance, as well as the armament, rigging, freighting, and maintenance of ships by all merchants, regardless of their nationality.[142]

By then urban authorities had already gone a long way toward the creation of a more comprehensive set of rules for contracting between merchants. Around 1300 towns in Flanders and Brabant began to record their customary law.[143] In 1413 the Amsterdam magistrate laid down prevailing customs and town ordinances in what is now the city's oldest keurboek (book of regulations).[144] Their continuous efforts to align local customs to business practice are most apparent from the frequent use of turben produced by local and foreign merchants, but also notaries, brokers, and attorneys.[145] The turbe differed from ordinary testimonies by witnesses in that it had legal force. It was common practice for local and foreign merchants in Antwerp and Amsterdam to deliver such testimonies on a variety of financial and commercial matters. From the fifteenth century both cities accommodated this legislation from below through the recording of the turben in official registers.[146]

Although legal records from Bruges in the mid-fifteenth century show foreign merchants referring to the city's local customs to support their claims, it was only in Antwerp that local customs seem to have gained universal acceptance by local and foreign residents.[147] Following an ordinance of Charles V, the Antwerp magistrate edited the *maniere van procederen* in 1532 and a full set of local customs in 1545. This first edition was revised and extended in 1570, 1582, and 1609. The foreword of the *Costumen* of 1582 is very clear about the rationale behind publication.

[141] Godding and de Smidt 1980: 179, 181; de Schepper and Cauchies 1993: 144–48; Breen 1902: 420–21.

[142] De Schepper and Cauchies 1993: 147; Wachter 1639: 90–92; Asaert 1976a.

[143] De Schepper and Cauchies 1993: 145–47.

[144] Breen 1902: vi–vii; Oldewelt 1967; Godding and de Smidt 1980: 181.

[145] In Antwerp, in 1571, the consul of the Genoese nation, together with other merchants, confirmed the terms of payments used for bills of exchange (De Smedt 1940–41: 23–24). In 1574 twelve Spanish merchants made a deposition concerning life insurances (Goris 1925: 287–88).

[146] For Antwerp: De Ruysscher 2006: 435; De Ruysscher 2009c: 31–98; Puttevils 2012: 219, 278–79. Amsterdam's magistrate kept a *compostboeck* with turben from the fifteenth century onward, but this register has not survived (Oldewelt 1967). The text of some declarations survives in seventeenth- and eighteenth-century collections of local customs, e.g., Noordkerk 1748: 2:502, 536.

[147] Gilliodt van Severen 1901–2: 1:82.

It was considered too time-consuming for merchants to mount a turbe every time the validity of a specific commercial practice had to be confirmed. The edition was meant to once and for all end

> the great confusion and manifold frivolous trials, protestations, and unbearable costs which parties that have to produce *turben* have to make; and to prevent other such irregularities and inconveniences; and to provide the community of this city with a certain base or rule to regulate those who are guilty of breaking the said rules.[148]

The editor added that the customs would be distributed among all the town magistrates and the entire legal profession—a measure that would give these officials the necessary background to take on responsibilities as arbiters and judges. To be sure, the officially edited customs were never the only legal texts available to merchants in Antwerp. Besides the obvious Roman law tracts and the maritime law of Damme, various more popular books were in circulation that informed them about prevailing laws and customs.[149]

Some historians have claimed that foreign merchants in Antwerp had fewer rights than local citizens, which would of course have given them some reason to continue to apply their own rules in consular courts.[150] There is little evidence for this, however. Most rules that explicitly referred to foreign merchants were to their benefit. Besides, the foreign nations were consulted when existing rules were adapted or amplified. For example, in 1558, before the implementation of an imperial ordinance on marine insurances, town officials consulted with the merchants from Portugal, Spain, Florence, Germany, Lucca, and the Low Countries.[151] Antwerp insurance law as such was largely based on Mediterranean customs.[152] Finally, legislators curtailed only commercial practices that were believed to harm other merchants, the local food supply, or foreign policy. Well-known examples include malpractices in marine insurance and forward trading in grain—both in the 1550s.

Amsterdam worked in similar ways toward the creation of a uniform set of rules. Already in the fifteenth century the magistrate treated all merchants, regardless of their origin, as equal before the law.[153] At the end of the sixteenth century, when the fall of Antwerp led Flemish, Por-

[148]*Rechten ende costuymen van Antwerpen* (Cologne 1597).

[149]Notably the *Practijke criminele* and *Practijke Civile* of Philips Wielant, a councilor with the Raad van Vlaanderen and the Grand Conseil of Malines, were often reprinted and even spread to Germany and Holland: Godding and de Smidt 1980: 177–78.

[150]Van Houtte 1961: 276.

[151]Génard 1882: 57–58.

[152]Génard 1882: 54–56; de Groote 1976.

[153]Breen 1902: 159–61, 222; Noordkerk 1748: 1:33–46; 2:495–502, 577.

tuguese, English, and German merchants to settle in Amsterdam, the city made determined efforts to adjust its customary law to changing business practices. The town magistrate invited Flemish immigrants to testify to the rules followed in the Scheldt port, for instance in marine insurance and exchange operations.[154] In several turben in Amsterdam's *compostboeck* these merchants from the southern provinces figured prominently. Notarial deeds also attest to the consultation of Flemish traders about business practices in southern provinces.[155] Indeed, the Antwerp Customs of 1582 were reprinted several times in Amsterdam, either separately or in combination with other legal texts.[156]

These combined editions, published by private editors from the late sixteenth century onward, also reveal other sources of Amsterdam's commercial customs. In addition to the most recent version of local customs, they included placards of the central authorities, the maritime law of Visby, ordinances of Charles V and Philip II, the customs of Antwerp, and prevailing procedural law.[157] Collections of maritime and insurance law also existed, including the sea law of Visby, the ordinances of Charles V and Philip II, and various local customs from different parts of the Dutch Republic.[158] Later in the century followed separate publication of turben by merchants concerning specific commercial practices.[159] Finally there was a six-volume edition of legal advice by professional jurists working for the Court of Holland.[160] These *Hollandsche Consultatiën* (1645–66) clearly demonstrate that lawyers of this higher court based their opinions

[154] Wachter 1639: 108; Oldewelt 1967; Asser 1987: 105–6, with references to the older literature.

[155] See, for instance, ACA NA 1967/325 (August 14, 1609).

[156] *Rechten ende costumen van Antvverpen*, published in Amsterdam in 1613 by Hendrick Barentsz; similar editions printed in Cologne and Hamburg may also have circulated in Amsterdam: Goris 1925: 34.

[157] Among them are the following editions (with titles abbreviated): *Handt-vesten ende privilegien van Amstelredam* (Amsterdam: Barent Adriaensz, Utrecht: Herman van Borculo, 1597 [1599]); *Handt-vesten ende Privilegien van Amstelredam* (Amsterdam: Jacob Pietersz Wachter, 1639); *Receuil van verscheyde Keuren, en Costumen. Midtsgaders Maniere van Procederen binnen de stadt Amsterdam* (Amsterdam: Gerrit Jansz, 1644; 2nd ed.: Amsterdam: Jan Hendricks, 1656); *Hand-vesten, privilegien, octroyen, costumen en willekeuren der Stad Amstelredam* (Amsterdam: Otto Barentsz. Smient and Jodocus Smient, 1662 [1663]). In addition there were more general texts that circulated in the merchant community, the best known of which was *'t Boeck der Zee-rechten*, first published in Amsterdam in 1648 (Lichtenauer 1956: 66–67).

[158] *Zee-rechten, inhoudende dat Oudste en Hoogste Water-recht, dat de Gemeene Kooplieden en Schippers hebben gemaekt in Wisbuy, etc.* (Amsterdam: Laurens Gunter, 1695).

[159] *Verzameling* 1793–1804.

[160] Given that the motivation of verdicts of the Hof van Holland and the Hoge Raad was never made public (Asser 1987: 110), the *Consultatien* (1657–66) is the principal source reflecting then prevailing legal opinions on commercial matters.

on a combination of Roman law, local and foreign customs, Habsburg ordinances, and Italian and Spanish mercantile law.[161]

To be sure, neither the reliance on different legal traditions nor the publication of compilations of contracting rules was typical for the Low Countries. After 1532 the mercantile court of Genoa applied contracting rules from a variety of sources, including local customs, Roman law, and the maritime law of the Consulado del Mar.[162] In Venice, in 1553, Benvenuto Stracca published *De Mercature*, a treatise that gave a survey of extant laws pertaining to long-distance trade, albeit without any intention of consolidating a universal commercial code. The concept of a border-crossing lex mercatoria was a seventeenth-century idea, promoted by English merchants who struggled against the king's attempts to obtain jurisdiction in commercial matters.[163] The most prominent advocate was Gerard Malynes, who in 1622 published *Consvetvdo, vel Lex Mercatoria* (The Ancient Law Merchant). On closer inspection his book is not a comprehensive legal code, but rather a survey of local and foreign customs, not unlike the collections of commercial laws and customs that circulated in Italy and the Low Countries in the seventeenth century.[164] In a similar vein, half a century later, the French *Ordonnances sur le Commerce de Negotians & Marchands* explicated the legal power of merchant books, the central role of arbitration in the resolution of conflicts, and the primary place of local courts in commercial litigation.[165] It was surely no coincidence that the compiler of the *Ordonnances*, Jacques Savary, was the first of several French writers to publish lengthy books on commercial practices in the Dutch Republic, and Amsterdam in particular.[166]

The preceding discussion should have made it abundantly clear that legal developments in the Low Countries in the sixteenth and seventeenth centuries never amounted to the creation of a lex mercatoria—in either substance or procedure. There is, however, an unmistakable international dimension to them. In the seventeenth century the contracting rules ap-

---

[161] See, for instance, the legal advice on the nature of partnerships: *Consultatien* 1657–66; 2:233, 277, 462; 3:217–19; 4:513. On shipmasters: 3:584–85; 6:537. On insolvencies: 1:328, 397–99, 413, 358; 2:74–75, 84, 238, 456, 529; 3:120, 536; 4:10ff., 184; 5:371, 600, 752; 6:9, 11, 12, 583. The actual influence of this legal advice on commercial customs in Amsterdam would require a separate and perhaps impossible analysis since Amsterdam's magistrate had the right to issue its own ordinances without reference to rules established by provincial or central courts: 3:238.

[162] Doehaerd 1941:1:146–48.

[163] Basile et al. 1998: 124.

[164] Munro 2003: 555. Note also that it was not until 1748 that a complete edition of Amsterdam's privileges, laws, and customs first appeared in print: Noordkerk 1748. See Oldewelt (1967) for a critical evaluation of this edition and its forerunners.

[165] The *Ordonnances* were published two years later in Amsterdam: Phoonsen 1676: 250.

[166] Jansen 1946.

plied in the Low Countries were exported to other parts of Europe, just like Italian and Spanish rules found their way to Bruges and Antwerp in previous centuries. In other words, the century-long concentration of foreign merchants turned the Low Countries into a *trait d'union* among Mediterranean, Northern European, and Anglo-Saxon legal traditions. Cities like Antwerp and Amsterdam obviously had their share in legal improvements, but the principal contribution of the Low Countries to the development of European commercial law was the amalgamation and legal acceptance of a wide range of already-existing contracting practices.[167]

Conclusion

Merchants at issue with trading partners valued private solutions that strained business relationships as little as possible. To avoid legal proceedings, the foreign merchants in Bruges, Antwerp, and Amsterdam put personal pressure on their agents, relied on arbiters to mediate, or simply took their losses. These private order solutions functioned in the shadow of the law, however. Merchants may have been very reluctant to go to court because of the time it took, the damage it could do to their reputation, or the uncertainty of the outcome, but all their letters and contracts were cast in terms facilitating the remote possibility of legal action. Thus, for all merchants trading at arm's length, regardless of their regional origin, access to a third party to resolve commercial disputes was indispensable to prevent agency problems.

The creation of a legal system to meet this requirement was a major achievement, not only from an organizational point of view, but also because the nature of contested transactions changed over time. Itinerant traders became permanent residents, merchants influenced each other's contracting practices, and as trade expanded in new directions they developed new contracting forms that upset conventional wisdom. In other words, securing contract enforcement at the lowest possible cost required the continuous adaptation of legal institutions, and this was exactly the strength of commercial cities like Bruges, Antwerp, and Amsterdam. Their legal autonomy allowed the town magistrates to adapt the local legal system to the changing demands of the mercantile community, and because they were keen to attract as many international traders as possible, they did so time and again.

In the medieval period, when trade was concentrated at the fairs of Flanders and Brabant, the aldermen's benches of Bruges and Antwerp

[167] De Ruysscher 2009a: 470–79.

committed to the speedy resolution of disputed spot transactions, very much like the proceedings dubbed lex mercatoria in English local courts. As foreign merchants began to settle for longer periods in the Low Countries, their home governments, often but not always cities, delegated legal authority to the community leaders abroad. The host cities in turn accepted the establishment of extraterritorial jurisdictions to allow the foreign consuls to adjudicate conflicts among fellow countrymen. These consulates functioned well for a long period, but eventually transactions between merchants from different cities and countries increased, raising new issues about which contracting rules to apply. The cities responded to this challenge in three ways. They stimulated the use of arbiters to allow merchants to apply the rules of their choice, they tried to incorporate as much as possible foreign mercantile usage in the local customs, and they set up subsidiary courts to adjudicate specific categories of commercial and financial conflicts such as marine insurance and insolvencies.

Thus Bruges, Antwerp, and Amsterdam were able to turn to their advantage the legal fragmentation caused by their own autonomy and that of other cities, through a series of legal interventions that teach important lessons about the dynamics of institutional change in international trade. The process of legal adaptation was set in motion by the expansion of trade and the related growth of a very diverse group of resident foreign merchants. This created a demand for legal support that surpassed the abilities of separate community leaders, but was met by town magistrates who wanted to reinforce their city's position as a major hub in the commercial networks of international traders. The legal changes were relatively inexpensive for these cities because they were designed to support private contracting and minimize formal intervention, while the actual improvements were grafted onto an already-existing legal apparatus whose costs were habitually deferred through modest fees paid by litigants. The upshot was the marginalization of the foreign nations whose members no longer needed the wide range of commercial, legal, social, and religious services they offered—a process of functional loss identical to that of the cities' hostellers in the same period.[168]

---

[168]Compare Mancur Olson's observation that collective organizations that offer multiple services to their members are more successful (Olson 1965: 73).

CHAPTER 6

The Protection of Trade

EVEN IF BRUGES, ANTWERP, AND AMSTERDAM DID EVERYTHING THEY could to support private contracting between international traders, the agency problems that issued from Europe's legal fragmentation may have been a minor concern compared with the violent threats merchants faced.[1] Traders traveling over land to distant markets were confronted with theft, robbery, or even outright warfare. Violence was at least as disruptive in maritime trade. Between the fourteenth and eighteenth centuries privateering was the principle means by which Europe's maritime powers tried to harm their adversaries.[2] In peacetime privateers often turned pirates and continued to pry on shipping. Merchants who got their money or merchandise safely to the place of destination might still fall victim to crime, corruption, confiscations, monetary manipulation, social unrest, religious persecution, or outright civil war. Yet, despite these violent threats international trade expanded.

There is no obvious solution to this paradox of violence and growth. Douglass North and others point to the rise of strong, centralized states with the ability to raise standing armies and navies as the source of improved protection.[3] This may be true for England and France in the eighteenth century, but in the late medieval period princes had to acknowledge the military superiority of city-states like Venice and Genoa.[4] Further evidence for a key role of local governments comes from the towns of the German Hanse. Their individual power was very limited indeed, but collectively the Hanseatic League managed to outfit large fleets to fight pirates and foreign competitors. In the sixteenth and seventeenth centuries commercial cities continued to have much influence on the military protection of merchants because they controlled a considerable share of fiscal revenues and a large stock of commercial wealth, both of which were indispensable for the funding of their sovereigns' warfare.[5] The cities' financial power did not automatically lead to the adequate protection

---

[1] Spufford 2002: 115–27; Horden and Purcell 2000: 154–59; Findlay and O'Rourke 2007: 187–94; Braudel 1949: 240–58, 661–722; Rosenthal and Bin Wong 2011: 92–93.

[2] Coornaert 1961: 1:59–61; Tenenti 1959; Pérotin-Dumon 1991: 211; Hillmann and Gathmann 2011.

[3] Bernard 1972: 314–15; North and Thomas 1973: 91–101; Glete 2002: 2–3, 214–15.

[4] Lane 1958, 1966.

[5] Tilly 1990.

of trade, however. On the one hand, commercial cities that resisted the centralizing efforts of their sovereigns could run into great difficulties, witness the Low Countries where the Flemish Revolt (1483–92) ended Bruges's commercial hegemony and the Dutch Revolt (1568–88) shifted the economic center from Antwerp to Amsterdam. On the other, when local elites had a very strong say in the central government, as in London or Amsterdam, the state's protective efforts increased together with their use of violence to obtain commercial advantages. As rival states repaid in kind, the safety of merchants from both sides came into play.

In this chapter and the next we analyze the protective measures of merchants and rulers in Bruges, Antwerp, and Amsterdam to develop a new explanation for the paradox of violence and growth. An important part of this explanation is the ability of merchants to deal with losses, a topic we will turn to in chapter 7. First, I demonstrate how the existence of an international network of commercial cities created strong incentives for local and central governments to offer protection to international traders to enhance the position of individual cities in this network. But I also show in this chapter that imminent changes in a city's position in the international urban hierarchy could lead to the massive use of force. In particular, I show that during the Flemish Revolt the Roman king, and future Holy Roman emperor, Maximilian I did not hesitate to come down hard on Bruges because he knew that its merchants would relocate elsewhere in his territories, that is, Antwerp. Conversely, in the last third of the sixteenth century Philip II put forth enormous military effort to restore his control over the entire Low Countries and retain Europe's principal market within his territory.

Merchants in Arms

Bruges emerged as the principal port of Northwestern Europe in a period of great political and military upheaval. At the turn of the fourteenth century warfare between the king of France and various German princes ended the primacy of the Champagne fairs, forcing merchants from Italy, Germany, France, England, and Flanders to find other places to exchange their goods. Thus began a regular traffic of galleys from Venice and Genoa, and later also Florence, to England and the Low Countries. Bruges in particular was a very attractive place because of its overland and overseas connections with all major markets in Northwestern Europe, a considerable local demand for foreign goods, and a ready supply of high-quality export products. But as commodity flows thickened in the North Sea area, political and economic rivalries coalesced and the risk of violent assaults against international traders increased.

To signal commitment to the protection of merchants and their goods, the city of Bruges and the Count of Flanders issued safe-conducts.[6] Between 1250 and 1450 virtually every group of foreign traders, even those who merely intended to come to Bruges, were promised free passage and safeguard against arbitrary confiscations and arrests. German merchants received such paper promises already in 1253, followed by traders from La Rochelle and Saint-Jean d'Angély (1331), Nuremburg (1362), and Castile (1366) in the fourteenth century and England (1408), Portugal (1411), and Scotland (1427) in the fifteenth.[7] The rulers of neighboring Brabant made similar promises to German and English merchants around 1300, and as early as 1243 merchants from Lübeck and Hamburg were given letters of safe-conduct by the Count of Holland, who hoped they would use Dutch inland waterways to reach Bruges.[8] In return for these safe-conducts merchants from Flanders, Holland, and Brabant were promised protection in Germany, England, and France.[9]

The safe-conducts did not suffice to prevent violent assaults, however. As we saw in chapter 3 Bruges, Antwerp, and Amsterdam were able to police their local market effectively, but they lacked the financial and military resources to protect merchants traveling to and from their cities. Instead the magistrates relied on their economic attraction as an incentive for neighboring rulers to secure the safety of traders outside their city walls. They applied what was known as the freedom of the fair. Antwerp, for instance, threatened to arrest the subjects of any town, domain, or state where visitors of the fairs of Brabant suffered theft, robbery, or arbitrary confiscations.[10] None of them would be allowed to trade at the fairs until reparations had been made. At the beginning of each fair the town authorities posted the names of those who were excluded from the freedom of the fairs. It was a powerful instrument to secure the protection of individual traders because the value of the money and goods they carried was typically much smaller than the combined loss that artisans and traders from various parts of the Low Countries would suffer if they could not visit Bruges or Antwerp. Therefore many local rulers felt the pressure of their local business communities to protect the property of traveling merchants.[11]

The rivalry between towns in this regional trade network did not cause a breakdown of trade between them because they all needed the supply

[6] Stützel 1998; Craeybeckx 1958: 108; Blockmans 1978: 481–83; Gilliodts-Van Severen 1871–85: 2:139; 4:495–500.
[7] Jenks 1995: 513–14, 521–22.
[8] Höhlbaum et al. 1876–1939: 1:106–7; Smit 1914: 2–3, 25–27.
[9] Stützel 1998: 57; de Boer 1996: 129, 147; Craeybeckx 1958: 123; Noordkerk 1748: 1:chaps. 19, 51–61.
[10] *Antwerpse Costumen* (1582), title 49; *Antwerpse Costumen* (1609), 48–50.
[11] See, e.g., Harreld 2004: 110.

and demand of each other's goods and services. This created a relatively stable equilibrium that was further enhanced by occasional interventions from the central government to uphold the freedom of the fairs. In 1410, for instance, the Duke of Brabant intervened on behalf of Antwerp to lift the arrest by a local lord of merchandise destined for the Bamis fair.[12] But even Antwerp was not faultless, of course. Twenty years earlier, in May 1391, several merchants from Louvain, traveling to the fair of Antwerp, had been arrested in Malines to make good Louvain's arrears in interest payments owed to citizens of Malines. As was to be expected, the magistrate of Antwerp reacted with arrests of Malines citizens, but then the magistrate accidently seized merchandise from traders who were not from Malines. Philip the Bold intervened and confirmed the shielding of fair visitors from arrests for debts originating outside the fairs.[13] The compliance of individual towns with the freedom of the fairs was important because otherwise the rulers of Flanders, Brabant, and Holland had few means to secure the safety of foreigners traveling through their territories. They did appoint bailiffs in towns and countryside to persecute criminals, but they lacked the resources to effectively police roads and rivers.[14] In the mid-fourteenth century German merchants deemed the security risks in Flanders big enough to claim the right to apprehend robbers themselves. After long deliberations the count and the Four Members accepted, and the article was added to the privileges of 1360.[15]

For the physical protection of their persons and goods merchants traveling in the Low Countries were mostly left to their own devices. They carried arms, moved in groups, and sometimes even organized their own armed escorts.[16] In 1281 Bruges confirmed the right of German and other merchants to carry weapons, and the Duke of Brabant allowed English traders to be armed in 1296.[17] In 1421 a merchant from London was allowed "to travel with five armored men, swords, and other weapons" through the towns and villages of Holland and Zeeland.[18] Merchants in arms, however, are not very inviting when it comes to the actual exchange of money and goods. Some of the more colorful descriptions of day-to-

[12] *Clementynboeck*: 78–79.
[13] Bartier and Nieuwenhuysen 1965: 2, 424–26.
[14] Blockmans 1978: 460–62.
[15] Gilliodts-Van Severen 1871–85: 2:53; Stützel 1998: 34–35. The Flemish towns were not responsible for the brigandage and murder committed by subjects of the French kings, even though Flanders was officially still a fief of the French king. German merchants and the cities of Flanders could prosecute these criminals in Flanders, however: Gilliodts-Van Severen 1871–85: 3:224–28, 232; see also Diegerick 1854: 2:268–71.
[16] Herborn 1984; Müller 1907; Spufford 2002: 19; Van Houtte 1982: 173; Craeybeckx 1958: 54–67, 74–76; Brulez 1962: 144.
[17] Stützel 1998: 47; Gilliodts-Van Severen 1871–85: 2:50, 79; Prims 1927–49: 2:2.
[18] Van Mieris 1753–56: 4:594.

day trade in Bruges, Antwerp, and Amsterdam suggest that feelings could run high between traders, and there was little use in adding knife fights to the occasional scoldings and scuffles.[19] From very early on, therefore, cities tried to enforce their local monopoly of violence. Shortly after 1300 Antwerp obliged all visitors to lay down any weapons they were carrying upon their arrival in town. The additional rule that hostellers had to inform their guests about the obligation—and notify the authorities in case visitors did carry arms—suggests merchants had to comply as well.[20] In fourteenth-century Bruges the carrying of arms, concealed or open, except knives with blades shorter than three palms, was also forbidden.[21]

VIOLENCE AT SEA

Robbers and thieves posed a real threat to merchants traveling around Europe, but this was a minor concern compared to the violence that resulted from the Continent's political fragmentation. Over time European markets may have become increasingly integrated, but that did not end political rivalries. Armed conflicts between England, France, Spain, and many other European countries were rife. Land routes were made unsafe by military campaigns and pillaging troops, while overseas trade was threatened by naval warfare, in particular privateering raids.[22] Almost always the aggression of one ruler led to retaliation by another and their attacks back and forth were often difficult to stop. The involvement of the rulers of the Low Countries in many of these conflicts created additional

[19] Goris 1925: 109–10; Jacob 2006: 79, 81.

[20] *Keurboeck metten doppen* (ACA PK 94), 2. Repeated prohibitions in 1386, 1394, 1395, 1410, and 1416: van Gerven 1999: 197–98. For the sixteenth century: *Antwerpse Costumen* (1545), title 2, art. 1; see also *Antwerpse Costumen* (1582), title 41, art. 101; Van Uytven 1982: 216; Jacob 2006: 164n44. In Amsterdam strangers were not allowed to carry arms from the first half of the sixteenth century: Boomgaard 1992: 212.

[21] Gilliodts-Van Severen 1871–85: 6:352.

[22] Privateers should not be cast as villains too easily. In many cases the hunt for spoils was as much a business as anything else. In Amsterdam privateering missions were organized just like any other commercial venture. For instance, the Walloon merchant Pieter Denijs, otherwise active as a brewer, civet trader, and general wholesale merchant, was active in at least eleven shipping companies that privateered between 1622 and 1632 (courtesy Ruud Koopman): ACA Notarial Archives 258/349, January 24, 1623; NA 221/9v, May 30, 1623; NA 717/459, June 28, 1623; NA 717/627, August 19, 1623; NA 719/219, June 18, 1625; NA 721/319, September 17, 1627; NA 723/436, January 5, 1629; NA 725/299, August 6, 1631; NA 26/416, August 5, 1632. At least one ship sailed on "free bounty"; six others had official letters of mark. Three of the latter ships made no profit for their owners because the shipmasters did not respect its commission and damaged several "free ships," after which the Admiralty repossessed their prizes (ACA NA 719/219, June 18, 1625; NA 725/299, August 6, 1631).

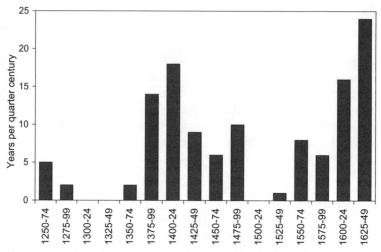

FIGURE 6.1. Number of years per quarter century in which privateers damaged the property of one or more communities of foreign merchants in Bruges, Antwerp, or Amsterdam, 1250–1650
Source: Appendix A.

safety risks for foreign merchants in Bruges, Antwerp, and Amsterdam. The danger of naval attacks was obviously biggest for merchants whose governments fought the Burgundian and Habsburg rulers—and after 1580, the Dutch Republic—but even neutral traders in possession of safe-conducts from both warring parties were not completely safe.

Privateering was the favorite weapon of rulers in late medieval Europe because it allowed the outsourcing of military operations to private parties whose remuneration depended on their own efforts. We cannot calculate the actual losses suffered from these operations, but we can estimate the number of years in which the trade of foreign merchants in the Low Countries was disrupted by privateers (Figure 6.1). Before the Dukes of Burgundy came to power in the 1380s, international warfare interfered with trade on average once every five years. This incidence of violence was low in comparison with the Burgundian period, which may explain why so many alien traders came to Bruges in the late thirteenth and early fourteenth century. But even the increase in privateering raids caused by the involvement of the house of Burgundy in the European power struggle did not stop merchants from coming to the Low Countries. In the fifteenth century leading international firms continued to manage their operations from Bruges, and at the same time Antwerp emerged as a major market in its own right. This commercial expansion in a period of increased warfare suggests that merchants and rulers found ways to reduce the risk of violent assaults to a level low enough to allow trade to continue.

When it came to the actual protection of their ships, foreign merchants had little to expect from the rulers of Low Countries. In the fourteenth century Flemish shipmasters occasionally sailed in convoys coordinated by the water bailiff of Sluis, but neither the cities nor the count were willing to finance armed escorts.[23] Military protection was offered only under very special circumstances, such as during a particularly violent episode of the war between England and the Dukes of Burgundy at the turn of the fifteenth century. In 1400 Bruges paid 80 percent of the costs of a garrison of one hundred soldiers and three ships in the harbor of Sluis to prevent raids on merchantmen by privateers from England and Zeeland. When the violence did not stop in 1402, more troops were sent, and Sluis's water bailiff and his aides began to travel the coast to punish wrongdoers.[24] In the long run these efforts were unsustainable, however, and already in 1401 Bruges began to push hard for a peace agreement with England.

While Bruges's means to protect merchants outside the city walls were extremely limited, foreign visitors did receive military support from their cities of origin.[25] Venice is the most notable example for it built its own galleys, equipped them, determined the routes to take, and then sold cargo space to individual merchants.[26] In Genoa the authorities did not own any ships, but they did appoint an admiral to supervise the galleys' and carracks' operations at sea. In the fifteenth century Florentine merchants used communal fleets modeled on the Venetian example, although they also shipped merchandise in private galleys to Flanders and England.[27] The Spanish wool fleets were financed and organized by the consulados of Bilbao and Burgos, who secured the proper functioning of their convoys by delegating the authority to discipline shipmasters and their crew to consuls in Bruges.[28]

The importance of coordination by the home government is also very clear from the attempts of Lübeck and other Hanseatic cities to fight the Vitalienbrüder at the end of the fourteenth century.[29] These privateers,

[23] Asaert 1976b: 63; Blockmans 1978: 450–54.

[24] Gilliodts-Van Severen 1871–85: 3:458, 462–63; Paviot 1995: 249.

[25] Horden and Purcell 2000: 157; Häpke 1908: 157; Vandewalle 2002: 27–30; Goris 1925: 254; Jenks 1992b: 1:305–20; Heers 1961: 270–71, 300–307.

[26] The older literature on the Venetian galley system is summarized in Mallett 1967: 17.

[27] Just like in Venice, the actual operation of the communal fleets between 1421 and 1480 was mostly auctioned off to private entrepreneurs, who made their money by charging freighters for the cargo space they hired. The state-appointed *consoli del mare*, however, supervised the building and equipment of the galleys, set the rules for their operations, decided on who was to hire cargo space, and determined departure times and sailing routes. Mallett 1967: 17–22, 82–103. See also Watson 1961, 1962.

[28] Gilliodts-Van Severen 1871–85: 2:130–39.

[29] The following is based on Puhle 1992. See also Smit 1914: 145–48 and Paviot 1995: 236.

first recruited by the Duke of Mecklenburg to fight the king of Denmark in 1376, posed a major threat to fishing and shipping in the Baltic up until 1398. A first attempt to equip *Friedeschiffe* (literally: peace ships) failed in 1379, but in following years men-of-war paid for by the Hanse towns did escort convoys of merchantmen on various occasions. Yet a plan to put a stop to the menace with a war fleet of forty ships fell apart in 1394 because the Prussian quarter—with Amsterdam in its wake—refused to contribute its share. Only in 1398, after a truce had been negotiated between the warring parties, did the Teutonic Order manage to chase the Vitalienbrüder off Gotland, robbing them of an operational basis and an outlet for their bounty. Still, it took two more naval expeditions and another four years to apprehend the remaining pirates on the North Sea.

The operations of the Vitalienbrüder marked the beginning of a secular rise in privateering in the North Sea. From the 1380s onward warfare between France and England, Lübeck's attempts to further German commercial interests, and in particular the renewed involvement of Flanders in international politics, all compromised the safety of merchantmen sailing to and from the Low Countries.[30] Single ships were obviously most vulnerable, but even convoys were at risk. In 1387, for instance, English ships attacked a Flemish fleet, allegedly carrying nine thousand tons of wine, en route from La Rochelle to Sluis. Some ships were destroyed, others carried off to England. The Count of Flanders responded by banning English traders, which in turn led to reprisals touching merchantmen from France, Flanders, Germany, Brittany, and Spain.[31] There were numerous incidents of this kind. For example, in 1419 a fleet of forty vessels sailing from Flanders to France was captured by Castilian corsairs.[32] In 1449 an English fleet captured more than 100 Dutch and Hanseatic merchantmen off the coast of France.[33] The ships from the Netherlands were released, but the Hanseatic ships were brought to England. In 1458 eighteen vessels from Lübeck were taken by the English governor of Calais.[34]

Political conflicts were not the only source of violence against trade. Commercial cities also took up arms to defend their position in international markets. Such deliberate use of force to advance commercial interests is clear from the conflict between Denmark and the Hanse in the 1430s over the Danish introduction of the Sound Toll for ships passing through the Sound. To force the Danish king to lift the toll, Lübeck attempted a naval blockade of the entry to the Baltic Sea but failed and

---

[30]Thielemans 1966.
[31]Gilliodts-Van Severen 1871–85: 2:188–227, 471–73; 3:95–96, 281–85, 454; 4:61; 9:11; Murray 2005: 245, 276.
[32]Craeybeckx 1958: 115–17.
[33]Thielemans 1966: 336.
[34]Dollinger 1964: 373.

subsequently reverted to the isthmus of Holstein to continue their trade with the Low Countries. This was unsustainable, however, as Dutch shipmasters took over the German trade with Scandinavian countries. Two years after a peace with Denmark was signed in 1436, war broke out between Holland and the Hanse. Officially this was a campaign by the Dukes of Burgundy, but it was entirely financed and organized by the towns of Holland.[35] Lübeck warships sank or captured various Dutch merchantmen, and Holland attacked the Lübeck fleet on at least three occasions. Eventually, in 1440, a Dutch fleet of seventeen or eighteen vessels managed to force its way into the Baltic Sea, and the subsequent Peace of Copenhagen (1441) secured free entry for all Dutch ships.

Privateering wars also affected merchants ashore.[36] In 1371 the Count of Flanders ordered the seizure of thirty-nine English ships in Sluis following attacks by English pirates and the destruction of a Flemish fleet of twenty-two ships off the coast of France. Most cargo found in the ships in Sluis turned out to be from Flemish, Italian, and German merchants, but the confiscation still yielded 8,340 pounds sterling of English property. Merchants from Genoa were arrested in Flanders in 1409 after Genoese attacks on Burgundian troops.[37] In 1453, at the very end of the Hundred Years' War, various English merchants were arrested in Hulst in retaliation for English attacks on Flemish ships carrying wine from La Rochelle.[38] In 1459 or 1460 a former captain of Burgundian men-of-war seized Genoese merchandise in Middelburg to recoup losses from the capture of one of these ships by Genoa in 1445.[39] In 1476 Genoese merchants, who were suspected of supporting the king of France in his struggle with Charles the Bold, were expelled from Bruges rather than arrested.[40]

Such local reprisals were potentially very disruptive, and as the rulers of the Low Countries became more involved in international politics they made firmer commitments to the safety of enemy subjects. Already

[35] Blockmans and Prevenier 1999: 93–94.

[36] Gilliodts-Van Severen 1871–85: 3:281–85; Paviot 1995: 202, 213, 228, 236; Watson 1961: 1088; Van Rompaey 1973: 189. Not every attachment of foreign goods was related to privateering, however. In 1377 Bruges's town magistrate attached German goods after it learned that the Germans were planning to leave the city in protest of the city's refusal to assume liability for the debts of local money changers. In 1443 and again in 1444 the Duchess of Burgundy, Isabelle of Portugal held up the Florentine galleys for the Florentine Republic, still owed interest on its Monte shares to her brother. In 1448 the Florentine fleet was detained in Sluis by Portuguese merchants, who claimed forty-five casks of sugar laden in the galleys. Mallett 1967: 88–89, 91.

[37] Gilliodts-Van Severen 1871–85: 4:342.

[38] Slootmans 1985: 1:99.

[39] Paviot 1995: 215–16.

[40] Goris 1925: 75.

in 1307 German merchants had been promised forty days to leave with all their belongings in case a conflict arose between Flanders and the Holy Roman Emperor or any of the *Reichsfürsten*.[41] Count Louis of Male (r. 1346–84) committed to a safe departure of English, Castilian, and Hanseatic merchants in case of violent threats.[42] Philip the Bold (r. 1384–1404) and his successors confirmed these privileges and created a similar possibility for merchants from Aragon, Portugal, Scotland, Ireland, Genoa, and Venice. Princes at war with each other also exercised restraint toward neutral traders—or at least they tried. A treaty signed in 1296 between the king of France and the Count of Holland already stipulated that neither party would attack "marchaanz sanz armes."[43] To protect neutral traders, the Dukes of Burgundy issued letters of mark that instructed privateers to attack enemy ships only.[44] In the words of the Great Privilege of 1477, "[I]t is prohibited to stop merchantmen on the pretext of letters of mark, countermark, seizure, or reprisal, except the accused, and in no way the innocent and guiltless."[45]

Bruges's dependence on the presence of foreign merchants made its magistrate weary of the dynastic ambitions of the Counts of Flanders. For instance, in the opening years of what is now known as the Hundred Years' War (1337–1453), the city pushed hard for restraint on behalf of the Count of Flanders whose initial support for France in its struggle over Guyenne had led the English king to forbid wool export to Flanders. Confiscations on both sides followed, and one English merchant even ended up in Bruges's prison.[46] To prevent further damage to their commercial and industrial interests the towns of Flanders decided to steer a neutral course in the Anglo-French conflict, forcing the Count of Flanders, Louis of Nevers (r. 1322–46), to leave the country.[47] His successor, Louis of Male, tried to stay out of the Anglo-French conflict as much as possible.[48] Even the Dukes of Burgundy were forced to take into account the economic interests of the major Flemish cities, if only because they needed their financial support. In 1400 the magistrate of Bruges initiated the talks that led to a truce between England and Burgundy, and for the next fifteen years the city participated in the ongoing negotiations.[49] In

[41] Stützel 1998: 56.
[42] Asaert 1976b: 63; Gilliodts-Van Severen 1871–85: 2:132; Stützel 1998: 56.
[43] De Boer 1996: 136.
[44] Gilliodts-Van Severen 1883–85: 1:466–72; see also Craeybeckx 1958: 120.
[45] Sicking 2004: 421; Gilliodts-Van Severen 1883–85: 1:466–72. For a similar rule laid down in the *Magnus Intercursus* (1496) between England and Burgundy, see De Smedt 1951: 101–2.
[46] Murray 2005: 265.
[47] Blockmans 1992b: 207.
[48] Blockmans 1978: 128–31, 170–92, 303; Vandermaesen 1982: 430–40.
[49] Blockmans 1978; Gilliodts-Van Severen 1871–85: 3:466–69, 494–96, 502–5, 511–12; 4:483–84; 9:12–13.

the fifteenth century the Estates of Flanders still maintained diplomatic ties with England, Castile, and the German Hanse—the countries whose merchants suffered most from privateering.[50]

Thus, the involvement of the Dukes of Burgundy in international politics repeatedly harmed foreign traders in Bruges but never to the extent that they turned their back on the city. The Burgundian rulers were careful not to destroy trade with their political and military endeavors because the prosperity of the Flemish economy was crucial to the funding of their operations. Bruges, in turn, used its financial contribution to secure the central government's restraint. The linchpin of this relatively stable equilibrium was Bruges's undisputed commercial leadership, or rather the lack of an equally suitable alternative home base for foreign merchants within the Burgundian Netherlands. All this would change with the rise of Antwerp in the fifteenth century.

THE FLEMISH REVOLTS

Between the thirteenth and fifteenth centuries the political situation within the county of Flanders was very unstable. In Bruges, Ghent, and Ypres aspiring artisans contested the power of the commercial and political elite, and at the same time these cities tried to strengthen their autonomy vis-à-vis the central government.[51] The Counts of Flanders in turn wanted to end the interference of their liege lord, the king of France, and they also meddled in the succession of rulers in neighboring Brabant, Holland, and Hainaut. Political tensions grew as the Dukes of Burgundy came to power in Flanders in the last quarter of the fourteenth century. Notably Ghent and Bruges resisted the attempts at political centralization of the new counts, and this resulted in a series of urban revolts. These rebellions disrupted the business of foreign merchants in Bruges on several occasions, either because they voluntarily chose to move elsewhere or because the Dukes of Burgundy forced them to leave (Figure 6.2).

The first time foreigners turned their back on Bruges was in 1279 and 1280 to underline concerns about the city's commercial policy. The magistrate had forbidden direct trade between alien merchants and also refused to lower weighage fees. To pressure the magistrate to change its policy Spanish and French merchants removed their trade to nearby Aardenburg. The Count of Flanders sided with the merchants as he gave formal permission to the Germans to move there as well. The foreigners returned only in 1282 upon the city's acceptance of the rules of taxation

[50]Gilliodts-Van Severen 1901–2: 531; Gilliodts-Van Severen 1871–85: 4:380–81; 5:9.
[51]Blockmans 1988: 145–54; Compare Boone and Prak 1995: passim.

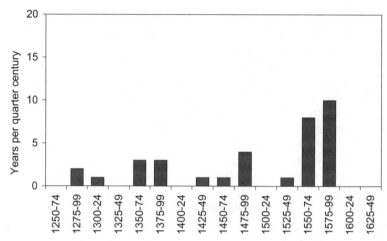

FIGURE 6.2. Number of years per quarter century in which internal conflicts in the Low Countries damaged the property of one or more communities of foreign merchants in Bruges, Antwerp, or Amsterdam, 1250–1650
   Source: Appendix A.

laid down by the count.[52] After 1290 the political situation in Bruges was again very unstable as local craftsmen fought for direct participation in the municipal government, but this did not interfere with the operations of the alien traders, and they continued to visit the Flemish port.[53] A second boycott by Spanish and German merchants followed in 1307 after repeated complaints about the city's monetary regime and the weighing of goods. The merchants once again moved to Aardenburg, and this time it took lengthy negotiations involving the Count of Flanders, and for the Germans the extension of new, more elaborate privileges, to secure their return to Bruges in 1309.

   Leaving Bruges would seem the most drastic of measures, but in this early period trade was still seasonal and few foreign merchants took up permanent residence in the city. The important thing for merchants from around Europe was to meet each other and local producers in a fixed location at regular intervals. The proximity of various other ports in the Low Countries with access to the same foreign and local markets made it relatively easy for merchants to relocate. The ease with which this was done is clear from the reaction of English merchants to the mounting tensions of their sovereign with France and Flanders in the late thirteenth century. In 1294 the Count of Flanders's support for France led the King of England to redirect his country's wool export to Dordrecht. As it

[52] Poeck 2000: 34; Dollinger 1964: 67–68; Vandermaesen 1982: 399–440.
[53] Blockmans 2010b: 295–323.

proved difficult to sell the wool there, the merchandise was transshipped to Antwerp, where English merchants received their first privileges in 1296. Until 1298 the English wool trade was fully centered upon Antwerp and nearby Malines.[54]

Bruges's commitment to the safety of merchants increased in the fourteenth century as the city developed a permanent market that thrived on the continuous presence of merchants from various parts of Europe. The power struggle within the city and between the city and the count did not harm the foreign merchants, perhaps with the exception of the Flemish Revolt of 1323–28, which led to the diversion of Venetian galleys to Antwerp. Only the attempt of Louis of Male to take control of Brabant in 1356 made a stir, but very much to Bruges's benefit. While carefully avoiding military involvement in the war between England and France, the count confiscated German vessels to carry out an attack on Antwerp and submit the city to his rule.[55] The Count of Flanders succeeded, gave staple rights to nearby Malines, and effectively curtailed the further growth of the Brabant fairs until the end of the annexation of Antwerp in 1405.[56] Throughout this period foreign merchants in Bruges were forbidden to visit the fairs of Brabant. Several merchants who did travel to the fairs were fined, for instance in Antwerp in 1389 and in Bergen-op-Zoom in 1401.[57]

By 1360 Bruges had become the undisputed leader of international trade in the North Sea area, and this situation defined the balance of power between the city and the central government. The Count of Flanders needed the foreign merchants to stay in Bruges, not because they brought in large tax revenues (the foreign nations were exempt from paying excises on wine and beer) or because they acted as bankers for the count (only a handful of Italians provided such services) but because their presence stimulated the local economy. The taxation of local traders, producers, and consumers allowed the city to raise considerable revenues, and in exchange for regular contributions to the central treasury, the Counts of Flanders were willing to leave the city to its own devices.

Because of its strong position in international trade, the situation in Bruges was decidedly more stable than that in Ghent, a city with an equally flourishing economy, but one that leaned much more heavily on the production of textiles and other manufactures. Due to Ghent's different economic outlook tensions between craftsmen and the urban elite ran much higher than in Bruges. In 1379 local artisans, with the help of English

[54] Jansen 1982: 174–75.
[55] See, for example, the fines paid by visitors of the fairs of Antwerp in 1389 and those of Bergen-op-Zoom in 1401: Gilliodts-Van Severen 1871–85: 4:158, 201.
[56] Prims 1927–49: 5:1, 11–80, 132–33.
[57] Gilliodts-Van Severen 1871–85: 4:158, 201.

soldiers and craftsmen from other cities, rebelled against Louis of Male. The revolt spread rapidly across Flanders, and in 1382 even Bruges was submitted to the rebels' rule. Louis of Male ordered all foreign merchants to move to Antwerp to try to break the revolt of the Flemish towns. Germans, Catalans, Genoese, Spaniards, Lombards, Scots, and Englishmen complied, but they could return only a few months later after the defeat of the rebel army at Westrozebeke.[58] In other parts of Flanders the revolt continued until 1384, however, when Philip the Bold, Duke of Burgundy, and successor to Louis of Male, offered amnesty to Ghent in exchange for the city's withdrawal of support for England.

In the meantime the central government in the Netherlands became gradually more powerful as Philip the Good took control of Namur in 1429, Brabant in 1430, Hainaut, Holland, and Zeeland in 1433, and Luxemburg in 1451. He implemented legal and administrative reforms to unify his possessions and requested greater subsidies from Flanders and the other provinces to fund his military operations. Bruges's population had to pay higher taxes, but the city retained a strong bargaining position all the same because the duke was always short of money and needed Bruges to raise loans to anticipate revenues from either his own domains or the provincial subsidies. The foreign nations were in equally good graces because they remained vital to Bruges's prosperity, that is, its fiscal capacity, in addition to which some of the Italian merchants lent money for Philip the Good's military endeavors.

The importance of Bruges for the Duke of Burgundy was demonstrated during the urban revolt of 1436–38. The failure of a costly military campaign against Calais brought disgruntled members of the local militia back before the gates of Bruges in August 1436, where they refused to put down their weapons and disband. The situation escalated as urban laborers called a general strike. Shortly afterward one of the count's officials, the sheriff, was killed and the mob imprisoned magistrates and urban tax receivers. To stop the violence and secure the resumption of the artisans' work the consuls of the foreign nations cast themselves as negotiators and actually managed to restore order. But the revolt continued in the spring of 1437 when the mayor of Bruges was murdered. The foreign merchants panicked and fled to Antwerp, while Philip the Good moved in with his troops. His initial intervention ended in a humiliating flight, but eventually the duke prevailed and in 1438 he punished the city with a public display of the magistrate's submission to his rule, a huge fine, and a reduction of the town's legal and administrative powers. It was not long before the alien merchants returned from Antwerp and continued their business as usual.

[58] Gilliodts-Van Severen 1871–85: 4:311; Prims 1927–49: 5:1, 99; Dollinger 1964: 101.

The swift return of the foreign nations shows their preference for Bruges as the mainstay of their operations in the Low Countries. But this began to change in the following decades as Antwerp began to attract growing numbers of foreign merchants. Exactly how vulnerable this alternative location had made Bruges in its dealings with the central government became clear during the Flemish Revolt (1483–92) when Bruges, Ghent, and various other towns once again contested the power of their sovereign. When Charles the Bold died on the battlefield in 1477, his daughter Mary of Burgundy became countess of Flanders. The Estates of Flanders seized the opportunity to exact extensive privileges from the new ruler, but when Mary died in 1482 her husband Maximilian was appointed regent on behalf of their son, and he set out to roll back the privileges. Bruges and Ghent, however, refused to recognize him as regent of the Netherlands. To force Bruges to comply, Maximilian in 1484 ordered all foreign merchants to continue their trade at the fairs of Brabant. His order was revoked within months, but in 1485 London merchants in Bergen-op-Zoom still did not want to travel to Bruges for fear of being robbed.[59]

The political situation remained unstable for several years before it spun out of control in January 1488 when the burghers of Bruges imprisoned Maximilian I. After three months of very tense deliberations the Habsburg prince was forced to renounce his claim to the regency, but immediately after he left the city he gathered an army to put down the Flemish Revolt, and he ordered all foreign merchants to leave the city. Hundreds of German, Italian, Portuguese, and Castilian traders moved to Antwerp, where they continued to trade among each other and with local merchants and manufacturers. As it turned out, this forced departure of the foreign nations marked the end of Bruges as a leading European market. When the revolt was finally over in 1492, the town magistrate managed to convince the leaders of the foreign nations to return to the Flemish port, but most merchants preferred to stay in Antwerp, which quickly became the principal center of international trade in the North Sea area.

THE HABSBURG UNIFICATION

While foreign merchants left Bruges several times in response to violent incidents, Antwerp rose to commercial primacy in the sixteenth century without any attempt of its foreign nations to remove their business. One explanation might be that the Habsburg rulers, first Maximilian's son Philip the Fair (r. 1493–1506) and then Charles V (r. 1515–55), committed

[59]Slootmans 1985: 1:139.

more resources to the protection of trade and the reduction of violence along the lines sketched by Douglass North. But it might also be that the interdependence between the city and the sovereigns was simply stronger than was the case in Bruges, as the Antwerp market produced higher tax revenues for the crown and Charles V heavily relied on the local financial market to borrow money.

When Charles V came to power in the Netherlands in 1515 he set out to complete the political unification begun by Philip the Good. Through a combination of military and diplomatic efforts, Tournai (1521), Friesland (1524), Overijssel and Utrecht (1528), and Groningen (1536) were submitted to Habsburg rule. Unification benefited Holland's trade in particular because it ended Frisian privateering on the Zuiderzee and reduced violence on the land routes to Germany.[60] The one remaining internal conflict in the 1530s was the fight the Dukes of Guelders put up against Charles V. As the dukes gradually lost ground in the eastern provinces, they solicited financial and military support from the king of France. Charles V was forced to commit considerable resources to the reduction of Guelders's armies whose guerrilla tactics were a menace to merchants traveling to Antwerp. In 1542 the city even fortified its city walls "for the security of the alien merchants [and] to retain their trade."[61] In the end, however, Charles V prevailed and the Treaty of Venlo (1543) brought Guelders under Habsburg rule.

Charles V's political ambitions went far beyond the Netherlands, however. His first priority was to succeed his grandfather, Maximilian I, as Holy Roman Emperor. To achieve this Charles had to make very large payments to the German electors, which in turn forced him to borrow heavily from Italian and German bankers.[62] The loans meant to secure his election marked the beginning of a long-standing and increasingly tight financial relationship between the Habsburg king and the Antwerp money market.[63] From 1520 onward short-term borrowing from foreign bankers through bills of exchange and promissory notes allowed Charles V to wage a prolonged war against France, but he also relied on life and term annuities sold by the principal cities of Flanders, Brabant, and Holland to their local elites in anticipation of the provincial subsidies to the central government.[64] When it took too long to raise money in this fashion, the provinces reverted to short-term loans on the Antwerp market to meet their obligations. The emperor's financial interests were such that throughout his military endeavors he paid close attention to

[60]Paviot 1995: 233–34; Sicking 2004: 290–301; Israel 1995: 34, 49.
[61]Goris 1925: 5.
[62]Tracy 2002: 99.
[63]Tracy 2002: 91–108; Braudel 1959: passim.
[64]Tracy 1985: passim.

the economic situation in Antwerp. For one, the Habsburg-Valois Wars (1521–59) did not hurt the city's merchants very much because most battles were fought in and over Italy. In 1525 Charles V limited the number of French ships allowed to anchor in Antwerp and other ports, but the measure did not last. The emperor also threatened to impound the merchandise of French subjects, but the city seems to have had sufficient financial leverage to keep him from doing so. Direct encounters between French and Habsburg troops on the southern border may have stopped merchants in 1530 and 1536, but trade resumed as soon as the fighting was over.[65] Perhaps more disruptive in the 1530s was the contested succession to the Danish crown with Holland and the Hanse on opposite sides. Merchants in Antwerp and Amsterdam suffered from privateering raids, naval warfare, and the temporary closure of the Sound for Dutch ships. The conflict ended in 1544 when Denmark and the Habsburg Empire signed the Peace of Speyer, which secured free access to the Baltic Sea for all of Charles' subjects.

The safety of merchants mattered to Charles V because it helped to secure Antwerp's taxes and loans, but seldom did he use these resources to protect trade. While the foreign nations continued to rely on their home government to organize convoys and armed escorts, the emperor merely offered free passage in case of conflicts with their rulers. In 1545 Antwerp's local customs specified that if war were to break out with a foreign prince, the merchants from the latter's realm would be free to continue their trade unless the Habsburg emperor forbade it. In that case foreign merchants would be given three months to leave the city, taking all their belongings with them.[66] The emperor took additional action only in 1550, when increased activity from French corsairs threatened to paralyze trade between the Netherlands and the Iberian Peninsula. His Ordinance on Navigation of 1550 stated that every privateer without a letter of mark would be considered a pirate before the law.[67] Charles V also ordered all merchants from the Low Countries carrying high-value commodities to arm their ships.[68] In addition, westbound ships had to sail in convoys escorted by navy vessels. Initially foreign merchants were exempted from the former obligation, but a revised ordinance issued in 1551 required their compliance as well.[69] At first sight, this would seem an important step toward naval protection of visiting merchants organized. However, alien traders were not interested, and a first attempt to equip

[65] Sicking 2004: 244, 249; Braudel 1959; Coornaert 1961: 1:83–84; Sicking 2004: 244, 249.
[66] *Antwerpse Costumen* (1545), title 9, no. 54.
[67] Sicking 2004: 428.
[68] An earlier attempt in the 1530s to provide structural protection for the Dutch herring fleet of 700 vessels failed: Sicking 2004: 132–204.
[69] Sicking 2004: 251–53; Asaert 1976a: 180–205.

a convoy failed in 1551. Notably the Castilian nation was content with the way it organized its wool fleets, including the use of maritime insurance to cover risks. Besides, animosity between merchants from Burgos still residing in Bruges and other Spanish traders in Antwerp prevented adequate registration of their trade and thus thwarted Charles V's plan to tax commercial transactions to pay for the fleet. Other foreigners and locals also objected to this funding strategy and preferred to continue business as before.[70]

Charles persevered, however, and in 1552 and 1553 imperial convoys did sail to the Iberian Peninsula.[71] Crucial for the equipment of these fleets was the support of Antwerp's town magistrate, which had decided to advance two-thirds of the total cost of the convoys. The local authorities did so because they feared a shortage of Spanish silver would jeopardize the repayment of Habsburg loans to Antwerp financiers, and upset trade in general. The silver crisis, in conjunction with French naval operations on the sea route to Spain, led Antwerp merchants to accept a 2 percent tax on trade to pay for their escort. To win over the Castilians, Charles V allowed two of them to oversee fleet preparations. It proved a Pyrrhic victory. The return of the first convoy was delayed by bad weather, angry crowds in the port of Cadiz, and Portuguese and Castilian authorities unwilling to load their spices, silver, and wool onto the ships. Despite the high costs incurred, a second convoy sailed in 1553, but this expedition was haunted by confiscation of some ships and the early return of others, due to arrears in sailors' pay. After these two failures Antwerp withdrew its financial support and the central government stopped organizing convoys.[72]

The emperor's dependence on the political and financial support of Antwerp also was demonstrated by his attempts to root out Protestantism. On April 29, 1550, the emperor issued his Eternal Edict, requiring all immigrants in the Low Countries to submit a certificate of orthodoxy signed by their parish priest.[73] This was a problem for Antwerp because alien traders threatened to leave the city if this were to happen. The town magistrate, which had already opposed a ban on the immigration of New Christians issued in 1548, was quick to respond to the worries of the foreign merchants.[74] The burgomasters and aldermen rallied the support

[70]Sicking 2004: 261–73.

[71]The following is based on Sicking 2004: 256–59; see also Asaert 1976a.

[72]Antwerp did contribute two warships to a squadron of eight that escorted two grain fleets in 1557. However, the Estates of Holland paid the other six vessels. Instead of organizing convoys, in a new edict in 1563 Philip II merely set rules for the armament, accompaniment, admiralship, and insurance of merchantmen.

[73]Mulder 1897: 7–12; Marnef 1996: 119.

[74]See the town ordinances from 1521, 1540, and 1544 (Thijs 1995). Already in 1490 the Bishop of Cambrai had guaranteed the citizens of Antwerp would be spared the Inquisition: Goris 1925: 546.

of other towns and the Council of Brabant, and they wrote to and visited Governess Mary of Hungary and managed to convince her to ask her brother to change his ordinance. In September 1550 Charles V expressly stated it was not his intention "to hinder in any way the course of trade and contracts between alien merchants and our subjects, nor to prevent them from disposing of their goods the way the rights and customs of the city specify."[75] He issued a new ordinance that no longer required alien merchants to prove their orthodoxy, but merely expected them not to give offense.[76]

Thus, the approach of Charles V toward the Antwerp market was fundamentally pragmatic. He never offered the kind of military support that economic historians today consider proof of a sovereign's commitment to the protection of trade, but he did consider the economic impact of his political choices. The rapprochement to England and the restoration of peace with the German Hanse were clearly intended to strengthen Antwerp's position, as was his turning a blind eye to the religious beliefs of Protestant and Jewish merchants. When Charles V abdicated in 1555 he also persuaded his son of the importance of this mutually beneficial relationship among the city, its merchants, and the crown, and in the first decade of his reign Philip II continued his father's pragmatic approach toward Antwerp and its international traders. However, the community of interest between the city and the sovereign fell apart after 1566 when a classic conflict over taxation merged with religious tensions and an acute food crisis to spark the Dutch Revolt.[77]

THE DUTCH REVOLT

In the early years of the Dutch Revolt nobody considered the possible demise of the Antwerp market. In 1488 Maximilian I had come down hard on Bruges because he knew the city's foreign merchants could continue their business elsewhere within his territory. At the outbreak of the Dutch Revolt this kind of rapid relocation was much less likely, however. Admittedly, Amsterdam had emerged as an important port of call for German and Flemish merchants, but the Dutch port remained loyal to the Spanish crown until 1578. Antwerp's other major satellite in the Low Countries, Middelburg, went over to the rebels in 1574, but its commercial fate remained equally uncertain for at least another decade. As a result of this unstable situation many foreigners either returned home or moved with merchants from the Low Countries to cities like London, Hamburg,

---

[75] Mulder 1897: 12.
[76] Mulder 1897: 12; Marnef 1996: 119.
[77] Marnef 1996: 37–46, 160–61; Parker 1998: 115–24.

Cologne, Frankfurt, and Rouen. Just like Amsterdam and Middelburg, these foreign ports had developed strong economic ties with Antwerp, and their commercial infrastructure was sufficiently well developed to accommodate newcomers and obtain a more central position in the international network of commercial cities.

Because of the ultimately far-reaching political and economic consequences of the Dutch Revolt, historians have often blamed Philip II for the escalation of the political and religious conflicts of the 1560s. The king's limited understanding of politics in the Netherlands, his preference for staying in Castile, and his staunch Catholicism would have prevented the careful balancing of opposing interests that had characterized Charles' V government. But this is not true. Philip II understood the financial and strategic importance of the Netherlands, and Antwerp in particular, at least as well as his father did. Admittedly, upon his accession in 1555, he immediately put pressure on the various provinces to obtain greater subsidies to fund his wars with France, but when confronted with their opposition he negotiated a nine-year financial agreement with the States General to create political stability. Even in religious matters Philip II was willing to make concessions to serve Antwerp's interests. In 1561 he appointed his trusted adviser Antoine Perrenot Granvelle as the first archbishop of Mechelen to carry out a major reorganization of the church in order to to strengthen the king's control over religious life, but then Antwerp's magistrate wrote to Governess Margaretha of Parma that it feared alien merchants would leave for Rouen or Hamburg if the king saw the reorganization through. Shortly afterward the city also sent envoys to Spain to ask Philip II to abandon the idea. The Catholic king was unimpressed at first, but popular protest continued, and eventually Granvelle was dismissed in December 1564.[78]

The situation started to spin out of control only in 1566 when tense negotiations about further tax increases coincided with rising grain prices and an outburst of religious fervor.[79] To quell the Iconoclastic fury that swept the country in August 1566, Margaret of Parma, pressured by William of Orange and other high nobles, decided to allow Protestants to openly profess their faith. Her intervention stopped the Iconoclasm and allowed the governess and the noblemen to punish several of the instigators. She even began to roll back the freedom of religion granted under duress, but it was not enough for Philip who decided to send the Duke of Alba to replace the governess, to punish the Protestants, and to wrest financial control from the States General.[80] In 1568 order was restored as

[78] Mulder 1897: 49–53; Israel: 1995: 143–44.
[79] Schöffer 1991: 103–14.
[80] Marnef 1996: 151–77.

Alba's troops crushed William of Orange's invasion army at Heiligerlee. In the following months Antwerp's local government was reorganized and hundreds of Anabaptists, Calvinists, and Lutherans were executed, banned, or stripped of their assets—unless, of course, they had fled to escape repression.

These events did not destroy Antwerp's international trade. Alba's persecution was primarily directed against the lower and middle classes, Anabaptists in particular, and only a small minority of the city's merchant community fled to Germany and England. One exception was the Company of Merchant Adventurers, which had moved to Stade near Hamburg as early as 1568, but their departure resulted from political tensions between Spain and England. In 1567 the Habsburg government had seized English ships in Antwerp in retaliation for the capture of Spanish ships laden with four million guilders worth of silver, destined for the Low Countries.[81] The Spanish attitude toward other local and foreign merchants did not change, however, and for several years they were able to continue their international business relatively undisturbed, even if privateering attacks from the Sea Beggars, Orange's seaborne guerilla army, caused losses to local and foreign merchants on several occasions.[82]

The pressure on Antwerp's merchant community started to grow after the Sea Beggars' capture of Brielle on April 1, 1572. This sparked a general revolt in Zeeland and Holland, forcing Alba to raise a large army and move into the northern provinces. It was very difficult for the Spanish king to pay for this military effort, however, and in 1574 Spanish troops garrisoned in the citadel threatened to mutiny to obtain their pay. An emergency loan from local and foreign merchants was necessary to prevent the ransacking of the city. Italian, Portuguese, and Spanish traders contributed more than 75,000 guilders, or 17.5 percent of the loan that totaled 430,000 guilders.[83] The Spanish crown's financial position continued to deteriorate, however, and in 1575 Philip's appointed governor, Requesens, was forced to start negotiations with the rebels.[84] The initial talks failed due to his refusal to allow religious freedom, but then the new governor died unexpectedly in March 1576. The southern provinces, led by Brabant, took control and convened the States General, including delegates from Holland and Zeeland, and in Ghent their assembly drafted a provisional peace agreement on October 28, 1576. But then, while the

[81] Read 1933.

[82] Pohl 1977: 140–41; Gelderblom 2000: 71–72.

[83] One merchant from Spain paid 90 guilders, a merchant from Florence paid 1,000 guilders, several merchants from Andalusia paid 3,100 guilders in all, the Milanese made a contribution of 10,000 guilders, the Portuguese 12,000 guilders, the Lucchese 20,000 guilders, and finally the Genoese 30,000 guilders. Van den Branden 1885: passim.

[84] Groenveld et al. 1979: 96–100.

provincial delegates returned home to obtain approval of the armistice, the Spanish garrison in Antwerp mutinied. This Spanish Fury left many houses burned as soldiers extorted payments from the local population. The violence led merchants to flee the city, with many Southern Europeans not returning because one year later a Calvinist Republic was proclaimed, which put Antwerp, like most other major towns in Brabant and Flanders, firmly in the rebel camp.

Antwerp's defection, quickly followed by Amsterdam switching sides in 1578, had far-reaching economic and political consequences because of the Low Countries' strategic importance in Spain's power struggle with England and France. Philip II needed a military and financial operating base in the North Sea area, and now that all major commercial cities in the Netherlands—Antwerp, Middelburg, and Amsterdam—had joined the Revolt, he had to defeat the rebels in the southern *and* northern provinces to secure the continuation of Antwerp's primacy. Anything less would have led to the scattering of merchants over different ports in England, France, Germany, and Holland and put end to the political primacy of the Habsburgs in Northwestern Europe.

Thus Philip II launched a new offensive, led by Alexander Farnese, to regain control over the cities and provinces that had turned against him. The course of this military campaign leaves no doubt that complete submission was the ultimate goal. Farnese first conquered the Protestant towns in the South, including the submission of Antwerp in 1585, and then continued all the way to Groningen in the northeast to encircle Holland and Zeeland. The actual conquest of the coastal provinces remained a daunting task because of the rivers, lakes, and marshes that had to be crossed, but Farnese never even got that far because of the assassination of the king of France in 1589.[85] As the leader of the Huguenots, Henry of Navarre, proclaimed himself the new king, Philip II decided to intervene and ordered Farnese to redeploy his troops in France. In retrospect, this decision secured the independence of the Dutch Republic, as Holland and Zeeland could now recuperate and recapture the eastern provinces.[86]

The failed submission of the Northern Netherlands to Spanish rule fundamentally changed the economic geography of the Netherlands as well as for the commercial and political geography of Europe. In the seventeenth century Northwestern Europe became the principal political theatre with England, France, and the Dutch Republic as its major players, and the North Sea area became the Continent's economic core. Contrary to Antwerp, which had relied heavily on the presence of foreign merchants, Amsterdam became the center of international trading

[85] Parker 1998: 284.
[86] Israel 1989: 38–42; Israel 1995: 241–62.

networks built by merchants born and raised in the Netherlands. What is more, the independence of the Dutch Republic from Spain allowed merchants in Amsterdam and other Dutch ports to extend their operations beyond Europe and establish direct connections with markets in Asia, Africa, and the Americas.

THE RISE OF THE DUTCH REPUBLIC

However advantageous the fall of Antwerp was for Amsterdam in the long run, in the first decade after 1585 the city's prospects remained bleak. Hans Thijs, who moved to Amsterdam in 1584 to marry Catharina Boel, the only child of his prospective business partner Augustijn Boel, left for Poland even before Antwerp's capitulation, while his father, brother, and sisters settled in various German cities. Only halfway through the 1590s did Hans Thijs return to the Dutch port whose prospects had now greatly improved. In a letter to a foreign correspondent he reported, "You would be surprised about the ships sailing to every part the world, there is no talk of war here, and without a fire arm you can travel the entire country from Emden to Middelburg in Zeeland."[87]

The ascent of Amsterdam was directly linked to war with Spain. For one, Philip II's choice to intervene in the French Civil War extinguished his plans to regain control over the coastal provinces in the north, which in turn allowed Amsterdam to regain its position as the principal transporter of Northwestern Europe. Spain continued to fight the young republic, but neither its trade embargoes nor its commissions to Dunkirk privateers could prevent Dutch forays into the Mediterranean, West Africa, Asia, and the Caribbean.[88] For another, the increased military capabilities of the Dutch Republic made it easier to defend Amsterdam's commercial interests.

In the 1590s the States General were able to raise a large land army to roll back the Spanish troops in the eastern provinces, and thereafter several garrisons were left behind to guard the frontier and secure rivers and roads. On several occasions towns in Holland explicitly asked the States General to deploy naval craft and cavalry to escort merchants on the way to Germany and the Spanish-ruled territories.[89] In 1605, for example, merchants from Amsterdam and other Dutch cities trading with Frankfurt, Nuremberg, Augsburg, and Cologne asked and received additional protection.

---

[87] Gelderblom 2000: 131.

[88] Van Loo 1999: 355.

[89] RSH 28-07-1570; RSG 1580, 180; RSG 1591, 470, 473–74; RSH 595/625 (December 2 and 21, 1596); RSH 234/253 (June 9 and 12, 1599); RSG 1610, p. 141 (no. 751).

During a trial period of eight to ten weeks the States General promised "six horsemen to escort, two by two, the wagons of the petitioners."[90] To be sure, this surveillance of rivers and roads also helped to obstruct military supplies to the enemy. In 1625 it was even decided to block all traffic on the rivers to Germany. This blockade lasted until 1630, but it mostly applied to foodstuffs and military supplies, and it was seldom enforced throughout the year.[91] And even if it harmed some traders in Amsterdam, the blockade also created new opportunities, for instance the shipment of supplies from Holland, via Bremen and Hamburg, to the south of Germany.[92]

Even more important for Amsterdam's commercial success was the creation of a standing navy. From the 1580s the United Provinces had a fleet of several dozens of men-of-war at their disposal, which could be used for offensive and defensive warfare, as well as the protection of the merchantmen and the fishing fleet. Whereas in the 1550s Charles V had failed to convince the Antwerp magistrate of the benefits of a stand- ing fleet, the war against Spain was sufficient reason for Amsterdam and other seaports in Holland and Zeeland to outfit a fleet, even if it was under the express condition that the individual cities remained respon- sible for the actual equipment and deployment of the ships. This led to the creation of a governance structure with five local Admiralty Boards, three in cities in Holland, one in Zeeland, and one in Friesland, whose funding was made dependent on the amount of shipping traffic. The local Admiralties levied customs duties according to tariffs set by the States General and used the revenue to pay their military expenses.[93]

This urban control over naval warfare had a long pedigree in the north. Already in 1440 the towns of Holland managed to equip a fleet of forty merchantmen-turned-warships to break through the blockade of the Sound by Lübeck and the Wendish towns and secure their trading interests in the Baltic area.[94] The Dutch ability to raise money to coun- ter violent threats to its merchant marine was proven time and again in later years. In April 1478, for instance, Amsterdam levied a special tax (pontgeld) to pay for the protection of merchants and fishermen against the French king, and in 1505 Amsterdam levied a lastgeld for similar pur- poses.[95] Hostellers were asked to inform shipmasters about the pontgeld and direct them to the local receiver, which suggests that foreign visitors

[90] RSG 1596, 184–85; RSG 1597, 535–36; RSG 1600, 340; RSG 1605, 490.

[91] Kernkamp 1931–34; Israel 1980: passim.

[92] It is telling that Holland, and Amsterdam in particular, supported a continued river blockade in 1626 and 1627: Israel 1980: 473–77.

[93] Sicking 2004; Lesger 2001: 257–66.

[94] Knevel 2004: 374–75.

[95] Breen 1902: 128–29, 437; Meilink 1923b.

shared the financial burden with the local community.[96] The key to success was the earmarking of these taxes for naval protection. Between 1506 and 1562 the cities of Holland fiercely resisted a permanent tax on the grain trade levied by the central government because this congégeld would deter foreign grain merchants. All the same, in 1541 the urban delegates to the Estates of Holland voted for incidental subsidies to fund military operations against the German Hanse.[97] Not surprisingly, when Amsterdam negotiated its defection to William of Orange in 1577, the city wanted its merchants to be exempted from the recently introduced customs duties. The parties indeed agreed to "free and unhampered exercise of navigation and trade," but William of Orange changed his mind and forced the city to accept import and export duties payable by all merchants, including foreigners. He did concede that *convooien en licenten* would be used only to pay for the protection of the merchant navy, and this would remain the guiding principle for the protection of trade in the Low Countries.[98]

From 1580 onward the principal ports of the Low Countries relied on the members of their Admiralty Boards, recruited from the local political elite, to negotiate the protection of maritime trade. The States General formally decided on all naval affairs, but their resolutions were made in concert with both the Orange stadtholders and the Admiralty Boards, who remained responsible for the building, repairing, manning, and deploying warships.[99] Written reports of the Admiralties allowed the States General to closely monitor the naval operations of rival states and the operations of pirates around Europe. Based on the perceived threats to Dutch merchantmen the federal state dispatched a varying numbers of navy vessels to Russia, the coasts of Germany, the North Sea fishing grounds, the English Channel, the Atlantic coasts of Europe and Africa, the Strait of Gibraltar, and eventually also the Mediterranean.[100]

One should be careful not to rate Dutch naval power too highly, however. In Western and Northern European waters, in peacetime at least, the navy was dominant enough to allow its merchantmen to merely sail in

[96] Breen 1902: 132.
[97] Van Tielhof 1995a: 132–38; Lesger 2006: 53.
[98] Noordkerk 1748: 1:chaps. 15 and 16.
[99] Bruijn 1993: 29–39; Bruijn 1998: 39–52.
[100] De Jong 2005: 35–39. Compare the close monitoring of the constantly changing requirements for the protection of European and colonial trade during the Twelve Years' Truce: RSG 1610, nos. 233, 268, 499, 968, 1095, 1202, 1209, 1362; RSG 1611, no. 924; RSG 1614, no. 290, 628; RSG 1617, no. 804. In 1617 the growing threat of Barbary pirates on both sides of the Strait of Gibraltar required a full revision of protective measures for all southbound merchantmen (including VOC ships) and the cancellation of projected operations in the Baltic Sea: RSG 1617, nos. 442, 633, 717, 734, 875, 882, 908, 971, 983, 1084, 1093, 1149, 1869.

admiralship, that is, together but without armed escorts.[101] Most notably
in the Baltic Sea the fledgling republic's ability to retaliate quickly and
forcefully was such that it kept most attackers from trying altogether.[102]
Adequate protection was far more difficult to organize in distant waters.
Dutch ventures into Africa, Asia, and America implied a direct confron-
tation with Spanish and Portuguese traders, and it was only through the
pooling of private resources in the East and West India Companies (VOC
and WIC) that Dutch merchants could muster enough strike power to
stand their ground. Within Europe the Mediterranean trade via the Strait
of Gibraltar was very risky because of Spain's proximity and constant
raids by Barbary pirates. In 1618 the United Provinces for once managed
to equip a joint fleet with England, France, and Venice to fight the pirates,
but this was a rare occurrence, feasible only because of the truce with
Spain between 1609 and 1621.[103]

As soon as the war with Spain resumed in 1621, expenditure for naval
operations soared and the Admiralties had to choose carefully where to
deploy their vessels.[104] In the Baltic trade light armament of individual
ships and sailing in convoys deterred most enemies, but elsewhere Dutch
merchantmen were under constant attack from Spanish warships and
corsairs from Dunkirk and Barbary.[105] Foreign merchants trading in the
Low Countries did not escape these attacks because they often used ships
from the United Provinces.[106] The considerable losses led Amsterdam to
allow its merchants to organize their own armed escorts.[107] Thus in 1625
a committee of merchants trading with the Mediterranean, the Direction
for the Levant Trade, was established.[108] The Direction, funded with an
additional tax payable by all Levant traders, set rules for the armament
of the merchant fleet and negotiated with the States General about the deployment of its navy vessels in the Mediterranean. For instance, In 1631
the Direction proposed a joint operation with Venice, France, England,
and the Hanse, either to force the Spanish king to do something about
the pirates of Barbary Coast and Tunesia or to mount a naval expedi-

---

[101] Bruijn 1998; van Tielhof 2002: 232–33.

[102] Israel 1989: 95.

[103] RSG 1618, nos. 1869, 2079, 2084, 2167, 2174, 2383, 2383, 2579, 2586, 2590, 2606, 2785, 2808, 3035, 3288, 3290, 3475, 3605, 3816. For Amsterdam's role in the prepara-
tions: RSH 94/591 (09-04-1618) and RSH 351/834 (10-11-1618). The Dutch Republic and England had already engaged in joint naval operations against Spain in 1596—and would do so again between 1626 and 1630. Wijffels and van Loo 1998.

[104] Bruijn 1998: 50–51.

[105] Van Loo 1999: 362.

[106] Stradling 1992: 212.

[107] Bruijn 1998: 36.

[108] Heeringa and Nanninga 1910: 509–16.

tion themselves to get rid of them.[109] In spite of these measures the costs of freighting and insurance soared in the 1630s, which led several merchants to seek alternative investment opportunities.[110]

Violence at sea was the price merchants in Amsterdam paid for the republic's political success. In the Baltic Sea, the traditional mainstay of the city's commercial dominance, the Dutch Republic dominated up to the point of creating a *Pax Neerlandica*, but elsewhere in Europe pirates and privateers regularly attacked Dutch merchantmen. In response to these threats the major ports were put in charge of the protection of overseas trade. Their Admiralty Boards could never secure complete safety at sea, but what they did achieve was the creation of calculable risks, which individual merchants could then try to spread, share, or transfer to others.

CONCLUSION

Premodern Europe had two distinct faces. Politically the Continent was extremely fragmented with almost continuous international warfare and sometimes very violent struggles between sovereigns and their subjects. Economically, however, there was growing integration as commerce across political boundaries expanded. This combination of conflict and commerce is the more remarkable as international trade was a prime target in many wars. The history of Bruges, Antwerp, and Amsterdam suggests that this paradox of violence and growth is at least partially resolved by the interchangeable position of individual towns in Europe's network of commercial cities. Violence bred violence, but it also triggered rulers to police local markets, to secure the freedom of the fairs, or to arrange for armed escorts to shield merchants from its consequences in those areas they deemed vital to their political interests. Contrary to what North and Acemoglu, Johnson, and Robinson have argued, these efforts to protect trade, whether through the exercise of restraint or actual military intervention, did not depend on the political voice of merchants. There was a more fundamental economic motivation behind it, which is shown to good effect by the shift of commercial leadership first from Bruges to Antwerp, and then from Antwerp to Amsterdam.

In the 1480s Maximilian I did not budge an inch in the conflict with Bruges because he could ask the foreign merchants trading in Bruges to move their business to Antwerp. The long-standing interaction between these cities made Antwerp an attractive alternative, the more so as the local government was willing to adapt the commercial, legal, and financial

[109] RSH 61/69, 08-04-1631.
[110] Israel 1986; Israel 1989: 135.

infrastructure to the needs of the newcomers. Once Maximilian had prevailed in the Flemish Revolt, foreign merchants in Antwerp were able to connect to local producers in Flanders directly, thus obviating Bruges's intermediation. One century later the situation was very different because there was no obvious alternative to Antwerp as the major gateway to the Low Countries. When the Dutch Revolt began in the late 1560s, Antwerp's merchants could not easily move to another place in the Habsburg Netherlands because political and religious tensions had degenerated into civil war in all the maritime provinces. In an attempt to restore Philip II's authority, Alexander Farnese managed to take control of Antwerp in 1585, but his troops failed to occupy Holland and Zeeland, and worse, the revolting provinces managed to block both the river Scheldt and the coast of Flanders. Amsterdam benefited in several ways, not least because of the migration of thousands of textile workers, manufacturers, and merchants, and because the separation from Spain allowed Holland's independent foray into markets outside Europe.

Thus merchants in cities that played a key role in international trading networks were exposed to many violent threats, but they were also under the constant care of their host government. Rulers were concerned with their safety because merchants were footloose and could always choose to go somewhere else if they deemed the risks too high. This constraint on the behavior of cities and sovereigns goes a long way toward explaining why European trade could grow in the face of criminal assaults, urban rebellions, and privateering wars. It does not fully solve the paradox of violence and growth, however, as individual merchants could still suffer losses large enough to put them out of businesses and reduce the overall level of commercial activity. Why did that not happen in Bruges, Antwerp, or Amsterdam?

CHAPTER 7

Dealing with Losses

IN SPITE OF AN OFTEN VERY HIGH INCIDENCE OF VIOLENCE, MANY INTER-national traders in Bruges, Antwerp, and Amsterdam managed to build very profitable businesses. These merchants were willing to take risks to clear big profits, but high margins alone were not enough to be success-ful, for the nature of violence was such that individual incidents, whether confiscation, embargo, or the capture of a ship, could lead to large in-come losses. Very big businesses like those of the Medici, Fugger, or Trip families were probably able to cushion these shocks within their own operations, witness their placing of balances to reserve for bad debts, but more modest merchants—who greatly outnumbered the very wealthy—did not make large enough profits to set off big income shocks. Moreover, the openness of the markets of Bruges, Antwerp, and Amsterdam stimu-lated a continuous entry of new competitors, which in turn pushed profit margins down. In such a competitive environment losses could obviously be dealt with systemically rather than individually, that is, unfortunate merchants simply could have been replaced by new entrants, and some of this certainly did happen. But there is no evidence for large-scale failures during or after major trade disruptions in Bruges, Antwerp, or Amster-dam, and this suggests individual merchants found other ways to deal with losses.

One way out for merchants may have been to act collectively, either through the creation of cartels to inflate profit margins or through joint demands for compensation in the case of damages.[1] For several centuries the German, English, and Portuguese nations in the Low Countries were certainly organized well enough to institute boycotts to obtain compen-sation for damages. Leaving together was crucial because the value indi-vidual traders added to the market was too small to pose a credible threat to the host ruler.[2] As a group the merchants stood much stronger because they were the unique suppliers of spices, woolens, or grain, and major buyers of local produce at that. This kind of bargaining also fitted the region's economic geography because the close proximity of competing ports created a credible threat for the foreigners to leave.[3]

---

[1] Greif, Milgrom, and Weingast 1994; Greif 2006b: 91–123; Ogilvie 2011: 100–125.
[2] Greif 2006b: 91–93.
[3] On the roots of this competition, see Blockmans 2010b: 100–102.

And yet one has to wonder whether collective action really was that important. Not all merchants in the Low Countries were able to delegate control to a corporate body, and those who did, like the English and the Germans, were increasingly hesitant after 1500 to use boycotts to claim damages for violent assaults. This may have been related to the growing power of the Burgundian and Habsburg rulers, whose wars with the home rulers of the foreign merchants of Bruges and Antwerp destroyed any hope for compensation or, on a more positive note, to the growing legal powers of the sovereigns to try prize cases and redress at least the losses of neutral traders. But the decline of collective action may also have resulted from the choice of foreign merchants to take up permanent residence in the Low Countries. We already established in previous chapters that fixed settlement reduced the benefits of belonging to a nation, while raising the cost of a forced departure. But how then did these stationary merchants cope with the vicissitudes of trade? The answer, I argue in this chapter, lay once again with the town magistrates who organized the local market in such a way that merchants could simply spread, share, or transfer the risks of losses from violence and opportunism, instead of organizing boycotts that hurt their own economic interests as much as those of their local hosts.

COLLECTIVE ACTION

The earliest recorded instance of foreign merchants leaving Bruges collectively to wrest concessions from their hosts was in 1279 when Spanish and possibly also French merchants removed their trade to nearby Aardenburg to force the city to lower its weighing and toll tariffs.[4] German merchants followed a year later after the Count of Flanders gave them formal permission to do so. The collective boycott lasted until 1282, when Bruges followed the count's orders to revise its fiscal regime.[5] No evidence survives of any compensation granted to the Spanish initiators of the boycott, but we do know that the Germans were able to improve themselves. The city allowed them to appoint proxies (*procureurs*) to settle internal disputes, and they were given permission to exchange goods with other foreigners, albeit through the mediation of brokers.

---

[4] It is possible that, already before this date, foreigners in Bruges acted collectively to obtain compensation for damages. For instance, in the eleventh and twelfth centuries German merchants traveling to the Low Countries were bound by a *Schwurbruderschaft*, also known as *Eidgenossenschaft* or *Conjuratio*: they swore an oath of trust that required them to stand up for each other in case of violent conflict. The otherwise very detailed account of H. Planitz of the history of these communities, however, does not mention any collective action for compensation. Planitz 1940: 46–52, 115–16.

[5] Poeck 2000: 34; Dollinger 1964: 67–68; Vandermaesen 1982.

A quarter century later the Spanish and German merchants left once again for Aardenburg to lend force to repeated complaints about weighing and money changing in Bruges. Negotiations among the city, the count, and town officials from Lübeck and Dortmund were necessary to establish the terms upon which the Germans would return to the Flemish port. Eventually, in 1309, the city confirmed a new set of privileges that once again implied an improvement of the German position. From now on a German staple was officially established in Bruges, and the community was granted a separate jurisdiction.[6] For a second time running there is no indication of a more privileged position for the Spanish merchants—their oldest privilege, a general safe-conduct, dates from 1343.[7] Neither community obtained pecuniary compensation for any losses they might have suffered.

A third group of merchants suffering from violence in the second half of the thirteenth century were English wool traders. England was an important trading partner for Flanders because the latter's drapers needed English wool to produce their cloth. Initially Flemish merchants bought the wool in England, but after 1270 they were replaced by English and Italian exporters.[8] Political relations between England and Flanders were tense in this period. In 1270 the English king defaulted on a Flemish loan, and this led the Countess of Flanders to seize the ships and goods of English merchants. On behalf of his subjects Henry III retaliated with the arrest of Flemish merchants, vessels, and merchandise in England. Trade was disrupted for almost a decade. A second incident followed in 1294, when King Edward I reacted to Flanders' siding with the king of France by redirecting the export of English wool to Dordrecht. The Dutch port had little demand for the wool, however, and merchants shipped their wares to Antwerp instead. In 1296 the Duke of Brabant granted the English community privileges very similar to those of the German Hanse in Bruges.[9]

The basic outcome of the German, Spanish, and English boycotts between 1270 and 1310 was the confirmation or extension of commercial privileges. What followed was a long period with very little collective action. One exception is the diversion of the Venetian galleys to Antwerp in 1327, which might explain the formal recognition of the Venetian nation by the Count of Flanders in 1332.[10] Admittedly, the English wool merchants left Bruges twice in the first half of the fourteenth century, in 1326 and again in 1348, but their departure was actually forced upon them. The Bruges magistrate allowed the English to sell their wool in 1325 and

[6] Dollinger 1964: 68, 71.
[7] Gilliodts-Van Severen 1871–85: 2:130.
[8] Murray 2005: 261–64.
[9] Jansen 1982: 174–75.
[10] De Roover 1948: 15.

again in 1340, but only to Flemish drapers. At the same time the city banned English cloth from the local market. Under these circumstances it was more profitable for the English wool exporters to supply the Flemish cloth producers from outside Flanders, that is, Calais.[11]

In the mid-fourteenth century the Hanseatic League raised the stakes of collective action as it began to demand financial compensation for damages as well (Table 7.1; see also Appendix B). In 1358 the German merchants in Bruges submitted a nine-page document, the *Claghe der Oosterlingen*, with complaints about English and Spanish privateers, local tolls and weighage facilities, the confiscation of German ships for a Flemish attack on Antwerp, and several other nuisances.[12] To enforce their claims the Hanseatic League moved the Bruges Kontor to Dordrecht in 1358. After prolonged negotiations the Germans returned to Bruges in 1360 with minor additions to their already extensive privileges and the award of damages to the value of 4,100 pounds Flemish.

A quarter century after the German removal to Dordrecht the trade of foreign merchants in Bruges was heavily disrupted by the Ghent war of 1379–85.[13] Many merchants temporarily left the city, but this was their own individual choice, not a collective attempt to negotiate damages.[14] Once the disturbances were over in 1387 the Count of Flanders did issue a new safe-conduct for visiting merchants, but this was for traders of all nations except the English.[15] Remarkably, the return of foreigners to Bruges was precisely when German merchants chose to issue a new boycott. In 1388 they moved once again to Dordrecht, to return only in 1392 after a promise of very substantial damages. To compensate for earlier arrests and damage from privateering, the Hanse received a record amount of 11,000 pounds and a public penance by Bruges's citizens.[16] In addition the towns of Flanders committed themselves, in new privileges, to com-

[11]Nicholas 1979: 23.

[12]The nine pages with complaints from individual members and merchants from specific towns were filed in October 1358: Gilliodts-Van Severen 1871–85: 2:36–45; Dollinger 1964: 85–91.

[13]See Appendix A.

[14]In 1383, following disturbances in Bruges, the duke of Brabant issued a safe-conduct for all merchants who wanted to travel to Antwerp: Bartier and Nieuwenhuysen 1965: 5–6. A clear indication for the individual nature of the response can be found in the annual membership of the Lucchese nation, which stood at fifty-three merchants between 1377 and 1379, then dropped to twenty-two merchants in 1387, then rose to over forty merchants in the early 1390s: Lazzareschi 1947.

[15]Bartier and Nieuwenhuysen 1965: 200–201. In 1397, 1398, 1401, and 1403, respectively, merchants from the English towns of Newcastle, Berwick-on-Tweed, and Norwich received safe-conducts promising them undisturbed trade in Flanders, and the right to leave with all their belongings within three months in case of war. Bartier and Nieuwenhuysen 1974: 242–44, 311–12, 491–92.

[16]Gilliodts-Van Severen 1871–85: 3:244–60.

TABLE 7.1. Pecuniary compensation paid to German merchants in Bruges
(1250–1500)

Date	Contested issues	Damages (£ Flemish)
1280–82	Toll and weighage tariffs	—
1305	Money standards and weighage	—
1307–9	Money standards, brokerage, weighage	—
1351	English attack on German ship; weighage; default by hosteller	—
1357–60	Staple rights, tolls, brokerage, wine excise; display of goods; confiscated vessels; preferential local debts	4,111
1377	Default by hostellers; assaults; taxes; quality of goods; import restrictions	—
1383	Flemish Revolt	—
1392	Confiscation of German goods	11,100
1397	Damage done in local hostel	107
1405	Attack by pirates from Nieuwpoort	703
1428	Conflicts between Hansa and Holland	—
1430	Damage done by local moneychanger	267
1431–32	Attack by pirates from Scotland	2,151
1434–35	Attacks by privateers from Zeeland	—
1438	Murder of Germans in Sluis	(8,000)[a]
1438	Attack of two German hostellers	108
1448	Establishment of German staple	—
1451	Establishment of German staple	—
1457	Various complaints	2,000
1498	Piracy and damages to Florentine merchant	18,000

[a] This money was never paid.

Source: Appendix B.

pensate the Germans for any future damage suffered at the hands of their
own subjects.[17]

Bruges took this promise to the German Hanse very seriously. In the
first half of the fifteenth century the city, sometimes in association with
the other Flemish towns, quickly made amends when German merchants
complained about infringements on their property. In 1397, 1430, and
1438 the town magistrate paid damages for the misbehavior of local
money changers and hostellers toward German merchants (Table 7.1).
In 1405 and 1432 payments were made to compensate for attacks by
pirates from Nieuwpoort and Scotland, respectively. A major incident

[17]Bartier and Nieuwenhuysen 1965: 473.

occurred in 1436 when allegedly more than eighty Hanseatic seamen and merchants were killed in Sluis by a mob suspecting their support for the English king.[18] The actual number of casualties was probably much lower, but nevertheless in 1438 the German Kontor temporarily moved to Antwerp to return only upon the promise of damages to the amount of 8,000 pounds Flemish.

It was during this period that English merchants in Antwerp for the first time reverted to a boycott to obtain compensation for damages. In 1430 they removed their business to Middelburg in response to violence against English visitors at the fairs of Antwerp.[19] The boycott produced little effect, however. The English returned to Antwerp after reassurances that their property would be secure, but no damages were paid.[20] In the following decades, war between England and Burgundy led to repeated bans on cloth imports, and although Antwerp's magistrate was supportive of English efforts to lift these bans, the city itself violated the nation's privileges on at least two occasions. In 1450 this led the English to stay away from the fair, but in 1457 mediation by arbiters sufficed to solve a conflict about the payment of excise duties.[21] In 1464 the English moved their business to Utrecht in response to yet another ban on their imports. Three years later a peace treaty between England and Burgundy secured their return, but without any financial compensation for losses suffered in the past.

The German merchants in Bruges were far more successful in obtaining compensation through boycotts. In 1450 the Hanse once again reverted to a collective boycott to obtain satisfaction for a number of infringements on their property. Damages promised in 1438 had not been paid, German ships had been attacked, and the merchants were dissatisfied with the enforcement of their staple rights. What followed in 1451 was a removal, first to Deventer and then to Utrecht. The boycott ended only in 1457 after lengthy negotiations, the confirmation of the German staple, the promise to construct a new nation house for the merchants, and the payment of damages to the amount of 2,000 pounds Flemish.

In 1497 came the highest payment of all time to German merchants in Bruges: 16,000 pounds Flemish.[22] One year earlier the Hanse had refused to follow an order by the Great Council to pay damages to Tomaso Portinari, the owner of a Florentine galley captured by a German privateer in 1473, more than twenty years earlier. Because of the political turmoil in

---

[18]Thielemans 1966: 85.

[19]De Smedt 1951: 87, 89–90.

[20]De Smedt 1951: 88, 90–94; Prims 1927–49: 6:2, 151.

[21]De Smedt 1951: 84, 94.

[22]The following is based on Gilliodts-Van Severen 1871–85: 6:410–57. See also Grunzweig 1931: xxxix; Mallett 1967: 98–102, sets the value of ship and cargo at 30,000 florins.

Flanders, German property in Bruges had been impounded in retaliation only in 1492, after the Kontor had been removed to Antwerp. In the year after the verdict of the Great Council, the Hanse, still unwilling to pay, threatened to leave Bruges for good, unless the town paid all damages to the Florentine shipowner. By then Bruges was so eager to restore its former glory that it even offered an extra 2,000 pounds to compensate for more recent assaults by pirates. Such was the town's predicament that one year later even the Castilian nation wrested 2,000 pounds from the magistrate in exchange for their promise to return to Bruges.

In brief, repeated boycotts of Bruges, mostly by the German Hanse but sometimes also by English and Spanish traders, show that collective action was used by merchants to discipline rulers. The successful execution of these boycotts hinged on the presence of neighboring ports where merchants could continue their work at relatively low cost. Still, only some of the violent incidents led to the collective departure of foreign merchants, while the compensation for commercial losses incurred often remained very limited. Moreover, many merchants, particularly those from France, Portugal, and the Italian city-states, never reverted to boycotts. This suggests a very specific combination of preconditions that had to be met for foreign nations to choose a boycott as the appropriate course of action.

The Narrow Margins of Success

The German success in obtaining new privileges and financial compensation in Bruges between the thirteenth and fifteenth centuries hinged on the value of the German contribution to Flemish trade and the ability of the Hanse, and Lübeck in particular, to coordinate collective action.[23] The procedure was straightforward. Once German merchants in Bruges had informed their home rulers about the problems they had encountered, the *Hansetag*, the general assembly of the Hanse, decided what action to take and then sent special envoys to lead negotiations with the host rulers. Sometimes, but certainly not always, demands were enforced by a collective boycott. Once an agreement about damages was reached, it was left to the aldermen of the Kontor to distribute the money among individual traders in Bruges.[24] It was probably no coincidence that the first successful demand for damages followed shortly after the Hanse's

[23]To be sure, this interference of home governments does not imply a conflict of interest between the German community in Bruges and the central authority of the Hanse. The delegates who decided on the boycott at the *Hansetage* in Lübeck often had considerable commercial interests in Flanders themselves: Poeck 2000: 41–43, 47–49; Jenks 1992a.

[24]Gilliodts-Van Severen 1871–85: 2:45–46.

formal recognition in 1356 of the internal Kontorordnung drafted by the German merchants in Bruges in 1347.[25]

Still, the internal organization of the German Hanse alone does not explain the privileges and compensation obtained by them. Italian, English, Spanish, and later also Portuguese merchants in Bruges equally belonged to corporate bodies strong enough to force members to impose penalties on the host city.[26] English wool exporters, for instance, were formally submitted to the authority of the Staple Company, whose monopoly in turn was enforced by the English king.[27] In the third quarter of the fourteenth century the consuls of the Lucchese nation disciplined individual merchants by excluding them from the religious ceremonies of the *communità* or denying other members the right to trade with them.[28] In 1420 and 1427 the internal cohesion of the Castilian nation in Bruges apparently was strong enough to convince their host they would leave collectively if their property was confiscated.[29]

As far as the internal organization of their communities was concerned, the consuls of the nations of Venice, Genoa, Florence, and Lucca were able to organize collective action. However, the cost of leaving Bruges was too high for their members. The merchants from the various city-states were each other's competitors in trade with Italy, hence the departure of one group would play into the hands of the others. What is more, from the second half of the fourteenth century the Italian trade with Northern Europe was based on their fixed residence in Bruges and London. Whereas German trade mostly consisted of straightforward sales and purchases with relatively simple credit requirements, the Italians developed sophisticated exchange operations and current accounting practices to organize payments and short-term credit. Hence it comes as no surprise that the Venetians could credibly threaten to continue their business in Antwerp only in the 1450s when the fairs of Brabant began to offer sufficient scope for more complex financial operations.[30]

---

[25]Henn 2008; Dollinger 1964: 86–88, 99–102; Stein 1902. Complete control over the operations of individual merchants was impossible, however. For instance, in 1392 the Hanse could not but accept that merchants continued their exportation of amber to Bruges and their visits of Brabant fairs and Malines. The Hanse town of Kampen also continued its trade with Bruges. Dollinger 1964; Rössner 2001: 63.

[26]Note also that granting new privileges was not always the result of collective action. It was standard procedure to confirm privileges upon the accession of a new ruler, and a new franchise could also be extended to confirm alliances. At the occasion of the marriage of Philip the Good with Isabella of Portugal in 1438, for instance, new privileges were given to Portuguese merchants in the Burgundian lands and to Flemish merchants in Portugal, for that matter: Goris 1925: 34, 38.

[27]Nicholas 1979: 23–32.

[28]Lazzareschi 1947: 32–33, 37, 41, 43–44.

[29]Paviot 1995: 216–17.

[30]Bolton and Guidi Bruscoli 2008.

The German merchants in Bruges were also better positioned than English and Spanish traders, whose sovereigns were repeatedly at war with the Dukes of Burgundy.[31] Admittedly, Holland and the Wendish quarter of the Hanse were embroiled from the 1430s onward, but Flanders stayed out of their conflicts, and thus the negotiating position of the Hanse in Bruges was unaffected.[32] Castilian and Aragonese merchants, on the other hand, were made to pay for damages inflicted by their home governments in the first half of the fifteenth century.[33] A Castilian attack on German and Flemish ships in 1417 left Castilian ships exposed to Flemish privateers in subsequent years.[34] To stop these reprisals the Castilian king wanted the merchants to withdraw from Bruges, but this was obviously not in their interest. Instead, after intensive talks in Spain and Flanders, they settled for a 5 percent levy on all sales of merchandise from Galicia, Asturia, Old Castile, and Biscay.[35] The Four Members of Flanders were to use the revenues to pay the costs of their diplomatic efforts and award damages to individual victims of the corsairs.[36] In the 1440s Aragonese merchants accepted a similar scheme to compensate for the seizure of Flemish ships in the Mediterranean in 1436 and 1440.[37] The obvious attraction of these financial solutions was the equal distribution of the burden over all traders, and the possibility to shift at least part of it to their customers. Yet once the Spaniards thought they had paid enough, they pushed for cancellation. In 1428 the Castilian levy was abolished after their king ordered his subjects to leave Flanders.[38] Protests by Bruges and merchants from Catalonia, Aragon, Venice, Genoa, Florence, Pisa, and Milan led to the withdrawal of the Aragonese levy in January 1450.[39]

In both the fourteenth and the fifteenth centuries England and Flanders so often captured and confiscated each other's ships and merchandise that mutual claims were simply cancelled out when peace negotiations

[31] Conflicts between Genoa and the Burgundian dukes were few and far between. In 1462 Genoese merchants paid 1,435 pounds to the captain of a Burgundian warship that had been captured by Genoa in 1445—seventeen years earlier. Paviot 1995: 216.

[32] Blockmans and Prevenier 1999: 93–94; Paviot 1995: 235–38; Dollinger 1964: 378–79; Slootmans 1985: 1:103–5.

[33] Watson 1961: 1088; Paviot 1995: 214–15.

[34] Gilliodts-Van Severen 1883–85: 1:466–72; Gilliodts-Van Severen 1871–85: 4:379, 381, 494.

[35] Gilliodts-Van Severen 1901–2: 23; Gilliodts-Van Severen 1871–85: 4:495–96.

[36] Gilliodts-Van Severen 1901–2: 26.

[37] In 1440 when talks with the Aragones consuls in Bruges failed to produce a result, the Duke set a levy of 1.66 percent on all imports from Aragon to be collected by the disenfranchised merchants. Five years later the levy was raised to 2.5 percent following the capture of a Burgundian ship in the Mediterranean. Paviot 1995: 214.

[38] Gilliodts-Van Severen 1871–85: 4:494, 496, 497; Paviot 1995: 217.

[39] Paviot 1995: 213–15.

were held. This happened for instance in 1414, when Burgundy signed a peace treaty with then still independent Holland and Zeeland. Damages before October 24, 1412, were simply considered not to have occurred, damages thereafter had to be compensated within the next year, and future infringements were to be severely punished.[40] In the first half of the fifteenth century political conflicts between the two countries undermined the bargaining position of English cloth merchants in Antwerp. To wage war against England, the Dukes of Burgundy impounded their goods on several occasions and repeatedly issued bans on their imports as well.[41] Only toward the end of the fifteenth century, when the regular import, finishing, and export of English cloth became indispensable to the functioning of the Antwerp market, did English merchants gain some leverage.[42] Building on a tighter internal organization and the active support of the English crown, they started using the competition between Bergen-op-Zoom and Antwerp to secure a most favorable treatment by both towns: "[T]hey dryve the townshippes, by feere of theyre withdrawing and absentyng, to reforme their wronges."[43] The payment of damages remained a bridge too far, however. Only once, in 1490, could the English make Antwerp pay for an armed convoy they had organized themselves to secure a safe crossing from England.[44]

In addition to their strong internal organization and the lack of political conflict with the Dukes of Burgundy, the Hanseatic merchants also benefited from their strong economic position in Bruges. They were the city's principal suppliers of Baltic grain and major buyers of textiles and other high-value commodities. In 1360 an imminent grain shortage was one of the reasons why Bruges complied with demands for new privileges and hefty compensation.[45] In 1436 the Hanse threatened to stop grain imports to get permission to move to Antwerp after the assault on their

[40] Gilliodts-Van Severen 1883–85: 1:466–72.

[41] De Smedt 1951: 90.

[42] Bisson 1993: 70–80.

[43] De Smedt 1951: 96.

[44] In 1492 English merchantmen were once again protected by an English war fleet, funded by the English. In 1493 a boycott and removal to Calais was instigated by the English king, not the merchant community. De Smedt 1951: 98–100.

[45] Bruges's account books reveal three payments of damages to the German Hanse. In 1357–58 a delegation of four was given 1,800 pounds Flemish as it left for Lübeck. In 1359–60 two merchants representing the German Hanse received 1,547 pounds Flemish for an outstanding claim on a Bruges citizen and for Scottish merchandise that had been seized on their behalf by the city of Bruges. One year later another German representative received 559 pounds Flemish as part of the damages awarded by Flanders to the Hanse (Gilliodts-Van Severen 1871–85: 2:48, 65). In addition to this Dollinger (1964: 89–90) mentions an otherwise unspecified amount of 155 pounds payable by both Bruges and Ypres. In 1365 the Hanse formally relieved Bruges of its suretyship for damages payable by the Count of Flanders. Gilliodts-Van Severen 1871–85: 2:127–28.

members in Sluis, and in 1438 they promised to deliver Prussian grain to facilitate their return.[46] In 1457 even the Spanish, Catalan, Florentine, Genoese, and Lucchese merchants asked Bruges to arrange for the return of the German Hanse—obviously to secure their own business with them.[47]

The value Bruges's magistrates attached to the presence of the German merchants is very clear from the cost they incurred to negotiate the return of the Hanse in the 1450s.[48] The city accounts reveal expenses of more than 4,000 pounds Flemish between 1452 and 1458. The travel expenses of envoys (not their salaries), the cost of meals and paperwork, and the interest payment on German debts to citizens of Bruges amounted to 500 pounds; the Duke of Burgundy received 600 pounds for his approval of the extension of new privileges; the expropriation of a parcel for the construction of a new nation house cost 574 pounds; and legal proceedings in Paris, involving Hanseatic merchants but also members of other nations, cost another 430 pounds. Finally the city paid its one-quarter share of the 8,000 pounds Flemish in damages that had been awarded, but never paid out, in 1438.[49]

The economic value of the Hanse to the host community also explains why German boycotts stopped in the sixteenth century.[50] With Holland gaining a foothold in the Baltic trade, the Hanse lost their position as sole supplier of Baltic goods; they had to allow Dutch exports to Germany, and consequently lost the ability to harm their hosts by staying away. At the same time the Dutch entry into the Baltic led to political tensions. For example, in 1510 the Habsburg rulers allowed Dutch merchants to capture whatever Wendish ship they could to compensate for damages of more than 100,000 guilders resulting from the capture of eleven merchantmen by a Lübeck fleet.[51] Likewise, the attachment of the goods of Hanseatic merchants in five Antwerp hostels in 1532 followed attacks on

[46] Rössner 2001: 71–72; Blockmans 1978: 467, referring to direct grain purchases by Bruges in Hainault between 1436 and 1438.
[47] Gilliodts-Van Severen 1871–85: 5:402.
[48] Gilliodts-Van Severen 1871–85: 5:409–18.
[49] Dollinger 1964: 368; Gilliodts-Van Severen 1871–85: 257.
[50] Pace Blockmans and Prevenier (1999), who stress the importance of Burgundian unification for the reduced efficiency of collective action by the Hanse. In their view, the growing political unity would have limited the possibilities to temporarily remove the staple to territories under a different rule. Compare also Dollinger (1964: 349). Both the removal of the German Hanse from Bruges to Antwerp in 1553 and the repeated relocation of the Court of Merchant Adventurers from Middelburg to Delft, Dordrecht, and Rotterdam in the Dutch Republic in the first half of the seventeenth century show that political unification does not keep foreign merchants from playing one city against the other as long as cities are sufficiently autonomous to negotiate with them.
[51] Sicking 2004: 207–41.

Netherlandish ships by Lübeck.[52] Admittedly, the Hanse did eventually obtain extensive privileges in Antwerp in 1553, but this was very much a defensive move of the Scheldt port, which by then also began to feel the negative effects of the Dutch domination of the Baltic trade.

Thus it was a combination of political and economic factors that allowed the German Hanse more than any other foreign nation in the Low Countries to use boycotts to try to improve its position. It is doubtful, however, whether this was either necessary or sufficient to deal with losses from violent assaults. We saw earlier that by 1400 virtually every merchant community had been given a general safe-conduct and consular jurisdiction. The Germans stand out because of the considerable damages awarded to them, but it is doubtful whether this sufficed to cover their losses. In 1438, for instance, the merchants and shipmasters of twenty-three Hanseatic ships captured by privateers from Zeeland and Holland off the coast of France suffered losses of 12,450 pounds Flemish.[53] Further attacks on dozens of other German ships in 1439 and 1440 doubled the total losses.[54] At 1,650 pounds Flemish, the Dutch capture of eight German ships between 1456 and 1458 alone cost merchants and ship-masters from Prussia and Latvia almost as much as the paltry compensation the German Hanse received in 1458, after a six-year boycott, for a different and much larger set of infringements.[55] In other words, the total value of German cargo lost in violent assaults was many times higher than the compensation paid by Bruges.

The cost of the actual boycotts was very high as well—in terms of the physical removal of merchants and their goods, the administrative burden, and, perhaps most important, the income lost by not being in the most favorable location. If these costs were anywhere near the expenses Bruges's magistrate made to secure a German return—a not unreasonable assumption given the speed with which both parties, at least until 1450, tried to renegotiate the German position in Bruges—it may well be that the damages covered only these costs and not the losses that had actually triggered the boycott. This then would suggest that the primary purpose of the Hanseatic boycotts was not to compensate for damages but rather to exploit their key role in the Bruges market to secure favorable trading conditions—most notably the confirmation of their staple rights. But if collective action could not make up for the actual losses, what other means of compensation could foreign merchants in the Low Countries revert to?

[52] Häpke 1913.
[53] Poelman 1917: 1:347, 2:796–807.
[54] Poelman 1917: 2:807–28.
[55] Poelman 1917: 2:833–34.

Prize Cases

From the very moment foreign merchants visited the ports of Bruges, Antwerp, and Amsterdam, their hosts considered various legal arrangements to compensate for the losses they might incur. Already in the thirteenth century Flanders had its Scabini Flandriae, a jury consisting of the aldermen from the five major towns that ruled in cases of damages inflicted on merchants and shipmasters.[56] In 1303 the Count of Flanders and the five towns named auditors to establish the damage done to foreign merchants.[57] We do not know what cases the Scabini Flandriae was supposed to deal with, but considering the attacks on English merchants in this period one might expect the committee's intervention to have focused on the consequences of interstate rivalry. The collaboration did not last, however, and in later years foreign merchants and shipmasters probably turned to local courts to claim damages. For instance, in 1432 a shipmaster from Zeeland who had captured a ship from Brittany was brought before the water bailiff of Sluis, the outport of Bruges.[58] In 1459 English and Italian merchants contested seizures of their goods before the local court of Bruges.[59]

In the first half of the fifteenth century provincial court proceedings emerged as an alternative road to compensation, often but not always in unison with the town magistrates. In 1440 the Duke of Burgundy ordered Amsterdam's bailiff to arrest the owners of ships that had attacked Norwegian vessels in order to try them before the Hof van Holland, the Court of Holland. To force the local court to comply, the duke threatened to allow the Norwegians to retaliate with the attachment of property of Amsterdam citizens.[60] In 1442 several merchants from the Dutch port appeared before the Court of Holland because their cog had taken a ship with its merchandise from a citizen of Copenhagen.[61] The Danish shipowner was unable to recoup the damage from the Amsterdam burghers, and the provincial judges had to ask Amsterdam's local judges to attach the shipowners' property in order to compensate the injured party.[62] In 1488, on the other hand, the Amsterdam magistrate independently took hostage several Englishmen in response to a request by local merchants whose ships and goods had been seized by English warships near Calais.[63]

[56] Gilliodts-Van Severen 1871–85: 4:268.
[57] Gilliodts-Van Severen 1871–85: 164–65.
[58] Paviot 1995: 219.
[59] Thielemans 1966: 264.
[60] Poelman 1917: 1:392, 395.
[61] Poelman 1917: 1:432.
[62] Poelman 1917: 1:437, 438.
[63] Breen 1902: 237–38.

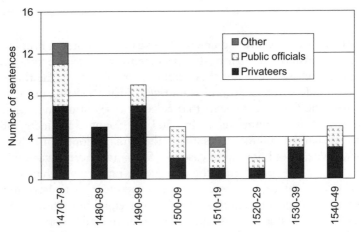

FIGURE 7.1. Different types of violence addressed in sentences of the Great Council of Malines in lawsuits involving foreign merchants, 1470–1550
    Source: de Smidt 1966–79: passim.

In a further attempt to discipline public officials, lower-level governments, and individual subjects, the Dukes of Burgundy set up the Great Council of Malines as a central court for the Low Countries.[64] Among its judgments passed between 1470 and 1550 were forty-seven sentences concerning violence against foreign merchants (Figure 7.1).[65] More than half of these sentences related to attacks by privateers from the Burgundian lands, England, France, and Germany, or subsequent attachments of property of alleged associates or fellow countrymen of the privateers. Another third of the cases involved disputed behavior of local magistrates, tax collectors, and other public officials. Finally, two cases dealt with the return of goods washed ashore after a shipwreck, and one concerned the refusal of Portuguese insurers in Bruges to honor a claim of an insured merchant.[66]

Both foreign and local traders could turn to the Great Council. Among the claimants in these forty-seven lawsuits were merchants from Spain, Brittany, England, Scotland, Florence, Genoa, Germany, and the Low Countries. The cases they filed involved the simple restitution of ships and cargo, but also damages claimed from merchants who had bought goods taken by privateers, and disputes about the legality of prizes. For instance, in 1494 representatives of the king of Scotland protested against letters of mark given to Hanseatic merchants, who claimed Scottish pri-

[64]Van Rompaey 1973.
[65]Some prize cases were heard already before 1470: Van Rompaey 1973: 282.
[66]de Smidt et al. 1966–79: De Counas and Lommelin v. Denis and Fernande 1478.

vateers had taken their merchandise. The Scotsmen referred to earlier privileges protecting their property from any reprisals in the Burgundian lands.[67] As for the cases involving public officials, they mostly concerned disputed confiscations that seem at least indirectly related to warfare and privateering. However, there also were a few contested arrests of the merchants (or their goods) whose agents had failed to pay tolls.[68] Even the Dukes of Burgundy did not escape the judges' scrutiny. In 1468 the Great Council confirmed the freedom of the fairs of Brabant by lifting the seizure of the goods of a French merchant on his journey home from Antwerp. In doing so the judges overruled the permission the dukes had given for the arrest.[69]

With one sentence every two years, on average, the number of cases heard by the Great Council was very minimal, however. One reason was that merchants turned to the central court only to appeal decisions of local and provincial courts.[70] Another reason, evidenced by the very limited number of prize cases after 1500, was the ducal decision in 1488 that Burgundian privateers had to present all their prizes to a specialized court to establish their lawfulness. From then on the Admiralty Court in Veere, and its subsidiary in Dunkirk, acted as court of first instance for neutral traders suffering from privateering in Zeeland and Flanders.[71] Following legal procedures similar to those of the Great Council, the justices of the Admiralty Court of Veere inspected the shipping documents, testimonies of both parties, and any letters of mark or countermark to establish the righteousness of the capture and restitute the property in case of unlawful capture.[72] The major concern of the Admiralty Court was to protect neutral traders against wrongful captures. Out of thirty-four prize cases brought before the Admiralty of Veere between 1537 and 1559, twenty-five

[67]de Smidt et al. 1966–79: Representatives of the Scottish King v. Gerard de la Maire and the City of Antwerp 1494.

[68]de Smidt et al. 1966–79: Comito v. Toll Collector of Iersekeroord and Arnemuyden 1513; Besselu and Mornault v. Toll Collector of Iersekeroord 1517; Philippe v. Toll Collectors of Grevelingen 1500.

[69]Van Rompaey 1973: 402.

[70]We can identify ten cases as appeals to verdicts of the Court of Holland. De Smidt et al. 1966–79: Alkmaar etc. v. Baldry 1478; Genoese Nation v. Towns of Flanders 1479; Bels v. Sersanders and Van Eygnhen 1484; Colins v. Huppenaer 1491; Scottish Merchants v. Bruynhille 1497; Van der Heyden v. Aelbrechtsz 1509; Brederode v. Scottish Nation 1519; Pietersz v. Jacobsz 1531; Viensz v. Luyden Zwinge 1536; Bodly v. Bailiff Veere 1540. Another five cases were appeals to verdicts of local courts in Zeeland and Flanders: Colins v. Huppenaer 1491; De Counas and Lommelin v. Denis and Fernande 1478; Somer and Schelton v. De Vos 1478; Le Marc v. Fonyer 1480; Scottish Nation v. Blackwort 1518. Finally, three cases were appeals to verdicts of the Admiralty of Zeeland: English Nation v. Symonsz 1540; Claes v. English Merchants 1542; Du Gal v. De Doot and Pietersz 1548.

[71]Sicking 2004: 442–43.

[72]Sicking 2004: 440–41, 445; Roelofsen 1991.

involved merchants from countries not at war with the Habsburgs. The Great Council of Malines continued to function as a court of appeal, but between 1488 and 1550 it served this purpose only three times in cases involving foreign merchants as claimants or defendants.[73]

In contrast, the province of Holland did not recognize the authority of the Admiralty of Veere.[74] Here the provincial court continued to deal with privateering cases initially.[75] It was only at the end of the sixteenth century that the Court of Holland lost its role in prize cases to five newly established Admiralty Courts in Amsterdam, Middelburg, Rotterdam, Hoorn/Enkhuizen, and Dokkum (in 1645 removed to Harlingen).[76] From the 1580s onward these courts adjudicated all prize cases with the High Court of Holland and Zeeland acting as the court of appeal.[77] Much like the earlier Admiralty of Veere, the courts used the ship's papers to determine within three days whether a capture constituted a lawful prize. If it did not, ship and cargo were immediately released.[78]

The central government exercised no direct control over the adjudication of prize cases by the Admiralty Courts, but the States General did occasionally intervene on behalf of foreign merchants.[79] Dutch but also

[73] De Smidt et al. 1966–79: English nation v. Symonsz 1540; Claes v. English Merchants 1542; Du Gal v. De Doot and Pietersz 1548.

[74] In 1560 the legal functions of the Admiralty of Veere devolved to the Court of Flanders. Roelofsen 1991: 7.

[75] Roelofsen 1991: xxii–xxiii; Sicking 2004: 432.

[76] In 1586 the Estates of Holland left it to the Admiralty to reach an agreement with an English merchant regarding two of his ships that had been taken by a Dutch privateer (RSH 20/22, 15-01-1586). Our sample of sentences (1582–1630) of the Court of Holland relating to Flemish and English merchants in Amsterdam analyzed in chapter 5 contains only two cases involving the payment of damages after the capture of a ship by pirates before the Flemish coast: NA 3.03.01.01 *Hof van Holland*: Sententiën, 1610/37, fiche 621*; 1624/209, fiche 666*.

[77] The Court of Holland continued to have jurisdiction over disputes involving public officials, but our analysis of sentences of the Court of Holland involving Flemish and English merchants between 1580 and 1632 reveals no such cases (see chapter 5).

[78] Already in 1577 goods wrongfully taken from merchants from befriended nations were returned by the Admiralties: RSH 11/258, 11-01-1577. For the procedures followed by the Admiralty of Middelburg at the turn of the eighteenth century: Bruijn 1993: 104.

[79] The States General, often at the instigation of local or provincial authorities, wrote letters to the rulers of Sweden, Denmark, the German order, England, the Spanish Netherlands, France, Spain, Algeria, Tuscany, and Venice asking them to return ships and merchandise, to free prisoners, or to compensate for damages. For Amsterdam's request to the States General for diplomatic support, see RSG 1600, 329–30; RSG 1610, no. 41; RSG 1618, no. 2292. For diplomatic efforts of the Estates of Holland: RSH 55/622, 19-03-1579; RSH 475/863, 09-09-1581; RSH 20-11-1585; RSH 175/193, 17-07-1627; RSH 163/786, 25-11-1626. On two occasions, in 1639 and 1642, the Estates of Holland asked diplomats to look into the lawfulness of capture of Dutch ships by Genoese privateers: RSH 175/435, 16-09-1639; also 210/474, 18-10-1639, and 214/479, 21-10-1639; RSH 119/521, 08-05-1642. In 1642 a similar action was undertaken toward the English authorities: RSH 299/718, 25-11-1642.

Portuguese, German, and Flemish merchants benefited from these interventions.[80] Thus, in 1589 they ordered the return to an Italian merchant of a ship laden with grain that had been taken by the Dutch navy. The merchant, Jehan Baptista Pelligrini, living in Sweden, had sought the support of the Polish king to recoup his loss. In order not to upset the king, the States General decided in his favor, with a friendly reminder to the king that Pelligrini, just like any other merchant, should have produced sufficient evidence to support his claim, and appear before a court in the Low Countries.[81] On a few other occasions the States General allowed the immediate treatment of a case by the High Court.[82] At least once they asked the judges of the High Court to proceed quickly in a case involving London merchants.[83]

The legal solution only went so far, however. Most of the time there was no counterparty to sue.[84] Foreign privateers obviously took their prizes abroad, but even attackers with letters of mark from the Dutch Republic often put in to foreign ports either to keep the Admiralties from taking their cut or to prevent other corsairs from robbing them of their prize.[85] Thus it comes as no surprise that several cases before courts in the Low Countries followed the chance spotting of an aggressor's ship or merchandise. Scottish merchants in Veere, for instance, were able to start legal proceedings against English privateers who in 1533 had captured their cargo only when another ship of one of the owners of the attackers' vessel moored in Zeeland two years later.[86]

At the same time court proceedings were time-consuming. With cases dragging on for years, it took strong convictions or very high stakes—as with the German capture of a Florentine galley in 1473—for merchants to choose to go to court.[87] This also explains why merchants and rulers, just like private parties involved in business disputes, sometimes tried to reach an amicable settlement instead. In 1458, for instance, arbitration resolved a conflict with English merchants about the payment of certain

[80] Suffice it to cite several individual recommendations involving merchants from Portugal, Germany, and Flanders: RSG 1610, no. 1358; RSG 1615, no. 1551; RSG 1618, nos. 3634, 3635; RSG 1620, 419; RSG 1611, no. 300; RSG 1610, nos. 751, 1065, 1411n, 1536; RSG 1611, no. 613; RSG 1617, nos. 964, 1610, 1763; RSG 1618, nos. 2799, 3549, 3835, 4001.

[81] RSG 1589, 633–34.

[82] RSG 1600, 339–40; RSG 1600, 613; RSG 1613: 11.

[83] RSG 1612, 800.

[84] Stradling 1992: 210–11; Wijffels and van Loo 1998: 652–53.

[85] Korteweg 2006: 91.

[86] Roelofsen 1991: xix–xxiii. For similar incidents see de Smidt et al. 1966–79: 1:152, 156.

[87] Compare the recovery of 39,000 pounds Flemish worth of goods confiscated by the English crown in the 1560s. The attempts of the Flemish merchants to obtain compensation in England cost almost 6,000 pounds Flemish worth of presents, travel expenses, and other expenses. Brulez 1959: 29–30.

excise taxes in Burgundian territory.[88] In 1467 the Great Council of Malines asked Bruges to arbitrate in a conflict between the aldermen of the
Kontor and the officers of Spanish warships who had taken an English
ship with cloth that partly belonged to German merchants. They proposed this informal solution "pour éviter longueur de process et despens,
et entre tenir paix et amour entre eux."[89]

RISK SPREADING

With collective action and court proceedings offering limited opportunities to deal with losses from violent assaults, merchants had to turn to
the market to organize compensation. There they could choose among
three ways to manage risks: spread investments over different products
and markets, share risks through joint operations with other merchants,
or transfer risks to third parties. The added advantage of all three strategies was that they allowed for compensation for more than just damage
resulting from violence. Shipwreck due to bad weather or incompetence
of a shipmaster and his crew, opportunistic behavior by trading partners,
and adverse market conditions could also cause considerable financial
damage, and thus put a premium on appropriate risk management.

For the thirteenth and early fourteenth centuries we lack detailed information on the organization of transactions, but we can already observe some of the basic strategies. A straightforward means to spread
risks was to send cargo in different vessels or wagons. In Venice, for instance, merchants bought shares in partnerships that rented and freighted
the state-owned galleys to Flanders. They participated in different companies and different galleys to minimize the commercial risks involved
in the sailings to Flanders.[90] In Northern Europe, shipping among the
Low Countries, England, and Germany was regular enough to create an
embryonic market for transportation service, with the related possibility to divide cargo between ships.[91] In the late thirteenth century fifteen
German merchants contracted with a Dutch shipmaster to export wool
from Boston, England—a transaction brokered by two merchants from
Lucca.[92] Hamburg beer exporters to Amsterdam in the second half of
the fourteenth century typically shared cargo space with between five
and twenty other merchants.[93] In the fifteenth century English and Italian merchants continued to spread their cargo over different ships when

[88] De Smedt 1951: 94.
[89] Gilliodts-Van Severen 1883–85: 1:467.
[90] Lane 1944b: 186–94.
[91] Nicholas 1979: 40–41, 47–55.
[92] De Boer 1996: 130–31.
[93] Smit 1914: 46, 47–48, 91–92; Slootmans 1985: 1:107–8, 111–12.

crossing the North Sea.[94] Thus, when a wool fleet chartered by Italian merchants was captured by English pirates in 1457, the damages were divided over all participants according to their share in the total cargo.[95] A report drafted in 1458 by Prussian authorities on the damages suffered by German merchants at the hands of privateers from Holland and Zeeland in the previous two decades reveals the importance of the distribution of cargo over different vessels.[96] First and foremost among the assaults on the Germans was the capture off the French coast of twenty-three ships returning from Portugal in 1438. The number of merchants with cargo in these ships varied between one and ten, and the average value of parcels loaded by individual traders probably did not exceed 100 pounds Flemish. The damages suffered as a result of the loss of another thirty-one ships in 1439 and 1440 amounted to 9,111 pounds Flemish. Although the report on these losses is much less detailed, the available data suggest an average cargo of at most 120 pounds Flemish per freighter.

The distribution of cargo over different ships continued in Antwerp and Amsterdam after 1500. A small sample of imports and exports registered for taxation by two Spanish merchants and one Portuguese merchant in Antwerp in 1553 and 1554 shows how they divided up their cargoes in dozens of separate shipments with an average value of 800 pounds Flemish.[97] The business administration of a Delft merchant in the late sixteenth century reveals that 40 percent of the voyages of his ships to the Baltic Sea included cargo of other merchants.[98] Swedish custom accounts between 1580 and 1650 reveal that 45 to 65 percent of all ships bound for the Low Countries counted between two and ten freighters, while an additional 20 to 25 percent of these ships even had more than ten freighters.[99] A report written by Amsterdam merchants in support of a project to establish a general insurance company for trade with the Mediterranean explicitly mentioned the customary division of freight over several ships in voyages to ports in Norway, Germany, England, and France.[100] Merchants involved in overland trade among the Low Countries, Germany, and Italy also reduced risks by dividing up their cargo.[101] In Antwerp the merchandise was left in the hands

[94] Nicholas 1979: 41; Hanham 1985. For the sixteenth century see Van der Wee 1963: 2:327.

[95] Slootmans 1985: 1:99–100. Slootmans reports a similar division of losses in 1446: Slootmans 1985: 1:97–98.

[96] Poelman 1917: 1:347; 2: nos. 796–834.

[97] Goris 1925: 307–16; Coornaert 1961: 2:38.

[98] Christensen 1941: 155.

[99] Christensen 1941: 166–67.

[100] Christensen 1941: 171–76; Blok 1900a, 1900b; Go 2009: 137–39.

[101] Harreld 2004: 125.

of specialized transporters, who carried the goods in single-axle carts to Cologne or in wide-gauged wagons with a loading capacity of two tons or more, to destinations further afield. Some of these transporters may even have run a regular service between major commercial towns.[102] Just like shipmasters, the transporters could not be held liable for criminal assaults or other damages, unless merchants could prove their negligence.[103]

A related strategy was to share not the cargo space but the actual ownership of the vessels sailing to and from the Low Countries. In medieval Genoa merchants used the *caratatio*, a partnership with transferable shares and a division of profits and losses proportional to the value of each share. The earliest mention of the caratatio in Bruges dates back to 1390. The key to the success of this type of shipping company was the limitation of the partners' losses to the total value of their joint investment, provided they had done everything in their power to prevent or counter violent attacks and natural disaster. This rule derived from a basic principle of maritime law: the owners of a ship and its cargo had the right to abandon their property in case of shipwreck.[104] The caratatio, however, did require shareholders to keep a close eye on their associates because they remained liable toward outside creditors for all debts made by coowners, even if these debts exceeded the value of their own share. Hence the shipmaster was required to draw up detailed accounts and was sometimes given shares to align his interests with those of the nonsailing partners.[105] Some historians have argued that the transferability of Genoese *carats* provided additional security because it allowed shareholders to end their involvement at any point in time. However, given the unlimited liability for debts incurred by other shareholders, the only persons willing to participate were those with sufficient insight into the company's operations, and as long as the books of shipping companies were kept in private this remained a closed circle of investors.

The buying of shares in ships became attractive to outsiders only once their liability could be limited to the value of their initial investment. This abolition of joint and several liability was achieved for the first time with

[102] Harreld 2004: 120–21, 123–24, 129.

[103] Slootmans 1985: 1:121.

[104] To be sure, the practice of dividing a maritime enterprise into shares existed already in Roman times. It was practiced again in the Mediterranean in the ninth and tenth centuries; witness the maritime customs of the island of Rhodes. Ashburner 1909: xiii–xv, clxiii–clxvi. Similar rules were laid down in Barcelona's Consulate of the Sea: arts. 195, 196, and 211 (Jados 1975: 99–100, 112–13).

[105] Record keeping aboard ships probably goes back to the early medieval *columna*. As early as the tenth century ships sailing from Amalfi and Ragusa in the Adriatic sea used a *column* to share profits and losses. In the ship's log they registered the contributions of labor and capital of each and every crew member. Lopez 1971: 75–76.

the *partenrederij* in Northwestern Europe.[106] This equity contract divided the ownership of a ship—and often also its cargo—into equal shares or *parten*. Shareholders bought one or more of eight, sixteen, or thirty-two shares (or multiples thereof) and delegated the authority to manage the shipping company to one of the owners in exchange for a 1 or 2 percent provision. The association was understood to be for one voyage only, shares were transferable, and proper accounting by the shipmaster was required.[107] However, unlike the caratatio, investors in a partenrederij could be held liable for each other's debts only to the amount of their individual investment.[108]

German, English, Dutch, and Flemish merchants invested in partenrederijen on a regular basis in the fifteenth century, and they even used them to transfer risks across national boundaries.[109] Starting in 1405 the German Hanse explicitly forbade its members from holding shares in Dutch companies five times in the fifteenth century—a clear indication that this was a common practice.[110] In 1473 Amsterdam accepted that its citizens participated in shipping companies (*paertscepen*) with strangers, provided these ships sailed to Amsterdam and not to other Dutch ports.[111] During the Habsburg-Valois Wars French and Flemish merchants in Antwerp teamed up deliberately to take advantage of each other's safe-conducts.[112] In the 1590s Dutch merchants tried to circumvent Spanish embargoes through shipments under the German flag, and in the seventeenth century Amsterdam's shipping companies habitually drew investors from the Dutch, Flemish, English, German, and Portuguese communities.[113]

[106] Gelderblom and Jonker 2004; Asser 1983: with references to older literature.

[107] In 1413 Amsterdam's magistrate confirmed the requirement for *partenrederijen* to keep proper accounts of their activities: the shipmaster was obliged to render accounts referring to his associates (*sinen veynoets*): Breen 1902: 28.

[108] Gilliodts-Van Severen 1871–85: 6:540; Lichtenauer 1935: 348.

[109] Slootmans 1985: 1:110, 118; Poelman 1917, 2:796–820; Thielemans 1966: 320–24.

[110] Greve 1999: 217; Jenks 1996b: 9–30. Amsterdam's customs in 1413 stipulated that partnerships between citizens and aliens were not allowed: Breen 1902: 19.

[111] The rule was confirmed in 1492 and 1496: Breen 1902: 70–71.

[112] Coornaert 1961: 2:42; Van der Wee 1963: 2:323.

[113] Kernkamp 1931–34; Hart 1977: 108–9; Winkelman 1971–83; van Gelder 1916; Gelderblom 2000: 280–83. Portuguese merchants in Amsterdam made extensive use of shipping shares; see, e.g., SR 59; 64; 83; 90; 111; 149; 306; 307; 319; 341; 404; 459; 666; 707; 833; 843; 1078; 1408; 1439; 1440; 1456; 1491; 1550; 1571; 1608; 1645; 1851; 1879; 1933; 1943; 1944; 1952; 1994; 2031; 2036; 2037; 2049; 2063; 2069; 2092; 2103; 2104; 2106; 2107; 2109; 2110; 2129; 2133; 2135; 2136; 2147; 2183; 2184; 2226; 2228; 2268; 2272; 2316; 2323; 2365; 2486; 2511; 2551; 2590; 2603; 2612; 2631; 2643; 2652; 2659; 2678; 2719; 2720; 2812; 2835; 2839; 2861; 2908; 2922; 2929; 2938; 2940; 2941; 2951; 2987; 3017; 3018; 3033; 3079; 3123; 3186; 3206; 3249; 3291; 3468; 3478; 3559; 3583; 3599; 3603; 3607.

The Transfer of Risk

The spreading of cargo or shared ship ownership did not always suffice to reduce risks, however. Cargo might simply have been too valuable or destined for markets where potential losses due to warfare or piracy were too high. Merchants who did not want to revert to excessive armament to counter these risks could choose to transfer the risk of violent assault to a third party. An early means to do so was the sea loan or *foenus nauticum*. The sea loan, widely used in Genoa and Venice during the early phases of the Commercial Revolution, was a personal loan extended to a shipmaster or merchant with one crucial clause, namely that the principal sum had to be repaid, with a considerable premium, only when the debtor had safely arrived at his destination.[114] The sea loan was intended as a credit instrument for men with little or no money who wanted to invest their labor in a commercial venture financed by a merchant. However, since redemption of the loan was contingent on the ship's safe arrival, the sea loan also was a very suitable vehicle for the debtor to transfer the risk of shipwreck—whether through natural disaster or violence—to his creditor.

Either one of these two functions made the contract useful to Italian merchants in Bruges into the thirteenth and fourteenth centuries, and to French and German merchants into the fifteenth century.[115] Even in seventeenth-century Amsterdam, where more sophisticated means of risk management were available to all merchants, sea loans (also called bottomry loans) continued to be taken out in the trade with France and the Baltic Sea, possibly as a cheap means of transferring funds back to the Dutch Republic.[116] On the other hand, merchants and shipmasters in Amsterdam used the sea loan to fund the very risky salt voyages to Venezuela around 1600 and the first whaling expeditions in the seas off Greenland shortly thereafter.[117]

The *maritime bill of exchange*, the preferred debt instrument of Genoese merchants trading with Bruges in the early fourteenth century, also

[114]The following is based on Liagre-De Sturler 1969: lxxxii–xc. See also Doehaerd 1941; De Roover 1953b; Edler de Roover 1945; Cordes 1998; Cordes, Friedland, and Sprandel 2003.

[115]Liagre-De Sturler 1969: lxxix–lxxxi; Gilliodts-Van Severen 1883–85: 2:86; Drost 1984, 1989.

[116]De Bruyn Kops 2007: 87–89; van Tielhof 2002: 224; Winkelman 1971–83.

[117]Compare the bottomry loans for the salt trade with Venezuela, contracted before Amsterdam notary Jan Frans Bruyning: ACA NA 80/135v, 17-07-1598; NA 83/126v, 26-04-1599; NA 85/58v, 10-11-1599; NA 85/80, 06-12-1599; NA 85/188v, 17-03-1600; NA 86/98, 04-04-1600; NA 86/121v, 04-04-1600; NA 33/387a, 22-04-1600; NA 86/148, 27-04-1600; NA 86/173, 14-05-1600; NA 92/97v, 18-04-1602; NA 93/86v, 29-11-1602; NA 95/24v, 20-08-1603; NA 96/105, 04-11-1603; NA 97/14, 03-05-1604. On whaling: Hart 1957: 33.

entailed the payment of a capital sum to a shipmaster, but here the ship-master pledged commodities, specified in the debt contract, as collateral, while at the same time the contract stipulated the repayment of the principal in a different currency, thus allowing the parties to disguise the payment of interest. Anticipating the development of marine insurance, Genoese merchants after 1345 experimented with a maritime bill of exchange that used the freightage as collateral for the loan. Here the ship-master received a sum of money from the freighter to be changed at the port of destination. Repayment was again conditional on the safe arrival of the ship. The few maritime bills of exchange that have survived suggest that the pledging of collateral resulted in interest rates that were considerably lower than those for the sea loan.[118]

The breakthrough in risk management, however, came with the invention of marine insurance in Italy in the fourteenth century. The galleys sailing from Venice, Genoa, and later also Florence were few, but their cargoes were very valuable. Hence the loss of one galley could cause considerable financial damage even if the number of participating merchants was large. To counter this risk the Venetian authorities initially chose to send out only convoys of heavily armed galleys—not unlike the Dutch and English East India traders in the seventeenth century. However, such an operation required large investments and a very tight organization. Genoese merchants did not want to revert to excessive armament and chose to insure their cargoes instead.

Marine insurance was developed to shift the financial burden of violent assaults and natural disaster to third parties who were willing to jointly bear the risk of losses at sea in exchange for a premium paid before the ship's departure. The premium was fixed according to the perceived risk of losses on a particular trade route. The first known policies were written in Genoa in the mid-fourteenth century, but half a century later merchants in Venice and Florence also regularly insured voyages to the Levant, England, and Flanders.[119] The insurance policies signed before notaries in Genoa from the 1340s onward give remarkable insight into the use of this instrument in the trade with the Low Countries. Figure 7.2 shows that a few early policies in the 1350s notwithstanding, insurance became common practice only in the late 1370s. Between 1370 and 1400 the Genoese wrote anywhere between zero and twenty policies per year for voyages to England and Flanders, with a peak of twenty-eight contracts in 1385. In the first half of the fifteenth century the annual number of policies fluctuated between zero and fifteen, with marked peaks in 1428, 1429, and 1432.

[118]Liagre-De Sturler 1969: lxxxiii.
[119]Hunt and Murray 1999: 158–59; van Niekerk 1998: 1:199; Liagre-De Sturler 1969.

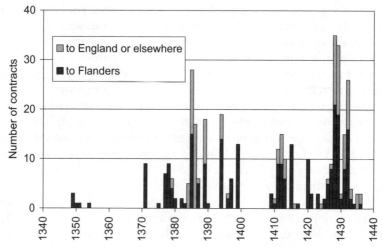

FIGURE 7.2. Insurance contracts for shipments to Northwestern Europe, signed by merchants before Genoese notaries (1340–1440)

    Sources: Liagre-De Sturler 1969: 2:947–66 (corrected tabulation after recounting all deeds); Doehaerd and Kerremans 1952: table 3.

    The Genoese insurance contracts reveal three different strategies to cope with risks at sea. The complete absence of policies in a large number of years could point to an incidence of violence so high that Genoese merchants simply did not sail to the North Sea. This strategy seems to have been followed between 1400 and 1408, when privateers from England, Flanders, and Holland attacked ships from virtually every nation trading in Bruges. The limited number of Genoese freight contracts, the few known captains of Genoese galleys, and the lack of other notarial deeds related to the Flemish trade would seem to confirm the reduced trade in these years.[120] The Venetian galleys did not come to Bruges either in this period.[121] A similar response might explain the lack of recorded policies in the second half of the 1430s when renewed warfare between France and England led to a spate of privateering attacks.[122]

    It was not just Italian merchants who decided not to trade in the face of violence. In the late fifteenth century English wool merchants did not

---

[120]Doehaerd and Kerremans 1952: tables 2 and 3.

[121]Liagre-De Sturler 1969: xxxvii.

[122]The lack of insurance policies in this period may also be an artifact of changes in insurance practices among Genoese merchants. Contracts were increasingly written in private in this period (see chapter 4), and the merchants may have started to take out insurance in Bruges. See, for instance, Doehaerd and Kerremans 1952: 602. In 1458 Bruges's insurance market was sufficiently developed for a shipowner from La Rochelle to buy insurance from two Spanish merchants through the intermediation of an Italian merchant banker. Craeybeckx 1958: 112–13.

travel to Calais, or from Calais to Bruges when French troops were campaigning.[123] Keeping away from military operations was also what first brought the Fuggers to Amsterdam. In 1511 warfare threatened their exports of Hungarian copper through Lübeck and Danzig, and they appointed a factor in the Dutch port to take over the sales.[124] The almost complete absence of French merchants in Antwerp in the most violent years of the Habsburg-Valois Wars (1522–23, 1530, 1541) and the Dutch Revolt (1566, 1574, 1583) suggests that they tried to stay away from turmoil.[125]

A second solution, clearly visible in Figure 7.2, is the diversion of trade to other ports, sometimes elsewhere in the Low Countries but more often in England. Between 1384 and 1388, when trade in Bruges was severely disrupted by the revolt of the Flemish towns, the majority—and in some years all—of the Genoese policies indicated ports other than Sluis (notably Southampton but also London and Middelburg) as the destination of their voyage. To be sure, these were regular ports of call in the Genoese run to the North Sea, but the civil war caused the Genoese to strike Bruges from their itinerary. Scattered references to the voyages of other nations suggest this was indeed a common strategy. In 1387 Portuguese merchants were granted a general safe-conduct on the explicit condition that they would sail to Flanders, not to England.[126] In 1320 and 1328 the Venetian galleys moored in Antwerp, not in Bruges, and in 1392 they sailed to London.[127]

The third strategy of the Genoese to cope with the risk of violence on their way to Flanders was of course to insure their merchandise. It seems no coincidence that the regular writing of policies by notaries in Genoa began in 1377 when political turmoil began in Flanders. In later years the coincidence between recorded violence and insurance taken out by Genoese merchants is equally striking. The 101 policies written between 1377 and 1389 were a direct response to the increased danger at sea. The 50 policies signed between 1411 and 1415 coincided with intensive privateering, and they followed shortly after the confiscation of Genoese property in Bruges in 1409. Between 1428 and 1432 again over 100 policies were signed, this time to counter the effects of attacks from Spanish, Dutch, Scottish, and German privateers.

By 1440 the insurance policies recorded by notaries in Genoa no longer reflect the importance of this instrument to Genoese merchants because judges in their hometowns, and presumably also the consular court

[123]Hanham 1985.
[124]Nübel 1972: 45–53.
[125]Coornaert 1961: 2: Annexe "Nombre de Marchands Français."
[126]Bartier and Nieuwenhuysen 1965: 201–2.
[127]Häpke 1908: 157–59.

in Bruges, recognized private contracts. By then marine insurance had also spread to other foreign nations. Between 1440 and 1470, for instance, merchants from Barcelona, Burgos, Venice, Seville, and Portugal appear in insurance conflicts before Bruges's local court.[128] Only in Antwerp in the second quarter of the sixteenth century did merchants from Northern Europe begin to rely on marine insurance to manage risks.[129] In 1531, a German vessel sailing from Lübeck to Arnemuyden near Middelburg was insured for 1,883 pounds Flemish by forty-two merchants and companies, all but three of them from Italy, Spain, and Portugal.[130] In 1557 merchants in Antwerp declared that some of their colleagues had specialized in marine insurance, and foreign merchant houses even commissioned their agents to take out insurance in the Scheldt port.[131] In the course of time the Southern European merchants became less dominant. In 1557 there were 50 merchants from the Low Countries, 10 from Germany, and 6 from England among 177 merchants protesting a reform of the insurance market.[132] In their petition to the town magistrate they stressed how even modest merchants were able to take out insurance on small freights on the Antwerp exchange.[133]

As with the spreading of cargo and the diversification of trade, marine insurance was feasible only in markets of sufficient scale and scope. The true importance of the existence of a sufficiently large and diverse crowd of insurers is apparent from the predicament Castilian merchants found themselves in after the capture of the annual wool fleet by Sea Beggars in Middelburg.[134] The Castilians did use insurance to secure compensation in case of shipwreck or privateering attacks. However, the vast majority of policies were underwritten by merchants who themselves participated in the wool trade. The one thing they had not envisaged was the capture of all ships, which left the entire community with losses they could not recoup.

Within a decade after the fall of Antwerp a thriving insurance market emerged in Amsterdam. Flemish and Portuguese immigrants from the Scheldt port, but also traders from Holland, Germany, and England, made intensive use of the emerging market.[135] Notarial deeds signed by Portuguese merchants in Amsterdam reveal their regular use of insurance

[128] Van Niekerk 1998: 1:199–201; Horden and Purcell 2000: 157; Gilliodts-Van Severen 1871–85: 5:276; Gilliodts-Van Severen 1883–85: 2:106.
[129] Strieder 1962: 194; Drost 1989: 12, 13, 45, 47, 49, 52, 141, 145, 149, 156, 262.
[130] Goris 1925: 181, citing Hofmeister 1888.
[131] Génard 1882: 34, 36.
[132] Génard 1882: 9–10, 20–22.
[133] Génard 1882: 33.
[134] Phillips and Rahn Phillips 1977.
[135] Barbour 1928–29: 581–83; van Tielhof 2002: 228–32; Go 2009: 61–158.

to compensate for damage done by privateers from the first decade of the seventeenth century onward.[136] By 1626 the city's price current included insurance rates for destinations in the Baltic, France, Italy, and the Levant.[137] It did not take long before merchants elsewhere in Europe began to order their agents in Amsterdam to take out insurance for them.[138]

The ease with which merchants in Amsterdam could obtain insurance is evident from the way Hans Thijs used the instrument from the very moment he settled in the Dutch port. Between 1596 and 1598 Thijs took out three policies for voyages of ships he partially owned.[139] In the following years the jeweler usually allowed the managers of the shipping companies he invested with to decide whether individual voyages had to be insured, but occasionally he acted alone. In 1602 Thijs even underwrote two policies for salt voyages to the West Indies in exchange for which the insured parties signed his policy for a similar voyage.[140] This is not to say that marine insurance made other forms of risk management redundant. Thijs also used the partial ownership of ships and their cargo to deal with losses. Between 1589 and 1609 he earned an average annual return of 10.5 percent on the shares he owned in thirty-one different ships, in spite of the fact that two ships sank and five others turned a loss. These shipping operations in turn were but a small part of Thijs's business, which also included trade in jewelry, leather, and miscellaneous other products, some of which he traded on his own account, and some on joint account in temporary or long-standing partnerships with others.

The importance of marine insurance relative to other strategies for risk management can be ascertained from a proposal submitted to the States General by four Amsterdam merchants in 1628 to create a general insurance company.[141] The promoters wanted the Ghenerale Compagnie van Asseurantie to offer compulsory insurance for all outbound voyages to destinations in Europe, in exchange for which the company would provide naval protection to merchantmen on these routes. The charter was to be for twenty-four years, and the company was also to be given a monopoly on trade with the western and northern coast of Africa and the Levant.[142] This, the promoters argued, was the best way to cover the

[136] Portuguese merchants appeared before the local Insurance Chamber from 1604 onward: SR 183, 221–24; 128, 143; 231, 248, 253; 376, 377, 427, 434, 513. Claims following attacks by privateers are recorded from 1608 onward: SR 280, 501, 546, 568, 572, 592, 595, 596, 606–10, 623. See also Ebert 2011.

[137] Spooner 1983: 163–65.

[138] Tenenti 1959: 64–65.

[139] BT 119, Grootboek Hans Thijs, 1595–99, fols. 55, 70, 108, 148.

[140] BT 119, Grootboek Hans Thijs, 1599–1603, fols. 15, 133, 163, 211; Grootboek Hans Thijs 1604–10, fols. 84, 110, 116, 128, 158.

[141] Blok 1900a, 1900b; Barbour 1928–29: 585–86; and van Tielhof 2002: 227–28.

[142] Blok 1900a: 10–11.

losses from the privateering war fought against Spain.[143] Amsterdam's merchant community was not impressed, however. It was feared that the scheme would eat up profits and divert trade to other countries. In particular, those who were opposed argued that ships sailing to Northern Europe were seldom insured. No more than 1 percent of all ships leaving the Dutch Republic and perhaps 10 percent of their cargo was ever insured. In all other cases merchants relied on the division of cargoes between ships, the partenrederij, and joint operations with other merchants.[144] As a result of the protests from Amsterdam and other Dutch towns the plan was first revised and then completely abandoned in 1635. Even if the protesters painted too bleak a picture of insurance practices in Amsterdam, their objections make abundantly clear that marine insurance was never more than a partial solution to the problem of violence.

Conclusion

In the thirteenth and fourteenth centuries the economic situation in the Low Countries allowed merchants to seek compensation through collective action. Competing cities were willing to grant privileges to attract traders, and many foreign groups were sufficiently tightly organized to credibly threaten their hosts with a collective departure. But in the fifteenth and sixteenth centuries, when trade in Bruges and Antwerp became permanent and the competition from local merchants increased, the opportunity costs of boycotts rose. Some of the best organized nations, notably the German Hanse in Bruges and the Company of Merchant Adventurers in Antwerp sought the confirmation of their staple rights. The extra profits this generated may have created a financial buffer for merchants to compensate for damages, but it is unlikely these extra profits were essential to deal with losses, as the same English and German merchants traded in Amsterdam without any recourse to collective action. Indeed, from the sixteenth century onward new groups of Walloon, Flemish, and Dutch merchants in Antwerp and Amsterdam entered the international market without any exclusive trading rights.

State intervention was even less important to obtain compensation for damages. The rulers of the Low Countries regularly fought with the sovereigns of foreign residents, and if they refrained from large-scale expropriations of foreign traders this was only because the ports of the Low Countries had sufficient fiscal and financial leverage to restrain them. But even with the help of their host cities it was difficult for foreign merchants

[143]Blok 1900a: 5–6.
[144]Blok 1900b: 46.

to obtain compensation for actual damages. Peace settlements typically led to a mutual write-down of losses instead of retributions to individual traders. The odds were slightly better for merchants whose rulers stood away from conflicts since the Dukes of Burgundy, the Habsburg kings, and later also the Dutch Republic allowed neutral traders to go to court to recoup losses, but the number of prize cases heard before the Admiralty courts suggests this was a mere palliative, not a structural, solution for the damages issuing from interstate rivalry.

There was only one solution that became decidedly more effective over time: private risk management.[145] In larger, more sophisticated markets it was easier for merchants to spread investments and compensate their losses in one area with profits from another. As the number of active traders in Bruges, Antwerp, and Amsterdam grew, the opportunities for merchants to reduce exposure to risks through joint investments in shipping and trading companies also increased. In addition to this, the growing supply of capital in the three cities helped to create insurance markets that allowed merchants to transfer risks to third parties who, in exchange for a premium paid in advance, assumed the possible losses suffered at sea. In comparison with collective action and court proceedings, these private arrangements had the considerable advantage that they could pay for damages from violent assaults as well as natural disasters or the dishonest behavior of trading partners. Still, these market solutions thrived only with the support of local governments willing to tailor their cities' commercial and legal infrastructure to the needs of the merchant community at large.

[145] North 1991: 28–29; Hunt and Murray 1999: 60–63; see also Tenenti 1959: 59–65.

CHAPTER 8

Conclusion

THE ORGANIZATION OF INTERNATIONAL TRADE IN THE LOW COUNTRIES shows how urban competition leads to the creation of inclusive institutions that facilitate exchange and help merchants deal with conflicts. Bruges, Antwerp, and Amsterdam built basically permanent vending locations and regulated brokers' work to support the local and international exchange of money, goods, and information. The cities continuously amended and adapted local customs to create a broader set of contracting rules that suited their heterogeneous business communities. They also supported a variety of institutions for conflict resolution to enable merchants a measured response to any kind of agency problem. In addition to this constant adaptation of contracting institutions, the three cities established a local monopoly of violence early on, and they were a major force against the centralizing tendencies of the houses of Burgundy and Habsburg, who had to delegate considerable administrative and fiscal authority to the individual cities. In the end Amsterdam's role as the guardian of commercial interests was perhaps the most pronounced. In the mid-sixteenth century Antwerp resisted the princely protection of its merchant fleet, but after 1580 Amsterdam worked with other cities in Holland and Zeeland to create a permanent Dutch fleet.

The history of Bruges, Antwerp, and Amsterdam forces us to reconsider current theories of institutional change, starting with those of North, Acemoglu, Johnson, and Robinson, and others who consider strong states with limited government a crucial prerequisite for the creation of inclusive, open access institutions. When Bruges emerged as a major international market in the late thirteenth century the Low Countries were fragmented politically, and even the strongest princes could not guarantee foreign merchants that their property would remain unharmed. The sovereigns' strength increased when the Dukes of Burgundy came to power in Flanders in 1384, but their attempts to carve out an independent state were accompanied by a sharp spike in internal and international conflicts, elevating rather than reducing the risk of violence against trade. The legal exploits of the new rulers did not help much either because the judges of their central court never managed to settle business disputes quickly and according to mercantile customs. A similar impotence characterized the Habsburg rulers in the sixteenth century. For his own benefit Charles V did intervene in the organization of credit operations on the Antwerp market, but the central court system remained unfit to adjudicate commercial conflicts, and the sovereign's attempt to put the naval protection of foreign and local merchants on a more permanent footing in the 1550s came to naught because Antwerp's merchant community immediately saw through Charles V's belligerent motive.

In the absence of strong states, Avner Greif has argued, merchants developed private solutions to deal with violence and opportunism. Indeed, up until the sixteenth century, foreigners trading in the Low Countries relied on their corporate bodies—the *foreign nations* of Bruges and Antwerp—to bargain with their hosts and resolve internal conflicts, and they created multilateral trading networks within which reputation and the prospect of repeat transactions offered strong incentives for distant agents to fulfill their obligations. These private order solutions were fundamental to the organization of international trade in the Low Countries, but they worked only because urban governments supported them. Every foreign nation in Bruges and Antwerp was formally recognized by its home ruler, and the privileges granted to them in the Low Countries were explicitly designed to embed their associations in the corporate structure of the host community. Likewise, the maintenance of international trading networks hinged on the ability of urban governments to support thriving local markets that could serve as central nodes in these networks.

Still, the fact that cities rather than sovereigns created inclusive, open access institutions in the Low Countries is not necessarily at odds with theories of institutional change that stress the importance of limited government. Douglass North, for instance, positioned Bruges, Antwerp, and Amsterdam in between the Italian city-states, where local and central government fully overlapped, and England, where local business elites had to push for political reforms at the central level in order to secure the sovereign's support for their trade.[1] David Stasavage found that limited government at the local level, that is, mercantile control over representative assemblies, gave city-states better access to credit, and he speculated that cities ruled by merchants were more inclined to create a legal environment favorable to economic growth.[2] The present study shows, however, that political constraints on the executive were of secondary importance for institutional change in the commercial cities of the Low Countries. International traders seldom participated in the political process. In Bruges and Antwerp local businessmen and public officeholders controlled the town council, while in Amsterdam the clique of local merchants who dominated the magistrate persistently tried to exclude other traders, local and foreign. Instead, the constraints on the rulers of Bruges, Antwerp,

[1] North 1981: 152–54; North 2005: 133–34.
[2] Stasavage 2011: 156–65.

and Amsterdam were economic. They adapted institutional arrangements to the needs of international traders because they faced strong competition from other potential gateways with good overseas and overland connections to each other and to a hinterland with marketable surpluses. To attract as many merchants as possible the municipal governments of the three cities tried to protect merchants to the best of their abilities against violence and opportunism, and these efforts created the kind of inclusive, open access international markets that institutional economists have long recognized as a key to the growth of European trade.

It may be tempting to consider the succession of Bruges, Antwerp, and Amsterdam as leading international markets as a unique success story predicated upon a favorable economic geography. The ports of the Low Countries obviously benefited from a highly developed industrial hinterland and a central position between major markets in Northern and Southern Europe. When the fairs of Champagne declined in the thirteenth century this combination of factors made cities like Bruges and Antwerp an attractive meeting place for merchants from different parts of Europe. However, there were many other cities across Europe with direct access to domestic and foreign markets, and even if open access institutions came early in the Low Countries, second only to those in the Italian city-states, the ongoing adaptation of trade-related institutions was a far more general phenomenon that eventually spread, with fits and starts, across Europe and beyond.

Our analysis sheds new light on the institutional foundations of international trade as it reveals the dynamic process through which competing commercial cities were able to transform an extremely heterogeneous institutional framework into a widely shared body of open access institutions. The basis for this transformation lay in a combination of three factors, the first of which was the large number of cities with direct access to tradable surpluses at home and abroad that vied for the presence of foreign traders. As international trade gravitated toward the coasts of Northwestern Europe the competitive pressure between ports in this area became much higher than in the Mediterranean and Baltic Seas or, for that matter, land-locked markets like Frankfurt, Cologne, or Lyons, whose *direct* connections with other major trading centers were more limited.[3] Only London's position was different at first because already in the late Middle Ages the city had obtained a firm hold over exports of regional products and redistribution of foreign imports throughout England.[4] But even London began to feel more pressure in the first half of the seventeenth century when merchants in other British ports engaged in

[3] Hohenberg and Lees 1995: 160–61.
[4] Keene 2004: 467–68, 470, 475.

direct trade with the Americas, and French and Dutch cities got increasingly involved in the transshipment of goods within Europe.

Second, international traders were footloose. They easily moved from one place to another, implying cities with equal economic opportunities had a real incentive to influence the cost-benefit calculus of individual traders to secure their prolonged presence. The opportunity for merchants to relocate was obviously greater in regions with multiple gateways, but what mattered even more was the possibility of choosing between cities with access to the same hinterland. In this respect the ports of the Low Countries offered considerably more freedom to foreign merchants than cities like Lübeck, Venice, or, until the sixteenth century, London, acting as the sole gatekeepers of their own hinterland. The same was true for the ports of the Levant, where foreign merchants were free to move between cities, but each of them restricted access to buyers and suppliers in their hinterland.

Third, the political autonomy of commercial cities in late medieval and early modern Europe gave their municipal government both the financial resources and the legal power to adapt institutional arrangements to changes in the scale and scope of trade.[5] It is worth noting that this adaptiveness did not require limited government at either the local or the central level because absolutist rulers also recognized the need for flexibility. This was true not just for the Burgundian and Habsburg rulers of the Netherlands, but also, for instance, for the Ottoman sultan who, fearing the departure of foreign merchants, allowed port cities, especially those in newly conquered territories, the freedom to organize their market as they desired, only forbidding foreigners to travel inland to purchase domestic products.[6] Nor is it a coincidence that Shanghai, in the second half of the nineteenth century, developed a commercial regime in which Chinese and foreign traders could use Western contracting institutions.[7] This policy change connected the Chinese port with a much larger network of Asian ports that already in the early modern period constantly adapted their commercial infrastructure to the needs of foreign merchants.[8]

It is clear that Bruges, Antwerp, and Amsterdam met all three conditions—access to domestic and foreign markets, footloose merchants, and urban autonomy—but even if they were able to attract large numbers of merchants from different parts of Europe, one still has to wonder why this led to institutional convergence rather than a continuation of the differences in contracting institutions between the foreigners. The present study

---

[5] Stasavage 2011: 25–46; see also Storper 2010: 2038–39.
[6] Pamuk 2009: 12; see also Bulut 2001: 107–28, 203–8.
[7] Ma 2008: 356, 370, 373–74; Rosenthal and Bin Wong 2011: 156–57.
[8] Pearson 1991: 70–77.

shows that the institutional adaptiveness of commercial cities hinged—paradoxically—on the freedom of merchants to choose their own rules and the institutional heterogeneity this created. The variation of solutions available to traders in commercial cities increased with the number of merchants from different parts of Europe, notably because rulers accepted the coexistence of alternative arrangements. Urban magistrates did not sanction specific contracting rules of resident traders or newcomers but instead amended local customs both with mercantile usages introduced by foreigners and with new practices that emerged from increased trading on the local market.

The long-term variation in contracting rules eventually spawned a more reduced and coherent set of institutions as merchants responded to changes in the relative costs and benefits of specific arrangements. They adapted their business organization when they recognized the cost advantages of using either a specific combination of institutions or an individual institution that served more than one purpose. The magistrates of Bruges, Antwerp, and Amsterdam, for their part, supported this ongoing selection process through adjustments and amendments of their local customs, including the incorporation of written declarations on mercantile practice by traders and other professionals. At the same time the cities refrained from the codification of a preferred set of contracting institutions, thus giving merchants the largest possible menu of choices. This constant adaptation of contracting institutions may be understood as an evolutionary process in which merchants and cities selected, from a variety of available institutions, those most fit to organize commercial and financial transactions. It is important to note, however, that variation remained the norm, even within the confines of single locations.[9]

The adaptive efficiency of both merchants and rulers is demonstrated to good effect by the changing role of hostellers, merchant guilds, and local courts in Bruges, Antwerp, and Amsterdam. From the moment foreign traders became regular visitors to the three ports hostellers played a key role in their business operations. They provided lodging and storage facilities for their guests, brokered deals for them on the local market, and acted as commission agents in their absence. This bundling of functions reduced costs for merchants as long as they traveled between markets, but once they settled permanently in the Low Countries they no longer needed temporary accommodation or local representation. When this happened each of the three cities responded with a further development of public vending locations, the confirmation of the individual legal responsibility of merchants, and, most important, the reduction of the hostellers-cum-brokers to a subservient position in the local market.

[9] On the notion of adaptive efficiency, see North 2005: 6, 169.

But institutional change did not stop here, as the permanent presence of foreign merchants immediately created a new problem. From their new domicile they now engaged in a much broader range of commercial transactions, including international shipments, credit operations, partnerships, and commission trade with foreign agents. Bruges and Antwerp, whose legal intervention in the business of the foreigners had so far been limited to their sales and purchases at the local fairs, decided to leave the enforcement of these new contracts to the foreign merchants themselves, and this created a new bundle of functions within the foreign merchant communities. In both cities the foreign nations were given their own chapel and administrative seat, from which their consuls liaised with the local authorities, supervised convoys, recorded commercial associations, and adjudicated conflicts.

Foreign merchants in Bruges and Antwerp benefited because these multiple functions turned their nations into a "one-stop shop," but this arrangement was once again undermined as trade continued to grow. The permanent presence of foreign merchants led to more regular business dealings with other foreigners that their respective consuls could not oversee. This in turn obliged the town magistrates to intervene and appropriate part of the administrative and legal functions of the foreign nations. Their intervention was substantial, including the integration of foreign usage into local customs, the public recording of private transactions by local notaries and town clerks, and the extension of the local court system with arbiters and specialized judges. This local legal support freed foreign merchants from the need to turn to their consuls to enforce contracts. This was already happening in Antwerp in the first half of the sixteenth century, and after 1585 Amsterdam's magistrate simply refused to create separate jurisdictions, which effectively reduced the corporate status of Portuguese, English, German, and Walloon traders to that of church congregations. Thus, it was the social capital created through direct interaction between merchants in combination with support from the local government that made the formalized collective action of merchant guilds redundant.

The freedom of merchants to choose their own contracting institutions helped to reduce transaction costs for each of them individually, but it also had systemic effects that explain why municipal governments were eager to append or even change local rules. The settlement of foreign traders could add new lines of business to the local economy, for instance the trading in bills of exchange, marine insurance, short-term credit operations, or freight services, and as the scope of trade widened, cities were more likely to become central nodes in international trading networks. To seize this opportunity and move up in the international hierarchy of markets, urban magistrates had to facilitate both local exchange and transactions with other cities. They had to set rules for international transfers of money and goods that matched those of other markets, and they had to support the private efforts of merchants to monitor distant agents, whereby the acceptance of business accounts and correspondence as legal proof in court proceedings turned out to be a big step forward. Thus urban competition was the driving force of institutional change in international trade, spurring not just local improvements of contracting rules but also institutional convergence between commercial cities.

Bruges, Antwerp, and Amsterdam were major conduits of institutional convergence because of their central location between markets, but the process of institutional adaptation was by no means unique to the Netherlands. Emily Kadens, for instance, has convincingly shown that local customs were permeable throughout Europe, and in a recent study on seventeenth-century Paris, Amalia Kessler demonstrates the willingness and ability of the city's mercantile court to adjust its mode of operation to changing economic circumstances.[10] The diffusion of merchant handbooks and the related emergence of an international culture of commerce in the seventeenth and eighteenth centuries confirm that merchants and rulers habitually turned to other commercial centers for inspiration.[11] But the process was even more general than that, witness the creation of a shared maritime law in the Mediterranean world and a similar legal evolution on the coasts of the Atlantic Ocean and Baltic Sea.[12] Likewise, the growing accordance in commercial customs between the towns that formed the Hanseatic League resulted from the obvious gains merchants could make when different places applied the same rules.[13] The adoption of international standard for weights and measures in Northwestern Europe, the establishment of monetary unions in the German lands in the late medieval and early modern period, and the introduction of European contracting practices in the New World all point to the same rationale: in all these cases trade within urban networks created opportunities for more efficient trading because local customs and mercantile practice were permeable.[14]

The determined efforts of commercial cities to support private contracting between international traders turned what could have been a very serious problem—the legal fragmentation of Europe—into a source of institutional improvement. This development lends support to the optimistic view of scholars who stress the dynamic role of commercial cities

[10] Kadens 2004; Kessler 2007.
[11] See an overview of surviving merchant manuals in Hoock et al. 1991; see also Jacob 2006: 66–94.
[12] Van Niekerk 1998: 1:245–46.
[13] Seifert 1997: 109.
[14] Spufford 2002: 146; Börner and Volckart 2011.

in the growth of the European economy before the Industrial Revolution.[15] However there is also evidence to suggest that powerful cities, even those controlled by merchants, could seriously hurt trade. Independent city-states could use their economic and military power to submit the surrounding countryside to their rule. The magistrates of commercial cities in larger territorial states sometimes chose to back the political and military ambitions of their sovereigns because they believed it would strengthen their competitive position, while other cities resisted the centralizing efforts of their sovereigns up to the point of urban revolt or outright civil war.[16]

We can observe most if not all of these problems in the history of Bruges, Antwerp, and Amsterdam, with the Flemish and Dutch Revolts actually shifting commercial hegemony from one city to the next. But the creation of inclusive institutional regimes never stopped, and trade in the Low Countries continued to grow. Urban competition can explain this paradox because it created strong incentives for cities and sovereigns to reduce the risk of conflicts to a level low enough for merchants to manage privately. This study reveals several incentive systems that led local and central governments to exercise restraint. One was a regional system within which the hosts of periodic fairs—Bruges and Antwerp—refused access to subjects of rulers who failed to protect merchants traveling to and from the fairs. Due to a lack of source material I have not been able to provide a detailed reconstruction of this mechanism, but the little scholars know suggests that Antwerp, for instance, could force rulers in its hinterland to secure a safe passage for the visitors to its fairs.

A second incentive system was international and hinged on the functional equivalence of competing cities. Since international traders were footloose, merchants who deemed the risk of violent assaults too high in one location could simply move to another. This exit strategy was institutionalized in the organization of merchant guilds. In the Low Countries the German Hanse repeatedly boycotted Bruges to obtain compensation for damages, and merchants from Italy, Spain, and England also departed on several occasions to punctuate their demand for damages. The privileges of the foreign nations in Bruges and Antwerp also stipulated the delay granted to merchants who had to leave because their rulers came into conflict with the rulers of the Low Countries. But group formation

---

[15] On urban centers as engines of growth: De Long and Shleifer 1993; Hohenberg and Lees 1995; Bosker, Buringh, and van Zanden 2008: 26–29; Rosenthal and Bin Wong 2011: 99–128; Stasavage 2011. For the Low Countries in particular, see Lesger 2006; Blockmans 2010b.

[16] On cities fighting for trade: Greif 2008: 772; on cities' control over their hinterland: Epstein 2000; on rent seeking and regulatory capture: Ogilvie 2011: passim; Stasavage 2011: 164–65.

was not necessary for merchants to exercise their exit option. When merchants deemed violent risks in one location too high, they made up their own mind about leaving. In the sixteenth century even the German Hanse lost its bargaining power because its members chose individually where to trade.

In premodern Europe it was relatively easy for merchants to move from one place to another because many cities competed for their presence and because merchants who left a particular city often left a sovereign realm as well, thus creating an extra stimulus for princes to exercise restraint. The potency of the latter incentive is very clear from the rise and decline of Antwerp as the leading port of the Low Countries. In 1488 Maximilian I did not flinch when he expelled the foreign nations from Bruges: he firmly controlled the nearby market of Antwerp, which offered an excellent refuge to these merchants. On the other hand, one century later, Philip II made every effort not just to recapture Antwerp but also to crush the revolt in the Northern Netherlands, because anything less than a complete victory would have shifted the center of international trade beyond his control.

Thus, in the politically fragmented world of Europe before 1800 urban competition had a positive, systemic effect on the safety of merchants. As long as foreign merchants had the opportunity to move their business to another place with more or less similar economic opportunities, local and central governments were very keen to exercise sufficient constraint to prevent them from leaving. This mechanism was not limited to the Low Countries. In fourteenth-century Germany, with its many small principalities, competition created a stable political environment for local businessmen, and in the Mediterranean it led to the creation of extensive compounds for foreign visitors in every major commercial city in the late Middle Ages. In the seventeenth century Livorno set a new standard for Italian ports with a very open attitude toward foreign merchants, which converted even Genoa to the creation of more inclusive institutions instead of attacking their commercial rivals.[17] In Britain, in stark contrast with the European Continent, the lack of urban competition created an exclusive relationship between London's business elite and the crown.[18] Britain's specific economic geography with only one city capable of competing with other ports in the North Sea allowed the merchants of London to monopolize exports to Europe—an outcome that was detrimental to other English ports, and perhaps to the economy in general, but nevertheless that exemplifies the impact of urban competition on the efforts rulers made to protect trade.[19]

[17] Kirk 2001: 8–13, 16–17; Trivellato 2009; Engels 1997.
[18] Volckart 2002: 56–93; Constable 2003; Keene 2004: 478.
[19] Gelderblom 2009: 226–32.

This is not to say that urban competition and the related exit option for international traders could ever stop violence against trade. They did restrain rulers up to the point of creating calculable risks of violent assaults, but the actual level of risk merchants were able to deal with depended on the contracting institutions they could use to spread, share, or transfer the risk. This is why merchants in major markets like Bruges, Antwerp, and Amsterdam could sustain very high levels of violence. Markets of greater scale and scope boasted more sophisticated instruments to pool resources and insure against natural and man-made disasters, and their central position in international commercial networks also gave merchants better opportunities to diversify their trade. In other words, the improvement of contracting institutions that resulted from Europe's legal fragmentation mitigated the insufficient security of private property rights caused by the Continent's political fragmentation.

Urban competition explains why inclusive, open access institutions emerged in major European markets between 1000 and 1800, but did this institutional change contribute to the growth of international trade? Surely the histories of Bruges, Antwerp, and Amsterdam, cities that for a very long time stood at the top of the urban hierarchy, offer compelling evidence that the ongoing process of institutional adaptation reduced transaction costs. Merchants in the Low Countries benefited from new combinations of institutions, for instance the introduction of VOC shares as collateral for loans that pushed down interest rates in Amsterdam after 1602 or, on a more general level, the protection offered by local and central governments that, in conjunction with improved contracting institutions, allowed merchants to sustain higher levels of violence against trade. Merchants also saved costs using institutions with multiple functions, like the hostellers who charged minimal brokerage fees because they earned money with other services as well, or the foreign nations that offered diplomatic, legal, economic, and religious services in exchange for very low membership fees. We cannot calculate the cost of contract enforcement in Bruges, Antwerp, and Amsterdam, but the rules they set for speedy court proceedings, their acceptance of business accounts and letters as legal proof, and the regular intervention of arbiters leave little doubt that urban magistrates tried very hard to keep the costs of conflict resolution down.

And yet we have to be cautious because many of the institutional changes we observe were necessary to repair the legal and political deficits that issued from Europe's extreme fragmentation. This repair in itself was very successful in Europe because commercial cities had the freedom to adapt institutional arrangements and the competition and cooperation between them ensured the benefits spread across the Continent. But even if Europe managed to mitigate the negative effects of its fragmentation, its adaptive efficiency need not have pushed down transaction cost below the levels attained by merchants in China or the Middle East already at the end of the first millennium. Europe may very well have experienced decreasing returns to institutional change. Once the biggest problems were resolved, and institutional improvements widely shared between merchants in different cities, the incentives to adapt institutions could have disappeared and the process of institutional change stalled. Cities that were unable to keep up with their competitors may also have been tempted to revert to more exclusive commercial regimes, witness Lübeck and Venice, which in the sixteenth century both tried to reserve their most lucrative outlets for local business elites. The magistrate of Bruges experienced a similar reflex in the late fifteenth century when it offered more extensive premises to German and Castilian merchants to keep them from moving to Antwerp, and even the latter city provided German and English merchants with abundant accommodation in the 1550s because their presence was deemed crucial to maintaining the city's competitive strength.

But the corporate reflex in some cities notwithstanding, institutional change did not stop. The overall trend in early modern Europe was undeniably toward more inclusive, open access institutions. The principal reason for this was that leading markets thrived on the confluence of merchants from more peripheral markets. Cities at the top of the urban hierarchy had a competitive advantage in specialized sectors that thrived on the spatial concentration of supply and demand, for example colonial wares, marine insurance, bullion, and bills of exchange. These offerings made cities like Venice, Bruges, Antwerp, Amsterdam, and London indispensable nodes in the multilateral trading networks of merchants all over Europe, and as foreign merchants continued to settle in the leading ports, their markets grew thicker. This stimulated the further improvement of commercial and financial techniques, like the acceptance of bills of exchange, derivatives trading, or fiat money, and it allowed merchants to diversify their investments at low cost and increase their resistance against shocks.

Finally, it is important to note that local rent seeking could never really reverse the adoption of more inclusive institutions. Regulatory capture obviously harmed outsiders in more peripheral cities, but the systemic costs remained small because the business elites of these cities, if they wanted to maintain some presence in international markets, could not afford to steer their own institutional course. Merchants in cities that were trapped in a situation of stable or even declining participation in international trade, even if they managed to exclude foreign or local competitors, still conformed to institutional best practices that emerged in Europe's commercial heartland. There was a latent benefit to this institutional copying because it allowed for easy catch-up when economic prospects improved. Thus, Venice had no difficulty accommodating large numbers of English and Dutch merchants after 1590, London made a very smooth transition to a more open market in the mid-seventeenth century, and, perhaps most spectacularly, Antwerp, after two centuries of relative isolation, managed to regain a dominant position within decades after the reopening of the river Scheldt in 1795. In other words, institutional best practice, initiated in the Mediterranean world, incorporated in the local customs of Bruges, Antwerp, and Amsterdam, described in Gerard Malynes *Lex Mercatoria* 1622, and then codified in Colbert's *Code de Commerce* in 1673, eventually became a public good shared by merchants from all over Europe and then, in the nineteenth century, was exported to the rest of the world.

The Incidence of Violence against Foreign Merchants in the Low Countries, 1250–1650

THIS APPENDIX CATALOGUES THE VIOLENT ASSAULTS THAT DISRUPTED THE trade of foreign merchants trading in Bruges, Antwerp, and Amsterdam between 1250 and 1650. This detailed description underlies Figures 6.1 and 6.2 in chapter 6.

1250–99

Between 1250 and 1299 three violent episodes damaged the interest of English, German, and Spanish merchants trading in the Low Countries. First, in 1270 there was the default of the English king on a long-standing loan, which led the Countess of Flanders to seize the ships and goods of English merchants in Flanders. Henry III retaliated with the arrest of Flemish merchants, and the seizure of their vessels and merchandise in England. Besides, merchants and shipmasters from England, Holland, and Zeeland fell victim to acts of piracy. As a result of these infringements English wool exports to Flanders stopped between 1270 and 1274 and remained below their normal level until at least 1278. Official restoration of commercial ties followed only in 1285. Since the English king gave licenses to English, German, Liégeois, Brabantine, French, Spanish, and Italian merchants to export wool to the Continent, English and Flemish traders were probably the only ones to suffer, notably between 1270 and 1275.[1]

In 1279 the interests of Spanish and southern French merchants in Bruges were harmed by a conflict between Bruges's merchant elite (and town council) and the Count of Flanders, over comital control over weighage and tolls, and committal policy toward the English. To avoid paying too high tariffs in Bruges, the Spanish and French merchants removed their trade to nearby Aardenburg. German merchants followed suit when in 1280 the Count of Flanders granted formal permission for the removal. Between 1280 and 1282 Spaniards, Germans, and French operated from the small port of Aardenburg. They returned only upon the city's acceptance of the rules of taxation laid down by the count.[2] Also

[1] Greif, Milgrom, and Weingast 1994; Greif 2006b: 91–123; Ogilvie 2011: 100–125.
[2] Poeck 2000: 34; Dollinger 1964: 67–68; Vandermaesen 1982: 399–440.

in 1280 two Flemish ships carrying merchandise of French traders were captured by English privateers.

A third conflict that damaged the trade of alien merchants in Bruges was that between France and England beginning in 1294. The Flemish support of France led the king of England to redirect his country's wool export to Dordrecht in 1294. However, the wool could not be sold here and was transshipped to Antwerp, where English merchants received their first privileges in 1296. Until 1298 the English wool trade was concentrated in Antwerp (and Malines) instead.[3] The years 1294 and 1295 are considered to have been disruptive.

French attempts to gain control over Flanders, enacted between 1297 and 1304 (and including the famous Battle of the Golden Spurs in 1302), are not included in the catalogue of violence, for despite open warfare on land and sea, there is no evidence of violent threats against foreign merchants trading in Bruges.[4] The same is true for the social and political upheaval that followed the murder of Floris V, Count of Holland in 1296. Although tensions in Holland dissipated only after 1305, there is no evidence of disruptions to the trade of Germans who often used Dutch waterways to reach Flanders.

1300–1349

The most important conflict to disrupt the trade of foreign merchants in the Low Countries between 1300 and 1349 was the beginning of the Hundred Years' War between England and France (1337–1453). Already in 1336 support of the Count of Flanders for France in its struggle over Guyenne had brought the English to forbid wool export to Flanders. What followed were confiscations on both sides in 1336 and 1337. One English merchant even ended up in Bruges's prison.[5] To prevent further damage to their commercial and industrial interests the towns of Flanders decided to steer a neutral course in the Anglo-French conflict—a decision that brought the Count of Flanders to leave the county for a period of ten years.[6] The defeat of a French war fleet by the English near Sluis in 1340 probably caused French merchants to stay away in 1340 and 1341 (when a truce was signed). Other foreign merchants do not seem to have suffered from the outbreak of the Hundred Years' War. Before the actual battle Genoese galleys, for instance, had managed to get away. Only in 1346, when the count in exile was killed at Crécy and an English war fleet

---

[3] Jansen 1982: 174–75.
[4] Blockmans 1992b: 207.
[5] Murray 2005: 265.
[6] Blockmans 1992b: 207.

threatened to take Zeeland, did various attacks on merchant ships occur in the North Sea. As the nationality of these ships is unknown, the attacks have not been included in the tabulation.[7] Once Bruges sided with the new Count Louis of Male in 1348, and this count during several decades shunned any involvement in the War, the threat of violence receded.[8]

In addition to the Hundred Years' War there was one other international conflict that damaged the commercial interests of foreign merchants in Bruges in the first half of the fourteenth century. In the first two decades of the fourteenth century warfare between Flanders and France made overland travel to the fairs of Champagne a hazardous undertaking. In 1315 the French king outright forbade Flemish merchants to visit the fairs of Champagne.[9] In 1316 and 1317 France and Flanders were once again at war. In 1316 four ships from Normandy were set on fire by Flemings in Bay of Bourgneuf, while Flemish ships were arrested in Holland, a county that sided with the French.[10] The damage military campaigns in the south of Flanders and the north of France did to trade is unknown, but it is safe to assume that at least French merchants and shipmasters perceived violent threats in 1316 and 1317.

The removal of German merchants to Aardenburg in 1307 was related to local issues, notably money changing and weighage. The year of the actual departure is considered disruptive for German trade. We know that in 1312 a notary in Bruges was asked to mediate in a lingering conflict between English and Flemish merchants, but we cannot determine the exact nature of the damages.[11] Evidence for damages due to the "peasant" rebellion in Flanders (1323–28) consists of the staying away of the Venetian galleys from 1327 onward. We mark 1327 and 1328 as disrupted by violence, even though the galleys returned only in 1332.[12] There is no evidence for violence against foreign merchants during the short war between Brabant and Flanders in 1334.[13] In the Northern Netherlands Amsterdam and Deventer were engaged in a commercial conflict that entailed repeated seizures of goods on both sides (1336, 1338, 1346, 1347, and 1368). Again, violent threats to foreign traders are not recorded.[14]

[7] Jim Murray has argued that the rule of Edward III (1327–77) damaged the English wool trade to Flanders through confiscations, taxation, and warfare. We lack information on individual assaults, however, and therefore we may underestimate damages to English traders: Murray 2005: 266.

[8] Vandermaesen 1982: 430–40.

[9] Doehaerd 1941: 222–26.

[10] Gilliodts-Van Severen 1871–85: 1:319–20.

[11] Murray 1995: 72.

[12] We do not consider the rerouting of the Venetian galleys to Antwerp in 1314, 1324, and 1325 a disruption of trade with the Netherlands. The same holds for the absence of Venetian galleys from 1337 until 1356: Liagre-De Sturler 1969: xxxxvii.

[13] Vandermaesen 1982: 424–25.

[14] Smit 1914: 70–71, 126.

1350–99

In 1351 an English corsair who had attacked a ship from Greifswald was arrested in Sluis and executed under pressure of the Hanse. This led to confiscations of German merchandise in England and England's removal of its wool staple from Antwerp back to England in 1353. The refusal of Bruges and the Count of Flanders to compensate Hanseatic merchants for losses following privateering by English and Spanish corsairs in subsequent years was one of the reasons why the Hanse removed its Kontor to Dordrecht in 1358. For lack of further evidence, for German traders only the year of the initial incident (1351), the two years leading up to their departure, and the year of their removal (1358) are considered to have been disruptive.[15]

In the 1350s Antwerp's trade suffered another serious blow after a Flemish fleet (consisting of German ships, confiscated for the occasion) attacked the town twice, in 1356 and 1357, and subsequently submitted it to Flemish rule. The Count of Flanders gave staple rights to Malines and effectively curtailed the further growth of the Brabant fairs until the end of his annexation in 1405.[16] Throughout this period foreign merchants in Bruges were forbidden to travel to the fairs of Brabant. Several merchants who did visit the fairs were fined, for instance in Antwerp in 1389 and in Bergen-op-Zoom in 1401.[17] After 1356 the Bruges market was opened to the English and German merchants who had previously traded in Antwerp, and therefore the Flemish reign over Antwerp is not considered disruptive.

The temporary allegiance of Holland and Zeeland to the Hanse, to fight Denmark between 1367 and 1369, may have been costly to traders, but the conflict was fought primarily in the Baltic area, and merely required a financial contribution from the merchants most directly involved—the Germans.[18] Therefore the episode is not considered disruptive. The years between 1369 and 1371 saw repeated English pirate attacks on Flemish ships, but although other sources suggest that Castilian, French, and English merchants transported their goods in these ships no actual damages are recorded.[19]

Notably the last three decades of the fourteenth century saw many trade disruptions. In 1371 the Count of Flanders ordered the seizure of thirty-nine English ships in Sluis following English piracy and the destruction of a Flemish fleet of twenty-two nefs off the coast of France. Most cargo in

[15] Dollinger 1964: 85–91.
[16] Prims 1927–49, 5:1, 11–80, 132–33.
[17] Gilliodts-Van Severen 1871–85: 4:158, 201.
[18] Dollinger 1964: 91–96.
[19] Nicholas 1979: 34–35.

Sluis turned out to be owned by Flemish, Italian, and German merchants, but the English capture still amounted to 8,340 pounds sterling. Other Flemish attacks in 1371 and early in 1372 added to the damage.[20] There is no evidence that warfare between Holland and Utrecht in the years 1372–74 disturbed foreign trade.[21]

Violence is recorded in 1377 when Bruges seized the goods of German merchants to prevent their collective departure and in 1382 when the Count of Flanders ordered all foreign merchants to leave Bruges to try to weaken the revolting Flemish towns. The vast majority of Germans, Catalans, Genoese, Spaniards, Lombards, Scots, and Englishmen complied.[22] They could resume their trade, however, after the defeat of the Flemish towns at the Battle of Westrosebeeke (1382). Social unrest within Flanders continued until 1384 when the new count, Philip the Bold of Burgundy, offered amnesty to Ghent in exchange for its withdrawal of support for England.

The year 1379 marked the beginning of repeated confrontations between England and Flanders, following the latter's renewed siding with France in the Hundred Years' War.[23] English and Flemish commerce was damaged on many occasions. In 1381 French pirates pillaged ships and damaged merchants and sailors from Flanders, Germany, Zeeland, Holland, and other countries near the Zwyn.[24] In 1382, when Ghent rebels occupied Bruges, six English ships were arrested and 117 sacks of wool impounded.[25]

In 1387 the English attacked a Flemish fleet (which probably included some French, German, and Spanish ships, or carried merchandise owned by merchants from these countries),[26] allegedly carrying nine thousand tons of wine, from La Rochelle to Sluis. Some ships were destroyed, others carried off to England.[27] The Dukes of Burgundy reacted by banning English traders from Flanders. There were also plans to mount an invasion of England, but despite an extensive loan from Bruges, and a fleet set up in Damme, the plans did not materialize.[28]

In 1392 and in the years between 1396 and 1403 attacks by pirates from France, Flanders, Zeeland, and Holland on English merchants and

[20] Murray 2005: 274; Nicholas 1979: 34–35; Craeybeckx 1958: 114.
[21] Smit 1914: 126.
[22] Gilliodts-Van Severen 1871–85: 4:311; Prims 1927–49: 5:1, 99; Vandermaesen 1982: 435–44.
[23] Blockmans 1978: 482.
[24] Gilliodts-Van Severen 1871–85: 2:471–73.
[25] Murray 2005: 245, 276.
[26] Craeybeckx 1958: 117.
[27] Asaert 1976b, 64; Craeybeckx 1958: 116–17, raised doubts about the amount of wine captured.
[28] Gilliodts-Van Severen 1871–85: 3:96–101.

their goods are recorded.[29] One attack on a Dutch ship carrying herring, eel, and other goods for English merchants is recorded in 1392.[30] In 1402 and 1403 these pirates also attacked Danish, Scottish, and German ships. To force the release of Flemish ships, in 1403 the Duke of Burgundy confiscated English goods and ships in his territories.[31] Bruges filed complaints with the Count of Holland, participated in conferences in Antwerp and Ghent in 1401, sent envoys to England, Scotland, and Ireland, and participated in another conference in Sluis in 1402.

Finally a truce was reached at a conference with the English king in 1403.[32] The truce was renewed in 1407, 1408, 1411, but also violated on several occasions.[33] In 1403 and 1410, the Duke of Burgundy confiscated English property in reaction to the capture of Flemish vessels; in 1403 Scottish goods were seized in Flanders.[34] Also in 1412, 1413, and 1415 Flemish privateers captured English ships.[35] Other foreigners trading with Flanders also suffered losses.

In 1387 German merchants asked Bruges for compensation for damages related to the Flemish involvement in the war between France and England.[36] When the city refused this, the Kontor was removed to Dordrecht in 1388, where it remained until 1392. The years 1387 and 1388 are considered disruptive for German trade.

Between 1378 and 1402 trade in the Baltic Sea was disrupted by the Vitalienbrüder, privateers for the Dukes of Mecklenburg who turned into outright pirates once their services were no longer needed.[37] Attacks on Hanseatic ships returning from the North Sea, or sailing there, appeared throughout this period. Major disruptions of German trade occurred in 1380–81, 1383–84, and 1391–97. Attacks in these years also harmed those Germans trading with the Low Countries. In 1393, 1394, and 1395 the Count of Holland issued letters of mark that allowed citizens from Amsterdam to recoup losses from citizens of Wismar, Rostock, and Mecklenburg, and from subjects of the king of Sweden.[38] In 1398 the Vitalienbrüder shifted their operations to the North Sea, where they were chased and rounded up by a Hamburg fleet shortly after 1400. In addition to this threat, merchants from Hamburg, Kampen, Saxony, and

[29] Gilliodts-Van Severen 1871–85: 1:466–72; Paviot 1995: 224–26.
[30] Van der Laan 1975: 382.
[31] Paviot 1995: 202.
[32] Gilliodts-Van Severen 1871–85: 3:453–67.
[33] Gilliodts-Van Severen 1871–85: 3:524–34; 4:37–42, 61, 70–74, 138.
[34] Paviot 1995: 202, 228.
[35] Paviot 1995: 224–26.
[36] Gilliodts-Van Severen 1871–85: 3:96.
[37] The following is based on Puhle 1992: passim.
[38] Van der Laan 1975: 420, 430–31, 435, 437, 444, 459, 464.

Brandenburg were the victims of Dutch freebooters engaged in war between Holland and Friesland in 1397, 1398, and 1400.[39]

1400–1449

In the first half of the fifteenth century violent incidents harmed the trade of almost all foreign merchant communities in the Low Countries. When Castilian corsairs attacked Flemish ships between 1417 and 1421, the Four Members of Flanders responded with the issue of letters of mark allowing Flemish traders to recoup their losses with the taking of Castilian ships.[40] In 1421 the council of the Duke of Burgundy issued a charter that set a 5 percent levy on all sales of merchandise from Galicia, Asturia, Old Castile, and Basque—with the explicit exception of Navarre—as compensation for damages done to the Flemish in the past four years. The Four Members of Flanders were to use the revenues to pay the costs of their diplomatic efforts, and award damages to individual victims of the corsairs.[41] Although this measure was meant to replace the letters of mark, new Castilian attacks led to new letters issued in 1423 and 1424.[42] New negotiations following a Castilian threat to leave Flanders in 1427 led to the revocation of the levy and the granting of new privileges to the Castilian nation in 1428. A committee was appointed to establish mutual damages.[43]

In 1438 Philip the Good allowed the Flemish and Italian owners of a ship confiscated in Valencia in 1436 to compensate their loss with the seizure of Catalan and Aragonese property in Flanders.[44] Initially the Four Members managed to postpone this measure, but fearing its application in the fall of 1439 the Aragonese crown ordered Catalan and Aragonese merchants to prepare for a departure from Burgundian territory. It did not come that far, however, for the Duke instituted a committee that proposed to set a levy of 1.66 percent on all imports from Aragon instead. The revenue (up to a total value of 1,288 pounds Flemish) was to be collected by the disenfranchised merchants. Following the capture of a Burgundian ship in the Mediterranean in 1440, talks started anew. To put pressure upon the Aragonese crown, its merchants were held shortly by the duke's bailiff in Bruges in 1443. Again talks continued, however, and eventually in 1444 or 1445 the levy was raised to 2.5 percent. The levy

[39]Smit 1914: 163–77.
[40]Gilliodts-Van Severen 1871–85: 4:379, 381, 494; Paviot 1995: 216–17.
[41]Gilliodts-Van Severen 1901–2: 23, 26; Gilliodts-Van Severen 1871–85: 4:495–96.
[42]Gilliodts-Van Severen 1871–85: 4:494, 496–97; Gilliodts-Van Severen 1883–85: 1:466–72.
[43]Paviot 1995: 217.
[44]Paviot 1995: 213.

was repealed in January 1450 after repeated protests of the city of Bruges (afraid that the city would lose its attraction), as well as merchants from Catalunya, Aragon, Venice, Genoa, Florence, Pisa, and Milan.[45]

German merchants trading with the Low Countries were confronted with piracy, privateering, and warfare on many occasions. In addition to the incidents already mentioned above, between 1403 and 1407 English privateers captured various German ships.[46] In 1418 French pirates attacked Hanseatic ships before the Flemish coast.[47] In the late 1420s Scottish privateers also attacked German ships.[48] In 1419 a fleet of forty Flemish and Hanseatic vessels was attacked by Castilians of the coast near La Rochelle.[49] With this incident commenced a privateering war between Castile and the Hanse that officially ended only in 1443.[50]

Meanwhile, between 1426 and 1435 the German Hanse was at war with Denmark, following the Danish introduction of the Sound Toll, payable by all ships passing through. Initially Hanseatic attempts to block the entry to the Baltic Sea failed, and German merchants had to revert to the isthmus of Holstein to continue their trade with the Low Countries. In these years privateers from Holland and Zeeland launched repeated attacks on merchants from the Wendish quarter.[51] On one occasion, in 1427, the capture of an Amsterdam ship, first by Danish and then by Hamburg privateers, led to the arrest of Hamburg citizens in Leyden.[52]

The war with Denmark immediately ushered in a new conflict. During the war Dutch ships had taken over the German trade with Scandinavian countries. War broke out between Holland and the Hanse in 1438. Officially this was a Burgundian campaign, but it was entirely financed and organized by the towns of Holland.[53] Lübeck warships sank or captured Dutch merchantmen. Holland engaged in privateering and attacked the fleet of Lübeck on at least three occasions. In 1440 a Dutch fleet of seventeen or eighteen vessels forced its way into the Baltic Sea. In 1441 the Peace of Copenhagen, a truce by the letter, secured free entry for Dutch ships.

After almost continuous privateering between England and the Burgundian lands in the years between 1395 and 1415, the Duke of Burgundy became the ally, and between 1420 and 1422 even the vassal, of the English king Henry V, who was also king of France in this period.[54]

[45] Watson 1961: 1088; Paviot 1995: 214–15.
[46] Smit 1914: 188–89.
[47] Gilliodts-Van Severen 1871–85: 4:377–78.
[48] Gilliodts-Van Severen 1871–85: 5:12–13.
[49] Dollinger 1964: 318; Gilliodts-Van Severen 1871–85: 4:379; Paviot 1995: 216.
[50] Dollinger 1964: 318, 479–81.
[51] Paviot 1995: 235–38.
[52] Paviot 1995: 236.
[53] Blockmans and Prevenier 1999: 93–94.
[54] Paviot 1995: 220–28.

However, in 1435 (Treaty of Arras) the Dukes of Burgundy sided with France again in its war against England. The Flemish towns did support him, but their troops backed of in the siege of Calais, and returned home precociously. The battle for Calais was lost, and English troops began ravaging the Flemish countryside. The war damaged trade because it led to repeated attacks by pirates and privateers in the North Sea. Particularly violent were the years 1436–40, 1443, 1446, 1449, 1453, 1455, 1457, and 1460.[55] In addition to merchants from England, France, and the Low Countries, Spaniards and Germans were also attacked.[56]

In addition to these larger conflicts, a number of other incidents occurred. Particularly worrisome for the Hanse was the killing of allegedly more than eighty Hanseatic seamen and merchants in Sluis in 1436 by a mob that suspected their support for the English king.[57] While urban revolt continued in Bruges, the German Kontor was temporarily removed to Antwerp. Violent threats to other foreigners during the Bruges Revolt of 1436–38 are not recorded, however. In 1439 Flemish traders went to Holland to buy goods from ships from Spain, Brittany, and other countries, taken by pirates from Holland and Zeeland.[58] In 1449 an English fleet captured more than one hundred Burgundian and Hanseatic merchantmen off the coast of France. The Burgundians were released, but the Hanseatic ships were brought to England. Other attacks of Hanseatic ships are recorded for 1439, 1443, and 1457.[59]

Finally, violent incidents in the first half of the fifteenth century included the confiscation of the goods of Genoese merchants in Bruges in 1409 by John the Fearless following the betrayal of one of his officers in Genoa.[60] In 1415 Scottish pirates captured four foreign ships before the coast of Nieuwpoort with goods belonging to English, Italian, and Flemish merchants.[61]

1450–99

The second half of the fifteenth century was hardly less disturbing for foreign merchants trading in the Low Countries. Particularly harmful was the Flemish Revolt (1483–92), which led to major trade disruptions in 1484, 1488, and 1489. The revolt ended officially in 1490, but Sluis continued

[55]Thielemans 1966: 261, 340–42; Slootmans 1985: 1:96–99, 101, 113; Gilliodts-Van Severen 1871–85: 5:380; Paviot 1995: 218, 226–28; Dollinger 1964: 373–74.
[56]Craeybeckx 1958: 110; Paviot 1995: 218; De Smedt 1951: 89–90.
[57]Thielemans 1966: 85.
[58]Gilliodts-Van Severen 1871–85: 5:197–98.
[59]Thielemans 1966: 337–38.
[60]Gilliodts-Van Severen 1871–85: 4:342; Van Rompaey 1973: 189.
[61]Gilliodts-Van Severen 1871–85: 4:334–35.

to resist until 1492.[62] Damage was done to the entire foreign merchant community, for in 1484 Maximilian forced all foreign merchants to temporarily leave Bruges. Although this order was revoked that same year, in 1485 London merchants in Bergen-op-Zoom still did not want to travel to Bruges for fear of being robbed.[63] In 1488 all foreign merchants were forced to leave Bruges again. This time it took until 1492 for Bruges to renegotiate the return of the foreign nations. However, foreign trade with the Low Countries was not disturbed after 1489, for alien traders continued their business in Antwerp in the meantime.

Rivalry between England and the German Hanse led to several violent incidents in the second half of the fifteenth century. In 1458 eighteen vessels from Lübeck were taken by the English governor of Calais.[64] Between 1470 and 1473 there was an armed conflict between Holland and England on one side, and the Hanse on the other. The Hanse forced Denmark to close the Sound for all ships from Holland and England, and German privateers attacked Brabantine ships they believed were laden with English goods. One of the ships turned out to be chartered by the city of Hamburg, forcing the principals of the privateering captain to indemnify the city.[65] In another attack, in 1473, the Florentine merchant Tomaso Portinari lost a ship carrying at least 40,000 pounds Flemish pounds of merchandise.[66]

Between 1470 and 1493 warfare between France and Burgundy reduced the import of French grain to a fraction of what it had been before. Military operations (including privateering) and trade embargoes kept French merchants and shipmasters from the ports of the Low Countries in this period.[67] Attacks of French privateers on ships from England and the Burgundian Netherlands are recorded in 1471, 1472, 1484, and 1485, but probably occurred more often than that.[68] According to Sicking the Atlantic coast was not safe between 1478 and 1483, nor between 1486 and 1489.[69] Émile Coornaert established that trade between France and the Burgundian Netherlands was disrupted by warfare in 1477–79, 1484–89, and 1491–93.[70]

Smaller incidents in the second half of the fifteenth century included the arrest of various English merchants in Hulst in 1453, following En-

[62] Sicking 2004: 65.
[63] Slootmans 1985: 1:139.
[64] Dollinger 1964: 373.
[65] Dollinger 1964: 378–79; Slootmans 1985: 1:103–6.
[66] Gilliodts-Van Severen, 1871–85: 6:410–57.
[67] Van Tielhof 1995a: 19–21; Blockmans and Prevenier 1999: 181–82.
[68] Sicking 2004: 65; Slootmans 1985: 1:104, 106, 136.
[69] Sicking 2004: 65.
[70] Coornaert 1961: 1:80.

glish attacks on Flemish ships carrying wine from La Rochelle.[71] In 1457 three ships laden with wool that belonged to merchants from Lombardy were captured by English pirates.[72] In 1459 or 1460 a former commander of Burgundian warships seized Genoese merchandise in Middelburg to recoup losses from the capture of one of these warships by Genoa in 1445.[73] In 1476, when Genoese merchants were suspected to support the king of France in his struggle with Charles the Bold, they were temporarily expelled from Bruges.[74] Pirates from Holland attacked English ships in 1480 and 1481. In 1488 the Amsterdam magistrate took hostage several Englishmen in response to a request by local merchants whose ships and goods had been seized by English warships near Calais.[75]

Again, the effect of violent incidents on trade is not always clear. The Revolt of Ghent between 1450 and 1453 did not lead to infringements on foreign property, but Ghent's absence from the meetings of the Four Members did stall negotiations with the German Hanse about their return to Bruges.[76] Besides, the fact that in 1452 the foreign nations of Bruges, together with the city of Ghent, sent delegates to the Duke of Burgundy in Dendermonde to ask for a six-month truce in the struggle between Ghent and the Duke suggests that at least in 1452 foreign trade was harmed by the revolt (the year is considered disruptive for all groups of traders).[77] Overland trade with Germany may have been disrupted by Maximilian's involvement in the succession of the murdered Princebishop of Liège (1482–93). Violence is recorded in 1482, 1485, and 1490, but there is no evidence of harm done to German traders.[78]

1500–1549

The major conflict harming foreign merchants in the Low Countries in the first half of the sixteenth century was the prolonged Habsburg-Valois Wars. According to Émile Coornaert trade between France and the Burgundian Netherlands was disrupted by warfare in 1506–8, 1513, 1521–25, 1528–29, 1536–38, and 1542–44.[79] Coornaert provides details about violence for several of these years. In 1513 a short campaign of English

[71] Slootmans 1985: 1:99.
[72] Slootmans 1985: 1:97–100.
[73] Paviot 1995: 215–16.
[74] Goris 1925: 75.
[75] Breen 1902: 237–38.
[76] Blockmans 1978: 251.
[77] Van Rompaey 1973: 85–86.
[78] Slootmans 1985: 1:120–24.
[79] Coornaert 1961: 1:80.

troops disrupted trade between France and Flanders.[80] In 1544 French corsairs were very active in the Channel.[81] In addition there were several announcement of confiscation of French goods in the Low Countries (1521, 1528, 1536, 1537, 1542, 1551, 1557).[82] In 1525 French merchants suffered from a limit of twelve set on the number of French ships allowed in ports in the Low Countries.[83] Although actual confiscations were limited, and French merchants continued to come to Antwerp, these years can be marked as disruptive for French trade with the Low Countries.[84]

The menace to Holland's maritime economy was even greater in the first half of the sixteenth century. Hostilities on land and sea, issuing from both the Habsburg attempt to control the Northern Netherlands, and repeated conflicts with the German Hanse, are recorded in eighteen years between 1500 and 1543.[85] In the 1540s Antwerp merchants complained about attacks by English, Scottish, and French privateers and pirates.[86] However, as far as foreign merchants are concerned, only German traders may have suffered from this violence. However, it is not clear in what years the closure of the Sound by the Hanse—meant to frustrate Dutch trade—also damaged German interests.[87]

Two other incidents should be mentioned. In an attempt to regain the Danish throne, in 1525 Christian II of Denmark outfitted privateers that attacked several Hanseatic ships sailing to the Low Countries.[88] The year 1542 can be identified as one of violent threats for all foreign merchants in Antwerp, for an army from Guelders, led by Maarten van Rossem, threatened to sack Antwerp. In 1543 fortifications were built "for the security of the alien merchants to retain their trade."[89]

1550–99

Especially the years between 1540 and 1565 may be considered relatively safe for foreign merchants in the Low Countries.[90] Charles V generally refrained from violence against foreign merchants. On one occasion, his attempts to root out Protestantism posed a real threat to foreign merchant

[80] Coornaert 1961: 1:80.
[81] Coornaert 1961: 1:81.
[82] Coornaert 1961: 1:83–84.
[83] Sicking 2004: 249.
[84] Sicking 2004: 244.
[85] Sicking 2004: 290–301; Israel 1995: 34, 49.
[86] Sicking 2004: 249.
[87] Sicking 2004: 239.
[88] Sicking 2004: 219–21.
[89] Goris 1925: 5.
[90] Brulez 1959: 32–33.

communities. On April 29, 1550, the emperor issued his Eternal Edict that required all immigrants in the Low Countries to submit a certificate of orthodoxy signed by their parish priest.[91]

The Habsburg-Valois Wars continued to disrupt trade between France and the Low Countries in the 1550s. According to Émile Coornaert, trade was disrupted throughout the entire decade, but he does not provide more detailed evidence.[92] We do know, however, that in 1551, French galleons captured several merchantmen returning from Spain, and some twenty hulks sailing to France and Spain to fetch salt.[93] In the 1560s England's trade with the Low Countries was hindered for several years. First, war between England and France blocked English cloth imports to Antwerp in 1563 and 1564.[94] The English capture of Spanish ships laden with 4 million guilders worth of silver, destined for the Low Countries, led to the attachment of English ships in Antwerp in 1567, and the subsequent removal of English merchants to Stade near Hamburg in 1568.[95]

The single most disruptive event in the second half of the sixteenth century was the Dutch Revolt. Between 1568 and 1578 it hit every single group of alien merchants. Trade interruptions included the religious persecution of Protestants and the suppression of any Protestant worshipping, especially in 1568–69; privateering attacks from the See Beggars between 1568 and 1572, and again between 1574 and 1576; the open warfare in Flanders, Brabant, Holland, and the Zeeland estuary between 1572 and 1576; and the violent attack on merchants by unpaid Spanish troops in 1576 (the Spanish Fury). Meanwhile German merchants in Amsterdam suffered from the city's allegiance to the Spanish king between 1572 and 1578.[96]

The years between 1578 and 1584 passed in relative peace both in Antwerp and Amsterdam, with the exception perhaps of the French Fury in Antwerp in 1583—though no attacks on merchants were reported. The siege of Antwerp in 1584 began a second period of military violence that harmed the commercial interests of many merchants. In 1584 and 1585 the remaining foreigners in Antwerp could hardly trade due to the siege.

In the second half of the 1580s Italian, Portuguese, and Flemish merchants, who had moved to Cologne and Frankfurt, as well as merchants from these areas themselves had difficulty reaching the Low Countries

[91] Mulder 1897: 7–12; Marnef 1996: 119.
[92] Coornaert 1961: 1:80. For lack of detailed evidence, these years have not been added to the tabulation of violent assaults.
[93] Sicking 2004: 254.
[94] Enthoven 1996: 18.
[95] Read 1933: passim.
[96] Van Loo 1999; Israel 1989.

due to the Spanish occupation of the eastern provinces. Between 1586 and 1589 followed a Spanish trade embargo for merchants from the revolting provinces, which was countered by an English and Dutch embargo on trade with Spain, Portugal, and the Spanish Netherlands. The latter embargo, issued by the Count of Leicester on April 4, 1586, explicitly forbade trade with the enemy for Dutch and foreign merchants.[97] The Spaniards at the time had up to twenty ships at sea attacking the Dutch, according to Leicester.[98] The result of the embargoes was a renewed increase of Dutch privateering in 1586 (partially because it absorbed surplus capital that could not be invested in regular trade), which hit French, Scottish, German, and other foreign merchants.[99] However, in 1587 privateering stopped again when the Dutch lifted their embargo.[100]

In 1598 Philip III launched a new embargo against all Dutch ships to Spain and Portugal, an act that led the Dutch to renew their embargo on trade with the Iberian Peninsula, for Dutch and foreign merchants alike.[101] It is difficult to establish the harm done to Spanish-Dutch trade, or to Dutch trade in general, in the years following the embargo. If anything, the years between 1598 and 1601 were the most disruptive, with more than twenty royal and private Spanish warships engaged in attacks on Dutch vessels—against ten to fifteen ships in the years before and afterward.[102] Between 1595 and 1609 Portuguese merchants recorded only one privateering attack in 1596 and another two in 1599 in deeds of Amsterdam notaries.[103] Evidence for more serious disruptions comes from the number of fishing ships from the Meuse estuary captured by privateers in the years 1596–1601. While between 1585 and 1596 every year only between one and five ships were captured, this number rose to eleven in 1597, twenty-eight in 1599, forty-eight in 1600, and thirty-six in 1601. In the following years privateering was back to its pre-1597 level, with the exception of 1606, when nineteen ships were taken by privateers.[104] Merchants from Portugal may not have suffered that much because the embargo was not strictly upheld in Portugal, and their access to Dutch markets was in no way restricted.

In the second half of the sixteenth century Elizabeth I did nothing to suppress the privately run pirate companies that operated a profitable business from various ports in Wales and Cornwall. However, the dam-

---

[97]Van Loo 1999: 354.
[98]Van Vliet 1994: 69.
[99]Oudendijk 1958: passim.
[100]Van Loo 1999: 355.
[101]Van Loo 1999: 356.
[102]Van Vliet 1994: 69–70.
[103]Koen 1973–2001, nos. 10, 61, 92.
[104]Van Vliet 1994: 319.

age done to ships sailing to and from the Low Countries was limited. Most pirates targeted the coastal trade in the Irish Sea and the Channel.[105]

1600–1649

Until 1608 merchants from the Low Countries felt the consequences of the Spanish embargo on Dutch ships. The Twelve Years' Truce (1609–21) put a temporary stop to warfare, but it did not end violent attacks on merchantmen. The demobilization of the navies of Spain and the Dutch Republic created a surplus of sailors, some of whom engaged in piracy to gain a living. Also English pirates were very active in this period.[106] Thus it comes as no surprise that Portuguese merchants recorded many more captures of ships and cargo. Notarial deeds drawn up after such events reveal the minimum number of ships and/or cargo belonging to Portuguese traders who were taken by pirates and privateers.[107] The data show that from 1608 onward every year (except 1615) saw the capture of at least one ship by pirates or privateers: 1596 (1), 1599 (2), 1608 (4), 1609 (1), 1610 (1), 1611 (3), 1612 (3), 1613 (5), 1614 (4), 1616 (4), 1617 (4), 1618 (16), 1619 (5), 1620 (6). In addition to this in 1618 and 1619 Portuguese merchants had to deal with the arrest of several of their agents in Portugal by the Spanish Inquisition.[108]

The resumption of war with Spain led to a renewed embargo, open warfare in the southern part of the Low Countries, privateering on the North Sea and the Atlantic Coast of France and Spain, and acts of piracy in that same area.[109] Portuguese, English, and Dutch merchants in Amsterdam suffered less from the embargo than from piracy, privateering, and warfare because the embargo was relatively easily circumvented

[105] Mathew 1924: passim.
[106] Bruijn 1998: 29–31.
[107] Koen 1973–2001, nos. 10, 61, 92, 270, 280, 285, 287, 343, 485, 501, 546, 572, 579, 586, 592, 623, 627, 656, 663, 711–13, 777, 842, 1026, 1031, 1113, 1313, 1330, 1417, 1430/1434, 1469, 1473, 1518, 1551, 1571, 1580, 1605, 1625, 1631, 1637, 1664, 1687, 1706, 1720, 1871, 1922, 1958, 1969, 2006, 2085, 2137, 2213, 2259, 2331, 2349, 2401, 2429, 2473, 2526, 2552, 2564, 2565, 2573, 2574, 2585, 2597–2601, 2613, 2644, 2660, 2684, 2685, 2693, 2699, 2706, 2714, 2722, 2723, 2729, 2744, 2764, 2778, 2780, 2789, 2801, 2808, 2831, 2886, 2887, 2905, 290, 2952, 2959, 2978, 2984, 3052, 3086, 3120, 3127, 3177, 3201, 3205, 3214, 3228, 3291, 3385, 3402, 3418, 3428, 3432, 3439, 3462, 3464, 3473, 3481, 3505, 3589, 3590, 3591, 3622, 3628, 2640.
[108] Koen 1973–2001: nos. 1548, 1553, 1554, 1555, 1556, 1557, 1573, 1585, 1587, 1615, 1548, 1594, 1647, 1695, 1696, 1697, 1728, 1731, 1739, 1754, 1759, 1760, 1774, 1776, 1810, 1813, 1845, 1858, 1865, 1873, 1928, 1937, 1938 1967, 2008, 2029. For goods impounded by Spain's fiscal authorities in 1618 and 1619: Koen 1973–2001: nos. 1737, 1748, 1751, 1754, 1759, 1760, 1719, 1810, 1833, 1858, 1937, 1938.
[109] Bruijn 1993: 19–28; Bruijn 1998: 32–38; Israel 1989: 121–96; van Vliet 1994: 143.

through long-established contacts with traders in northern Germany, southern France, and Portugal.[110] Between 1621 and 1648 merchantmen sailing to the Dutch Republic had to deal with continuous attacks from Dunkirk pirates. Dutch and Portuguese merchants were hit every year. Evidence collected by van Vliet for the period 1626–46 shows that every single year at least 100 merchantmen and fishing ships were captured, with 1632 as the most "successful" year, with 350 ships. On average, every year 229 ships were captured—at least half of which were from the Dutch Republic.[111] Most English merchantmen were captured in 1630, and French ships almost exclusively in 1638.[112]

Furthermore, Italian, Flemish, and Dutch merchants trading in the Mediterranean had to deal with Spanish attempts to frustrate trade between Holland, Italy, and the Levant from 1621 onward.[113] Dutch and German merchants involved in Continental trade had to deal with the river blockade between 1625 and 1630. Between 1628 and 1630 Dutch and German merchants in Amsterdam also suffered from military operations in their trade with the Baltic area.

[110]Kernkamp 1931–34: passim.

[111]Van Vliet 1994: 204–6, 306–19; Israel 1989: 121–96. Notarial deeds signed by Portuguese merchants between 1621 and 1627 reveal the capture of ships in every year between 1621 and 1627: 1621 (14), 1622 (20), 1623 (13), 1624 (8), 1625 (4), 1626 (12), 1627 (60): Koen 1973–2001: passim.

[112]According to Stradling (1980) 64 percent of the ships captured by Dunkirque privateers were Dutch, almost 20 percent English (almost all captured in 1630), and another 15 percent French (mostly captured in 1638). In the 1640s the majority of ships captured were also Dutch: Baetens 1976.

[113]Bruijn 1998: 32–38.

The Motivation, Organization, and Outcome of
Collective Action by Merchants of the German
Hanse in Bruges, 1250–1500

Date	Motivation	Action taken	German principals	Outcome
1252–53	Official establishment in Flanders; establishment of fenced community near Damme	Talks	Merchants from Hamburg and Lübeck	Initial privileges, but no separate premises
1280–82	Bruges refuses to apply toll and weighage tariffs agreed upon by Count of Flanders	Removal to Aardenburg, following initiative of Spanish (and possibly French) merchants	Official from Lübeck, also on behalf of eight other towns, supported by Flemish Count	Internal disciplining by procureurs; trade with foreigners through brokers allowed
1305	Disagreement about Bruges's monetary regime and the weighage of goods	Talks, with threat to leave	Officials from Lübeck	None
1307–9	Disagreement about Bruges's monetary regime and the weighage and brokerage of goods	Removal to Aardenburg, together with Spanish merchants	Officials from Lübeck and Dortmund, supported by Flemish Count	Consular jurisdiction; German *concession:* staple fixed *in Bruges*
1351	English attack on German ship; weighage	Talks and permission from Hansetag for Kontor to leave; threat not executed.	German Kontor in Bruges, without consulting Lübeck	New weighage facility
1357	Bruges's staple rights; higher tolls, brokerage, and wine excise; confiscation of German vessels for military purposes; denial of preferential debts over Bruges's citizens; display of goods limited to Mondays in urban vending locations (Cologne)	Mediation between Bruges and German Kontor	Officials from Lübeck and Cologne, independently	None

1358–60	Bruges's staple rights; higher tolls, brokerage, and wine excise; confiscation of German vessels for military purposes; denial of preferential debts over Bruges's citizens; display of goods limited to Mondays in urban vending locations (Cologne)	German boycott of trade with Flanders; removal of Kontor to Dordrecht	Lübeck and Greifswald carrying out decisions of the Hansetag	4,111 pounds Flemish paid by Bruges.[a] Privileges apply to all of Flanders; Count cannot recall privileges; Germans may arrest robbers inside and outside Flanders; retail trade allowed; sales allowed every day; exemption from Bruges's staple right (1323); brokers cannot own goods they purvey; suretyship of Bruges for debts of hostellers (proved unenforceable later); several minor amendments regarding brokerage, tolls, lading of ships. *Implicit concession:* tolls on re-exports.
1377	Bruges refused liability for hostellers; refused to punish those that had aggressed and injured Germans; tax levied on imported codfish; interdiction to import Hamburg beer; bad quality of certain cloth sold to Germans	Failed attempt to leave Bruges collectively	Bruges Kontor without notifying Hanse	Count of Flanders found out and confiscated German goods

continued

Date	Motivation	Action taken	German principals	Outcome
1383	Confiscation of German goods in 1377; trade disruption due to revolt of Flemish towns against Count; in 1382 Count forced temporary removal of all foreigners to Antwerp	Talks with Count of Holland about removal to Dordrecht	Hansetag	Hanse declines invitation
1388–92	Confiscation of German goods in 1377; other damages in following years, including Flemish capture of German ship on the Zwyn	German boycott of trade with Flanders; removal of Kontor to Dordrecht	Hansetag, led by Lübeck officials	11,100 Pounds Flemish paid by Count and Four Members.[b] Confirmation of old privileges; public penance by Bruges citizens.
1397	Damage done in local hostel	Talks with Bruges		107 pounds Flemish paid by Bruges
1405	Attack by pirates from Nieuwpoort	Talks with Four Members of Flanders		703 pounds Flemish paid by Four Members
1428	Repeated conflicts between Hanse and towns in Holland	Threat to boycott trade with Flanders	Bruges Kontor, with envoys from Hanse	None
1430	Damage done by local money changer	Talks with Bruges		267 pounds Flemish paid by Bruges

1431–32	Scottish pirates attack	Talks with Bruges and Four Members		2,151 pounds Flemish paid by Bruges and Four Members[c]
1434–35	Repeated attacks by privateers from Zeeland	Talks with Bruges and Four Members		None
1437–38	In 1436 up to 80 Germans killed in Sluis; social unrest following revolt of Bruges (1436–38) against Count	German stoppage of grain imports, to acquire right to move with other foreigners to Antwerp	Hanse	8,000 pounds Flemish, promised by Four Members; not paid
1438	Two German hostellers attacked	Talks		108 pounds Flemish paid by Bruges
1448	Hanseatic towns wish to organize formal German staple in Bruges	Talks with Bruges	Hanse	None
1451	Hanseatic towns wish to organize formal German staple in Bruges (internal dissension between merchants from Prussia, Cologne, and Lübeck)	Boycott of Flanders. Removal to Deventer	Hanse	None

continued

Date	Motivation	Action taken	German principals	Outcome
1452–57	Hanseatic towns wish to organize formal German staple in Bruges (internal dissension between merchants from Prussia, Cologne, and Lübeck)	Additional boycott of Brabant fairs (1453); removal to Utrecht to be closer to Amsterdam; intensive talks with Burgundian duke and Bruges since 1456	Hanse	Duke of Burgundy names committee of "notables" to look into conflicts between him and the Hanse; Bruges grants the Hanse the right to build new premises; 2,000 pounds Flemish (of 1438 promise) paid by Four Members[d]
1498	Piracy; Hanseatic refusal to comply with verdict of Great Council regarding the restitution of the value of the goods loaded in a Florentine galley	Talks	Hanse	2,000 Pounds Flemish paid to Hanse by Bruges for damage by pirates and 16,000 pounds Flemish to pay off the Florentine owners of the ship that had been captured by Hanse in 1473

[a] The compensation consisted of 3,911 pounds Flemish paid by Bruges, and 1500 ecu d'or payable by the Count of Flanders with Bruges standing surety. To convert the ecu d'or to pounds Flemish we use the exchange rate set in 1270 by Louis IX: 1 ecu d'or = ½ livre tournois. Given that in 1360 one pound Flemish equaled 7.5 Livre tournois, the compensation of the Count of Flanders amounted to 200 pounds Flemish. If we use the exchange rate of the mid-fifteenth century instead (1 ecu d'or = 49 groats Flemish; Paviot 1995: 216), the compensation would amount to somewhat over 300 pounds Flemish.

[b] In exchange for the promise of the Hanse to return to Flanders, 5,550 pounds Flemish was paid in Amsterdam on Assumption (August 15). The sum had to be paid in full before the end of 1394.

[c] This compensation consisted of 751 pounds Flemish paid by the Four Members and 1,400 pounds Flemish paid by Bruges.

[d] The payment is mentioned in a treaty between Hanse and Bruges, signed March 3, 1458; Bruges paid its share and stood surety for payments by the other Three Members.

Sources: Gilliodts-Van Severen 1871–85: 2:58, 64–65, 127–28; 3:244, 246, 257–59, 411, 523, 524; 5:10, 12–13, 201, 402, 406–7; 6:410–57; Dollinger 1964: 85–91, 99–102; Poeck 2000: passim; Stützel 1998: passim; Paviot 1995: 235; Mallett 1967: 101–2; Greve 2001: passim; Greve 1997: passim.

List of Abbreviations

ACA	Amsterdam City Archives
ACA NA	Amsterdam City Archives, Notarial Archives
Antwerp Customs (1545)	*Coutumes de la ville d'Anvers, dites Antiquissimae, d'après un manuscrit reposant aux Archives de la ville d'Anvers* (1545)
Antwerp Customs (1582)	*Coutumes du pays et duché de Brabant. Quartier d'Anvers. Coutumes de la ville d'Anvers* (1582). Edited by G. De Longé. Brussels: Gobbaerts, 1870, 1:429–705
BT	Biblioteca Thysiana, University Library Leiden
FA	Felix Archief (Antwerp City Archives)
NA	National Archives, The Hague.
Ordonnantie (1532)	*Ordonnantie ende Verhael vanden Stijl ende Maniere van Procederen* (1532)
RSG	Nicolaas Japikse and Hermina Hendrina Petronella Rijperman. *Resolutiën der Staten-Generaal van 1576 tot 1609.* 14 vols. The Hague: Nijhoff, 1915–70. *Resolutiën der Staten-Generaal Oude en Nieuwe reeks, 1576–1625.* http://www.inghist.nl/retroboeken/statengeneraal/
RSH	National Archives, *Generaale Index op Resoluties Staten van Holland*
SR	E. M. Koen. "Notarial Records Relating to the Portuguese Jews in Amsterdam up to 1639." *Studia Rosenthaliana* (1973–2001)

Bibliography

Abraham-Thisse, Simone. 2002. "De lakenhandel in Brugge." In *Hanzekooplui en Medicibankiers. Brugge, wisselmarkt van Europese culturen*, edited by André Vandewalle. Oostkamp: Stichting Kunstboek. 65–72.

Acemoglu, Daron, Simon Johnson, and James Robinson. 2005. "The Rise of Europe: Atlantic Trade, Institutional Change, and Economic Growth." *American Economic Review* 95 (3): 546–79.

Acemoglu, Daron, and James Robinson. 2005a. *Economic Origins of Dictatorship and Democracy*. New York: Cambridge University Press.

———. 2005b. "Unbundling Institutions." *Journal of Political Economy* 113: 949–95.

———. 2012. *Why Nations Fail: The Origins of Power, Prosperity, and Poverty*. London: Profile Books.

Aert, Laura van. 2005. "Tussen norm en praktijk. Een terreinverkenning over het juridische statuut van vrouwen in het zestiende-eeuwse Antwerpen." *Tijdschrift voor Sociale en Economische Geschiedenis* 2 (3): 22–42.

Allison Kirk, Thomas. 2005. *Genoa and the Sea: Policy and Power in an Early Modern Maritime Republic, 1559–1684*. Baltimore: Johns Hopkins University Press.

Ammann, Hektor. 1954. "Deutschland und die Tuchindustrie Nordwesteuropas im Mittelalter." *Hansische Geschichtsblätter* 72: 1–63.

Answaarden, Robert van. 1990. "Het drenken der heiligen, of de perikelen van een jonge Amsterdamse graanhandelaar in Portugal (1558)." *Jaarboek van het Genootschap Amstelodamum* 82: 11–22.

———. 1991. *Les Portugais devant le Grand Conseil des Pays-Bas (1460–1580)*. Paris: Fondation Calouste Gulbenkian, Centre Culturel Portugais.

Antunes, Cátia. 2004. *Globalisation in the Early Modern Period. The Economic Relationship between Amsterdam and Lisbon, 1640–1705*. Amsterdam: Aksant.

Arlinghaus, Franz-Josef. 2002. "Die Bedeutung des Mediums 'Schrift' für die unterschiedliche Entwicklung deutscher und italienischer Rechnungsbücher." In *Vom Nutzen des Schreibens*, edited by Walter Pohl and Paul Herold. Wien: Verlag der Österreichischen Akademie der Wissenschaften.

Asaert, Gustaaf. 1976a. "Scheepsbezit en havens." In *Maritieme Geschiedenis der Nederlanden*, edited by G. Asaert, J. van Beylen, and H. P. H. Jansen. Bussum: De Boer Maritiem. 1:180–205.

———. 1976b. "Scheepvaart van het zuiden tot 1400." In *Maritieme Geschiedenis der Nederlanden*, edited by G. Asaert, J. van Beylen, and H. P. H. Jansen. Bussum: De Boer Maritiem. 1:37–74.

Ash, Eric H. 2002. "'A Note and a Caveat for the Merchant': Mercantile Advisors in Elizabethan England." *Sixteenth Century Journal* 33: 1–31.

Ashburner, Walter. 1909. *The Rhodian Sea-Laws. Edited from the Manuscripts*. Oxford: Clarendon Press.

Asser, Willem Daniel Hendrik. 1983. *In solidum of pro parte: een onderzoek naar de ontwikkelingsgeschiedenis van de hoofdelijke en gedeelde aansprakelijkheid van vennoten tegenover derden.* Leiden: Brill.

———. 1987. "Bills of Exchange and Agency in the 18th Century Law of Holland and Zeeland. Decisions of the Supreme Court of Holland and Zeeland." In *The Courts and the Development of Commercial Law,* edited by Vito Piergiovanni. Berlin: Duncker & Humblot. 103–30.

Auweele, Dirk van den. 1977. "Zeerecht." In *Maritieme Geschiedenis der Nederlanden,* edited by Leo M. Akveld, Simon Hart, and Willem J. van Hoboken. Bussum: De Boer Maritiem. 2:220–26.

Baetens, Roland. 1972. *De Nazomer van Antwerpens welvaart. De diaspora en het handelshuis De Groote tijdens de eerste helft der 17de eeuw.* 2 vols. Brussels: Gemeentekrediet van België.

———. 1976. "The Organization and Effects of Flemish Privateering in the Seventeenth Century." *Acta Historiae Neerdandicae. Studies on the History of the Netherlands* 9: 48–75.

Baghdiantz, Ina, Iōanna MacCabe, Pepelasē Minoglou, and Gelina Harlaftis. 2005. *Diaspora Entrepreneurial Networks: Four Centuries of History.* Oxford: Berg.

Bailly, Marie Charlotte Le. 2001. *Recht voor de Raad: Rechtspraak voor het Hof van Holland, Zeeland en West-Friesland in het midden van de vijftiende eeuw.* Hilversum: Verloren.

Bailyn, Bernard. 1955. *The New England Merchants in the Seventeenth Century.* Cambridge, Mass.: Harvard University Press.

Bairoch, Paul. 1988. *Cities and Economic Development: From the Dawn of History to the Present.* London: Mansell.

Baker, John Hamilton. 1986. "The Law Merchant and the Common Law before 1700." In John Hamilton Baker, *The Legal Profession and the Common Law* London: Hambleton Press. 341–68.

———. 2000. "The Law Merchant as a Source of English Law." In *The Search for Principle: Essays in Honour of Lord Goff of Chieveley,* edited by William Swadling and Gareth Jones. Oxford: Oxford University Press. 79–96.

Ballaux, Bart. 1999. "De Mechelse huidenvetterij in het Ancien Régime: van exportindustrie tot nijverheid van regionaal belang." *Bijdragen tot de Geschiedenis* 82: 9–30.

Banaji, Jairus. 2007. "Islam, the Mediterranean and the Rise of Capitalism." *Historical Materialism* 15 (1): 47–74.

Barbour, Violet. 1928–29. "Marine Risks and Insurance in the Seventeenth Century." *Journal of Economic and Business History* 1 (1): 561–96.

———. 1950. *Capitalism in Amsterdam in the Seventeenth Century.* Baltimore: Johns Hopkins University Press.

Bartier, John, and Andrée Nieuwenhuysen. 1965. *Recueil des anciennes ordonnances de la Belgique. Première Section. Ordonnances de Philippe le Hardi, de Marguerite de Male et de Jean sans Peur, 1381–1419. Tome 1. 16 Octobre 1381–31 Décembre 1393.* 2 vols. Brussels: Recueil des Ordonnances des Pays-Bas.

Basile, Mary Elizabeth, Jane Fair Bestor, Daniel R. Cocquillette, and Charles Donahue Jr., eds. 1998. *Lex Mercatoria and Legal Pluralism: A Late Thirteenth-Century Treatise and Its Afterlife.* Cambridge, Mass.: Ames Foundation.

Bautier, Robert-Henry. 1953. "Les Foires de Champagne. Recherches sur une Evolution Historique." In *La Foire*. Brussels: Recueils de la Société Jean Bodin. 5:97–147.

Beck, Colette. 1982. "Éléments sociaux et économiques de la vie des marchands génois à Anvers entre 1528 et 1555." *Revue du Nord* 64: 759–84.

Benedict, Philip. "Rouen's Foreign Trade during the Era of the Religious Wars (1560–1600)." *Journal of European Economic History* 13: 29–74.

Benson, Bruce L. 2002. "Justice without Government: The Merchant Courts of Medieval Europe and Their Modern Counterparts." In *The Voluntary City: Choice, Community, and Civil Society*, edited by David T. Beito, Peter Gordon, and Alexander Tabarrok. Ann Arbor: University of Michigan Press. 127–50.

Berman, Harold J. 1983. *Law and Revolution: The Formation of the Western Legal Tradition*. Cambridge, Mass.: Harvard University Press.

———. 2003. *Law and Revolution. Volume 2, The Impact of the Protestant Reformations on the Western Legal Tradition*. Cambridge, Mass.: Belknap.

Bernard, J. 1972. "Trade and Finance in the Middle Ages 900–1500." In *The Fontana Economic History of Europe, 1. The Middle Ages*. London: Franklin Watts. 274–338.

Bernstein, Lisa. 1992. "Opting Out of the Legal System: Extralegal Contractual Relations in the Diamond Industry." *Journal of Legal Studies* 21 (1): 115–57.

Beuken, Jozef Hubert Aloysius. 1950. *De Hanze en Vlaanderen*. Maastricht: Ernest van Aelst.

Bicci, Antonella. 1981. "Mercanti Italiani in Amsterdam." *Saggi e Documenti* 2: 463–501.

———. 1990. "Italiani ad Amsterdam nel seicento." *Rivista Storica italiana* 102: 899–934.

Bijtelaar, B. M. 1957. "De Hamburgerkapel in de Oude Kerk." *Jaarboek Amstelodamum* 49: 10–26.

Bisson, Douglas R. 1993. *The Merchant Adventurers of England. The Company and the Crown, 1474–1564*. Newark: University of Delaware Press.

Blockmans, Willem Pieter. 1978. *De volksvertegenwoordiging in Vlaanderen in de overgang van middeleeuwen naar nieuwe tijden (1384–1506)*. Brussels: Paleis der Academiën.

———. 1988. "Alternatives to Monarchical Centralisation: The Great Tradition of Revolt in Flanders and Brabant." In *Republiken und Republikanismus im Europa der frühen Neuzeit*, edited by Helmut Georg Königsberger and Elisabeth Müller-Luckner. Munich: Oldenbourg. 145–54.

———. 1992a. "Bruges, a European Trading Centre." In *Bruges and Europe*, edited by Valentin Vermeersch. Antwerp: Mercatorfonds. 40–55.

———. 1992b. "Bruges and France." In *Bruges and Europe*, edited by Valentin Vermeersch. Antwerp: Mercatorfonds. 206–23.

———. 1993. "The Economic Expansion of Holland and Zeeland in the Fourteenth-Sixteenth Centuries." In *Studia Historica Œconomica. Liber Amicorum Herman van der Wee*, edited by Erik Aerts et al. Leuven: Leuven University Press. 41–58.

———. 1994. "Voracious States and Obstructing Cities: An Aspect of State Formation in Preindustrial Europe." In *Cities and the Rise of States in Europe,*

A.D. 1000 to 1800, edited by Charles Tilly and Wim P. Blockmans. Boulder, Colo.: Westview. 218–50.

———. 2010a. "Constructing a sense of community in rapidly growing European cities in the eleventh to thirteenth centuries." *Historical Research* 83 (222): 575–87.

———. 2010b. *Metropolen aan de Noordzee: de geschiedenis van Nederland, 1100–1560*. Amsterdam: Bert Bakker.

Blockmans, Willem Pieter, and Walter Prevenier. 1999. *The Promised Lands: The Low Countries under Burgundian Rule, 1369–1530*. Philadelphia: University of Pennsylvania Press.

Blok, Petrus Johannes. 1900a. "Het plan tot oprichting eener compagnie van assurantie." *Bijdragen voor vaderlandsche geschiedenis en oudheidkunde* 1: 1–41.

———. 1900b. "Koopmansadviezen aangaande het plan tot oprichting eener compagnie van assurantie (1629–1635)." *Bijdragen en mededeelingen van het Historisch Genootschap* 21: 1–161.

Boer, Dick Edward Herman de. 1996. "Florerend vanuit de delta: de handelsbetrekkingen van Holland en Zeeland in de tweede helft van de dertiende eeuw." In *Wi Florens . . . De Hollandse graaf Floris V in de samenleving van de 13de eeuw*, edited by Dick E. H. de Boer. Utrecht: Matrijs. 126–52.

Bogart, Daniel, and Gary Richardson. 2008. "Institutional Adaptability and Economic Development: The Property Rights Revolution in Britain, 1700 to 1830." NBER Working Paper 13757. http://www.nber.org/papers/w13757.pdf.

Bogucka, Maria. 1984. "Danzig an der Wende zur Neuzeit: Von der Aktiven Handelsstadt zum Stapel und Produktionszentrum." *Hansische Geschichtsblätter* 102: 91–103.

Bolton, Jim L., and Francesco Guidi Bruscoli. 2008. "When Did Antwerp Replace Bruges as the Commercial and Financial Centre of North-Western Europe? The Evidence of the Borromei Ledger for 1438." *Economic History Review* 61 (2): 360–79.

Boomgaard, Jan E. A. 1992. *Misdaad en straf in Amsterdam: een onderzoek naar de strafrechtspleging van de Amsterdamse schepenbank 1490–1552*. Zwolle: Waanders.

Boone, Marc. 1996. "Les gens de métiers à l'époque corporative à Gand et les litiges professionnels (1340–1450)." In *Individual, Corporate and Judicical Status in European Cities*, edited by Marc Boone and Maarten Prak. Leuven: Garant. 23–48.

Boone, Marc, Karel Davids, and Paul Janssens, eds. 2003. *Urban Public Debts: Urban Government and the Market for Annuities in Western Europe (14th–18th centuries)*. Turnhout: Brepols.

Boone, Marc, and Maarten Prak. 1995. "Rulers, Patricians, and Burghers: The Great and Little Traditions of Urban Revolt in the Low Countries." In *A Miracle Mirrored: The Dutch Republic in European Perspective*, edited by Karel Davids and Jan Lucassen. Cambridge: Cambridge University Press. 99–134.

Börner, Lars. 2006. "Medieval Market Clearing: The Evolution of Brokerage Rules from the Late Middle Ages to the Early Modern Period." Manuscript, European Institute Florence.

Börner, Lars, and Daniel Quint. 2010. "Medieval Matching Markets." Working paper, Freie Universität Berlin. http://www.ssc.wisc.edu/~dquint/papers/boerner-quint-medieval-matching-markets.pdf.

Börner, Lars, and Albrecht Ritschl. 2002. "Individual Enforcement of Collective Liability in Premodern Europe." *Journal of Institutional and Theoretical Economics* 158: 205–13.

———. 2009. "The Economic History of Sovereignty: Communal Responsibility, the Extended Family, and the Firm." *Journal of Institutional and Theoretical Economics* 165: 99–112.

Börner, Lars, and Oliver Volckart. 2011. "The Utility of a Common Coinage: Currency Unions and the Integration of Money Markets in Late Medieval Central Europe." *Explorations in Economic History* 48: 53–65.

Bosker, Maarten, Eltjo Buringh, and Jan Luiten van Zanden. 2008. *From Baghdad to London. The Dynamics of Urban Growth in Europe and the Arab world, 800–1800*. London: Centre for Economic Policy Research.

Bracker, Jörgen, Volker Henn, and Rainer Postel. 1999. *Die Hanse. Lebenswirklichkeit und Mythos*. Lübeck: Schmidt Römild.

Brand, Paul. 1992. *The Making of the Common Law*. London: Hambledon Press.

Branden, Frans Jozef Peter, ed. 1885. "De Spaansche muiterij ten Jare 1574." *Antwerpsch Archievenblad* 22: 133–480.

———, ed. 1888. "Clementynboeck 1288–1414." *Antwerpsch Archievenblad* 25: 101–465.

———, ed. 1889. "Clementynboeck 1288–1414 (vervolg)." *Antwerpsch Archievenblad* 26: 1–136.

Braudel, Fernand. 1949. *La Méditerranée et le monde méditerranéen à l'époque de Philippe II*. Paris: Colin.

———. 1959. "Les emprunts de Charles-Quint sur la place d'Anvers." In *Charles Quint et son temps: colloque international du Centre National de la Recherche Scientifique. Paris du 30 septembre au 3 octobre 1958*. Paris: Editions du Centre National de la Recherche Scientifique. 191–200.

———. 1977. *Afterthoughts on Material Civilization and Capitalism*. Baltimore: Johns Hopkins University Press.

———. 1979. *Civilisation Matérielle, économie et capitalisme, XVe-XVIIIe siècles*. 3 vols. Paris: Colin.

Breen, Johannes Christiaan. 1902. *Rechtsbronnen der stad Amsterdam*. The Hague: Nijhoff.

Brenner, Robert. 1993. *Merchants and Revolution: Commercial Change, Political Conflict, and London's Overseas Traders, 1550–1653*. Cambridge: Cambridge University Press.

Briels, Jan G.C.A. 1971. "Zuidnederlandse goud- en zilversmeden in Noordnederland omstreeks 1576–1625. Bijdrage tot de kennis van de Zuidnederlandse immigratie." *Bijdragen tot de Geschiedenis* 54: 87–142.

———. 1972. "Zuidnederlandse goud- en zilversmeden in Noordnederland omstreeks 1576–1625. Bijdrage tot de kennis van de Zuidnederlandse immigratie (vervolg)." *Bijdragen tot de Geschiedenis* 55: 89–112.

———. 1985. *Zuid-Nederlanders in de Republiek, 1572–1630. Een demografische en cultuurhistorisch studie*. Sint-Niklaas: Dante.

Britnell, Richard. 2009. *Markets, Trade and Economic Development in England and Europe, 1050–1550*. Farnham: Ashgate.

Bruijn, Jaap R. 1993. *The Dutch Navy of the Seventeenth and Eighteenth Centuries*. Columbia: University of South Carolina Press.

———. 1998. *Varend verleden. De Nederlandse oorlogsvloot in de zeventiende en achttiende eeuw*. Amsterdam: Balans.

Brulez, Wilfrid. 1959. *De firma Della Faille en de internationale handel van Vlaamse firma's in de 16e eeuw*. Brussels: Paleis der Academiën.

———. 1960. De diaspora der Antwerpse kooplui op het einde van de 16de eeuw. *Bijdragen voor de Geschiedenis der Nederlanden* 1: 461–91.

———. 1962. "Les routes commerciales d'Angleterre en Italie au XVIe siècle." In *Studi in Onore di Amintore Fanfani. IV. Evo moderno*. Milan: Dott. A. Giuffrè. 123–84.

———. 1973. "Bruges and Antwerp in the 15th and 16th Centuries: An Antithesis?" *Acta historiae Neerlandicae* 6: 1–26.

———. 1975. "De handel." In *Antwerpen in de XVIde eeuw*, edited by Walter Couvreur. Antwerp: Mercurius. 109–42.

Brunelle, Gayle K. 1989. "Competition and Casualty in Rouennais Trade with the New World." *Terrae Incognitae* 21: 41–53.

Bullard, Melissa Meriam, S. R. (Larry) Epstein, Benjamin G. Kohl, and Susan Mosher Stuard. 2004. "Where History and Theory Interact. Fredric C. Lane on the Emergence of Capitalism." *Speculum* 79 (1): 88–119.

Bulut, Mehmet. 2001. *Ottoman-Dutch Economic Relations in the Early Modern Period*. Hilversum: Verloren.

Carasso-Kok, Marijke, and Cornelis L. Verkerk. 2004. "Eenheid en verdeeldheid. Politieke en sociale geschiedenis tot in de zestiende eeuw." In *Geschiedenis van Amsterdam. Een stad uit het niets*, edited by Marijke Carasso-Kok. Amsterdam: SUN. 204–49.

Carlos, Ann M. 1992. "Principal-Agent Problems in Early Chartered Companies: A Tale of Two Firms." *American Economic Review* 82 (2): 140–45.

Carlos, Ann M., and Frank D. Lewis. 2010. *Commerce by a Frozen Sea Native Americans and the European Fur Trade*. Philadelphia: University of Pennsylvania Press.

Carlos, Ann, and Larry Neal. 2011. "Amsterdam and London as Financial Centers in the Eighteenth Century." *Financial History Review* 18: 21–46.

Carlos, Ann M., and Stephen Nicholas. 1996. "Theory and History: Seventeenth Century Joint-Stock Chartered Trading Companies." *Journal of Economic History* 56 (4): 916–24.

Carson, Patricia. 1992. Bruges and the British Isles. In *Bruges and Europe*, edited by Valentin Vermeersch. Antwerp: Mercatorfonds. 128–45.

Carter, Alice Clare. 1964. *The English Reformed Church in Amsterdam in the Seventeenth Century*. Amsterdam: Scheltema & Holkema NV.

Cavaciocchi, Simonetta, ed. 2001. *Fiere e mercati nella integrazione delle economie Europee secc. XIII-XVIII*. Florence: Le Monnier.

Christensen, Aksel E. 1941. *Dutch Trade to the Baltic about 1600: Studies in the Sound Toll Register and Dutch Shipping Records*. Copenhagen: Munksgaard.

Cieślak, Edmund, and Csezlaw Biernat. 1995. *History of Gdansk*. Gdansk: Fundacja Biblioteki Gdańskiej.

Cipolla, Carlo. 1993. *Before the Industrial Revolution. European Society and Economy 1000–1700*. 3rd ed. London: Routledge.

Clark, Gregory. 2007. "A Review of Avner Greif's Institutions and the Path to the Modern Economy: Lessons from Medieval Trade." *Journal of Economic Literature* 45: 727–43.

Coase, Ronald H. 1937. "Nature of the Firm." *Economica* 4 (16): 386–405.

Constable, Olivia Remie. 2003. *Housing the Stranger in the Mediterranean World. Lodging, Trade, and Travel in Late Antiquity and the Middle Ages*. Cambridge: Cambridge University Press.

Consultatien, advyzen en advertissementen, gegeven bij verscheiden treffelijke rechtsgeleerden in Holland 1657–1666. 6 vols. Rotterdam: Joannes Næranus.

Coornaert, Émile. 1936. "La genése du système capitaliste: grand capitalisme et économie traditionnelle à Anvers au XVIe siècle." *Annales d'histoire économique et sociale: revue trimestrielle* 8 (38): 127–50.

———. 1961. *Les Français et le commerce international à Anvers, fin du XVe–XVIe siècle*. 2 vols. Paris: M. Rivière.

Cooter, Robert D., and Janet T. Landa. 1984. "Personal versus Impersonal Trade: The Size of Trading Groups and Contract Law." *International Review of Law and Economics* 4: 15–22.

Cordes, Albrecht, ed. 1998. *Spätmittelalterlicher Gesellschaftshandel im Hanseraum*. Köln: Böhlau Verlag.

———. 2005. "The Search for a Medieval *Lex Mercatoria*." In *From lex mercatoria to commercial law*, edited by Vito Piergiovanni. Berlin: Duncker & Humblot. 53–68.

Cordes, Albrecht, Klaus Friedland, and Rolf Sprandel, eds. 2003. *Societates. Das Verzeichnis der Handelsgesellschaften im Lübecker Niederstadtbuch 1311–1361*. Köln: Böhlau Verlag.

Craeybeckx, Jan. 1958. *Un grand commerce d'importation: Les vins de France aux anciens Pays Bas, XIIIe–XVIe siecles*. Paris: S.E.V.P.E.N.

Curtin, Philip. 1984. *Cross-Cultural Trade in World History*. Cambridge: Cambridge University Press.

Damen, Mario. 2003. "Het Hof van Holland in de Middeleeuwen." *Holland* 35: 1–8.

Davids, Karel. 1996. "Neringen, hallen en gilden. Kapitalisten, kleine ondernemers en de stedelijke overheid in de tijd van de Republiek." In *Kapitaal, ondernemerschap en beleid. Studies over economie en politiek in Nederland, Europa en Azië*, edited by Karel Davids, Wantje Fritschy, and Loes van der Valk. Amsterdam: Nederlands Economisch-Historisch Archief. 95–119.

———. 1998. "Successful and Failed Transitions. A Comparison of Innovations in Windmill Technology in Britain and the Netherlands in the Early Modern Period." *History and Technology* 14: 225–47.

———. 2004. "The Bookkeeper's Tale: Learning Merchant Skills in the Northern Netherlands in the Sixteenth Century." In *Education and Learning in the Netherlands, 1400–1600: Essays in Honour of Hilde de Ridder-Symoens*, edited by Koen Goudriaan, Jaap van Moolenbroek, and Ad Tervoort. Leiden: Brill. 235–52.

———. 2008. *The Rise and Decline of Dutch Technological Leadership: Technology, Economy and Culture in the Netherlands, 1350–1800.* Leiden: Brill.

De Bruyn Kops, Henriette. 2007. *A Spirited Exchange. The Wine and Brandy Trade between France and the Dutch Republic in Its Atlantic Framework.* Leiden: Brill.

De Long, J. Bradford, and Andrei Shleifer. 1993. "Princes and Merchants: European City Growth before the Industrial Revolution." *Journal of Law and Economics* 36: 671–702.

De Roover, Raymond. 1948. *Money, Banking and Credit in Mediaeval Bruges: Italian Merchant-Bankers Lombards and Money-Changers: A Study in the Origins of Banking.* Cambridge, Mass.: Mediaeval Academy of America.

———. 1949. "La communauté des marchands Lucquois à Bruges de 1377 à 1404." *Handelingen van het genootschap voor geschiedenis, gesticht onder de benaming Société d'Émulation te Brugge* 86: 23–89.

———. 1953a. "Anvers comme marché monétaire au XVIe siècle." *Revue Belge de Philologie et d'Histoire* 31 (2): 1003–47.

———. 1953b. *L'évolution de la lettre de change: XIVe-XVIIIe siècles.* Paris: Armand Colin.

———. 1956. "The Business Organisation of the Plantin Press in the Setting of Sixteenth Century Antwerp." *De Gulden Passer* 34: 104–20.

———. 1963. *The Rise and Decline of the Medici Bank 1397–1494. Harvard Studies in Business History 21.* Cambridge, Mass.: Harvard University Press.

De Ruysscher, Dave. 2006. "Law Merchant in the Mould. The Transfer and Transformation of Commercial Practices into Antwerp Customary Law (16th–17th Centuries)." In *Rechtstransfer in der Geschichte—Legal transfer in history.* Munich: Martin Meidenbauer. 433–45.

———. 2008. "Designing the Limits of Creditworthiness. Insolvency in Antwerp Bankruptcy Legislation and Practice (16th–17th Centuries)." *Tijdschrift voor rechtsgeschiedenis* 76: 307–27.

———. 2009a. "Antwerp Commercial Legislation in Amsterdam in the 17th Century. Legal Transplant or Jumping Board?" *Tijdschrift voor Rechtsgeschiedenis* 77 (3/4): 459–79.

———. 2009b. "From Individual Debt Recovery to Collective Liquidation Procedures. New Ideas on Creditors' Rights in Sixteenth-Century Antwerp." In *Turning Points and Breaklines,* edited by S. Peréz. Munich: Martin Meidenbauer. 193–206.

———. 2009c. *"Naer het Romeinsch recht alsmede den stiel mercantiel." Handel en recht in de Antwerpse rechtbank (16de-17de eeuw).* Kortrijk: UGA.

———. 2009d. "Spaanse Brabanders en hun regels. Antwerps handelsrecht te Amsterdam in de 17de eeuw." *Histoire du droit et de la justice. Une nouvelle génération de recherches. Een nieuwe generatie in het onderzoek over de geschiedenis van het recht en van de justitie.* Edited by Dirk Heirbaut, Xavier Rousseau, and Alain Wijffels. Louvain: Presses Universitaires de Louvain. 319–36.

De Smedt, Oskar. 1940–41. "De keizerlijke verordeningen van 1537 en 1539 op de obligaties en wisselbrieven." *Nederlandsche historiebladen. Driemaandelijks tijdschrift voor de geschiedenis en kunstgeschiedenis van de Nederlanden* 3: 15–35.

———. 1951. *De Engelse natie te Antwerpen in de 16e eeuw (1496–1582)*. Vol. 1. Antwerp: De Sikkel.

———. 1954. *De Engelse Natie te Antwerpen in de 16e eeuw (1496–1582)*. Vol. 2. Antwerp: De Sikkel.

Degryse, Karel. 1990. *Pieter Seghers. Een koopmansleven in troebele tijden* Antwerp: Hadewych.

———. 2001. "Boekhouders, notarissen, stadsboden en factors. Het succesverhaal van sommige 'financiële experten' te Antwerpen tijdens de 18de eeuw." *Bijdragen tot de Geschiedenis* 84: 43–62.

Denucé, Jan. 1934. *Inventaire des Affaitadi, Banquiers italiens à Anvers de l'Année 1568*. Antwerp: Chambre de Commerce d'Anvers.

———. 1938. *De Hanze en de Antwerpsche handelscompagnieën op de Oostzeelanden*. Antwerp: De Sikkel.

Des Marez, Guillaume. 1901. *La lettre de foire à Ypres au XIIIe siècle. Contribution à l'étude des papiers de crédit*. Brussels: H. Lamertin.

Despars, Nicolaes. 1840. *Cronycke van den lande ende graefscepe van Vlaenderen* Brugge: W. Messchert.

Dessí, Roberta, and Sheilagh Ogilvie. 2003. "Social Capital and Collusion: The Case of Merchant Guilds." CESifo Working Papers. http://papers.ssrn.com/sol3/papers.cfm?abstract_id=449263.

Diegerick, Isidore L. A. 1854. *Inventaire analytique et chronologique des chartes et documents appartenant aux Archives de la Ville d'Ypres*. Bruges: Vandecasteele-Werbrouck.

Dietz, Alexander. 1910. *Frankfurter Handelsgeschichte*. 4 vols. Frankfurt: Minjon.

Dijck, Maarten van. 2007. "De pacificering van de Europese samenleving. Repressie, gedragspatronen en verstedelijking in Brabant tijdens de lange zestiende eeuw." Unpublished doctoral dissertation, Antwerp University.

Dijkman, Jessica. 2002. "Giles Sylvester, an English merchant in Amsterdam." Manuscript, University Utrecht.

———. 2011. *Shaping Medieval Markets: The Organisation of Commodity Markets in Holland, c. 1200–c. 1450*. Leiden: Brill.

Dilis, Emile. 1910. "Les courtiers anversois sous l'ancien régime." *Annales de l'Académie royale d'Archéologie de Belgique* 72: 299–462.

Dillen, Johannes Gerard van, ed. 1925. *Bronnen tot de geschiedenis der Wisselbanken (Amsterdam, Middelburg, Delft, Rotterdam)*. 2 vols. The Hague: Nijhoff.

———, ed. 1929. *Bronnen tot de geschiedenis van het bedrijfsleven en het gildewezen van Amsterdam, I, 1512–1611*. The Hague: Nijhoff.

———, ed. 1933. *Bronnen tot de geschiedenis van het bedrijfsleven en het gildewezen van Amsterdam, II, 1612–1635*. The Hague: Nijhoff.

———. 1958. *Het oudste aandeelhoudersregister van de Kamer Amsterdam der Oost-Indische Compagnie*. The Hague: Nijhoff.

———. 1970. *Van rijkdom en regenten: handboek tot de economische en sociale geschiedenis van Nederland tijdens de republiek*. The Hague: Nijhoff.

Dincecco, Mark. 2011. *Political Transformations and Public Finances*. Cambridge: Cambridge University Press.

Dixit, Avinash K. 2004. *Lawlessness and Economics: Alternative Modes of Governance*. Princeton: Princeton University Press.

Doehaerd, Renée. 1941. *Les relations commerciales entre Gênes, la Belgique et l'outremont d'après les archives notariales gênoises aux XIII et XIV siècles*. 3 vols. Brussels: Palais des Academies/Academia Belgica.

———. 1962–63. *Études Anversoises. Documents sur le commerce international à Anvers 1488–1514*. 3 vols. Paris: Ecole Pratique des Hautes Etudes.

Doehaerd, Renée, and Charles Kerremans. 1952. *Les Relations commerciales entre Gênes, la Belgique et l'outremont d'après les archives notariales gênoises 1400–1440*. Rome: Institut Historique Belge de Rome.

Doerflinger, Thomas M. 1986. *A Vigorous Spirit of Enterprise: Merchants and Economic Development in Revolutionary Philadelphia*. London: Chapel Hill.

Dollinger, Philippe. 1964. *La Hanse (XIIe-XVIIe siècles)*. Paris: Aubier.

Donahue, Charles Jr. 2004. "Medieval and Early Modern *Lex mercatoria*: An Attempt at the *probatio diabolica*." *Chicago Journal of International Law* 5 (1): 21–37.

———. 2005. "Benvenuto Stracca's *De Mercatura*: Was There a *Lex Mercatoria* in Sixteenth-Century Italy?" In *From Lex Mercatoria to Commercial Law*, edited by Vito Piergiovanni. Berlin: Duncker & Humblot. 69–120.

Drost, M. A., ed. 1984. *Documents pour servir à l'histoire du commerce des Pays-Bas avec la France jusqu'à 1585, Vol. I Actes Notariés de la Rochelle 1423–1585*. The Hague: Nijhoff.

———, ed. 1989. *Documents pour servir à l'histoire du commerce des Pays-Bas avec la France jusqu'à 1585. Vol. II Actes Notariés de Bordeaux 1470–1520*. The Hague: Nijhoff.

Dudok van Heel, Sebastiaan Abraham Cornelis. 1984. "Oligarchieën in Amsterdam voor de Alteratie van 1578." In *Van stadskern tot stadsgewest. Stedebouwkundige geschiedenis van Amsterdam*, edited by Michiel Jonker, Leo Noordegraaf, and Michiel Wagenaar. Amsterdam: Verloren. 35–61.

———. 1990. "Vroege brouwerijen aan de Amstel in de vijftiende en zestiende eeuw." *Jaarboek Amstelodamum* 82: 23–74.

———. 1991. "Een grote concentratie van zeepzieders aan het Damrak. Amsterdamse zeepziederijen in de 16e en vroege 17e eeuw." *Jaarboek Amstelodamum* 83: 45–112.

Dugger, William M. 2010. "Review of Avner Greif, Institutions and the Path to the Modern Economy: Lessons from Medieval Trade (2006)." *Review of Radical Political Economics* 42 (3): 396–99.

Dumolyn, Jan. 1997. *De Brugse opstand van 1436–1438*. Kortrijk-Heule: UGA.

Dumolyn, Jan, and Jelle Haemers. 2005. "Patterns of Urban Rebellion in Medieval Flanders." *Journal of Medieval History* 31: 369–93.

DuPlessis, Robert S., and Martha C. Howell. 1982. "Reconsidering the Early Modern Urban Economy: The Cases of Leiden and Lille." *Past and Present* 94: 49–84.

Dursteler, Eric R. 2006. *Venetians in Constantinople: Nation, Identity, and Coexistence in the Early Modern Mediterranean*. Baltimore: Johns Hopkins University Press.

Ebert, Christopher. 2011. "Early Modern Atlantic Trade and the Development of Maritime Insurance to 1630." *Past and Present* 213: 87–114.

Edler, Florence. 1937. "Cost Accounting in the Sixteenth Century. The Books of Account of Christopher Plantin, Antwerp, Printer and Publisher." *Accounting Review* 12 (3): 226–37.

Edler de Roover, Florence. 1941. "Partnership Account in Twelfth Century Genoa." *Bulletin of the Business Historical Society* 15 (6): 87–92.

———. 1945. "Early Examples of Marine Insurance." *Journal of Economic History* 5 (2): 172–200.

Edwards, Jeremy, and Sheilagh Ogilvie. 2013. "What Lessons for Economic Development Can We Draw from the Champagne Fairs?" *Explorations in Economic History* 49(2): 131–48.

———. 2012. "Contract Enforcement, Institutions and Social Capital: The Maghribi Traders Reappraised." *Economic History Review* 65: 421–44.

Ehrenberg, Richard. 1885. "Makler, Hosteliers und Börse in Brügge vom 13. bis zum 16. Jahrhundert." *Zeitschrift für das gesamte Handelsrecht* 30: 403–68.

———. 1896. *Das Zeitalter der Fugger, Geldkapital und Creditverkehr im 16. Jahrhundert, Band II, Die Weltbörsen und Finanzkrisen des 16. Jahrhunderts.* Jena: Fischer.

Engels, Marie-Christine. 1997. *Merchants, Interlopers, Seamen and Corsairs. The 'Flemish Community in Livorno and Genoa (1615–1635).* Hilversum: Verloren.

English, Edward D. 1988. *Enterprise and Liability in Sienese Banking, 1230–1350.* Cambridge, Mass.: Medieval Academy of America.

Enthoven, Victor. 1996. *Zeeland en de opkomst van de Republiek. Handel en strijd in de Scheldedelta c. 1550–1621.* Rijksuniversiteit Leiden, Leiden.

Epstein, Stephan. R. 1994. "Regional Fairs, Institutional Innovation and Economic Growth in Late Medieval Europe." *Economic History Review* 47 (3): 459–82.

———. 2000. *Freedom and Growth: The Rise of States and Markets in Europe, 1300–1750.* London: Routledge.

Estié, Paul. 1987. *Het plaatselijk bestuur van de Nederlandse Lutherse gemeenten: ontstaan en ontwikkeling in de jaren 1566 tot 1686.* Amsterdam: Rodopi.

Ewert, Ulf-Christian, and Stephan Selzer. 2010. "Wirtschaftliche Stärke durck Vernetzung Zu den Erfolgsfaktoren des hansischen Handels." In *Praktiken des Handels in Spätmittelalter und Früher Neuzeit,* edited by Mark Häberlein and Christof Jeggle. Konstanz: UVK. 3–70.

Feenstra, Robert. 1953. "Les foires aux Pays-Bas septentrionaux." In *La Foire.* Brussels: Recueils de la Société Jean Bodin. 5:209–39.

Findlay, Ronald, and Kevin H. O'Rourke. 2007. *Power and Plenty: Trade, War, and the World Economy in the Second Millennium.* Princeton: Princeton University Press.

Fortunati, Maura. 1996. *Scrittura e prova. I libri di commercio nel diritto medievale e moderno. Vol. 35, Biblioteca della Rivista di Storia del Diritto Italiano.* Rome: Fondazione Sergio Mochi Onory.

———. 2005. "The Fairs between *Lex Mercatoria* and *Ius Mercatorum.*" In *From lex mercatoria to commercial law,* edited by Vito Piergiovanni. Berlin: Duncker & Humblot. 143–64.

Foster, Nicholas H. D. 2005. "Foundation Myth as Legal Formant: The Medieval Law Merchant and the New Lex Mercatoria." *Forum Historiae Iuris.* http://www.rewi.hu-berlin.de/online/fhi/articles/0503foster.htm.

Friedland, Klaus. 1990. *Brügge-Colloquium des Hansischen Geschichtsvereins 26–29. Mai 1988: Referate und Diskussionen*. Köln: Böhlau.

———. 1991. *Die Hanse*. Stuttgart: Kohlhammer.

Frijhoff, Willem. 1995. "La formation des négociants de la République hollandaise." In *Cultures et formations négociantes dans l'Europe moderne*, edited by Franco Angiolini and Daniel Roche. Paris: Éditions de l'École des Hautes Études en Sciences Sociales. 175–98.

———. 2003. "Uncertain Brotherhood: The Huguenots in the Dutch Republic." In *Memory and Identity: The Huguenots in France and the Atlantic Diaspora*, edited by Bertrand van Ruymbeke and Randy J. Sparks. Columbia: University of South Carolina Press. 128–71.

Funnell, Warwick, and Jeffrey Robertson. 2011. "Capitalist Accounting in Sixteenth Century Holland: Hanseatic Influences and the Sombart Thesis." *Accounting, Auditing & Accountability Journal* 24 (5): 560–86.

Fusaro, Maria. 2012. "Cooperating Mercantile Networks in the Early Modern Mediterranean." *Economic History Review* 65 (2): 701–19.

Geirnaert, Noel. 1992. "Bruges and the Northern Netherlands." In *Bruges and Europe*, edited by Valentin Vermeersch. Antwerp: Mercatorfonds. 72–98.

Gelder, Herman Arend Enno van. 1916. "Zestiende-eeuwse vrachtvaarten." *Oud-Holland* 34: 18–148.

———. 1917. "Een Italiaansch reiziger over ons land in 1517." *Oud-Holland* 35: 12–33.

Gelder, Maartje van. 2009. *Trading Places: The Netherlandish Merchant Community in Early Modern Venice*. Leiden: Brill.

Gelder, Roelof van, and Renée Kistemaker. 1983. *Amsterdam 1275–1795. De ontwikkeling van een handelsmetropool*. Amsterdam: Meulenhoff Informatief.

Gelderblom, Oscar. 1999. "De Deelname van Zuid-Nederlandse kooplieden aan het openbare leven van Amsterdam (1578–1650)." In *Ondernemers & bestuurders. Economie en politiek in de Noordelijke Nederlanden in de late middeleeuwen en vroegmoderne tijd*, edited by Clé Lesger and Leo Noordegraaf. Amsterdam: NEHA. 237–58.

———. 2000. *Zuid-Nederlandse kooplieden en de opkomst van de Amsterdamse stapelmarkt (1578–1630)*. Hilversum: Verloren.

———. 2002. "Een Antwerpse 'cruydenier' in Amsterdam: Hans Martens (1555–1613)." *Jaarboek Oud-Utrecht*: 16–33.

———. 2003a. "Coping with the Perils of the Sea: The Last Voyage of Vrouw Maria in 1771." *International Journal of Maritime History* 15 (2): 95–116.

———. 2003b. "From Antwerp to Amsterdam. The Contribution of Merchants from the Southern Netherlands to the Commercial Expansion of Amsterdam (c. 1540–1609)." *Review. A Journal of the Fernand Braudel Center* 26 (3): 247–83.

———. 2003c. "The Governance of Early Modern Trade: The Case of Hans Thijs (1556–1611)." *Enterprise & Society* 4 (4): 606–39.

———. 2004. "The Decline of Fairs and Merchant Guilds in the Low Countries, 1250–1650." *Jaarboek voor Middeleeuwse Geschiedenis* 7: 199–238.

———. 2008. "Het juweliersbedrijf in de Lage Landen, 1450–1650." Manuscript, Utrecht University.

———. 2009. "The Organization of Long-Distance Trade in England and the Dutch Republic, 1550–1650." In *The Political Economy of the Dutch Republic*, edited by Oscar Gelderblom. Aldershot: Ashgate. 223–54.

———. 2011. "The Golden Age of the Dutch Republic." In *The Invention of Enterprise: Entrepreneurship from Ancient Mesopotamia to Modern Times*, edited by David S. Landes, Joel Mokyr, and William J. Baumol. Princeton: Princeton University Press. 156–82.

Gelderblom, Oscar, Abe de Jong, and Joost Jonker. 2011. "An Admiralty for Asia, Business Organization and the Evolution of Corporate Governance in the Dutch Republic, 1590–1610." In *The Origins of Shareholder Advocacy*, edited by Jonathan Koppell. New York: Palgrave Macmillan. 29–60.

Gelderblom, Oscar, and Regina Grafe. 2010. "The Rise, Persistence, and Decline of Merchants Guilds. Re-thinking the Comparative Study of Commercial Institutions in Pre-modern Europe." *Journal of Interdisciplinary History* 40: 477–511.

Gelderblom, Oscar, and Joost Jonker. 2004. "Completing a Financial Revolution: The Finance of the Dutch East India Trade and the Rise of the Amsterdam Capital Market, 1595–1612." *Journal of Economic History* 64 (3): 641–72.

———. 2005. "Amsterdam as the Cradle of Modern Futures Trading and Options Trading, 1550–1650." In *The Origins of Value: The Financial Innovations that Created Modern Capital Markets*, edited by W. G. Goetzmann and K. G. Rouwenhorst. Oxford: Oxford University Press. 189–205.

Génard, P. 1882. "Jean Baptiste Ferufini et les assurances maritime à Anvers au XVIe Siècle." *Bulletins de la Société Royale de Géographie d'Anvers* 7: 193–268.

Gerven, Jan van. 1999. "War, Violence and an Urban Society: The Brabantine Towns in the Later Middle Ages." In *Secretum Scriptorum. Liber Amicorum Walter Prevenier*, edited by Wim Blockmans, Marc Boone, and Thérèse d'Hemptinne. Leuven: Garant. 183–211.

Gijsbers, Wilma M. 1999. *Kapitale ossen. De internationale handel in slachtvee in Noordwest-Europa (1300–1750)*. Hilversum: Verloren.

Gilissen, John. 1958. "Le statut des étrangers en Belgique du XIIIe au XXe siècle." In *L'étranger*, edited by John Gilissen. Brussels: Editions de la Librairie encyclopédique.

Gillard, Lucien. 2004. *La banque d'Amsterdam et le florin européen au temps de la République néerlandaise (1610–1820)*. Paris: Éditions de l'École des Hautes Études en Sciences Sociales.

Gilliodts-Van Severen, Louis. 1871–85. *Inventaire des archives de la ville de Bruges*. 7 vols. Bruges: Gailliard.

———, ed. 1883–85. *Coutumes des Pays et Comté de Flandre. Quartier de Bruges*. 3 vols. Brussels: Fr. Gobbaerts.

———. 1901–2. *Cartulaire de l'ancien Consulat d'Espagne à Bruges. Recueil de documents concernant le commerce maritime et interieur, le droit des gens public et privé, et l'histoire économique de la Flandre*. 2 vols. Bruges: Louis de Plancke.

Glete, Jan. 2002. *War and State in Early Modern Europe*. London: Routledge.

Go, Sabine. 2009. *Marine Insurance in the Netherlands 1600–1870. A Comparative Institutional Approach*. Amsterdam: Aksant.

Godding, Philippe. 1987. *Le droit privé dans les Pays-Bas méridionaux, du 12e au 18e siècle*. Brussels: Académie Royale de Belgique.

Godding, Philippe, and Jacobus Thomas de Smidt. 1980. "Evolutie van het recht in samenhang met instellingen." In *Algemene Geschiedenis der Nederlanden*. Haarlem: Fibula-Van Dishoeck. 4:172–81.

Godfrey, Mark. 2002. "Arbitration and Dispute Resolution in Sixteenth Century Scotland." *Tijdschrift voor rechtsgeschiedenis* 70 (1/2): 109–35.

Goldberg, Jessica. 2011. "Making Reputation Work: Re-examining Law, Labor and Enforcement among Geniza Businessmen." Paper presented at the Before and Beyond Europe: Economic Change in Historical Perspective conference, Yale University.

———. 2012. *Trade and Institutions in the Medieval Mediterranean The Geniza Merchants and their Business World*. Cambridge: Cambridge University Press.

Goldgar, Anne. 2007. *Tulipmania: Money, Honor, and Knowledge in the Dutch Golden Age*. Chicago: University of Chicago Press.

Goldschmidt, Ernst Philip. 1939. "Le voyage de Hieronimus Monetarius à travers la France, 17 septembre 1494–14 avril 1495." *Humanisme et Renaissance* 6: 55–75, 198–220, 324–48, 529–39.

González De Lara, Yadira. 2001. "Enforceability and Risk-Sharing in Financial Contracts: From the Sea Loan to the Commenda in Late Medieval Venice." *Journal of Economic History* 61 (2): 500–504.

———. 2002. "Institutions for Contract Enforcement and Risk-Sharing: From Debt to Equity in Late Medieval Venice." Manuscript, Ente Enaudi.

———. 2008. "The Secret of Venetian Success: A Public-order, Reputation-based Institution." *European Review of Economic History* 12 (3): 247–86.

González de Lara, Yadira, Avner Greif, and Saumitra Jha. 2008. "The Administrative Foundations of Self-Enforcing Institutions." *American Economic Review: Papers & Proceedings* 98 (2): 105–9.

Goris, Jan Albert. 1925. *Étude sur les colonies marchandes méridionales (Portugais, Espagnols, Italiens) à Anvers de 1488 à 1567. Contribution à l'histoire des débuts du capitalisme moderne*. Louvain: Librairie Universitaire.

Gotzen, Marcel. 1951. "Het Oud-Antwerps burgerlijk procesrecht volgens de Costumiere Redacties van de 16e–17e eeuw." *Rechtskundig tijdschrift voor België* 41: 291–315, 424–68.

Goudsmit, Marinus Theodorus. 1882. *Geschiedenis van het Nederlandsche zeerecht*. The Hague: Nijhoff.

Grafe, Regina. 2001. "Northern Spain between the Iberian and Atlantic Worlds: Trade and Regional Specialization, 1550–1650." Unpublished doctoral dissertation, London School of Economics.

———. 2005. "When Merchants Choose Not to Organise: The English in Seventeenth Century Bilbao." Unpublished manuscript.

———. 2012. *Distant Tyranny: Markets, Power, and Backwardness in Spain, 1650–1800*. Princeton: Princeton University Press.

Granovetter, Mark. 1985. "Economic Action and Social Structure. The Problem of Embeddedness." *American Journal of Sociology* 91 (3): 481–510.

Greefs, Hilde. 1995. "Foreign Entrepreneurs in Early Nineteenth-Century Antwerp." In *Entrepreneurs and Entrepreneurship in Early Modern Times: Mer-*

chants and Industrialists within the Orbit of the Dutch Staple Market, edited by Clemens Maria Lesger and Leo Noordegraaf. The Hague: Stichting Hollandse Historische Reeks. 101–17.

———. 2008. "De terugkeer van Mercurius: de divergerende keuzes van de zakenelite in Antwerpen en het belang van relatienetwerken na de heropening van de Schelde (1795–1850)." *Tijdschrift voor sociale en economische geschiedenis* 5 (2): 55–86.

Greif, Avner. 1989. "Reputation and Coalitions in Medieval Trade: Evidence on the Maghribi Traders." *Journal of Economic History* 49 (4): 857–82.

———. 1992. "Institutions and International Trade: Lessons from the Commercial Revolution." *American Economic Review* 82: 128–33.

———. 1993. "Contract Enforceability and Economic Institutions in Early Trade: The Maghribi Traders Coalition." *American Economic Review* 83: 525–48.

———. 1994a. "Cultural Beliefs and the Organization of Society: A Historical and Theoretical Reflection on Collectivist and Individualist Societies." *Journal of Political Economy* 102 (5): 912–50.

———. 1994b. "On the Political Foundations of the Late Medieval Commercial Revolution: Genoa during the Twelfth and Thirteenth Centuries." *Journal of Economic History* 54 (2): 271–89.

———. 1998. "Self-Enforcing Political Systems and Economic Growth: Late Medieval Genoa." In *Analytic Narratives*, edited by Robert H. Bates, Avner Greif, Margaret Levi, Jean-Laurent Rosenthal, and Barry R. Weingast. Princeton: Princeton University Press. 23–63.

———. 2000. "The Fundamental Problem of Exchange: A Research Agenda in Historical Institutional Analysis." *European Review of Economic History* 4 (3): 251–84.

———. 2001. "Impersonal Exchange and the Origin of Markets: From the Community Responsibility System to Individual Legal Responsibility in Pre-modern Europe." In *Communities and Markets in Economic Development*, edited by Masahiki Aoki and Yujiro Hayami. Oxford: Oxford University Press. 3–41.

———. 2002. "Institutions and Impersonal Exchange: From Communal to Individual Responsibility." *Journal of Institutional and Theoretical Economics* 158: 168–204.

———. 2005. "Commitment, Coercion, and Markets: The Nature and Dynamics of Institutions Supporting Exchange." In *Handbook in New Institutional Economics*, edited by Claude Menard and Mary M. Shirley. Norwell: Kluwer Press. 727–86.

———. 2006a. "History Lessons: The Birth of Impersonal Exchange: The Community Responsibility System and Impartial Justice." *Journal of Economic Perspectives* 20 (2): 221–36.

———. 2006b. *Institutions and the Path to the Modern Economy: Lessons from Medieval Trade*. New York: Cambridge University Press.

———. 2008. Commitment, Coercion, and Markets: The Nature and Dynamics of Institutions Supporting Exchange." In *Handbook of New Institutional Economics*, edited by C. Ménard and M. M. Shirley. Dordrecht: Springer. 727–86.

———. 2009. "The Curious Commentary on the Citation Practices of Avner Greif." *Public Choice* 141 (3–4): 273–75.

———. 2012. "The Maghribi Traders: A Reappraisal?" *Economic History Review* 65 (2): 445–69.

Greif, Avner, Paul Milgrom, and Barry R. Weingast. 1994. "Coordination, Commitment and Enforcement: The Case of the Merchant Guild." *Journal of Political Economy* 102 (4): 745–76.

Greve, Anke. 1997. "Vreemdelingen in de stad: integratie of uitsluiting." In *Hart en Marge in de Laat-Middeleeuwse Maatschappij. Handelingen van het colloquium (22–23 Augustus 1996)*, edited by M. Carlier, A. Greve, W. Prevenier, and P. Stabel. Leuven: Garant. 153–63.

———. 1999. "Jacob Sconebergh and His Short Career as a Hosteller in Fourteenth-Century Bruges." In *Secretum Scriptorum. Liber Amicorum Walter Prevenier*, edited by Wim Blockmans, Marc Boone, and Thérèse d'Hemptinne. Leuven: Garant. 213–24.

———. 2000. "Brokerage and Trade in Medieval Bruges: Regulation and Reality." In *International Trade in the Low Countries (14th–16th centuries). Merchants, Organization and Infrastructure*. Edited by Peter Stabel, Bruno Blondé, and Anke Greve. Leuven: Garant. 37–44.

———. 2001. "Die Bedeutung der Brügger Hosteliers fuer hansische Kaufleute im 14. und 15. Jahrhundert." *Jaarboek voor Middeleeuwse Geschiedenis* 4: 259–96.

Groenveld, Simon, H. L. Ph. Leeuwenberg, Nicolette Mout, and W. M. Zappey. 1979. *De kogel door de kerk? De opstand in de Nederlanden en de rol van de Unie van Utrecht, 1559–1609*. Zutphen: Walburg Pers.

Groote, Henry L. V. de. 1976. "Zeeverzekering." In *Maritieme Geschiedenis der Nederlanden*, edited by Gustaaf Asaert, Philippus M. Bosscher, Jaap R. Bruijn, and Willem J. van Hoboken. Bussum: De Boer Maritiem. 1:206–19.

Grunzweig, Armand. 1931. *Correspondance de la filiale de Bruges des Medici*. Brussels: Lamertin.

Guinnane, Timothy W., Ron Harris, Naomi R. Lamoreaux, and Jean-Laurent Rosenthal. 2007. "Putting the Corporation in Its Place." *Enterprise and Society* 8 (3): 687–729.

Häberlein, Mark. 1998. *Brüder, Freunde und Betrüger. Soziale Beziehungen, Normen und Konflikte in der Augsburger Kaufmannschaft um die Mitte des 16. Jahrhunderts*. Berlin: Akademie Verlag.

Hagoort, Lydia. 1997. "The Del Sottos, A Portuguese Jewish Family in Amsterdam in the Seventeenth Century." *Studia Rosenthaliana* 31 (1): 31–57.

Halberstadt, A. 1910. "Botermarkt en kaasplein." *Jaarboek Amstelodamum* 8: 155–80.

Hamilton, Gary. G. 1991. "The Organizational Foundations of Western and Chinese Commerce: A Historical and Comparative Analysis." In *Business Networks and Economic Development in East and Southeast Asia*, edited by Gary G. Hamilton. Hong Kong: Centre for Asian Studies. 48–65.

Handt-vesten ende privilegien van Amstelredam. 1597. Utrecht: Herman van Borculo for Barent Adriaensz.

Handt-vesten ende privilegien van Amstelredam. 1599. Amsterdam: Barent Adriaensz.

Handt-vesten ende Privilegien van Amstelredam. 1639. Amsterdam: Jacob Pietersz Wachter.

Handt-vesten, privilegien, octroyen, costumen en willekeuren der Stad Amstelredam. 1662. Amsterdam: Otto Barentsz. Smient and Jodocus Smient.

Hanham, Alison. 1985. *The Celys and Their World. An English Merchant Family of the Fifteenth Century.* Cambridge: Cambridge University Press.

Hanus, Jord. 2007. *Tussen stad en eigen gewin. Stadsfinanciën, renteniers en kredietmarkten in 's-Hertogenbosch (begin zestiende eeuw).* Amsterdam: Aksant.

Häpke, Rudolf. 1908. *Brügges Entwicklung zum Mittlelalterlichen Weltmarkt.* Berlin: Karl Curtius.

———, ed. 1913. *Niederländische Akten und Urkunden zur Geschichte der Hanse und zur deutschen Seegeschichte, I, 1531–1557.* Munich: Duncker & Humblot.

Harkness, Deborah E. 2008. "Accounting for Science: How a Merchant Kept His Books in Elizabethan England." In *The Self-Perception of Early Modern Capitalists,* edited by Margaret C. Jacob and Catherine Secretan. Basingstoke: Palgrave Macmillan. 205–28.

Harreld, Donald J. 2004. *High Germans in the Low Countries: German Merchants and Commerce in Golden Age Antwerp.* Leiden: Brill.

———. 2006. "An Education in Commerce: Transmitting Business Information in Early Modern Europe." Paper presented at the 14th International Economic History Congress, Helsinki. http://www.helsinki.fi/iehc2006/papers1/Harreld.pdf.

Harris, Ron. 2000. *Industrializing English Law: Entrepreneurship and Business Organization, 1720–1844.* Cambridge: Cambridge University Press.

———. 2008. "The Institutional Dynamics of Early Modern Eurasian Trade: The Commenda and the Corporation." http://ssrn.com/abstract=1294095.

Hart, Marjolein 't, and Manon van der Heijden. 2006. "Het geld van de stad. Recente historiografische trends in het onderzoek naar stedelijke financiën in de Nederlanden." *Tijdschrift voor Sociale en Economische Geschiedenis* 3 (3): 3–35.

Hart, Simon. 1957. "De eerste Nederlandse tochten ter walvisvaart." *Jaarboek Amstelodamum* 49: 27–64.

———. 1977. "Rederij." In *Maritieme Geschiedenis der Nederlanden,* edited by Leo M. Akveld, Simon Hart, and Willem J. van Hoboken. Bussum: De Boer Maritiem. 2:106–25.

———. 1978. "De Italië-vaart 1590–1620." *Jaarboek Amstelodamum* 70: 42–60.

Heeringa, Klaas, and Jan Garbrand Nanninga. 1910. *Bronnen tot de geschiedenis van den Levantschen handel. Deel 1, 1590–1660.* The Hague: Nijhoff.

Heers, Jacques. 1961. *Gênes au XVe siècle. Activité économique et problèmes sociaux.* Paris: S.E.V.P.E.N.

Heijden, Manon van der. 2001. "Misdrijf of zonde? Sociale controle van huwelijksgedrag in Holland tijdens de vroegmoderne tijd." *Tijdschrift voor Sociale Geschiedenis* 27: 281–308.

———. 2006. *Geldschieters van de stad. Financiële relaties tussen stad, burgers en overheden 1550–1650.* Amsterdam: Bert Bakker.

Heijer, Henk den. 1994. *De geschiedenis van de W.I.C.* Zutphen: Walburg Pers.

Helmholz, Richard H. 1979. "Debt Claims and Probate Jurisdiction in Historical Perspective." *American Journal of Legal History* 23: 68–82.

———. 1986. "Usury and the Medieval English Church Courts Source." *Speculum* 61 (2): 364–80.

———. 1990. *Roman Canon Law in Reformation England. Cambridge Studies in English Legal History.* Cambridge: Cambridge University Press.

Henn, Volker. 1996. "Mißglückte Messegründungen." In *Europäische Messen und Märktsysteme in Mittelalter und Neuzeit,* edited by Peter Johanek and Heinz Stoob. Köln: Böhlau. 205–22.

———. 1999a. "Das Brügger Kontor." In *Die Hanse. Lebenswirklichkeit und Mythos,* edited by Jörgen Bracker, Volker Henn, and Reiner Postel. Lübeck: Schmidt Römild. 216–22.

———. 1999b. "Entfaltung im Westen: 'Hansen' auf den niederländischen Märkten." In *Die Hanse. Lebenswirklichkeit und Mythos,* edited by Jörgen Bracker, Volker Henn, and Reiner Postel. Lübeck: Schmidt Römild. 50–56.

———. 1999c. "Wachsende Spannungen in den hansisch-niederländischen Beziehungen." In *Die Hanse. Lebenswirklichkeit und Mythos,* edited by Jörgen Bracker, Volker Henn, and Reiner Postel. Lübeck: Schmidt Römild. 73–79.

———. 2008. "Eine unbeachtete Brügger Kontorordnung aus dem 15. Jahrhundert." In *Von Nowgorod bis London: Studien zu Handel, Wirtschaft und Gesellschaft im mittelalterlichen Europa: Festschrift für Stuart Jenks zum 60. Geburtstag,* edited by Marie-Louise Heckmann and Jens Röhrkasten. Göttingen: Vandenhoeck & Ruprecht. 31–50.

Herborn, Wolfgang. 1984. "Frammersbacher auf den Antwerpener Messen. Miszelle zu den bedeutendsten Fernfuhrleuten des deutschsprachigen Raumes um 1500." In *Civitatum communitas. Studien zum europäischen Städtewesen. Festschrift Heinz Stoob zum 65. Geburtstag,* edited by Helmut Jäger, Franz Petri, and Heinz Quirin. Cologne: Böhlau. 832–43.

Heuvel, Danielle van de. 2007. *Women and Entrepreneurship. Female Traders in the Northern Netherlands c. 1580–1815.* Amsterdam: Aksant.

Heyden, J. van der. 1983. "Misdrijf in Antwerpen—Een onderzoek naar de criminaliteit in de periode 1404–1429." In *Justicie ende Gerechticheyt. Handelingen van het zevende Belgisch-Nederlands rechtshistorisch colloquium. Colloquium gehouden op 17 en 18 mei 1982 aan de Faculteit der Rechtsgeleerdheid van de K.U. Leuven, Afdeling Kortrijk,* edited by G. v. Dievoet and G. Macours. Antwerpen: Kluwer Rechtswetenschappen. 223–40.

Hillmann, Henning, and Christina Gathmann. 2011. "Overseas Trade and the Decline of Privateering." *Journal of Economic History* 71 (3): 730–61.

Hirsch, Jean-Pierre. 1989. "Revolutionary France, Cradle of Free Enterprise." *American Historical Review* 94 (5): 1281–89.

———. 1991. *Les deux rêves du commerce. Entreprise et institution dan la région lilloise (1780–1860).* Paris: École des Hautes Études en Sciences Sociales.

Hirschfelder, Gunther. 1994. *Die Kölner Handelsbeziehungen im Spätmittelalter.* Köln: Kölnischen Stadtmuseum.

Hirschman, Albert O. 1970. *Exit, Voice and Loyalty. Responses to Decline in Firms, Organizations, and States.* Cambridge, Mass.: Harvard University Press.

Hofmeister, Adolf. 1888. "Eine Hansische Seeversicherung aus dem Jahre 1531." *Hansische Geschichtsblätter* 15: 169–77.

Hohenberg, Paul, and Lynn Lees. 1995. *The Making of Urban Europe, 1000–1994*. 2nd ed. Cambridge, Mass.: Harvard University Press.

Höhlbaum, Konstantin, Karl Kunze, Hans-Gerd Rundstedt, and Walther Stein, eds. 1876–1939. *Hansisches Urkundenbuch*. Halle: Weissenhaus.

Hoock, Jochen, Pierre Jeannin, Bernadette Duval, and Wolfgang Kaiser. 1991. *Ars mercatoria. Handbücher und Traktate für den Gebrauch des Kaufmanns, 1470–1820: eine analytische Bibliographie in 6 Bänden*. Paderborn: Schöningh.

Horden, Peregrine, and Nicholas Purcell. 2000. *The Corrupting Sea: A Study of Mediterranean History*. Oxford: Blackwell.

Huffman, Joseph P. 1998. *Family, Commerce, and Religion in London and Cologne. Anglo-German Emigrants, c. 1000–c. 1300*. Cambridge: Cambridge University Press.

Hunt, Edwin S. 1994. *The Medieval Super-companies. A Study of the Peruzzi Company of Florence*. Cambridge: Cambridge University Press.

Hunt, Edwin S., and James M. Murray. 1999. *A History of Business in Medieval Europe, 1200–1550*. Cambridge: Cambridge University Press.

IJzerman, Jan Willem. 1931. "Amsterdamsche bevrachtingscontracten 1591–1602: I, De vaart op Spanje en Portugal." *Economisch-Historisch Jaarboek* 17: 163–291.

Irsigler, Franz. 1985. "Der Alltag einer Hansischen Kaufmannsfamilie im Spiegel der Veckinchusen-Briefe." *Hansische Geschichtsblätter* 103: 75–99.

———. 1996. "Jahrmärkte und Messesysteme im westlichen Reichsgebiet bis ca. 1250." In *Europäische Messen und Märktsysteme in Mittelalter und Neuzeit*, edited by Peter Johanek und Heinz Stoob. Köln: Böhlau. 1–33.

———. 1999. "Fernhandel, Märkte und Messen in vor- und frühhansischer Zeit." In *Die Hanse. Lebenswirklichkeit und Mythos*, edited by Jörgen Bracker, Volker Henn, and Reiner Postel. Lübeck: Schmidt Römild. 22–27.

Israel, Jonathan Irvine. 1980. "The States General and the Strategic Regulation of Dutch River Trade, 1621–1636." *Bijdragen en Mededelingen betreffende de Geschiedenis der Nederlanden* 95 (3): 461–91.

———. 1983. "The Economic Contribution of Dutch Sephardi Jewry to Holland's Golden Age, 1595–1713." *Tijdschrift voor Geschiedenis* 96 (4): 505–35.

———. 1986. "The Phases of the Dutch *Straatvaart* (1590–1713): A Chapter in the Economic History of the Mediterranean." *Tijdschrift voor geschiedenis* 99: 1–30.

———. 1986. "The Dutch Merchant Colonies in the Mediterranean during the Seventeenth Century." *Renaissance and Modern Studies* 30: 87–108.

———. 1989. *Dutch Primacy in World Trade, 1585–1740*. New York: Oxford University Press.

———. 1992. "England's Mercantilist Response to Dutch World Trade Primacy, 1647–1674." In *State and Trade: Government and the Economy in Britain and the Netherlands since the Middle Ages*, edited by Simon Groenveld and Michael Wintle. Zutphen: Walburg Pers. 50–61.

———. 1994. "Lopo Ramirez (Davied Curiel) and the Attempt to Establish a Sephardi Community in Antwerp in 1653–1654." *Studia Rosenthaliana* 28 (1): 99–119.

———. 1995. *The Dutch Republic: Its Rise, Greatness, and Fall, 1477–1806.* Oxford: Clarendon.

———. 1997. "England, the Dutch Republic, and Europe in the Seventeenth Century." *Historical Journal* 40: 1117–21.

———. 2002. *Diasporas within a Diaspora. Jews, Crypto-Jews and the World Maritime Empires (1540–1740).* Leiden: Brill.

Jacob, Margaret C. 2006. *Strangers Nowhere in the World. The Rise of Cosmopolitanism in Early Modern Europe.* Philadelphia: University of Pennsylvania Press.

Jacob, Margaret C., and Catherine Secretan, eds. 2008. *The Self-Perception of Early Modern Capitalists.* New York: Palgrave Macmillan.

Jados, Stanley S., ed. 1975. *Consulate of the Sea and Related Documents.* Alabama: University of Alabama Press.

Jahnke, Carsten, and Antjekathrin Graßmann. 2003. *Seerecht im Hanseraum des 15. Jahrhunderts. Edition und Kommentar zum Flandrischen Copiar Nr. 9.* Lübeck: Schmidt Rönhild.

Jansen, H. P. H. 1982. "Handel en Nijverheid, 1000–1300." In *Algemene Geschiedenis der Nederlanden*, edited by Dirk Peter Blok. Haarlem: Fibula-van Dishoeck. 2:148–86.

Jansen, Lucas. 1946. *"De koophandel van Amsterdam." Een critische studie over het koopmanshandboek van Jacques Le Moine de l'Espine en Isaac le Long.* Amsterdam: Nieuwe Uitgevers Maatschappij.

Jansma, T. S. 1943. "De betekenis van Dordrecht en Rotterdam omstreeks het midden der zestiende eeuw." *De Economist* 92 (1): 202–50.

Japikse, Nicolaas, and Hermina Hendrina Petronella Rijperman. 1915–70. *Resolutiën der Staten-Generaal van 1576 tot 1609.* 14 vols. The Hague: Nijhoff.

Jeannin, Pierre. 1957. *Les marchands au XVIe siecle.* Paris: Seuil.

———. 1982. "The Sea-Borne and the Overland Trade Routes of Northern Europe in the XVIth and XVIIth Centuries." *Journal of European Economic History* 11: 5–60.

Jenks, Stuart. 1992a. "A Capital without a State: Lübeck *caput tocius hanze* (to 1474)." *Historical Research* 65 (157): 134–49.

———, ed. 1992b. *England, die Hanse und Preußen. Handel und Diplomatie 1377–1474.* 3 vols. Köln: Böhlau.

———. 1993. "Der Frieden von Utrecht 1474." In *Der hansische Sonderweg? Beiträge zur Sozial- und Wirtschaftsgeschichte der Hanse*, edited by Stuart Jenks and Michael North. Köln: Böhlau. 59–76.

———. 1995. "Die Welfen, Lübeck und die werdende Hanse." In *Die Welfen und ihr Braunschweiger Hof im Die hohen Mittelalter*, edited by Bernd Schneidmüller. Wiesbaden: Harrassowitz. 483–522.

———. 1996a. "England und die Kontinentalen Messen im 15. Jahrhundert und die Entstehung der Merchant Adventurers." In *Europäische Messen und Märktsysteme in Mittelalter und Neuzeit*, edited by P. Johanek and H. Stoob. Köln: Böhlau. 57–86.

———. 1996b. "Zum hansisches Gästerecht." *Hansische Geschichtsblätter* 114: 3–60.

———. 2006. "Small Is Beautiful: Why Small Northern European Firms Survived in the Late Middle Ages." Manuscript, University of Erlangen.

Johanek, Peter, and Heinz Stoob. 1996. *Europäische Messen und Märktsysteme in Mittelalter und Neuzeit.* Köln: Böhlau.

Jones, Eric. 2003. *The European Miracle. Environments, Economies and Geopolitics in the History of Europa and Asia.* 3rd ed. New York: Cambridge University Press.

Jones, S. R. H. 1997. "Transaction Costs and the Theory of the Firm: The Scope and Limitations of the New Institutional Approach." *Business History* 39 (4): 9–25.

Jong, Michiel de. 2005. *"Staat van oorlog." Wapenbedrijf en militaire hervorming in de Republiek der Verenigde Nederlanden, 1585–1621.* Hilversum: Verloren.

Jongbloet-Van Houtte, Gisela. 1986. *Brieven en andere bescheiden betreffende Daniel van der Meulen, 1584–1600, Rijks Geschiedkundige Publicatiën.* The Hague: Nijhoff.

Jonker, Joost P. B., and Keetie E. Sluyterman. 2000. *At Home on the World Markets: Dutch International Trading Companies from the 16th Century until the Present.* The Hague: Sdu Uitgevers.

Kadens, Emily. 2004. "Order within Law, Variety within Custom: The Character of the Medieval Merchant Law." *Chicago Journal of International Law* 5 (1): 39–65.

———. 2012. "The Myth of the Customary Law Merchant." *Texas Law Review* 90: 1153–1206.

Kannegieter, Jan Z. 1963. "De Elandsstraat in haar eerste stadium. Grepen uit de geschiedenis van de vroegere Amsterdamse zeemleerindustrie." *Jaarboek Amstelodamum* 55: 77–105.

Kaptein, Herman. 1998. *De Hollandse textielnijverheid 1350–1600. Conjunctuur & continuïteit.* Hilversum: Verloren.

———. 2004. "De poort van Holland. De economische ontwikkeling 1200–1578." In *Geschiedenis van Amsterdam tot 1578. Een stad uit het niets,* edited by Marijke Carasso-Kok. Amsterdam: SUN. 109–73.

Karpinski, Louis C. 1936. "The First Printed Arithmetic of Spain: Francesch Sanct Climent: Suma de la Art de Arismetrica Barcelona, 1482." *Osiris* 1: 411–20.

Keene, Derek. 1989. "New Discoveries at the Hanseatic Steelyard in London." *Hansische Geschichtsblätter* 107: 15–25.

———. 1999. "Ein Haus in London: Von der Guildhall zum Stahlhof." In *Die Hanse. Lebenswirklichkeit und Mythos,* edited by Jörgen Bracker, Volker Henn, and Reiner Postel. Lübeck: Schmidt Römild. 46–49.

———. 2004. "Metropolitan Comparisons: London as a City-State." *Historical Research* 77 (198): 459–80.

Kellenbenz, Hermann. 1954. *Unternehmerkräfte im Hamburger Portugal- und Spanienhandel 1590–1620.* Hamburg: Verlag der Hamburgischen Bücherei.

Kernkamp, Johannes Hermann. 1931–34. *De handel op de vijand.* 2 vols. Utrecht: Kemink.

Kessler, Amalia D. 2007. *A Revolution in Commerce. The Parisian Merchant Court and the Rise of Commercial Society in Eighteenth-Century France.* New Haven: Yale University Press.

Khan, B. Zhorina. 2000. "Commerce and Cooperation: Litigation and Settlement of Civil Disputes on the Australian Frontier, 1860–1900." *Journal of Economic History* 60 (4): 1088–1117.

Kint, An. 1996a. "Becoming Civic Community: Citizenship in Sixteenth-Century Antwerp." In *Individual, Corporate and Judicial Status in European Cities (Late Middle Ages and Early Modern Period)*, edited by Marc Boone and Maarten Prak. Leuven: Garant. 157–69.

———. 1996b. "The Community of Commerce: Social Relations in Sixteenth-Century Antwerp." Unpublished doctoral dissertation, Columbia University.

Kirk, Thomas. 2001. "Genoa and Livorno: Sixteenth and Seventeenth-Century Commercial Rivalry as a Stimulus to Policy Development." *History* 86 (281): 3–17.

Klein, Peter Wolfgang. 1965. *De Trippen in de 17e eeuw: een studie over het ondernemersgedrag op de Hollandse stapelmarkt*. Assen: Van Gorcum.

———. 1992. "A New Look at an Old Subject. Dutch Trade Policies in the Age of Mercantilism" In *State and Trade. Government and the Economy in Britain and the Netherlands since the Middle Ages*, edited by Simon Groenveld and Michael Wintle. Zutphen: Walburg Pers. 39–49.

Klein, Peter Wolfgang, and Jan-Willem Veluwenkamp. 1993. "The Role of the Entrepreneur in the Economic Expansion of the Dutch Republic." In *The Dutch Economy in the Golden Age: Nine Studies*, edited by C. A. Davids and L. Noordegraaf. Amsterdam: NEHA. 27–54.

Klep, Paul M.M. 1990. "Het Brabantse stedensysteem en de scheiding der Nederlanden." *Bijdragen tot de Geschiedenis* 73: 101–29.

Klerman, Daniel. 2007. "Jurisdictional Competition and the Evolution of the Common Law." *University of Chicago Law Review* 74: 1179–1226.

Kloek, Els. 2003. "De gezeefde werkelijkheid van Lysbeth Philips de Bisschop (1566–1652): sporen van een remonstrantse koopmansvrouw uit Amsterdam." *De zeventiende eeuw* 19 (1): 90–115.

Knevel, Paul. 2004. "Vijfde stad in Holland." In *Geschiedenis van Amsterdam. Een stad uit het niets*, edited by Marijke Carasso-Kok. Amsterdam: SUN. 365–91.

Knight, Frank H. 1921. *Risk, Uncertainty, and Profit*. Boston: Houghton Mifflin.

Koen, E. M. 1973–2001. "Notarial Records Relating to the Portuguese Jews in Amsterdam up to 1639." *Studia Rosenthaliana*.

Kooijmans, Luuc. 1995. "Risk and Reputation. On the Mentality of Merchants in the Early Modern Period." In *Entrepreneurs and Entrepreneurship in Early Modern Times: Merchants and Industrialists within the Orbit of the Dutch Staple Market*, edited by Clemens Maria Lesger and Leo Noordegraaf. The Hague: Stichting Hollandse Historische Reeks. 25–34.

———. 1997. *Vriendschap en de kunst van het overleven in de zeventiende en achttiende eeuw*. Amsterdam: Bert Bakker.

Korteweg, Joke E. 2006. *Kaperbloed en koopmansgeest. "Legale zeeroof" door de eeuwen heen*. Amsterdam: Balans.

Korthals Altes, A. 1973. *Prijs der Zee. Raakvlak van reding, strandrecht en wrakwetrechtgeving*. Zwolle: W.E.J. Tjeenk Willink.

Kortlever, Yolande E. 2001. "The Easter and Cold Fairs of Bergen op Zoom (14th–16th centuries)." In *Fiere e mercati nella integrazione delle economie Europee secc. XIII–XVIII*, edited by Simonetta Cavaciocchi. Florence: Le Monnier. 625–43.

Kowaleski, Maryanne. 1995. *Local Markets and Regional Trade in Medieval Exeter*. Cambridge: Cambridge University Press.

Krieger, Karl-Friedrich. 1970. *Ursprung und Wurzeln der Rôles d'Oléron*. Köln: Böhlau.

Kuran, Timur. 2010. *The Long Divergence: How Islamic Law Held Back the Middle East*. Princeton: Princeton University Press.

Kuske, Bruno, ed. 1923. *Quellen zur Geschichte des Kölner Handels und Verkehrs im Mittelalter*. Bonn: P. Hanstein.

La Foire. 1953. Vol 5. Brussels: Recueils de la Société Jean Bodin.

Laan, P. H. J. van der, ed. 1975. *Oorkondenboek van Amsterdam*. Amsterdam: Gemeentelijke Archiefdienst.

Lambert, Bart. 2006. *The City, the Duke and Their Bank: The Rapondi Family and the Formation of the Burgundian State (1384–1430)*. Turnhout: Brepols.

Lamoreaux, Naomi R., Daniel M. G. Raff, and Peter Temin. 2003. "Beyond Markets and Hierarchies: Toward a New Synthesis of American Business History." *American Historical Review* 108 (2): 404–33.

Lamoreaux, Naomi R., and Jean-Laurent Rosenthal. 2005. "Legal Regime and Contractual Flexibility: A Comparison of Business's Organizational Choices in France and the United States during the Era of Industrialization." *American Law and Economics Review* 7 (1): 28–61.

Landa, Janet T. 1994. *Trust, Ethnicity, and Identity: The New Institutional Economics of Ethnic Trading Networks, Contract Law, and Gift-Exchange*. Ann Arbor: University of Michigan Press.

Lane, Frederic Chapin. 1944a. *Andrea Barbarigo, Merchant of Venice, 1418–1449*. Baltimore: Johns Hopkins University Press.

———. 1944b. "Family Partnerships and Joint Ventures in the Venetian Republic." *Journal of Economic History* 4 (2): 178–96.

———. 1958. "Economic Consequences of Organized Violence." *Journal of Economic History* 18 (4): 401–17.

———. 1962. "Venetian Maritime Law and Administration (1250–1350)." In *Studi in Onore di Amintore Fanfani. III. Medioevo*. Milan: Dott. A. Giuffrè. 19–50.

———. 1966. "National Wealth and Protection Costs." In *Venice and History: The Collected Papers of Frederic C. Lane*, ed. committee of colleagues and former students. Baltimore: Johns Hopkins University Press. 373–82.

Lazzareschi, Eugenio. 1947. *Libro della Comunità dei Mercanti Lucchesi in Bruges*. Milan: Dott. Rodolfo Malfasi.

Leeuw-Kistemaker, R. E. van der. 1974. *Wonen en werken in de Warmoesstraat van de 14de tot het midden van de 16de eeuw*. Vol. 7. Amsterdam: Werkschift Historisch Seminarium Universiteit van Amsterdam.

Leeuwen, Marco H. D. van. 2000. *De rijke Republiek. Gilden, assuradeurs en armenzorg, 1500–1800*. The Hague: Verbond van verzekeraars/NEHA.

Lesger, Clemens Maria. 1990. *Hoorn als stedelijk knooppunt*. Hilversum: Verloren.

———. 1993. "Intraregional Trade and the Port System in Holland 1400–1700." In *The Dutch Economy in the Golden Age*, edited by Karel Davids and Leo Noordegraaf. Amsterdam: Nederlandsch Economisch-Historisch Archief. 186–217.

———. 1996. "Over het nut van huwelijk, opportunisme en bedrog. Ondernemers en ondernemerschap tijdens de vroegmoderne tijd in theoretisch perspectief."

In *Kapitaal, ondernemerschap en beleid. Studies over economie en politiek in Nederland, Europa en Azië*, edited by Karel Davids, Wantje Fritschy, and Loes van der Valk. Amsterdam: Nederlands Economisch-Historisch Archief. 55–75.

———. 2001. *Handel in Amsterdam ten tijde van de Opstand: kooplieden, commerciële expansie en verandering in de ruimtelijke economie van de Nederlanden ca. 1550–ca. 1630.* Hilversum: Verloren.

———. 2006. *The Rise of the Amsterdam Market and Information Exchange: Merchants, Commercial Expansion and Change in the Spatial Economy of the Low Countries, c. 1550–1630.* Burlington, Vt.: Ashgate.

Lesger, Clemens Maria, and Leo Noordegraaf, eds. 1995. *Entrepreneurs and Entrepreneurship in Early Modern Times: Merchants and Industrialists within the Orbit of the Dutch Staple Market.* The Hague: Stichting Hollandse Historische Reeks.

———, eds. 1999. *Ondernemers & bestuurders. Economie en politiek in de Noordelijke Nederlanden in de late Middeleeuwen en vroegmoderne tijd.* Amsterdam: NEHA.

Lesnikov, Michail P. 1973. *Die Handelsbücher des Hansischen Kaufmanns Veckinckhusen.* Berlin: Akademie Verlag.

Liagre-De Sturler, Léone. 1969. *Les relations commerciales entre Gênes, la Belgique et l'Outremont: d'après les archives notariales gênoises, 1320–1400.* 2 vols. Brussels: Institut Historique Belge de Rome.

Lichtenauer, W. F. 1935. *Burgerlijk en handelsrecht.* Zwolle: Tjeenk Willink.

———. 1956. *Geschiedenis van de wetenschap van het handelsrecht in Nederland tot 1809.* Amsterdam: Noord-Hollandsche Uitgevers Maatschappij.

Lindberg, Erik. 2007. "Merchant Guilds and Urban Growth in the Baltic Sea Area, 1650–1850." In *The Dynamics of Economic Culture in the North Sea and Baltic Region, c. 1250–1700*, edited by Hanno Brand and Leos Müller. Hilversum: Verloren. 47–64.

———. 2009. "Club Goods and Inefficient Institutions: Why Danzig and Lübeck Failed in the Early Modern Period." *Economic History Review* 62 (3): 604–28.

Lingelbach, William E. 1904. "The Merchant Adventurers at Hamburg." *American Historical Review* 9 (2): 265–87.

Liste Chronologique des édits et ordonnances des Pays-Bas. Règne de Charles-Quint (1506–1555). 1885. Brussels: Fr. Gobbaerts.

Loo, Ivo J. van. 1998. "Organising and Financing Zeeland Privateering, 1598–1609." *Leidschrift* 13 (2): 67–95.

———. 1999. "Kaapvaart, handel en staatsbelang: het gebruik van kaapvaart als maritiem machtsmiddel en vorm van ondernemerschap tijdens de Nederlandse Opstand, 1568–1648." In *Ondernemers & bestuurders. Economie en politiek in de Noordelijke Nederlanden in de late Middeleeuwen en vroegmoderne tijd*, edited by Clé M. Lesger and Leo Noordegraaf. Amsterdam: NEHA. 349–68.

Lopez, Robert S. 1971. *The Commercial Revolution of the Middle Ages, 950–1350.* Englewood Cliffs, N.J.: Prentice Hall.

Lopez, Robert S., and Irving W. Raymond. 1955. *Medieval Trade in the Mediterranean World.* New York: Columbia University Press.

Ma, Debin. 2008. "Economic Growth in the Lower Yangzi Region of China in 1911–1937: A Quantitative and Historical Analysis." *Journal of Economic History* 68 (2): 355–92.

Mallett, Michael E. 1967. *The Florentine Galleys in the Fifteenth Century, with the Diary of Luca di Maso degli Albizzi, Captain of the Galleys 1429–1430.* Oxford: Clarendon.

Marche, Olivier de la. 1850 (1566). *Les memoires de Messire Olivier de La Marche, augmentés d'un Estat particulier de la maison du duc Charles le Hardy, composé du même auteur.* Paris: Guyot.

Maréchal, J. 1951. "Le départ de Bruges des marchands étrangers (XVe–XVIe siècles)." *Handelingen van het genootschap 'Société d'Emulation' te Brugge* 88: 26–74.

Marnef, Guido. 1996. *Antwerpen in de tijd van de Reformatie: ondergronds protestantisme in een handelsmetropool 1550–1577.* Amsterdam: Meulenhoff.

Mathew, D. 1924. "The Cornish and Welsh Pirates in the Reign of Elizabeth." *English Historical Review* 39: 337–48.

Mathias, Peter. 1995. "Strategies for Reducing Risk by Entrepreneurs in the Early Modern Period." In *Entrepreneurs and Entrepreneurship in Early Modern Times: Merchants and Industrialists within the Orbit of the Dutch Staple Market,* edited by Clemens Maria Lesger and Leo Noordegraaf. The Hague: Stichting Hollandse Historische Reeks. 5–24.

———. 2000. "Risk, Credit and Kinship in Early Modern Enterprise." In *The Early Modern Atlantic Economy,* edited by John J. McCusker and Kenneth Morgan. Cambridge: Cambridge University Press. 15–35.

Mauro, Frederic. 1990. "Merchant Communities, 1350–1750." In *The Rise of Merchant Empires: Long-Distance Trade in the Early Modern World, 1350–1750,* edited by James D. Tracy. Cambridge: Cambridge University Press. 255–86.

McCormick, Michael. 2002. *Origins of the European Economy: Communications and Commerce, AD 300–900.* New York: Cambridge University Press.

McCusker, John J. 1996. "The Role of Antwerp in the Emergence of Commercial and Financial Newspapers in Early Modern Europe." In *La ville et la transmission des valeurs culturelles au bas Moyen Âge et aux temps modernes—Die Stade und die Übertragung von kulturellen Werten im Spätmittelalter und in die Neuzeit—Cities and the Transmission of Cultural Values in the Late Middle Ages and Early Modern Period.* Brussels: Gemeentekrediet van België/Crédit Communal de Belgique. 303–32.

———. 2005. "The Demise of Distance: The Business Press and the Origins of the Information Revolution in the Early Modern Atlantic World." *American Historical Review* 110 (2): 295–321.

McCusker, John J., and Cora Gravesteijn. 1991. *The Beginnings of Commercial and Financial Journalism. The Commodity Price Currents, Exchange Rate Currents, and Money Currents of Early Modern Europe.* Amsterdam: NEHA.

Meewis, Wim. 1992. *De Vierschaar. De Criminele Rechtspraak in het Oude Antwerpen.* Kapellen: Pelckmans.

Meilink, P. A. 1922. "Gegevens aangaande bedrijfskapitalen in den Hollandschen en Zeeuwschen handel in 1543." *Economisch-Historisch Jaarboek* 8: 254–77.

———. 1923a. "Rapporten en betoogen nopens het congégeld op granen, 1530–1541." *Bijdragen en Mededelingen van het Historisch Genootschap* 44: 1–125.

———. 1923b. "Rekening van het lastgeld in Amsterdam, Waterland en het Noorderkwartier van Holland in 1507." *Bijdragen en Mededelingen van het Historisch Genootschap* 44: 187–230.

Melker, Bas R. de. 2002. "Metamorfose van stad en devotie. Onstaan en conjunctuur van kerkelijke, religieuze en charitatieve instellingen in Amsterdam in het licht van de stedelijke ontwikkeling, 1385–1435." Unpublished doctoral thesis, University of Amsterdam.

Mieris, Frans van. 1753–56. *Groot charterboek der graaven van Holland, van Zeeland en Heeren van Vriesland, beginnende met de eerste en oudste brieven van die landstreeken, en eindigende met den dood van onze graavinne, Vrouwe Jacoba van Beijere.* 4 vols. Leiden: Pieter vander Eyk.

Milgrom, Paul R., Douglass C. North, and Barry R. Weingast. 1990. "The Role of Institutions in the Revival of Trade: The Law Merchant, Private Judges and the Champagne Fairs." *Economics and Politics* 2 (1): 1–23.

Mokyr, Joel. 1994. "Cardwell's Law and the Political Economy of Technological Progress." *Research Policy* 23: 561–74.

———. 2007. "The Market for Ideas and the Origins of Economic Growth in Eighteenth Century Europe." *Tijdschrift voor Sociale en Economische Geschiedenis* 4 (1): 3–38.

———. 2010. "Entrepreneurship and the Industrial Revolution in Britain." In *The Invention of Enterprise: Entrepreneurship from Ancient Mesopotamia to Modern Times,* edited by David S. Landes, Joel Mokyr, and William J. Baumol. Princeton: Princeton University Press. 183–210.

Montias, John Michael. 1990. "Socio-economic Aspects of Netherlandish Art from the Fifteenth to the Seventeenth Century: A Survey." *Art Bulletin* 72: 358–73.

Mulder, J. J. 1897. *Twee verhandelingen over de Inquisitie in de Nederlanden tijdens de 16de eeuw. De uitvoering der geloofsplakkaten en het stedelijk verzet tegen de inquisitie te Antwerpen.* Gent: J. Vuylsteke.

Müller, Johannes. 1907. "Geleitswesen und Güterverkehr zwischen Nürnberg und Frankfurt a.M. im 15. Jahrhundert." *Vierteljahrschrift für Sozial- und Wirtschaftsgeschichte* 5: 173–96, 361–409.

Munro, John H. 1966. "Bruges and the Abortive Staple in English Cloth." *Revue Belge de Philologie et d'Histoire* 44: 1137–59.

———. 1972. *Wool, Cloth and Gold. The Struggle for Bullion in Anglo-Burgundian Trade, 1340–1478.* Toronto: University of Toronto Press.

———. 1990. "The International Law Merchant and the Evolution of Negotiable Credit in Late-Medieval England and the Low Countries." In *Banchi Pubblici, Banchi Privati e Monti di Piet'a nell'Europa Preindustriale,* edited by Dino Puncuh. Genoa: Societ'a Ligure de Storia Patria. 1:49–80.

———. 1999. "The Low Countries' Export Trade in Textiles with the Mediterranean Basin, 1200–1600: A Cost-Benefit Analysis of Comparative Advantages in Overland and Maritime Trade Routes." *International Journal of Maritime History* 11 (2): 1–30.

———. 2001. "'The New Institutional Economics' and the Changing Fortunes of Fairs in Medieval and Early Modern Europe: The Textile Trades, Warfare, and Transaction Costs." *Vierteljahrschrift fuer Sozial- und Wirtschaftsgeschichte* 88 (1): 1–47.

———. 2003. "The Medieval Origins of the Financial Revolution: Usury, *Rentes,* and Negotiability." *International History Review* 25 (3): 505–62.

————. 2008. "Hanseatic Commerce in Textiles from the Low Countries and England during the Later Middle Ages: Changing Trends in Textiles, Markets, Prices, and Values, 1290–1570." In *Von Nowgorod bis London: Studien zu Handel, Wirtschaft und Gesellschaft im mittelalterlichen Europa: Festschrift für Stuart Jenks zum 60. Geburtstag*, edited by Marie-Louise Heckmann and Jens Röhrkasten. Göttingen: Vandenhoeck & Ruprecht. 97–182.

Murphy, Anne L. 2010. *The Origins of English Financial Markets: Investment and Speculation before the South Sea Bubble*. Cambridge: Cambridge University Press.

Murray, David. 1923. "The Mediaeval Law and Practice in Regard to Accounts." *Journal of Comparative Legislation and International Law* 5 (1): 63–72.

Murray, James Michael. 1983. "Notaries Public in Flanders in the Late Middle Ages." Unpublished doctoral thesis. Northwestern University, Evanston, Ill.

————. 1988. "Family, Marriage and Moneychanging in Medieval Bruges." *Journal of Medieval History* 14 (2): 115–25.

————. 2000. "Of Nodes and Networks: Bruges and the Infrastructure of Trade in Fourteenth-Century Europe." In *International Trade in the Low Countries (14th–16th centuries). Merchants, Organization and Infrastructure*. Edited by Peter Stabel, Bruno Blondé, and Anke Greve. Leuven: Garant. 1–14.

————. 2005. *Bruges, Cradle of Capitalism 1280–1390*. Cambridge: Cambridge University Press.

Murray, James Michael, Walter Prevenier, and Michel Oosterbosch. 1995. *Notarial Instruments in Flanders between 1280 and 1452*. Brussels: Académie Royale de Belgique, Commission Royale d'Histoire.

Mus, Octaaf. 1964. "De Brugse compagnie Despars op het einde van de 15e eeuw." *Handelingen van het genootschap voor geschiedenis* 101: 5–118.

Nanninga-Uitterdijk, Jurjen. 1904. *Een Kamper Handelshuis te Lissabon 1572–1594. Handelscorrespondentie, rekeningen en bescheiden*. Zwolle: Erven J.J. Tijl.

Neal, Larry. 1981. "The Finance of Business during the Industrial Revolution." In *Economic History of Britain since 1700*, edited by R. Floud and D. N. MacCloskey. Cambridge: Cambridge University Press. 151–81.

Neal, Larry, and Stephen Quinn. 2001. "Networks of Information, Markets, and Institutions in the Rise of London as a Financial Center in the Seventeenth Century." *Financial History Review* 7: 117–40.

Nève, Paul L. 1975. "Van Ius commune naar Ius Particulare. Het 'europees' notariaat op weg naar een 'nationaal' statuut." In *Collatio Iuris Romani. Études dédiées à Hans Ankum à l'occasion de son 65e Anniversaire*, edited by Robert Feenstra et al. 2 vols. Amsterdam: J.C. Gieben. 2:379–87.

Nicholas, David. 1979. "The English Trade at Bruges in the Last Years of Edward III." *Journal of Medieval History* 5: 23–69.

————. 2006. "Capital Market and Central Place Function in Thirteenth-Century Ypres." In *Money, Markets and Trade in Late Medieval Europe: Essays in Honour of John H.A. Munro*, edited by L. Armstrong, M. M. Elbl, and I. Elbl. Leyden: Brill. 310–48.

Niekerk, J. P. van. 1998. *The Development of the Principles of Insurance Law in the Netherlands from 1500 to 1800*. 2 vols. Johannesburg: Juta.

Nieuwenhuysen, Andrée, and John Bartier. 1974. *Recueil des anciennes ordonnances de la Belgique. Première Section. Ordonnances de Philippe le Hardi, de Marguerite de Male et de Jean sans Peur, 1381–1419. Tome 2. 17 janvier 1394– 25 février 1405.* Brussels: Ministère de la Justice.

Noordkerk, Hermanus. 1748. *Handvesten ofte privilegien ende octroyen: mitsgaders willekeuren, costuimen, ordonnantien en handelingen der stad Amstelredam . . . tot den eersten February 1747 vervolgt, met verscheide stukken vermeerdert, mitsgaders in eene andere schikking gebragt.* 3 vols. Amsterdam.

Nörr, K. W. 1987. "Procedure in Mercantile Matters: Some Comparative Aspects." In *The Courts and the Development of Commercial Law*, edited by Vito Piergiovanni. Berlin: Duncker & Humblot. 195–201.

North, Douglass Cecil. 1981. *Structure and Change in Economic History.* New York: Norton.

———. 1990. *Institutions, Institutional Change, and Economic Performance: The Political Economy of Institutions and Decisions.* Cambridge: Cambridge University Press.

———. 1991. "Institutions, Transaction Costs, and the Rise of the Merchant Empires." In *The Political Economy of Merchant Empires*, edited by James D. Tracy. Cambridge: Cambridge University Press. 22–40.

———. 1992. *Transaction Costs, Institutions, and Economic Performance.* San Francisco: ICS Press.

———. 2005. *Understanding the Process of Economic Change.* Princeton: Princeton University Press.

North, Douglass C., John Joseph Wallis, and Barry R. Weingast. 2009. *Violence and Social Orders: A Conceptual Framework for Interpreting Recorded Human History.* New York: Cambridge University Press.

North, Douglass Cecil, and Robert Paul Thomas. 1973. *The Rise of the Western World: A New Economic History.* Cambridge: Cambridge University Press.

North, Douglass C., and Barry R. Weingast. 1989. "Constitutions and Commitment: Evolution of Institutions Governing Public Choice." *Journal of Economic History* 49 (4): 803–32.

North, Michael. 1984. "A Small Baltic Port in the Early Modern Period: The Port of Elbing in the Sixteenth and Seventeenth Century." *Journal of European Economic History* 13 (1): 117–27.

Nübel, Otto. 1972. *Pompejus Occo 1483 bis 1537. Fuggerfaktor in Amsterdam.* Tübingen: J.C.B. Mohr (Paul Siebeck).

O'Brien, Patrick. 1982. "European Economic Development: The Contribution of the Periphery." *Economic History Review*, Second Series 35 (1): 1–18.

———. 2000. "Mercantilism and Imperialism in the Rise and Decline of the Dutch and British Economies 1585–1815." *De Economist* 148: 469–501.

———. 2001. *Urban Achievement in Early Modern Europe: Golden Ages in Antwerp, Amsterdam and London.* Cambridge: Cambridge University Press.

Oexle, Otto Gerhard. 1981. "Gilden als soziale Gruppen in der Karolingerzeit." In *Das Handwerk in vor- und frühgeschichtlicher Zeit*, edited by H. Jankuhn, W. Janssen, R. Schmidt-Wiegand, and H. Tiefenbach. Göttingen: Vandenhoeck & Ruprecht. 284–354.

———. 1985. "Conjuratio und Gilde im frühe Mittelalter. Ein Beitrag zum Problem der sozialgeschichtlichen Kontinuität zwischen Antike und Mittelalter." In *Gilden und Zünfte. Kaufmännische und gewerbliche Genossenschaften im frühen und hohen Mittelalter*, edited by B. Schwineköper. Sigmarigen: Jan Thorbecke. 151–214.

Ogilvie, Sheilagh. 2007. "'Whatever Is, Is Right'? Economic Institutions in Pre-industrial Europe." *Economic History Review* 60 (4): 649–84.

———. 2011. *Institutions and European Trade: Merchant Guilds 1000–1800*. New York: Cambridge University Press.

Oldewelt, W. F. H. 1962. "Twee eeuwen Amsterdamse faillissementen en het verloop van de conjunctuur (1636 tot 1838)." *Tijdschrift voor Geschiedenis* 75: 421–35.

———. 1967. "De pogingen tot 'Codificatie' van het Amsterdamse recht." *Vereeniging tot uitgaaf der bronnen van het oud-vaderlandsch recht. Verslagen en Mededelingen* 13 (1): 57–73.

Olson, Mancur. 1965. *The Logic of Collective Action. Public Goods and the Theory of Groups*. Cambridge, Mass.: Harvard University Press.

———. 2000. *Power and Prosperity: Outgrowing Communist and Capitalist Dictatorships*. Oxford: Oxford University Press.

Oosterbosch, Michel, Monique Vleeschouwers-Van Melkebeek, Paulette Pieyens Rigo, and Philippe Godding. 1998. "Het Notariaat in de Belgische Territoria tijdens de Middeleeuwen." In *Het notariaat in België van de Middeleeuwen tot heden*, edited by Claude Bruneel, Philippe Godding, and Fred Stevens. Brussels: Gemeentekrediet. 11–94.

Ormrod, David. 2003. *The Rise of Commercial Empires. England and the Netherlands in the Age of Mercantilism, 1650–1700*. Cambridge: Cambridge University Press.

Oudendijk, J. K. 1958. "Een episode uit het begin van onze 'Tien Jaren.' " *Bijdragen en Mededelingen van het Historisch Genootschap* 72: 47–70.

Oudkerk, E. H. 1938. "De commissarissen van Kleine Zaken, een rechterlijk college in Amsterdam, (1611–1811)." In *Jaarboek van het Genootschap Amstelodamum* 35: 23–38.

Padgett, John. 2005. "Early Partnerships Memo." Manuscript. http://home.uchicago.edu/%7ejpadgett/papers/unpublished/early.part.pdf.

Pamuk, Şevket. 2009. "Changes in Factor Markets in the Ottoman Empire, 1500–1800." *Continuity and Change* 24 (1): 107–36.

Paravicini, Werner. 1992. "Bruges and Germany." In *Bruges and Europe*, edited by Valentin Vermeersch. Antwerp: Mercatorfonds. 98–127.

Parker, Geoffrey. 1974. "The Emergence of Modern Finance in Europe 1500–1750." In *The Fontana Economic History of Europe. Vol. 2. The Sixteenth and Seventeenth Century*, edited by C. Cipolla. Glasgow: Fontana. 527–94.

———. 1998. *The Grand Strategy of Philip II*. New Haven: Yale University Press.

Paviot, Jacques. 1995. *La politique navale des ducs de Bourgogne, 1384–1482*. Lille: Presses Universitaires de Lille.

———. 2002. *Bruges 1300–1500*. Paris: Editions Autrement.

Pearson, Michael N. 1991. "Merchants and States." In *The Political Economy of Merchant Empires*, edited by James D. Tracy. Cambridge: Cambridge University Press. 41–116.

Pearson, Robin, and David Richardson. 2001. "Business Networking in the Industrial Revolution." *Economic History Review* 54 (4): 657–79.

Pérotin-Dumon, Anne. 1991. "The Pirate and the Emperor: Power and the Law of the Sea, 1450–1850." In *The Political Economy of Merchant Empires*, edited by James D. Tracy. Cambridge: Cambridge University Press. 196–227.

Perroy, Edouard. 1974. "Le commerce anglo-flamand au XIIIe siècle: la Hanse flamande de Londres." *Revue Historique* 511: 3–18.

Petram, Lodewijk. 2011. "The World's First Stock Exchange. How the Amsterdam Market for Dutch East India Company Shares Became a Modern Securities Market, 1602–1700." Unpublished doctoral dissertation, University of Amsterdam.

———. 2012. *De bakermat van de beurs. Hoe in zeventiende-eeuws Amsterdam de moderne aandelenhandel ontstond*. Amsterdam: 2012.

Pettegree, Andrew. 1986. *Foreign Protestant Communities in Sixteenth-Century London*. Oxford: Oxford University Press.

Peyer, H. C., ed. 1983. *Gastfreundschaft, Taverne und Gasthaus im Mittelalter*. Munich: R. Oldenbourg.

Phillips, William D., and Carla Rahn Phillips. 1977. "Spanish Wool and the Dutch Rebels: The Middelburg Incident of 1574." *American Historical Review* 82 (2): 312–30.

Phoonsen, Johannes. 1676. *Wissel-Styl tot Amsterdam*. Amsterdam.

Piergiovanni, Vito. 1987a. "Courts and Commercial Law at the Beginning of the Modern Age." In *The Courts and the Development of Commercial Law*, edited by Vito Piergiovanni. Berlin: Duncker & Humblot. 11–21.

———. 1987b. "The Rise of the Genoese Civil Rota in the XVIth Century: The 'Decisiones De Mercatura' Concerning Insurance." In *The Courts and the Development of Commercial Law*, edited by Vito Piergiovanni. Berlin: Duncker & Humblot. 23–38

Pirenne, Henri. 1970 (1927). *Medieval Cities: Their Origins and the Revival of Trade*. Princeton: Princeton University Press.

Planitz, H. 1940. "Kaufmannsgilde und städtische Eidgenossenschaft in niederfränkischen Städten im 11. und 12. Jahrhunder." *Zeitschrift der Savigny-Stiftung für Rechtsgeschichte, Germanistische Abteilung* 60: 1–116.

Poeck, Dietrich W. 2000. "Kontorverlegung als Mittel hansischer Diplomatie." In *Hansekaufleute in Brügge. Teil 4: Beiträge der Internationalen Tagung in Brügge April 1996*, edited by Nils Jörn, Werner Paravicini, and Horst Wernicke. Frankfurt: Peter Lang. 33–53.

Poelman, Huibert Antonie, ed. 1917. *Bronnen tot de geschiedenis van den Oostzeehandel*. 2 vols. The Hague: Nijhoff.

Pohl, Hans. 1977. *Die Portugiesen in Antwerpen (1567–1648). Zur Geschichte einer Minderheit*. Wiesbaden: Steiner.

Pomeranz, Kenneth. 2000. *The Great Divergence: China, Europe, and the Making of the Modern World Economy*. Princeton: Princeton University Press.

Posner, Eric A. 2000. *Law and Social Norms*. Cambridge Mass.: Harvard University Press.

Postan, Michael Moissey. 1973. *Medieval Trade and Finance*. Cambridge: Cambridge University Press.

———. 1987 (1952). "The Trade of Medieval Europe: The North." In *The Cambridge Economic History of Europe. Volume II. Trade and Industry in the Middle Ages*, edited by Michael Moissey Postan and Edward Miller. Cambridge: Cambridge University Press. 168–305.

Posthumus, Nicolaas Wilhelmus. 1953. *De Oosterse handel te Amsterdam: het oudst bewaarde koopmansboek van een Amsterdamsche vennootschap betreffende de handel op de Oostzee 1485–1490*. Leiden: Brill.

———. 1964. *Nederlandse prijsgeschiedenis*. 2 vols. Leiden: Brill.

———. 1971. *De uitvoer van Amsterdam 1543–1545*. Leiden: Brill.

Prak, Maarten R. 2005. *The Dutch Republic in the Seventeenth Century: The Golden Age*. Cambridge: Cambridge University Press.

Prak, Maarten R., and Erika M. E. P. Kuijpers. 2002. "Burger, ingezetene, vreemdeling: burgerschap in Amsterdam in de 17e en 18e eeuw." In *Burger. Een geschiedenis van het begrip "burger" in de Nederlanden van de Middeleeuwen tot de 21ste eeuw*, edited by Joost Kloek and Tilmans. Amsterdam: Amsterdam University Press. 113–32.

Prims, Floris Hubert Lodewijk. 1927–49. *Geschiedenis van Antwerpen*. 10 vols. Antwerpen: N.V. Standaardboekhandel.

Pryor, John H. 1977. "The Origins of the Commenda Contract." *Speculum* 52 (1): 5–37.

Puhle, Matthias. 1992. *Die Vitalienbrüder. Klaus Störtebeker und die Seeräuber der Hansezeit*. Frankfurt: Campus Verlag.

Puttevils, Jeroen. 2007. "A servitio di vostri sempre siamo. De effecten van de handel tussen Antwerpen en Italië op de koopmansfamilie Van der Molen (midden zestiende eeuw)." Unpublished master's thesis, University of Antwerp.

———. 2009. "Klein gewin brengt rijkdom in: de Zuid-Nederlandse handelaars in de export naar Italië in de jaren 1540." *Tijdschrift voor sociale en economische geschiedenis* 6 (1): 26–52.

———. 2012. "The Ascent of Merchants from the Southern Low Countries. From Antwerp to Europe 1480–1585." Unpublished doctoral dissertation, Antwerp University, Antwerp.

Quinn, Stephen, and William Roberds. 2007. "Monetary Systems: Transitions and Experiments—The Bank of Amsterdam and the Leap to Central Bank Money." *American Economic Review* 97 (2): 262–65.

———. 2009. "An Economic Explanation of the Early Bank of Amsterdam, Debasement, Bills of Exchange and the Emergence of the First Central Bank." In *The Origins and Development of Financial Markets and Institutions: From the Seventeenth Century to the Present*, edited by Jeremy Atack and Larry Neal. New York: Cambridge University Press. 32–70.

Ramsay, G. D., ed. 1962. *John Isham: Mercer and Merchant, Adventurer. Two Account Books of a London Merchant in the Reign of Elizabeth I*. Durham: Northamptonshire Record Society.

Read, Conyers. 1933. "Queen Elizabeth's Seizure of the Duke of Alva's Pay-Ships." *Journal of Modern History* 1: 443–64.

Receuil van verscheyde Keuren, en Costumen. Midtsgaders Maniere van Procederen binnen de stadt Amsterdam. 1644. Amsterdam: Gerrit Jansz.

Receuil van verscheyde Keuren, en Costumen. Midtsgaders Maniere van Proce-deren binnen de stadt Amsterdam. 1656. 2nd ed. Amsterdam: Jan Hendricks.

Reincke, Heinrich. 1942–43. "Die Deutschlandfahrt der Flandrer während der hansischen Frühzeit." *Hansische Geschichtsblätter* 67/68: 51–164.

Reinert, Erik S. 2009. "Emulating Success: Contemporary Views of the Dutch Economy before 1800." In *The Political Economy of the Dutch Republic,* edited by Oscar Gelderblom. Aldershot: Ashgate. 19–39.

Révész-Alexander, Magda. 1954. *Die Alten Lagerhaüser Amsterdam. Eine Kunstgeschichtliche Studie.* The Hague: Nijhoff.

Reyerson, Kathryn Louise. 2002. *The Art of the Deal: Intermediaries of Trade in Medieval Montpellier.* Leiden: Brill.

Richman, Barak. 2006. "How Community Institutions Create Economic Advantage: Jewish Diamond Merchants in New York." *Law & Social Inquiry* 31 (2): 383–420.

Rijswijk, B. van. 1900. *Geschiedenis van het Dordtse stapelrecht.* The Hague: Nijhoff.

Robbins, Kevin C. 1997. *City on the Ocean Sea: La Rochelle, 1530–1650: Urban Society, Religion, and Politics on the French Atlantic Frontier.* Leiden: Brill.

Roelofsen, Cornelis Gerrit. 1991. *Studies in the History of International Law: Practice and Doctrine in Particular with Regard to the Law of Naval Warfare in the Low Countries from Circa 1450 until the Early 17th Century.* Utrecht: Rijksuniversiteit.

Roey, Jan van. 1963. "De sociale structuur en de godsdienstige gezindheid van de Antwerpse bevolking aan de vooravond van de Reconciliatie met Farnèse (17 augustus 1585)." Unpublished doctoral dissertation, University of Ghent.

Rogers, James Steven. 1995. *The Early History of the Law of Bills and Notes. A Study of the Origins of Anglo-American Commercial Law.* Cambridge: Cambridge University Press.

Rommelse, Gijs. 2010. "The Role of Mercantilism in Anglo-Dutch Political Relations, 1650–74." *Economic History Review* 63 (3): 591–611.

Roodenburg, Herman. 1990. *Onder censuur. De kerkelijke tucht in de gereformeerde gemeente van Amsterdam, 1578–1700.* Hilversum: Verloren.

Rooseboom, Gerard, ed. 1656. *Receuil van verscheyde Keuren en Costumen. Midtsgaders Maniere van Procederen binnen de stadt Amsterdam. Eerst gecollecteert en beschreven door Gerard Rooseboom, in sijn leven Secretaris de voorsz. Stadt.* 2nd ed. Amsterdam: Jan Hendricks.

Rooseboom, Matthijs P. 1910. *The Scottish Staple in the Netherlands. An Account of the Trade Relations between Scotland and the Low Countries from 1292 till 1676 with a Calendar of Illustrative Documents.* The Hague: Nijhoff.

Rorke, Martin. 2008. "Trade and Traders: Edinburgh's Sixteenth Century Exporting Community." *Historical Research* 81: 447–62.

Rosenthal, Jean-Laurent, and R. Bin Wong. 2011. *Before and Beyond Divergence. The Politics of Economic Change in China and Europe.* Cambridge, Mass.: Harvard University Press.

Rössner, Renée. 2001. *Hansische Memoria in Flandern. Alltagsleben und Totengedenken der Osterlinge in Brügge und Antwerpen (13. bis 16. Jahrhundert).* Frankfurt: Peter Lang.

Rothmann, Michael. 1998. *Die Frankfurter Messen im Mittelalter*. Stuttgart: Franz Steiner Verlag.

Rowley, C. K. 2009. "The Curious Citation Practices of Avner Greif: Janet Landa Comes to Grief." *Public Choice* 140 (3–4): 275–85.

Royen, Paul C. van. 1990. "The First Phase of the Dutch Straatvaart (1591–1605): Fact and Fiction." *International Journal of Maritime History* 2: 69–102.

Safley, Thomas Max. 2009. "Business Failure and Civil Scandal in Early Modern Europe." *Business History Review* 83 (1): 35–60.

Sargent, Thomas J., and François R. Velde. 2003. *The Big Problem of Small Change*. Princeton: Princeton University Press.

Schepper, Hugo de, and Jean-Marie Cauchies. 1993. "Justice, gracie en wetgeving: juridische instrumenten van de landsheerlijke macht in de Nederlanden, 1200–1600." In *Beleid en bestuur in de oude Nederlanden: liber amicorum prof. dr. M. Baelde*, edited by Michel E. J. Baelde, Hugo Soly, and René Vermeir. Gent: Universiteit Gent. 127–81.

Schlugleit, Dora. 1938–39. "De Predikheerenpand en St-Niklaasgilde te Antwerpen (1445–1553)." *Bijdragen voor de Geschiedenis* 29: 99–119.

Schöffer, Ivo. 1956. "De vonnissen in averij grosse van de Kamer van Assurantie en Avarij te Amsterdam in de 18e eeuw. Onderzoek naar hun economisch-historische waarde voor de geschiedenis van handel en scheepvaart van Amsterdam op de Oostzee 1700–1770." *Economisch-Historisch Jaarboek* 26: 73–132.

———. 1991. "De Opstand in de Nederlanden, 1566–1609." In *De Lage Landen, 1500–1780*, edited by Ivo Schöffer, Herman van der Wee, and J. A. Bornewasser. Amsterdam: Agon. 103–65.

Schreiner, Agnes T. M., Henny Bouwmeester, Anne van Dooren, and Dolph Heyning. 1991. *In de ban van het recht*. Amsterdam: Duizend & Een.

Schutte, O. 1982. *Repertorium der buitenlandse vertegenwoordigers residerende in Nederland 1584–1810*. The Hague: Nijhoff.

Seifert, Dieter. 1995. "Der Hollandhandel und seine Träger im 14. und 15. Jahrhundert." *Hansische Geschichtsblätter* 113: 71–92.

———. 1997. *Kompagnons und Konkurrenten. Holland und die Hanse im späten Mittelalter*. Köln: Böhlau.

———. 2000. "Hildebrand Veckinchusen: A Typical Hanseatic Merchant in the Low Countries?" In *International Trade in the Low Countries (14th–16th centuries). Merchants, Organization and Infrastructure*, edited by Peter Stabel, Bruno Blondé, and Anke Greve. Leuven: Garant. 45–53.

Selzer, Stephan, and Ulf-Christian Ewert. 2001. "Verhandeln und Verkaufen, Vernetzen und Vertrauen. Über die Netzwerkstruktur des hansischen Handels." *Hansische Geschichtsblätter* 119: 135–62.

Sicking, Louis. 2004. *Neptune and the Netherlands. State, Economy and War at Sea in the Renaissance*. Leiden: Brill.

Slootmans, Cornelis Johannes Franciscus. 1935. "De Bergen-op-Zoomsche jaarmarkten en de bezoekers uit Zuid-Nederland." *Sinte Geertruydtsbronne. Driemaandelijksch tijdschrift gewijd aan de Geschiedenis en Volkskunde van West-Brabant en omgeving, vermeerderd met "Bredaniana"* 12: 8–20.

———. 1985. *Paas- en koudemarkten te Bergen op Zoom, 1365–1565*. 3 vols. Tilburg: Stichting Zuidelijk Historisch Contact.

Smidt, Jacobus Thomas de, et al., eds. 1966–79. *Chronologische lijsten van de geëxtendeerde sententiën en procesbundels (dossiers) berustende in het archief van de Grote Raad van Mechelen*. 6 vols. Brussels: Koninklijke Commissie voor de Uitgave der Oude Wetten en Verordeningen van België.

Smit, Homme Jacob. 1914. *De opkomst van de handel van Amsterdam. Onderzoekingen naar de economische ontwikkeling der stad tot 1441* Amsterdam: A.H. Kruyt.

Smith, Woodruff D. 1984. "The Function of Commercial Centers in the Modernization of European Capitalism: Amsterdam as an Information Exchange in the Seventeenth Century." *Journal of Economic History* 44: 985–1005.

Sneller, Zeger Willem. 1936. *Deventer, die Stadt der Jahrmärkte*. Weimar: Hermann Böhlaus Nachfolger.

Soly, Hugo. 1975. "Nijverheid en kapitalisme te Antwerpen in de 16e eeuw." In *Album aangeboden aan Charles Verlinden ter gelegenheid van zijn dertig jaar professoraat*. Gent: Universa. 331–52.

———. 1977. *Urbanisme en kapitalisme te Antwerpen in de 16de eeuw: de stedebouwkundige en industriële ondernemingen van Gilbert van Schoonbeke*. Brussels: Gemeentekrediet van België.

———. 1999. "Introduction. Charles V and His Time." In *Charles V and His Time. 1500–1558*, edited by Hugo Soly. Antwerp: Mercatorfonds. 11–25.

Spooner, Frank. 1983. *Risks at Sea: Amsterdam Insurance and Maritime Europe, 1766–1780*. New York: Cambridge University Press.

Spufford, Peter. 1988. *Money and Its Use in Medieval Europe*. Cambridge: Cambridge University Press.

———. 2002. *Power and Profit: The Merchant in Medieval Europe*. London: Thames & Hudson.

———. 2005. *From Antwerp to London: The Decline of Financial Centres in Europe*. Ortelius lecture. Wassenaar: NIAS.

Stabel, Peter. 1996. "Entre commerce international et économie locale. Le monde financier de Wouter Ameyde (Bruges, fin XVe-début XVIe siècle)." In *Finances publiques et finances privées au bas moyen âge*, edited by Marc Boone and Walter Prevenier. Leuven: Garant. 75–99.

———. 1997. *Dwarfs among Giants. The Flemish Urban Network in the Late Middle Ages*. Leuven: Garant.

———. 2001. "De gewenste vreemdeling. Italiaanse kooplieden en stedelijke maatschappij in het laat-middeleeuws Brugge." *Jaarboek voor Middeleeuwse Geschiedenis* 4: 189–221.

———. 2002. "Kooplieden in de stad." In *Hanzekooplui en Medicibankiers. Brugge, wisselmarkt van Europese culturen*, edited by André Vandewalle. Oostkamp: Stichting Kunstboek. 85–96.

Stasavage, David. 2011. *States of Credit. Size, Power, and the Development of European Politics*. Princeton: Princeton University Press.

Stein, Walter. 1902. "Über die ältesten Privilegien der deutschen Hanse in Flandern und die ältere Handelspolitik Lübecks." *Hansische Geschichtsblätter* 30: 51–137.

Stieda, Wilhelm. 1921. *Hildebrand Veckinchusen. Briefwechsel eines deutschen Kaufmanns im 15. Jahrhundert*. Leipzig: Hirzel.

Stols, Eddy. 1971. *De Spaanse Brabanders of de Handelsbetrekkngen der Zuidelijke Nederlanden met de Iberische Wereld 1598–1648*. 2 vols. Brussels: Paleis der Academiën.

Storper, Michael. 2010. "Why Does a City Grow? Specialisation, Human Capital or Institutions?" *Urban Studies* 47: 2027–50.

Stradling, Robert A. 1980. "The Spanish Dunkirkers, 1621–48: A Record of Plunder and Destruction." *Tijdschrift voor Geschiedenis* 93 (4): 541–58.

———. 1992. *The Armada of Flanders: Spanish Maritime Policy and European War, 1568–1668*. Cambridge: Cambridge University Press.

Strieder, Jakob. 1962. *Aus Antwerpener Notariatsarchiven, Quellen zur Deutschen Wirtschaftsgeschichte des 16. Jahrhunderts*. Wiesbaden: Franz Steiner Verlag GMBH.

Stringham, Edward. 2003. "The Extralegal Development of Securities Trading in Seventeenth Century Amsterdam." *Quarterly Review of Economics and Finance* 43: 321–44.

Stromer, Wolfgang von. 1967. "Das Schriftwesen der Nürnberger Wirtschaft vom 14. bis zum 16. Jahrhundert." *Beiträge zur Wirtschaftsgeschichte Nürnbergs* 2: 751–99.

Stuart, T. 1879. *De Amsterdamse makelaardij. Bijdrage tot de geschiedenis onzer handelswetgeving*. Amsterdam: C.A. Spin & Zoon.

Studnicki-Gizbert, Daviken. 2007. *A Nation upon the Ocean Sea: Portugal's Atlantic Diaspora and the Crisis of the Spanish Empire, 1492–1640*. Oxford: Oxford University Press.

Stützel, Peter. 1998. "Die Privilegien des Deutschen Kaufmanns in Brügge im 13. und 14. Jahrhundert." *Hansische Geschichtsblätter* 116: 23–64.

Subacchi, P. 1995. "Italians in Antwerp in the Second Half of the Sixteenth Century." In *Minderheden in Westeuropese steden (16de–20ste eeuw)/Minorities in Western European Cities (Sixteenth–Twentieth Centuries)*, edited by A. K. L. Thijs and H. Soly. Brussels: Institut Historique Belge de Rome. 73–90.

Swetschinski, Daniel M. 2000. *Reluctant Cosmopolitans. The Portuguese Jews of Seventeenth-Century Amsterdam*. London: Littman Library of Jewish Civilization.

Szabó, T. 1983. "Xenodochia, Hospitäler und Herbergen—kirchliche und kommerzielle Gastung im mittelalterlichen Italien (7. bis 14. Jahrhundert)." In *Gastfreundschaft, Taverne und Gasthaus im Mittelalter*, edited by H. C. Peyer. Munich: R. Oldenbourg.

Tebeaux, Elizabeth. 2000. "Visual Texts: Format and the Evolution of English Accounting Texts, 1100–1700." *Journal of Technical Writing and Communication* 30 (4): 307–41.

Tenenti, Alberto. 1959. *Naufrages, corsairs et assurances maritimes à Venice*. Paris: Éditions EHESS.

Thielemans, Marie-Rose. 1966. *Bourgogne et Angleterre: relations politiques et économiques entre les Pays-Bas bourguignons et l'Angleterre, 1435–1467*. Brussels: Presses Universitaires de Bruxelles.

Thijs, Alfons K. L. 1995. "Minderheden te Antwerpen (16de-20ste eeuw)." In *Minderheden in Westeuropese steden (16de–20ste eeuw)/Minorities in Western European Cities (Sixteenth–Twentieth Centuries)*. Edited by Alfons K. L. Thijs and Hugo Soly. BrusselsBruxelles: Institut Historique Belge de Rome. 17–42.

Thomas, Heinz. 1977. "Beiträge zur Geschichte der Champagne-Messen im 14. Jahrhundert." *Vierteljahrschrift für Sozial- und Wirtschaftsgeschichte* 64: 433–67.

Thomson, Janice E. 1994. *Mercenaries, Pirates, and Sovereigns: State-Building and Extra-Territorial Violence in Early Modern Europe.* Princeton: Princeton University Press.

Tielhof, Milja van. 1995a. *De Hollandse graanhandel, 1470–1570. Koren op de Amsterdamse molen.* The Hague: Stichting Hollandse Historische Reeks.

———. 1995b. "Der Getreidehandel der Danziger Kaufleute in Amsterdam um die Mitte des 16. Jahrhunderts." *Hansische Geschichtsblätter* 113: 93–110.

———. 1997. "Handel en politiek in de 16e eeuw: een Amsterdamse Oostzee-handelaar tijdens de eerste jaren van de Opstand." *Tijdschrift Holland* 29 (1): 37–52.

———. 2002. *The "Mother of All Trades." The Baltic Grain Trade in Amsterdam from the Late 16th to the Early 19th Century.* Leiden: Brill.

Tilly, Charles. 1990. *Coercion, Capital and European States, AD 990–1990.* Cambridge: Blackwell.

Tilly, Charles, and Wim P. Blockmans, eds. 1994. *Cities and the Rise of States in Europe, A.D. 1000 to 1800.* Boulder, Colo.: Westview.

Tracy, James D. 1983. "Habsburg Grain Policy and Amsterdam Politics: The Career of Sheriff Willem Dirkszoon Baerdes, 1542–1566." *Sixteenth Century Journal* 14: 193–319.

———. 1985. *A Financial Revolution in the Habsburg Netherlands. Renten and Renteniers in the County of Holland, 1515–1565.* Berkeley: University of California Press.

———. 1990a. *Holland under Habsburg rule, 1506–1566. The Formation of a Body Politic.* Berkeley: University of California Press.

———, ed. 1990b. *The Rise of the Merchant Empires. Long-Distance Trade in the Early Modern World, 1350–1750.* Cambridge: Cambridge University Press.

———. 2002. *Emperor Charles V, Impresario of War: Campaign Strategy, International Finance, and Domestic Politics.* Cambridge: Cambridge University Press.

Trakman, Leon E. 1983. *The Law Merchant: The Evolution of Commercial Law.* Littleton, Colo.: Fred B. Rothman.

Trivellato, Francesca. 2009. *The Familiarity of Strangers: The Sephardic Diaspora, Livorno, and Cross-Cultural Trade in the Early Modern Period.* New Haven: Yale University Press.

Udovitch, Abraham L. 1970. *Partnership and Profit in Medieval Islam.* Princeton: Princeton University Press.

Ulbert, Jörg, and Gérard le Bouëdec, eds. 2006. *La fonction consulaire à l'époque moderne. L'affirmation d'une institution économique et politique (1500–1800).* Rennes: Presses Universitaires de Rennes.

Van Caenegem, Raoul Charles. 1965. "La preuve dans le droit du moyen âge occidental." *Studia historica gandensia* 23: 1–66.

Van Damme, Ilja. 2010. "Scaldis geketend: percepties van het economisch welvaren van de stad Antwerpen of de genese van een handelsideologie (zestiende-negentiendeeuw)." *Tijdschrift voor geschiedenis* 123 (4): 486–503.

Van den Branden, F. 1885. "De Spaansche muiterij ten Jare 1574." *Antwerpsch Archievenblad* 22: 133–480.

Van der Kooy, Tjalling Pieter. 1931. *Hollands stapelmarkt en haar verval*. Amsterdam: H.J. Paris.

Van der Wee, Herman. 1962. "L'échec de la réforme monétaire de 1407 en Flandre, vu par les marchands italiens de Bruges." In *Studi in Onore di Amintore Fanfani. III. Medioevo*. Milan: Dott. A. Giuffrè. 3:579–90.

———. 1963. *The Growth of the Antwerp Market and the European Economy (14th–16th centuries)*. 3 vols. The Hague: Nijhoff.

———. 1967. "Anvers et les innovations de la technique financière aux XVIe et XVIIe siècles." *Annales ESC* 22: 1067–89.

———. 1970. "Un modèle dynamique de croissance interséculaire du commerce mondial (XIIe–XVIIIe siècles)." *Annales ESC* 25: 100–126.

Van Doosselaere, Quentin. 2009. *Commercial Agreements and Social Dynamics in Medieval Genoa*. Cambridge: Cambridge University Press.

Van Houtte, Jan Arthur. 1936. "Les Courtiers au moyen age. Origine et caractéristiques d'une institution commerciale en Europe occidentale." *Revue Historique de droit français et étranger*, 4ème serie 15: 105–41.

———. 1940. "La genèse du grand marché international d'Anvers à la fin du Moyen Age." *Revue Belge de Philologie et Histoire* 19: 87–126.

———. 1950–51. "Makelaars en waarden te Brugge van de 13e tot de 16e eeuw." *Bijdragen voor de geschiedenis der Nederlanden* 5: 1–30, 177–97.

———. 1952. "Bruges et Anvers, marchés nationaux ou internationaux du XIVème au XVIème siècle." *Revue du Nord* 24: 89–108.

———. 1953. "Les Foires dans la Belgique ancienne." In *La Foire*. Brussels: Recueils de la Société Jean Bodin. 5:175–207.

———. 1961. "Anvers aux XVe et XVIe siècles. Expansion et Apogée." *Annales ESC* 16: 248–78.

———. 1966. "The Rise and Decline of the Market of Bruges." *Economic History Review*, New Series 19 (1): 29–47.

———. 1982. *De geschiedenis van Brugge*. Tielt: Lannoo.

———. 1983. "Herbergwesen und Gastlichkeit im Mittelalterlichen Brügge." In *Gastfreundschaft, Taverne und Gasthaus im Mittelalter*, edited by H. C. Peyer. Munich: R. Oldenbourg. 177–88.

Van Rompaey, Jan. 1973. *De Grote Raad van de hertogen van Boergondië en het Parlement van Mechelen*. Brussels: Paleis der Academieën.

Van Uytven, Raymond. 1982. "Stadsgeschiedenis in het Noorden en Zuiden." In *Algemene Geschiedenis der Nederlanden*. Haarlem: Fibula-Van Dishoeck. 2:188–253.

———. 1995. "Stages of Economic Decline: Late Medieval Bruges." In *Peasants and Townsmen in Medieval Europe. Studia in Honorem Adriaan Verhulst*, edited by Jean Marie Duvosquel and Erik Thoen. Gent: Snoeck-Ducaju & Zoon. 259–69.

———. 2004. "Het gewicht van de goede steden." In *Geschiedenis van Brabant: van het hertogdom tot heden*, edited by Raymond Van Uytven. Zwolle: Waanders Uitgeverij. 118–25.

Van Werveke, Hans. 1936. "Der flandrische Eigenhandel im Mittelalter." *Hansische Geschichtsblätter* 61: 7–24.

———. 1941. *Brugge en Antwerpen. Acht eeuwen Vlaamsche handel.* Gent: Willems-fonds.

———. 1953a. "'Hansa' in Vlaanderen en aangrenzende gebieden." *Handelingen van het genootschap 'Société d'Émulation' te Brugge* 90: 5–42.

———. 1953b. "Les 'statuts' latins et les 'statuts' français de la Hanse flamande à Londres." *Bulletin de la Commission Royale d'Histoire (Académie Royale de Belgique)* 118: 289–320.

———. 1963. "Die Beziehungen Flanderns zu Osteuropa in der Hansezeit." *Arbeitsgemeinschaft für Forschung des Landes Nordrhein-Westfalen*, Band 28: 59–77.

———. 1965. "Die Stellung des Hansischen Kaufmanns dem Flandrischen Tuchproduzenten gegenüber." In *Beiträge zur Wirtschafts- undt Stadtgeschichte. Festschrift für Hektor Ammann.* Wiesbaden: Steiner. 296–304.

Vandermaesen, M. 1982. "Politieke ontwikkeling circa 1100–1400. Vlaanderen en Henegouwen onder het Huis van Dampierre." In *Algemene Geschiedenis der Nederlanden*, edited by D. P. Blok et al. Haarlem: Fibula-van Dishoeck. 2:399–440.

Vandewalle, André. 2002. "De vreemde naties in Brugge." In *Hanzekooplui en Medicibankiers. Brugge, wisselmarkt van Europese culturen*, edited by André Vandewalle. Oostkamp: Stichting Kunstboek. 27–42.

Vanneste, Tijl. 2011. *Global Trade and Commercial Networks: Eighteenth-Century Diamond Merchants.* London: Pickering and Chatto.

Vasquez de Prada, V. 1960. *Lettres marchandes d'Anvers. Affaires et gens d'affaires.* 4 vols. Paris: S.E.V.P.E.N.

Veluwenkamp, Jan Willem. 1996. "Merchant Colonies in the Dutch Trade System (1550–1750)." In *Kapitaal, ondernemerschap en beleid. Studies over economie en politiek in Nederland, Europa en Azië*, edited by Karel Davids, Wantje Fritschy, and Loes van der Valk. Amsterdam: Nederlands Economisch-Historisch Archief. 141–64.

———. 2000. *Archangel. Nederlandse ondernemers in Rusland 1550–1785.* Amsterdam: Balans.

———. 2006. "International Business Communication Patterns in the Dutch Commercial System, 1500–1800." In *Your humble Servant. Agents in Early Modern Europe*, edited by Hans Cools, Marika Keblusek, and Badeloch Noldus. Hilversum: Verloren. 121–34.

Vergouwen, J. P. 1944. "De makelaardij in assurantiën in Italië, Spanje en Vlaanderen voor 1575." *Het Verzekerings-Archief. Wetenschappelijk orgaan van de bedrijfgroep levensverzekering* 25: 157–76.

Verhas, Christel Madeleine Odile. 1997. *De beginjaren van de Hoge Raad van Holland, Zeeland en West-Friesland: . . . tot onderhoudinge van de Politique ordre ende staet der Landen van Hollandt, Zeelandt, Vrieslant.* Den Haag: Algemeen Rijksarchief.

Verkerk, Cornelis L. 2004. "De goede lieden van het gerecht." In *Geschiedenis van Amsterdam. Een stad uit het niets*, edited by Marijke Carasso-Kok. Amsterdam: SUN. 175–203.

Verlinden, Charles. 1939. "The Rise of Spanish Trade in the Middle Ages." *Economic History Review* 10: 44–61.

———. 1963. "Markets and Fairs." In *Cambridge Economic History of Europe. III, Economic Organization and Policies in the Middle Ages*, edited by M. M. Postan, E. E. Rich, and E. Miller. Cambridge: Cambridge University Press. 119–56.

Verlinden, Charles, Jan Craeybeckx, and E. Scholliers. 1959–73. *Dokumenten voor de geschiedenis van prijzen en lonen in Vlaanderen en Brabant.* 4 vols. Brugge: De Tempel.

Verzameling van casus positien, voorstellingen en declaratien, betrekkelyk tot voorvallende omstandigheden in den koophandel, van tyd tot tyd binnen deeze stad beoordeeld en ondertekend 1793–1804. 2 vols. Amsterdam: Pieter Hendrik Dronsberg.

Visser, N. 1997. "Adriaentgen Adriaens (+/-1590–1648), Herbergierster." In *Utrechtse biografieën. Levensbeschrijvingen van bekende en onbekende Utrechters*, edited by Willem van de Broeke et al. Amsterdam: Boom. 11–17.

Vlessing, Odette. 1995. "The Portuguese-Jewish Mercantile Community in Seventeenth-Century Amsterdam." In *Entrepreneurs and Entrepreneurship in Early Modern Times: Merchants and Industrialists within the Orbit of the Dutch Staple Market*, edited by Clemens Maria Lesger and Leo Noordegraaf. The Hague: Stichting Hollandse Historische Reeks. 223–44.

Vliet, Adrianus Paulus van. 1994. *Vissers en kapers: de zeevisserij vanuit het Maasmondgebied en de Duinkerker kapers (ca. 1580–1648).* The Hague: Stichting Hollandse Historische Reeks.

———. 1998. "Foundation, Organization and Effects of the Dutch Navy (1568–1648)." In *Exercise of Arms. Warfare in the Netherlands, 1568–1648*, edited by M. V. D. Hoeven. Leiden: Brill. 153–72.

Voet, Léon. 1973. *Antwerp, the Golden Age: The Rise and Glory of the Metropolis in the Sixteenth Century.* Antwerp: Mercatorfonds.

Volckart, Oliver. 1999. "Political Fragmentation and the Emergence of Market Economics: The Case of Germany, c. 1000–1800 AD." MPI Discussion Papers No. 9901.

———. 2002. *Wettbewerb und Wettbewerbsbeschränkung im vormodernen Deutschland 1000–1800.* Tübingen: Mohr Siebeck Verlag.

———. 2004. "The Economics of Feuding in Late Medieval Germany." *Explorations in Economic History* 41: 282–99.

Volckart, Oliver, and Antje Mangels. 1999. "Are the Roots of the Modern 'Lex Mercatoria' Really Medieval?" *Southern Economic Journal* 65: 427–50.

Vries, Jan de. 1984. *European Urbanization 1500–1800.* Cambridge, Mass.: Harvard University Press.

Vries, Jan de, and Ad Van der Woude. 1997. *The First Modern Economy. Success, Failure, and Perseverance of the Dutch Economy, 1500–1815.* Cambridge: Cambridge University Press.

Waal, P. G. A. de. 1927. *Van Paciolo tot Stevin: een bijdrage tot de leer van het boekhouden in de Nederlanden.* Roermond: Romen.

———. 1934. "De Engelsche vertaling van Jan Impyn's Nieuwe Instructie." *Economisch Historisch Jaarboek* 18: 1–58.

Wachter, Jacob Pietersz, ed. 1639. *Handtvesten, ofte privilegien, handelingen, costumen ende willekeuren der stadt Aemstelredam. Mitsgaders, concept vande geraemde poincten op 't stuck vande iustitie, ofte maniere van prccoederen in Civile Saecken binnen deser Stede: Met verscheyden Placcaten dienstigh in diversche saecken. Als mede de Zee ende Scheeps-rechten van Wisbuy, vande Oude Hansesteden, van Keyser Karel ende Koningh Philips: Met een Tractaet van Avarije.* Amsterdam: Jacob Pietersz Wachter.

Wallerstein, Immanuel. 1976. *The Modern World-System: Capitalist Agriculture and the Origins of the European World-Economy in the Sixteenth Century.* New York: Academic Press.

Watson, W. B. 1961. "The Structure of the Florentine Galley Trade with Flanders and England in the Fifteenth Century: Some Evidence about Profits and the Balance of Trade. I." *Revue belge de Philologie et d'Histoire* 39: 1073–91.

———. 1962. "The Structure of the Florentine Galley Trade with Flanders and England in the Fifteenth Century: Some Evidence about Profits and the Balance of Trade. II." *Revue belge de Philologie et d'Histoire* 40. 317–47.

Wedemeyer Moore, Ellen. 1985. *The Fairs of Medieval England. An Introductory Study.* Toronto: Pontifical Institute of Mediaeval Studies.

Weststrate, Job Andries. 2000. "'Des kopmans Hense ende vrijheden': organisatie en structuur van de Hanze, ca. 1300–ca. 1450." *Leidschrift: historisch tijdschrift* 15 (2): 21–47.

———. 2008. *In het kielzog van moderne markten. Handel en scheepvaart op de Rijn, Waal en IJssel, ca. 1360–1560.* Hilversum: Verloren.

Wijffels, Alain. 2003. "Ius Commune and International Wine Trade. A Revision (Middelburg c. Antwerp 1548–1559," *Tijdschrift voor Rechtsgeschiedenis* 71 (3–4): 289–317.

Wijffels, Alain, and Ivo van Loo. 1998. "Zealand Privateering and the Anglo-Spanish Peace Treaty of 1630." In *Een Rijk Gerecht. Opstellen aangeboden aan prof. Mr. P.L. Nève*, edited by B. C. M. Jacobs and E. C. Coppens. Nijmegen: Gerard Noodt Instituut. 635–73.

Wijnman, H. F. 1963. "De herberg de Gulden Hand in de Warmoesstraat als centrum van de Oosterse handel te Amsterdam." *Jaarboek Amstelodamum* 55: 57–76.

Wijnroks, Eric H. 2003. *Handel tussen Rusland en de Nederlanden, 1560–1640, Een netwerkanalyse van de Antwerpse en Amsterdamse kooplieden, handelend op Rusland.* Hilversum: Verloren.

Williamson, Dean V. 2002. "Transparency, Contract Selection and the Maritime Trade of Venetian Crete, 1303–1351." Manuscript.

Williamson, Oliver. 1985. *The Economic Institutions of Capitalism.* New York: Free Press.

Wilson, Charles H. 1978. *Profit and Power. A Study of England and the Dutch Wars.* 2nd ed. The Hague: Nijhoff.

Winkelman, Petrus Henricus. 1971–83. *Bronnen voor de geschiedenis van de Nederlandse Oostzeehandel in de zeventiende eeuw.* 6 vols. The Hague: Nijhoff.

Wouters, Koen. 2004. "Een open oligarchie? De machtsstructuur in de Antwerpse magistraat tijdens de periode 1520–1555." *Revue belge de philologie et d'histoire* 82 (4): 905–34.

Yamey, Basil S. 1949. "Scientific Bookkeeping and the Rise of Capitalism." *Economic History Review* 1 (2/3): 99–113.

Yogev, Gedalia. 1978. *Diamonds and Coral: Anglo-Dutch Jews and Eighteenth-Century Trade*. Leicester: Leicester University Press.

Zanden, Jan Luiten van. 1993a. "Economic growth in the Golden Age: The Development of the Economy of Holland, 1500–1650." In *The Dutch Economy in the Golden Age*, edited by Karel Davids and Leo Noordegraaf. Amsterdam: Nederlandsch Economisch-Historisch Archief. 5–26.

———. 1993b. "Holland en de Zuidelijke Nederlanden in de periode 1500–1570: divergerende ontwikkelingen of voortgaande economische integratie." In *Studia Historica Oeconomica. Liber amicorum Herman van der Wee*, edited by Erik Aerts et al. Leuven: Leuven University Press. 357–67.

———. 2009. *The Long Road to the Industrial Revolution. The European Economy in a Global Perspective*. Leiden/Boston: Brill.

Zijlstra, Suzanne. 2012. "To Build and Sustain Trust: Long-Distance Correspondence of Dutch Seventeenth-Century Merchants." *Dutch Crossing: Journal of Low Countries Studies* 36 (2): 114–31.

Zimmermann, Reinhard. 1990. *The Law of Obligations. Roman Foundations of the Civilian Tradition*. Oxford: Clarendon.

Zuijderduijn, Jaco. 2009. *Medieval Capital Markets. Markets for Renten, State Formation and Private Investment in Holland (1300–1550)*. Leiden/Boston: Brill.

Index

Aardenburg, 151, 152, 170, 171, 211, 213
account books, 7, 49, 82, 87, 98, 101; and
    double-entry bookkeeping, 86, 87,
    94–100; as legal proof, 17, 88, 89,
    90n84, 94–101, 204, 207. *See also*
    registration
Acemoglu, Daron, 2, 5, 6, 167, 198
Admiralty Boards, 164, 165, 166, 167, 185
Admiralty Courts, 132, 183–84, 197
Adrichem, Claes van, 81
Africa, 37, 62, 66, 163, 166
Alba, Duke of, 32, 120, 160–61
America, 37, 62, 66, 163, 166
Amsterdam: accommodation and storage
    facilities in, 70; and Antwerp, 1, 34,
    36, 37, 38, 60, 61, 70, 121, 137,
    162–63; arbitration in, 17, 106, 107,
    108, 125; Bank of Exchange (Wis-
    selbank), 38, 70–71, 126; Bourse of, 7,
    71, 72, 73; brokers in, 57–62, 66, 67,
    70–74, 75, 122, 198; and Bruges, 15,
    25, 38, 123; cashiers in, 71; churches
    in, 121–22, 125; commission trade
    in, 79; and Company of Merchant
    Adventurers, 38–39; conflict resolu-
    tion in, 17, 70, 106, 107, 108, 121–26;
    and Deventer, 213; Direction for the
    Levant Trade, 166–67; and Dukes of
    Burgundy, 34; and Dutch Revolt, 36,
    59, 142, 162, 163, 223, 225; English
    merchants in, 1, 38–39, 121–22, 123;
    Flemish merchants in, 1, 37, 59, 121,
    122, 123, 159; French merchants in,
    121; and German Hanse, 34, 38, 58;
    German merchants in, 1, 35, 38, 39,
    58, 59, 121, 123, 159, 223; and Haar-
    lem, 38; hinterland access to, 201;
    hostellers/hostels in, 36, 43, 58, 59,
    60, 70, 71, 73; inclusive institutions
    in, 2, 16, 40, 70, 136, 197, 199, 200,
    201; information in, 57–74; insolven-
    cies/bankruptcies in, 70, 122, 124–25;
    institutional adaptation by, 16, 41, 74,
    99, 125, 126, 202; insurance in, 38,
    70, 73, 120, 121, 124, 194–96; inter-
national payments in, 38, 71; Italian
    merchants in, 1, 37, 38, 121; laws
    of, 35, 58, 70, 94, 98, 99, 101, 135,
    137; legal autonomy of, 139, 140,
    201; legal proof in, 94, 97, 98, 101;
    and Leyden, 38; magistrate of, 36, 39,
    40, 70, 71, 72, 73, 99, 121, 123, 125,
    135, 137, 181, 199, 202, 221; money
    market in, 67–70, 101; notaries of,
    92–94, 98, 99; political autonomy of,
    201; political elite of, 3, 39, 199; Por-
    tuguese merchants in, 1, 38, 39, 83,
    106, 108, 121, 123, 125; price cur-
    rents in, 61, 73–74, 195; privileges of
    merchants, 1, 38–40, 121; protection
    of merchants in, 1, 146, 157, 163–64,
    166–67, 198; residence (permanent)
    in, 35, 36, 38, 43, 57, 58, 59, 60, 70;
    risk management in, 190, 197; ship-
    ping services in, 34, 35, 62, 94, 163,
    189; and Spain, 36; and taxation,
    35, 36, 58, 124, 164–66; and urban
    competition, 1, 4, 11, 37, 39–41; Wal-
    loon merchants in, 39; and William of
    Orange, 36–37, 165
—: courts of: absence of consular, 1, 18,
    121, 124, 203; Admiralty Court in,
    184; Chamber of Insolvent Estates,
    124, 125–26; Chamber of Insurance,
    126; Chamber of Maritime Affairs,
    126; Commissioners of Minor Affairs
    (Kleine Zaken), 124, 125; consular,
    35; local, 58, 122–26; Orphan Cham-
    ber, 124, 125
—: and trade: with Baltic region, 16, 34,
    35, 36, 37, 59, 87, 121, 167; in beer,
    25, 35; in colonial wares, 37, 38, 62;
    in grain, 34, 35, 36, 38, 57–58, 59; in
    jewelry, 62, 63–65; in textiles, 34, 35,
    38, 61
Anabaptists, 161
Answaarden, Robert van, 127
Antwerp: accommodation and storage
    facilities in, 31, 32, 52, 54–55, 208;
    and Amsterdam, 1, 34, 36, 37, 38, 60,

25, 44n8, 45, 114, 142, 147, 150,
171, 186; consular jurisdiction of,
114, 117; and marine insurance, 194;
and risk management, 186
Venezuela, 190
Venice, 2, 3, 4, 6, 13, 25, 42, 77, 83, 96,
138, 141, 190, 191, 201, 208; and
Barbary pirates, 166; English and
Dutch merchants in, 209; Fondaco dei
Tedeschi, 55; galley fleets from, 22,
142, 147, 171, 192, 193, 213
Vereenigde Oost-Indische Companie
(VOC; Dutch East India Company),
39, 66, 67, 130, 132, 133, 166, 207
violence, 1, 76; avoidance of, 18, 205–6;
effect of competition in reducing, 14,
206, 207; incidence of, 14, 146, 152,
169, 212–26; and marine insurance,
191, 192, 193; profits despite, 169;
by public officials, 182–83; and state
formation, 2, 5, 141–42, 154, 167–68,
198. See also imprisonment, of merchants; privateering/privateers; property, protection of; property, seizure
of; risks; war
Visby, maritime law of, 35, 113, 117, 123,
135, 137
Vitalienbrüder, 147–48, 216
vreemde naties. See foreign nations
(vreemde naties)

Wallis, John, 2
Wallony, merchants from, 39, 60, 196
war, 14, 145, 167, 170; of Burgundy with
England, 147, 150, 174, 177–78, 219;
of Burgundy with France, 170, 220;
of Burgundy with Spain, 170, 177; of

Dutch Republic with Spain, 1, 38; of
England with France, 148, 150, 153,
192, 212–13, 216, 219, 223; of Flanders with Brabant, 213; of Flanders
with France, 213; of German Hanse
with Castile, 218; of Habsburg mon-
archy with France, 156, 160, 170;
restricted travel during, 192–93. See
also Dutch Revolt; Hundred Years' War
Watergeuzen, 36
weapons, merchants' right to carry, 144–45
weights and measures, international standard for, 204
Weingast, Barry R., 2, 14
Westindische Compagnie (WIC; Dutch
West India Company), 166
Westphalia, merchants from, 25, 54
Westrozebeke, Battle of, 154, 215, 1382)
Widerlegung (wederlegginge), 83–84, 89,
90
William of Orange, 160, 161, 165, 36–37
wills, 91, 125, 130
Wismar, 216
Wisselbank. See under Amsterdam
wool trade, 22, 24, 30, 33, 111, 120, 147,
171–72, 193, 194, 211, 212

Ympyn, Jan, 96, 100
Ypres, 88–89, 151; fairs of, 20

Zeeland, 1, 144, 154, 164, 168, 178, 198,
214; and Dutch Revolt, 161, 162, 223;
merchants from, 211, 215; privateers
from, 147, 215–16, 218; Scottish
staple removed to, 30
Zwolle, 61
Zwyn, 20, 215

THE PRINCETON ECONOMIC HISTORY OF THE WESTERN WORLD

Joel Mokyr, Series Editor

Growth in a Traditional Society: The French Countryside, 1450–1815, by Philip T. Hoffman

The Vanishing Irish: Households, Migration, and the Rural Economy in Ireland, 1850–1914, by Timothy W. Guinnane

Black '47 and Beyond: The Great Irish Famine in History, Economy, and Memory, by Cormac O Grada

The Great Divergence: China, Europe, and the Making of the Modern World Economy, by Kenneth Pomeranz

The Big Problem of Small Change, by Thomas J. Sargent and Francois R. Velde

Farm to Factory: A Reinterpretation of the Soviet Industrial Revolution, by Robert C. Allen

Quarter Notes and Bank Notes: The Economics of Music Composition in the Eighteenth and Nineteenth Centuries, by F. M. Scherer

The Strictures of Inheritance: The Dutch Economy in the Nineteenth Century, by Jan Luiten van Zanden and Arthur van Riel

Understanding the Process of Economic Change, by Douglass C. North

Feeding the World: An Economic History of Agriculture, 1800–2000, by Giovanni Federico

Cultures Merging: A Historical and Economic Critique of Culture, by Eric L. Jones

The European Economy since 1945: Coordinated Capitalism and Beyond, by Barry Eichengreen

War, Wine, and Taxes: The Political Economy of Anglo-French Trade, 1689–1900, by John V. C. Nye

A Farewell to Alms: A Brief Economic History of the World, by Gregory Clark

Power and Plenty: Trade, War, and the World Economy in the Second Millennium, by Ronald Findlay and Kevin O'Rourke

Power over Peoples: Technology, Environments, and Western Imperialism, 1400 to the Present, by Daniel R. Headrick

Unsettled Account: The Evolution of Banking in the Industrialized World since 1800, by Richard S. Grossman

States of Credit: Size, Power, and the Development of European Polities, by David Stasavage

Creating Wine: The Emergence of a World Industry, 1840–1914, by James Simpson

The Evolution of a Nation: How Geography and Law Shaped the American States, by Daniel Berkowitz and Karen B. Clay

Distant Tyranny: Markets, Power, and Backwardness in Spain, 1650–1800, by Regina Grafe

The Chosen Few: How Education Shaped Jewish History, 70–1492, by Maristella Botticini and Zvi Eckstein